Herbert A. Simon, George J. Stigler and Ronald H. Coase

The Pioneering Papers of the Nobel Memorial Laureates in Economics

Edited by: Howard R. Vane
Professor of Economics, Liverpool Business School, Liverpool John Moores University, UK
and
Chris Mulhearn
Reader in Economics, Liverpool Business School, Liverpool John Moores University, UK

1. *Milton Friedman, Robert E. Lucas, Jr. and Edmund S. Phelps*
2. *Harry M. Markowitz, Merton H. Miller, William F. Sharpe, Robert C. Merton and Myron S. Scholes*
3. *Trygve Haavelmo, James J. Heckman, David L. McFadden, Robert F. Engle and Clive W.J. Granger*
4. *Wassily W. Leontief, Leonid V. Kantorovich, Tjalling C. Koopmans and J. Richard N. Stone*
5. *John C. Harsanyi, John F. Nash, Jr., Reinhard Selten, Robert J. Aumann and Thomas C. Schelling*
6. *James A. Mirrlees, William S. Vickrey, George A. Akerlof, A. Michael Spence and Joseph E. Stiglitz*
7. *James Tobin, Franco Modigliani, Finn E. Kydland and Edward C. Prescott*
8. *Paul A. Samuelson, John R. Hicks, Kenneth J. Arrow, Gerard Debreu and Maurice F.C. Allais*
9. *Simon S. Kuznets, Theodore W. Schultz, W. Arthur Lewis and Robert M. Solow*
10. *Bertil G. Ohlin, James E. Meade and Robert A. Mundell*
11. *Herbert A. Simon, George J. Stigler and Ronald H. Coase*
12. *James M. Buchanan, Gary S. Becker, Daniel Kahneman and Vernon L. Smith*
13. *Gunnar Myrdal, Friedrich A. von Hayek, Robert W. Fogel, Douglass C. North and Amartya K. Sen*
14. *Ragnar A.K. Frisch, Jan Tinbergen and Lawrence R. Klein*

Wherever possible, the articles in these volumes have been reproduced as originally published using facsimile reproduction, inclusive of footnotes and pagination to facilitate ease of reference.

Herbert A. Simon, George J. Stigler and Ronald H. Coase

Edited by

Howard R. Vane

Emeritus Professor of Economics
Liverpool John Moores University, UK

and

Chris Mulhearn

Reader in Economics
Liverpool John Moores University, UK

PIONEERING PAPERS OF THE NOBEL MEMORIAL LAUREATES IN ECONOMICS

An Elgar Research Collection
Cheltenham, UK • Northampton, MA, USA

Published by
Edward Elgar Publishing Limited
The Lypiatts
15 Lansdown Road
Cheltenham
Glos GL50 2JA
UK

Edward Elgar Publishing, Inc.
William Pratt House
9 Dewey Court
Northampton
Massachusetts 01060
USA

A catalogue record for this book is available from the British Library

Library of Congress Control Number: 2011926263

MIX
Paper from responsible sources
FSC® C018575
FSC www.fsc.org

ISBN 978 1 84980 399 1

Printed and bound by MPG Books Group, UK

Contents

Acknowledgements

The editors and publishers wish to thank the authors and the following publishers who have kindly given permission for the use of copyright material.

American Economic Association for articles: Herbert A. Simon (1959), 'Theories of Decision-Making in Economics and Behavioral Science', *American Economic Review*, **XLIX** (3), June, 253–83; Herbert A. Simon (1978), 'Rationality as a Process and as Product of Thought', *American Economic Review*, **68** (2), May, 1–16; Herbert A. Simon (1979), 'Rational Decision Making in Business Organizations', *American Economic Review*, **69** (4), September, 493–513.

American Philosophical Society via the Copyright Clearance Center for article: Herbert A. Simon (1962), 'The Architecture of Complexity', *Proceedings of the American Philosophical Society*, **106** (6), December, 467–82.

Blackwell Publishing Ltd (Wiley-Blackwell) for article: R.H. Coase (1937), 'The Nature of the Firm', *Economica*, **4** (16), November, 386–405.

Katherine Simon Frank for excerpt: Herbert A. Simon (1972), 'Theories of Bounded Rationality', in C.B. McGuire and Roy Radner (eds), *Decision and Organization: A Volume in Honor of Jacob Marschak*, Chapter 8, 161–76, references.

MIT Press Journals for article: Herbert A. Simon (1955), 'A Behavioral Model of Rational Choice', *Quarterly Journal of Economics*, **69** (1), February, 99–118.

Oxford University Press for article: George J. Stigler (1945), 'The Cost of Subsistence', *Journal of Farm Economics*, **27** (2), May, 303–14.

RAND Corporation for article: George J. Stigler (1971), 'The Theory of Economic Regulation', *Bell Journal of Economics and Management Science*, **2** (1), Spring, 3–21.

University of Chicago Press for articles: George J. Stigler (1947), 'The Kinky Oligopoly Demand Curve and Rigid Prices', *Journal of Political Economy*, **55** (5), October, 432–49; R.H. Coase (1960), 'The Problem of Social Cost', *Journal of Law and Economics*, **3**, October, 1–44; George J. Stigler (1961), 'The Economics of Information', *Journal of Political Economy*, **LXIX** (3), June, 213–25; George J. Stigler (1962), 'Information in the Labor Market', *Journal of Political Economy*, **70** (5, Part 2), October, 94–105; George J. Stigler (1964), 'A Theory of Oligopoly', *Journal of Political Economy*, **72** (1), February, 44–61.

Every effort has been made to trace all the copyright holders but if any have been inadvertently overlooked the publishers will be pleased to make the necessary arrangement at the first opportunity.

In addition the publishers wish to thank the Library of Indiana University at Bloomington, USA for their assistance in obtaining these articles.

General Introduction

Howard R. Vane and Chris Mulhearn

The 'Sveriges Riksbank (Bank of Sweden) Prize in Economic Sciences in Memory of Alfred Nobel', popularly known as the Nobel Prize in Economics, was first awarded in 1969. At the time of writing (July 2010), over the 41 years since its inception there have been some 64 Nobel Laureates in economics. The Prize, like the Nobel awards in other disciplines, recognizes specific discoveries, achievements or breakthroughs in economic science, rather than outstanding economists or a person's lifetime work.[1]

The aim of this series is to bring together, in a number of volumes, *some* of the pioneering papers of the Nobel Memorial Laureates that have helped shape the development of modern economic thought. Because the work of the Prize winners spans a wide range of fields, it is possible to categorize the awards in a number of ways. However, as Lindbeck (1985; 2001) acknowledges, any chosen classification is going to be 'rather arbitrary' because of the 'overlapping' and, in some cases, 'multidimensional nature' of the Laureates' contributions (see also Chapter 1 of Vane and Mulhearn, 2005). Wherever possible, we have sought to include in each volume Laureates working in the same *broad* area of study. In some cases, deciding which Laureates' papers should be grouped together was relatively straightforward because the sub-disciplines were readily identifiable – for example, in the case of the pioneering game-theory papers of Harsanyi, Nash, Selten, Aumann and Schelling. For other volumes we have sought to identify a common link underlying the Laureates' work. For example, in the case of the volume containing work by Friedman, Lucas and Phelps an initial unifying theme is their research in macroeconomics and, more specifically, their analyses of tradeoffs, most notably between inflation and unemployment. In some of the volumes where it is less clear that there is a single common thread, we have grouped together the papers of Laureates working in two or more fields.

In this general introduction to the series we would like to highlight six main points.

- First, in order to keep the length and cost (given copyright permission fees) of each volume to manageable proportions we have imposed an arbitrary limit of not more than six papers under each Laureate's name per volume (with one exception, Paul Samuelson, whose influence on economics has been so profound and wide-ranging).
- Second, to avoid duplication across the series, no paper appears in more than one volume. For example, the joint papers by Franco Modigliani and Merton Miller in the field of financial economics appear only under Merton's name and not in the volume containing papers by Modigliani.
- Third, the pioneering contributions of certain Laureates appear in book form rather than in papers. For example, some of Milton Friedman's most influential work appears in his book *A Monetary History of the United States, 1867–1960*, co-authored with Anna J. Schwartz (Princeton: Princeton University Press, 1963). In cases such as this we have

sought to include some representative paper (e.g. Friedman and Schwartz's 1963 *Review of Economics and Statistics* paper on 'Money and Business Cycles'), or the Laureate's Nobel Lecture.

- Fourth, the impact of a Laureate's work is not necessarily confined to one field of study or, within one field, a particular topic or theme. For example, in the case of Robert E. Lucas Jr. his classic 1988 *Journal of Monetary Economics* paper 'On the Mechanics of Economic Development', in which he highlighted the importance of human capital accumulation and learning by doing, has (together with the work of Paul Romer) led to a resurgence of interest in the analysis of economic growth and, most notably, the development of endogenous growth theory. This important contribution might not be apparent to someone looking at the Prize citation for Lucas, which is 'for having developed and applied the hypothesis of rational expectations, and thereby transformed macroeconomic analysis and deepened our understanding of economic policy' (Nobel Foundation, 2010).
- Fifth, while the pioneering papers of some Laureates are easily identifiable, for others who have made numerous breakthroughs – such as Paul Samuelson, who has contributed fundamental insights into nearly every major area of economic theory – we need to stress that, at the margin, the selection of papers involves a degree of personal judgement. No doubt other economists would have preferences different from our own. In choosing the papers for each volume we have been guided, in part, by the Laureates' statements of their principal contributions to economics as *they* perceive them (see Blaug, 1999; Blaug and Vane, 2003), and in certain cases by Laureates who, in correspondence, have indicated which papers they wanted included under their name.
- Finally, it is important to stress that the rationale behind this series is *not* to produce either the *Collected Works* of individual Nobel Laureates or the *Collected Writings* of one or more Laureates on a particular topic. Instead our intention is to bring together in a series of volumes some of the pioneering papers of the Nobel Memorial Laureates that have shaped the development of modern economic thought and to set in context the selection of papers chosen for each volume by an editorial introduction to the Laureates' careers and main published works.

Note

1. The five original Nobel Prizes – in Physics, Chemistry, Physiology or Medicine, Literature and Peace – have been awarded annually since 1901.

References

Blaug, Mark (ed.) (1999), *Who's Who in Economics*, 3rd edn, Cheltenham, UK and Northampton, MA, USA: Edward Elgar.

Blaug, Mark and Howard R. Vane (eds) (2003), *Who's Who in Economics*, 4th edn, Cheltenham, UK and Northampton, MA, USA: Edward Elgar.

Lindbeck, Assar (1985), 'The Prize in Economic Science in Memory of Alfred Nobel', *Journal of Economic Literature*, **23**, March, pp. 37–56.

Lindbeck, Assar (2001), 'The Sveriges Riksbank (Bank of Sweden) Prize in Economic Sciences in Memory of Alfred Nobel 1969–2000', in A.W. Levinovitz and N. Ringertz (eds), *The Nobel Prize: The First 100 Years*, London: Imperial College Press and World Scientific Publishing Co., pp. 197–220.
Nobel Foundation (2010), Official Web Site, www.nobelprize.org.
Vane, Howard R. and Chris Mulhearn (2005), *The Nobel Memorial Laureates in Economics: An Introduction to Their Careers and Main Published Works*, Cheltenham, UK and Northampton, MA, USA: Edward Elgar.

Part I
Herbert A. Simon

Introduction to Part I: Herbert A. Simon (1916–2001)

Herbert Simon was born in Milwaukee, Wisconsin, USA in 1916. He studied political science at the University of Chicago, where he obtained a BA in 1936 and a PhD in 1943. His early posts included a position at the International City Managers' Association in Chicago from 1938 to 1939. Subsequently he became Director of Administrative Measurement Studies at the Bureau of Public Administration of the University of California at Berkeley from 1939 to 1942. In 1942 Simon returned to Chicago, where he was appointed initially as an Assistant Professor of Political Science at Illinois Institute of Technology, before becoming a full professor in 1947. In 1949 he moved to Pittsburgh, where he was Professor of Administration and Psychology at the Carnegie Institute of Technology (later renamed Carnegie-Mellon University) from 1949 to 1955, and Professor of Computer Science and Psychology from 1955 until he retired in 1988.

Simon's many offices and honours included: the Distinguished Scientific Contribution Award of the American Psychological Association in 1969; the A.M. Turing Award of the Association for Computing Machinery (with Allen Newell) in 1975; a Distinguished Fellowship of the American Economic Association (1976); the James Madison Award of the American Political Science Association in 1984; the award of the National Medal of Science in 1986; the John von Neumann Theory Prize of the Operations Research Society of America and the Institute of Management Sciences in 1988; the Research Excellence Award of the International Joint Conference on Artificial Intelligence in 1995; and the award of numerous honorary degrees from universities around the world. In 1978, Simon was awarded the Nobel Memorial Prize in Economics 'for his pioneering research into the decision-making process within economic organizations' (Nobel Foundation, 2010).

In economics Simon is best known for his important contributions to the field of behavioural decision making, especially in large organizations. His pioneering research in this area can be traced back to his PhD thesis on decision-making processes in administrative organizations, which was published (in revised form) in 1947 in his first major book entitled *Administrative Behaviour*. Central to this work is the idea that human decision making results in satisficing, rather than optimizing, behaviour. The traditional theory of the firm is based on the assumption of an omniscient, fully rational, profit-maximizing entrepreneur. In Simon's approach, the single entrepreneur is replaced by a constellation of decision makers whose rationality is limited and who cooperate to find satisfactory solutions to the problems they face. In consequence, firms are unable to maximize profits. He argued that, in reality, people in large organizations cannot obtain or process all the information needed to make fully rational decisions. Instead, due to limitations of knowledge (for example, about the uncertain future) and the capacity to process information, people 'satisfice' by making decisions that result in acceptable outcomes. In other words, people make decisions that are 'good enough', settling for certain aspiration levels that they adjust occasionally (either upwards or downwards) when outcomes do not match targets. In his book he rejected the idea of 'economic man' who 'optimizes', instead introducing the concept of 'administrative man' who 'satisfices'. This view of human decision making, based on 'limited' rationality, or what he subsequently called 'bounded' rationality, results in 'satisficing', not optimizing, behaviour.

A central aim of Simon's research was to investigate human rationality. In another influential book entitled *Models of Man* (Simon, 1957), he presented a collection of essays on rational human behaviour in a social setting. This work combined economic with philosophical and psychological perspectives specifically addressing: causation and influence relationships; social processes; motivation; and rationality and administrative decision making. In a series of books published with others in the 1950s and 1960s (Simon et al., 1950; 1960a; March and Simon, 1958; Simon, 1960b; 1965) he developed the ideas first put forward in his classic book, *Administrative Behaviour*. His interest in human decision making also led him to undertake research in the disciplines of political science, psychology and computer science. In the last case, for example, from the mid-1950s onwards he undertook research with Allen Newell to program computers to simulate human problem-solving behaviour using heuristics based on bounded rationality. This research led to the pioneering idea that computers can exhibit an 'artificial intelligence' that mirrors human thinking (Simon, 1969; Newell and Simon, 1972a) and to the 'information-processing revolution' in cognitive psychology. His extensive knowledge of, and research in, political science, economics, psychology and computer science allowed him to make insightful links between the disciplines. This led him to make important contributions to a number of fields, most notably human cognition, artificial intelligence and management science. Furthermore he explored the implications of this wide-ranging research for economics (see Earl, 2001). While he will be remembered in economics, first and foremost, for his analysis of decision making and its applications, he also undertook work in other areas of the discipline. For example, he made important contributions to mathematical economics, including a theorem concerned with the existence of a solution to an input–output process (Hawkins and Simon, 1949).

As should be evident from this brief overview, Simon was a truly remarkable and talented individual. Over the course of a long and distinguished career he held professorships in political science, administration, psychology and computer science. Through detailed and wide-ranging research he made lasting contributions to a number of disciplines and fields. The common theme running through all his work is human decision-making and problem-solving processes. Many of Simon's most important papers have been gathered together in six volumes: *Models of Discovery* (Simon, 1977), a collection of his papers on the philosophy of science; *Models of Thought* (Simon, 1979a), a two-volume collection of his papers in psychology; and *Models of Bounded Rationality* (Simon, 1982a; 1982b; 1997), a three-volume collection, containing more than 80 articles, of his papers in economics. Given Simon's prolific output of published papers, many of which have appeared in the world's top-ranked academic journals, the six papers chosen to appear in this volume are both among his most heavily cited and convey the basic tenor of his views in relation to economics. In chronological order of publication:

- Simon (1955 – paper 1) considers a behavioural model of rational choice in which he sought 'to replace the global rationality of economic man with a kind of rational behavior that is compatible with the access to information and the computational capacities that are actually possessed by organisms, including man, in the kinds of environments in which such organisms exist' (p. 99);

- Simon (1959 – paper 2) critically surveys developments in theories of decision making in economics and behavioural science;
- Simon (1962 – paper 3) considers complex systems 'made up of a large number of parts that interact in a non simple way' and argues that 'hierarchy ... is one of the central structural schemes that the architect of complexity uses' (p. 468), while 'in their dynamics, hierarchies have a property, near-decomposability, that greatly simplifies their behavior' (p. 482);
- Simon (1972b – paper 4) is a summary paper on theories of bounded rationality which Simon wrote for a *Festschrift* held to honour Jacob Marschak, a Russian-born economist who helped pioneer the development of economic theories of information, organization and decision under uncertainty, and who was Professor of Economics at the University of California, Los Angeles from 1960 until his death in 1977;
- Simon (1978 – paper 5), the Richard T. Ely Lecture, in which he emphasized rationality as a process of choice and as a product of thought; and
- Simon (1979 – paper 6), his 1978 Nobel Memorial Prize Lecture, in which he considered rational decision making in business organizations, concluding that 'we do understand today many of the mechanisms of human rational choice. We do know the information processing system called Man, faced with complexity beyond his ken, uses his information processing capacities to seek out alternatives, to calculate consequences, to resolve uncertainties, and thereby – sometimes, not always – to find ways of action that are sufficient unto the day, that satisfices' (p. 511).

The legacy of Herbert Simon in economic analysis is considered in a two-volume collection of 50 papers (Earl, 2001).

Main Published Works

(1947), *Administrative Behaviour*, New York: Macmillan; 4th edn 1997, New York: Free Press.
(1949), 'Note: Some Conditions of Macroeconomic Stability' (with D. Hawkins), *Econometrica*, **17**, July–October, pp. 245–8.
(1950), *Public Administration* (with V.A. Thompson and D.W. Smithburg), New York: Alfred A. Knopf.
(1955), 'A Behavioral Model of Rational Choice', *Quarterly Journal of Economics*, **69**, February, pp. 99–118.
(1957), *Models of Man*, New York: John Wiley.
(1958), *Organizations* (with J.G. March), New York: John Wiley; 2nd edn 1993, Cambridge, MA: Blackwell.
(1959), 'Theories of Decision-Making in Economics and Behavioral Science', *American Economic Review*, **49**, June, pp. 253–83.
(1960a), *Planning Production, Inventories and Work Forces* (with C.C. Holt, F. Modigliani and J. Muth), Englewood Cliffs, NJ: Prentice-Hall.
(1960b), *The New Science of Management Decision*, New York: Harper & Row; rev. edn 1977, Englewood Cliffs, NJ: Prentice-Hall.
(1962), 'The Architecture of Complexity', *Proceedings of the American Philosophical Society*, **106**, December, pp. 467–82.
(1965), *The Shape of Automation for Men and Management*, New York: Harper & Row.

(1969), *The Sciences of the Artificial*, Cambridge, MA: MIT Press; 3rd edn 1996.
(1972a), *Human Problem Solving* (with A. Newell), Englewood Cliffs, NJ: Prentice-Hall.
(1972b), 'Theories of Bounded Rationality', in C.B. McGuire and R. Radner (eds), *Decision and Organization: A Volume in Honor of Jacob Marschak*, Chapter 8, Amsterdam: North-Holland Publishing Company, pp. 161–76.
(1977), *Models of Discovery*, Dordrecht: Reidel.
(1978), 'Rationality as Process and as Product of Thought', *American Economic Review*, **68**, May, pp. 1–16.
(1979a), *Models of Thought*, New Haven, CT: Yale University Press.
(1979b), 'Rational Decision Making in Business Organizations', *American Economic Review*, **69**, September, pp. 493–513.
(1982a), *Models of Bounded Rationality, Volume I: Economic Analysis and Public Policy*, Cambridge, MA: MIT Press.
(1982b), *Models of Bounded Rationality, Volume II: Behavioral Economics and Business Organization*, Cambridge, MA: MIT Press.
(1992), *Economics, Bounded Rationality and Cognitive Revolution* (with M. Egidi, R. Marris and R. Viale, ed. M. Egidi and R. Marris), Aldershot, UK and Brookfield, US: Edward Elgar.
(1997), *Models of Bounded Rationality, Volume III: Empirically Grounded Economic Reason*, Cambridge, MA: MIT Press.

Secondary Literature

Ando, A. (1979), 'On the Contributions of Herbert A. Simon to Economics', *Scandinavian Journal of Economics*, **81** (1), pp. 83–114.
Baumol, W.J. (1979), 'On the Contributions of Herbert A. Simon to Economics', *Scandinavian Journal of Economics*, **81** (1), pp. 74–82 and 94–114.
Earl, P.E. (ed.) (2001), *The Legacy of Herbert Simon in Economic Analysis*, 2 vols, Cheltenham, UK and Northampton, MA, USA: Edward Elgar.
Nobel Foundation (2010), Official Web Site, www.nobelprize.org.

[1]

A BEHAVIORAL MODEL OF RATIONAL CHOICE

By HERBERT A. SIMON*

Traditional economic theory postulates an "economic man," who, in the course of being "economic" is also "rational." This man is assumed to have knowledge of the relevant aspects of his environment which, if not absolutely complete, is at least impressively clear and voluminous. He is assumed also to have a well-organized and stable system of preferences, and a skill in computation that enables him to calculate, for the alternative courses of action that are available to him, which of these will permit him to reach the highest attainable point on his preference scale.

Recent developments in economics, and particularly in the theory of the business firm, have raised great doubts as to whether this schematized model of economic man provides a suitable foundation on which to erect a theory — whether it be a theory of how firms *do* behave, or of how they "should" rationally behave. It is not the purpose of this paper to discuss these doubts, or to determine whether they are justified. Rather, I shall assume that the concept of "economic man" (and, I might add, of his brother "administrative man") is in need of fairly drastic revision, and shall put forth some suggestions as to the direction the revision might take.

Broadly stated, the task is to replace the global rationality of economic man with a kind of rational behavior that is compatible with the access to information and the computational capacities that are actually possessed by organisms, including man, in the kinds of environments in which such organisms exist. One is tempted to turn

* The ideas embodied in this paper were initially developed in a series of discussions with Herbert Bohnert, Norman Dalkey, Gerald Thompson, and Robert Wolfson during the summer of 1952. These collaborators deserve a large share of the credit for whatever merit this approach to rational choice may possess. A first draft of this paper was prepared in my capacity as a consultant to the RAND Corporation. It has been developed further (including the Appendix) in work with the Cowles Commission for Research in Economics on "Decision Making Under Uncertainty," under contract with the Office of Naval Research, and has been completed with the aid of a grant from the Ford Foundation.

to the literature of psychology for the answer. Psychologists have certainly been concerned with rational behavior, particularly in their interest in learning phenomena. But the distance is so great between our present psychological knowledge of the learning and choice processes and the kinds of knowledge needed for economic and administrative theory that a marking stone placed halfway between might help travellers from both directions to keep to their courses.

Lacking the kinds of empirical knowledge of the decisional processes that will be required for a definitive theory, the hard facts of the actual world can, at the present stage, enter the theory only in a relatively unsystematic and unrigorous way. But none of us is completely innocent of acquaintance with the gross characteristics of human choice, or of the broad features of the environment in which this choice takes place. I shall feel free to call on this common experience as a source of the hypotheses needed for the theory about the nature of man and his world.

The problem can be approached initially either by inquiring into the properties of the choosing organism, or by inquiring into the environment of choice. In this paper, I shall take the former approach. I propose, in a sequel, to deal with the characteristics of the environment and the interrelations of environment and organism.

The present paper, then, attempts to include explicitly some of the properties of the choosing organism as elements in defining what is meant by rational behavior in specific situations and in selecting a rational behavior in terms of such a definition. In part, this involves making more explicit what is already implicit in some of the recent work on the problem — that the state of information may as well be regarded as a characteristic of the decision-maker as a characteristic of his environment. In part, it involves some new considerations — in particular taking into account the simplifications the choosing organism may deliberately introduce into its model of the situation in order to bring the model within the range of its computing capacity.

I. Some General Features of Rational Choice

The "flavor" of various models of rational choice stems primarily from the specific kinds of assumptions that are introduced as to the "givens" or constraints within which rational adaptation must take place. Among the common constraints — which are not themselves the objects of rational calculation — are (1) the set of alternatives open to choice, (2) the relationships that determine the pay-offs ("satisfactions," "goal attainment") as a function of the alternative that is chosen, and (3) the preference-orderings among pay-offs. The selection of particular constraints and the rejection of others for incorporation in the model of rational behavior involves implicit assumptions as to what variables the rational organism "controls" — and hence can "optimize" as a means to rational adaptation — and what variables it must take as fixed. It also involves assumptions as to the character of the variables that are fixed. For example, by making different assumptions about the amount of information the organism has with respect to the relations between alternatives and pay-offs, optimization might involve selection of a certain maximum, of an expected value, or a minimax.

Another way of characterizing the givens and the behavior variables is to say that the latter refer to the organism itself, the former to its environment. But if we adopt this viewpoint, we must be prepared to accept the possibility that what we call "the environment" may lie, in part, within the skin of the biological organism. That is, some of the constraints that must be taken as givens in an optimization problem may be physiological and psychological limitations of the organism (biologically defined) itself. For example, the maximum speed at which an organism can move establishes a boundary on the set of its available behavior alternatives. Similarly, limits on computational capacity may be important constraints entering into the definition of rational choice under particular circumstances. We shall explore possible ways of formulating the process of rational choice in situations where we wish to take explicit account of the "internal" as well as the "external" constraints that define the problem of rationality for the organism.

Whether our interests lie in the normative or in the descriptive aspects of rational choice, the construction of models of this kind should prove instructive. Because of the psychological limits of the organism (particularly with respect to computational and predictive ability), actual human rationality-striving can at best be an extremely crude and simplified approximation to the kind of global rationality that is implied, for example, by game-theoretical models. While the approximations that organisms employ may not be the best — even at the levels of computational complexity they are able to handle — it is probable that a great deal can be learned about possible mechanisms from an examination of the schemes of approximation that are actually employed by human and other organisms.

In describing the proposed model, we shall begin with elements it has in common with the more global models, and then proceed to introduce simplifying assumptions and (what is the same thing) approximating procedures.

1.1 *Primitive Terms and Definitions*

Models of rational behavior — both the global kinds usually constructed, and the more limited kinds to be discussed here — generally require some or all of the following elements:

1. A set of *behavior alternatives* (alternatives of choice or decision). In a mathematical model, these can be represented by a point set, A.

2. The subset of *behavior alternatives that the organism "considers"* or "perceives." That is, the organism may make its choice within a set of alternatives more limited than the whole range objectively available to it. The "considered" subset can be represented by a point set $\mathring{A}$, with $\mathring{A}$ included in A ($\mathring{A} \subset A$).

3. *The possible future states of affairs*, or outcomes of choice, represented by a point set, S. (For the moment it is not necessary to distinguish between actual and perceived outcomes.)

4. A *"pay-off"* function, representing the "value" or "utility" placed by the organism upon each of the possible outcomes of choice. The pay-off may be represented by a real function, $V(s)$ defined for all elements, s, of S. For many purposes there is needed only an ordering relation on pairs of elements of S — i.e., a relation that states that s_1 is preferred to s_2 or vice versa — but to avoid unnecessary complications in the present discussion, we will assume that a cardinal utility, $V(s)$, has been defined.

5. *Information as to which outcomes in S will actually occur* if a particular alternative, a, in A (or in $\mathring{A}$) is chosen. This information may be incomplete — that is, there may be more than one possible outcome, s, for each behavior alternative, a. We represent the information, then, by a mapping of each element, a, in A upon a subset, S_a — the set of outcomes that may ensue if a is the chosen behavior alternative.

6. *Information as to the probability that a particular outcome will ensue* if a particular behavior alternative is chosen. This is a more precise kind of information than that postulated in (5), for it associates with each element, s, in the set S_a, a probability, $P_a(s)$ — the probability that s will occur if a is chosen. The probability $P_a(s)$ is a real, non-negative function with $\sum_{S_a} P_a(s) = 1$.

Attention is directed to the threefold distinction drawn by the definitions among the set of behavior alternatives, A, the set of outcomes or future states of affairs, S, and the pay-off, V. In the ordinary representation of a game, in reduced form, by its pay-off matrix, the set S corresponds to the cells of the matrix, the set A to the strategies of the first player, and the function V to the values in the cells. The set S_a is then the set of cells in the ath row. By keeping in mind this interpretation, the reader may compare the present formulation with "classical" game theory.

1.2 *"Classical" Concepts of Rationality*

With these elements, we can define procedures of rational choice corresponding to the ordinary game-theoretical and probabilistic models.[1]

A. *Max-min Rule.* Assume that whatever alternative is chosen, the worst possible outcome will ensue — the smallest $V(s)$ for s in S_a will be realized. Then select that alternative, a, for which this worst pay-off is as large as possible.

$$\hat{V}(\hat{a}) = \min_{s \epsilon S_{\hat{a}}} V(s) = \max_{a \epsilon A} \min_{s \epsilon S_a} V(s)$$

Instead of the maximum with respect to the set, A, of actual alternatives, we can substitute the maximum with respect to the set, $\mathring{A}$, of "considered" alternatives. The probability distribution of outcomes, (6) does not play any role in the max-min rule.

B. *Probabilistic Rule.* Maximize the expected value of $V(s)$ for the (assumed known) probability distribution, $P_a(s)$.

$$\hat{V}(\hat{a}) = \sum_{s \epsilon S_{\hat{a}}} V(s) P_{\hat{a}}(s) = \max_{a \epsilon A} \sum_{s \epsilon S_a} V(s) P_a(s)$$

C. *Certainty Rule.* Given the information that each a in A (or in $\mathring{A}$) maps upon a specified s_a in S, select the behavior alternative whose outcome has the largest pay-off.

$$\hat{V}(\hat{a}) = V(S_{\hat{a}}) = \max_{a \epsilon A} V(S_a)$$

II. The Essential Simplifications

If we examine closely the "classical" concepts of rationality outlined above, we see immediately what severe demands they make upon the choosing organism. The organism must be able to attach definite pay-offs (or at least a definite range of pay-offs) to each possible outcome. This, of course, involves also the ability to specify the exact nature of the outcomes — there is no room in the scheme for "unanticipated consequences." The pay-offs must be completely ordered —

1. See Kenneth J. Arrow, "Alternative Approaches to the Theory of Choice in Risk-Taking Situations," *Econometrica*, XIX, 404–37 (Oct. 1951).

it must always be possible to specify, in a consistent way, that one outcome is better than, as good as, or worse than any other. And, if the certainty or probabilistic rules are employed, either the outcomes of particular alternatives must be known with certainty, or at least it must be possible to attach definite probabilities to outcomes.

My first empirical proposition is that there is a complete lack of evidence that, in actual human choice situations of any complexity, these computations can be, or are in fact, performed. The introspective evidence is certainly clear enough, but we cannot, of course, rule out the possibility that the unconscious is a better decision-maker than the conscious. Nevertheless, in the absence of evidence that the classical concepts do describe the decision-making process, it seems reasonable to examine the possibility that the actual process is quite different from the ones the rules describe.

Our procedure will be to introduce some modifications that appear (on the basis of casual empiricism) to correspond to observed behavior processes in humans, and that lead to substantial computational simplifications in the making of a choice. There is no implication that human beings use all of these modifications and simplifications all the time. Nor is this the place to attempt the formidable empirical task of determining the extent to which, and the circumstances under which humans actually employ these simplifications. The point is rather that these are procedures which appear often to be employed by human beings in complex choice situations to find an approximate model of manageable proportions.

2.1 *"Simple" Pay-off Functions*

One route to simplification is to assume that $V(s)$ necessarily assumes one of two values, $(1, 0)$, or of three values, $(1, 0, -1)$, for all s in S. Depending on the circumstances, we might want to interpret these values, as (a) (satisfactory or unsatisfactory), or (b) (win, draw or lose).

As an example of (b), let S represent the possible positions in a chess game at White's 20th move. Then a $(+1)$ position is one in which White possesses a strategy leading to a win whatever Black does. A (0) position is one in which White can enforce a draw, but not a win. A (-1) position is one in which Black can force a win.

As an example of (a) let S represent possible prices for a house an individual is selling. He may regard $15,000 as an "acceptable" price, anything over this amount as "satisfactory," anything less as "unsatisfactory." In psychological theory we would fix the boundary at the "aspiration level"; in economic theory we would fix the boundary at the price which evokes indifference between selling and not selling (an opportunity cost concept).

The objection may be raised that, although $16,000 and $25,000 are both "very satisfactory" prices for the house, a rational individual would prefer to sell at the higher price, and hence, that the simple pay-off function is an inadequate representation of the choice situation. The objection may be answered in several different ways, each answer corresponding to a class of situations in which the simple function might be appropriate.

First, the individual may not be confronted simultaneously with

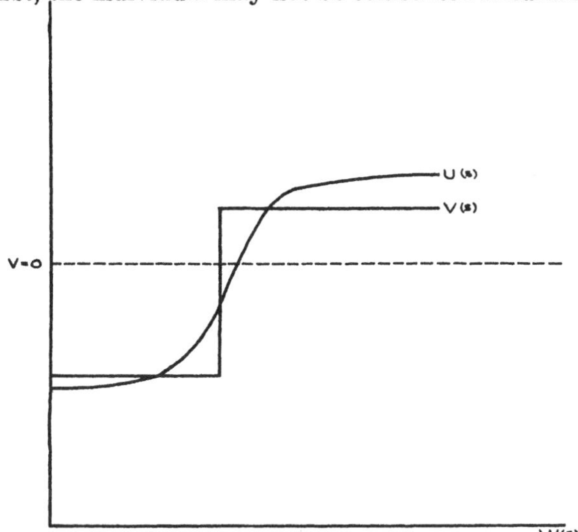

FIGURE I

a number of buyers offering to purchase the house at different prices, but may receive a sequence of offers, and may have to decide to accept or reject each one before he receives the next. (Or, more generally, he may receive a sequence of pairs or triplets or n-tuples of offers, and may have to decide whether to accept the highest of an n-tuple before the next n-tuple is received.) Then, if the elements S correspond to n-tuples of offers, $V(s)$ would be 1 whenever the highest offer in the n-tuple exceeded the "acceptance price" the seller had determined upon at that time. We can then raise the further question of what would be a rational process for determining the acceptance price.[2]

2. See the Appendix. It might be remarked here that the simple risk function, introduced by Wald to bring problems in statistical decision theory within the bounds of computability, is an example of a simple pay-off function as that term is defined here.

Second, even if there were a more general pay-off function, $W(s)$, capable of assuming more than two different values, the simplified $V(s)$ might be a satisfactory approximation to $W(s)$. Suppose, for example, that there were some way of introducing a cardinal utility function, defined over S, say $U(s)$. Suppose further that $U(W)$ is a monotonic increasing function with a strongly negative second derivative (decreasing marginal utility). Then $V(s) = V\{W(s)\}$ might be the approximation as shown on page 107.

When a simple $V(s)$, assuming only the values $(+1, 0)$ is admissible, under the circumstances just discussed or under other circumstances, then a (fourth) rational decision-process could be defined as follows:

D. (i) Search for a set of possible outcomes (a subset, S' in S) such that the pay-off is satisfactory ($V(s) = 1$) for all these possible outcomes (for all s in S').

(ii) Search for a behavior alternative (an a in $\mathring{A}$) whose possible outcomes all are in S' (such that a maps upon a set, S_a, that is contained in S').

If a behavior alternative can be found by this procedure, then a satisfactory outcome is assured. The procedure does not, of course, guarantee the existence or uniqueness of an a with the desired properties.

2.2 *Information Gathering*

One element of realism we may wish to introduce is that, while $V(s)$ may be known in advance, the mapping of A on subsets of S may not. In the extreme case, at the outset each element, a, may be mapped on the whole set, S. We may then introduce into the decision-making process information-gathering steps that produce a more precise mapping of the various elements of A on nonidentical subsets of S. If the information-gathering process is not costless, then one element in the decision will be the determination of how far the mapping is to be refined.

Now in the case of the simple pay-off functions, $(+1, 0)$, the information-gathering process can be streamlined in an important respect. First, we suppose that the individual has initially a very coarse mapping of A on S. Second, he looks for an S' in S such that $V(s) = 1$ for s in S'. Third, he gathers information to refine that part of the mapping of A on S in which elements of S' are involved. Fourth, having refined the mapping, he looks for an a that maps on to a subset of S'.

Under favorable circumstances, this procedure may require the individual to gather only a small amount of information — an insignificant part of the whole mapping of elements of A on individual elements of S. If the search for an a having the desirable properties is successful, he is certain that he cannot better his choice by securing additional information.[3]

It appears that the decision process just described is one of the important means employed by chess players to select a move in the middle and end game. Let A be the set of moves available to White on his 20th move. Let S be a set of positions that might be reached, say, by the 30th move. Let S' be some subset of S that consists of clearly "won" positions. From a very rough knowledge of the mapping of A on S, White tentatively selects a move, a, that (if Black plays in a certain way) maps on S'. By then considering alternative replies for Black, White "explores" the whole mapping of a. His exploration may lead to points, s, that are not in S', but which are now recognized also as winning positions. These can be adjoined to S'. On the other hand, a sequence may be discovered that permits Black to bring about a position that is clearly not "won" for White. Then White may reject the original point, a, and try another.

Whether this procedure leads to any essential simplification of the computation depends on certain empirical facts about the game. Clearly all positions can be categorized as "won," "lost," or "drawn" in an objective sense. But from the standpoint of the player, positions may be categorized as "clearly won," "clearly lost," "clearly drawn," "won or drawn," "drawn or lost," and so forth — depending on the adequacy of this mapping. If the "clearly won" positions represent a significant subset of the objectively "won" positions, then the combinatorics involved in seeing whether a position can be transformed into a clearly won position, for all possible replies by Black, may not be unmanageable.[4] The advantage of this procedure over the more common notion (which may, however, be applicable in the opening) of a general valuation function for positions, taking on values from -1 to 1, is that it implies much less complex and subtle evaluation criteria. All that is required is that the evaluation func-

3. This procedure also dispenses with the necessity of estimating explicitly the cost of obtaining additional information. For further discussion of this point see the comments on dynamics in the last section of this paper.

4. I have estimated roughly the actual degree of simplification that might be realized in the middle game in chess by experimentation with two middle-game positions. A sequence of sixteen moves, eight by each player, might be expected to yield a total of about 10^{24} (one septilion) legally permissible variations. By following the general kind of program just described, it was possible to reduce the number of lines of play examined in each of these positions to fewer than 100 variations — a rather spectacular simplification of the choice problem.

tion be reasonably sensitive in detecting when a position in one of the three states — won, lost, or drawn — has been transformed into a position in another state. The player, instead of seeking for a "best" move, needs only to look for a "good" move.

We see that, by the introduction of a simple pay-off function and of a process for gradually improving the mapping of behavior alternatives upon possible outcomes, the process of reaching a rational decision may be drastically simplified from a computational standpoint. In the theory and practice of linear programming, the distinction is commonly drawn between computations to determine the *feasibility* of a program, and computations to discover the *optimal* program. Feasibility testing consists in determining whether a program satisfies certain linear inequalities that are given at the outset. For example, a mobilization plan may take as given the maximum work force and the steel-making capacity of the economy. Then a feasible program is one that does not require a work force or steel-making facilities exceeding the given limits.

An optimal program is that one of the feasible programs which maximizes a given pay-off function. If, instead of requiring that the pay-off be maximized, we require only that the pay-off exceed some given amount, then we can find a program that satisfies this requirement by the usual methods of feasibility testing. The pay-off requirement is represented simply by an additional linear inequality that must be satisfied. Once this requirement is met, it is not necessary to determine whether there exists an alternative plan with a still higher pay-off.

For all practical purposes, this procedure may represent a sufficient approach to optimization, provided the minimum required pay-off can be set "reasonably." In later sections of this paper we will discuss how this might be done, and we shall show also how the scheme can be extended to vector pay-off functions with multiple components (Optimization requires, of course, a complete ordering of pay-offs).

2.3 *Partial Ordering of Pay-Offs*

The classical theory does not tolerate the incomparability of oranges and apples. It requires a scalar pay-off function, that is, a complete ordering of pay-offs. Instead of a scalar pay-off function, $V(s)$, we might have a vector function, $\mathrm{V}(s)$; where V has the components V_1, V_2, . . . A vector pay-off function may be introduced to handle a number of situations:

1. In the case of a decision to be made by a *group of persons*, components may represent the pay-off functions of the individual

members of the group. What is preferred by one may not be preferred by the others.

2. In the case of an individual, he may be trying to implement a number of *values that do not have a common denominator* — e.g., he compares two jobs in terms of salary, climate, pleasantness of work, prestige, etc.;

3. Where each behavior alternative, *a*, maps on a set of *n possible consequences*, S_a, we may replace the model by one in which each alternative maps on a single consequence, but each consequence has

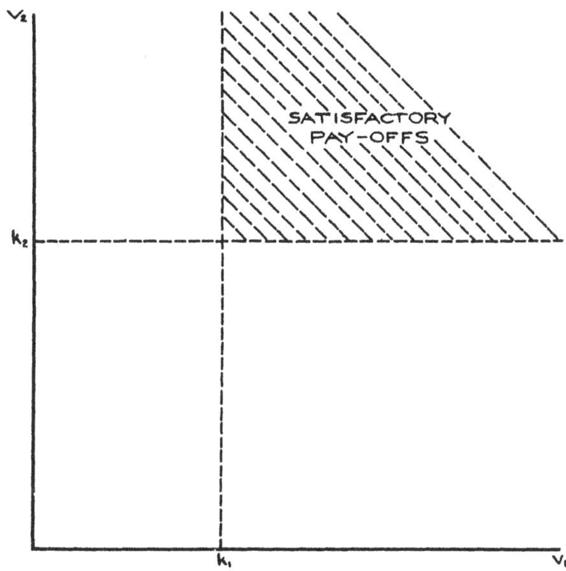

FIGURE II

Partial Ordering of Pay-Offs

as its pay-off the *n*-dimensional vector whose components are the pay-offs of the elements of S_a.

This representation exhibits a striking similarity among these three important cases where the traditional maximizing model breaks down for lack of a complete ordering of the pay-offs. The first case has never been satisfactorily treated — the theory of the *n*-person game is the most ambitious attempt to deal with it, and the so-called "weak welfare principles" of economic theory are attempts to avoid it. The second case is usually handled by superimposing a complete ordering on the points in the vector space ("indifference curves"). The third case has been handled by introducing probabilities as weights for summing the vector components, or by using principles like minimaxing satisfaction or regret.

An extension of the notion of a simplified pay-off function permits us to treat all three cases in much the same fashion. Suppose we regard a pay-off as *satisfactory* provided that $V_i \geqslant k_i$ for all i. Then a reasonable decision rule is the following:

E. Search for a subset S' in S such that V(s) is satisfactory for all s in S' (i.e., $\underset{s \epsilon S'}{V(s)} \geqslant k$).

Then search for an a in A such that S_a lies in S'.

Again existence and uniqueness of solutions are not guaranteed. Rule E is illustrated in Figure II for the case of a 2-component pay-off vector.

In the first of the three cases mentioned above, the satisfactory pay-off corresponds to what I have called a *viable* solution in "A Formal Theory of the Employment Relation" and "A Comparison of Organization Theories."[5] In the second case, the components of V define the *aspiration levels* with respect to several components of pay-off. In the third case (in this case it is most plausible to assume that all the components of k are equal), k_i may be interpreted as the *minimum guaranteed pay-off* — also an aspiration level concept.

III. Existence and Uniqueness of Solutions

Throughout our discussion we have admitted decision procedures that do not guarantee the existence or uniqueness of solutions. This was done in order to construct a model that parallels as nearly as possible the decision procedures that appear to be used by humans in complex decision-making settings. We now proceed to add supplementary rules to fill this gap.

3.1 *Obtaining a Unique Solution*

In most global models of rational choice, all alternatives are evaluated before a choice is made. In actual human decision-making, alternatives are often examined sequentially. We may, or may not, know the mechanism that determines the order of procedure. When alternatives are examined sequentially, we may regard the first satisfactory alternative that is evaluated as such as the one actually selected.

If a chess player finds an alternative that leads to a forced mate for his opponent, he generally adopts this alternative without worry-

5. *Econometrica*, XIX (July 1951), 293–305 and *Review of Economic Studies*, XX (1952–53, No. 1), 40–49.

ing about whether another alternative also leads to a forced mate. In this case we would find it very hard to predict which alternative would be chosen, for we have no theory that predicts the order in which alternatives will be examined. But in another case discussed above — the sale of a house — the environment presents the seller with alternatives in a definite sequence, and the selection of the *first* satisfactory alternative has precise meaning.

However, there are certain dynamic considerations, having a good psychological foundation, that we should introduce at this point. Let us consider, instead of a single static choice situation, a sequence of such situations. The *aspiration level*, which defines a satisfactory alternative, may change from point to point in this sequence of trials. A vague principle would be that as the individual, in his exploration of alternatives, finds it *easy* to discover satisfactory alternatives, his aspiration level rises; as he finds it *difficult* to discover satisfactory alternatives, his aspiration level falls. Perhaps it would be possible to express the ease or difficulty of exploration in terms of the cost of obtaining better information about the mapping of A on S, or the combinatorial magnitude of the task of refining this mapping. There are a number of ways in which this process could be defined formally.

Such changes in aspiration level would tend to bring about a "near-uniqueness" of the satisfactory solutions and would also tend to guarantee the existence of satisfactory solutions. For the failure to discover a solution would depress the aspiration level and bring satisfactory solutions into existence.

3.2 *Existence of Solutions: Further Possibilities*

We have already discussed one mechanism by which the existence of solutions, in the long run, is assured. There is another way of representing the processes already described. Up to this point little use has been made of the distinction between A, the set of behavior alternatives, and $\mathring{A}$, the set of behavior alternatives that the organism considers. Suppose now that the latter is a proper subset of the former. Then, the failure to find a satisfactory alternative in $\mathring{A}$ may lead to a search for additional alternatives in A that can be adjoined to $\mathring{A}$.[6] This procedure is simply an elaboration of the information-

6. I might mention that, in the spirit of crude empiricism, I have presented a number of students and friends with a problem involving a multiple pay-off — in which the pay-off depends violently upon a very contingent and uncertain event — and have found them extremely reluctant to restrict themselves to a set of behavior alternatives allowed by the problem. They were averse to an alternative that promised very large profit or ruin, where the relevant probability could not be computed, and tried to invent new alternatives whose pay-offs were less sensitive to the contingent event. The problem in question is Modigliani's "hot-

gathering process previously described. (We can regard the elements of A that are not in $\mathring{A}$ as elements that are initially mapped on the whole set, S.)

In one organism, dynamic adjustment over a sequence of choices may depend primarily upon adjustments of the aspiration level. In another organism, the adjustments may be primarily in the set $\mathring{A}$: if satisfactory alternatives are discovered easily, $\mathring{A}$ narrows; if it becomes difficult to find satisfactory alternatives, $\mathring{A}$ broadens. The more *persistent* the organism, the greater the role played by the adjustment of $\mathring{A}$, relative to the role played by the adjustment of the aspiration level. (It is possible, of course, and even probable, that there is an asymmetry between adjustments upward and downward.)

If the pay-off were measurable in money or utility terms, and *if* the cost of discovering alternatives were similarly measurable, we could replace the partial ordering of alternatives exhibited in Figure II by a complete ordering (an ordering in terms of a weighted sum of the pay-off and the cost of discovering alternatives). Then we could speak of the optimal degree of persistence in behavior — we could say that the more persistent organism was more rational than the other, or vice versa. But the central argument of the present paper is that the behaving organism does *not* in general know these costs, nor does it have a set of weights for comparing the components of a multiple pay-off. It is precisely because of these limitations on its knowledge and capabilities that the less global models of rationality described here are significant and useful. The question of how it is to behave "rationally," given these limitations, is distinct from the question of how its capabilities could be increased to permit action that would be more "rational" judged from the mountain-top of a more complete model.[7]

The two viewpoints are not, of course, completely different, much less antithetical. We have already pointed out that the organism may possess a whole hierarchy of rational mechanisms — that, for example, the aspiration level itself may be subject to an adjustment process that is rational in some dynamic sense. Moreover, in many situations we may be interested in the precise question of whether one decision-making procedure is more rational than another, and to answer this question we will usually have to construct a broader criterion of rationality that encompasses both procedures as approximations. Our whole point is that it is important to make explicit what level we are considering in such a hierarchy of models, and that

dog stand" problem described in *American Economic Review, Proceedings*, XXXIX (1949), 201–8.

7. One might add: "or judged in terms of the survival value of its choice mechanism."

for many purposes we are interested in models of "limited" rationality rather than models of relatively "global" rationality.

IV. Further Comments on Dynamics

The models thus far discussed are dynamic only in a very special sense: the aspiration level at time t depends upon the previous history of the system (previous aspiration levels and previous levels of attainment). Another kind of dynamic linkage might be very important. The pay-offs in a particular trial might depend not only on the alternative chosen in that trial but also on the alternatives chosen in previous trials.

The most direct representation of this situation is to include, as components of a vector pay-off function, the pay-offs for the whole sequence of trials. But then optimization would require the selection, at the beginning of the sequence, of a strategy for the whole sequence (see the Appendix). Such a procedure would again rapidly complicate the problem beyond the computational capacity of the organism. A possible middle ground is to define for each trial a pay-off function with two components. One would be the "immediate" pay-off (consumption), the other, the "position" in which the organism is left for future trials (saving, liquidity).

Let us consider a chess game in which the players are paid off at the end of each ten moves in proportion to arbitrarily assigned values of their pieces left on the board (say, queen, 1; rook, 10; etc.). Then a player could adopt some kind of planning horizon and include in his estimated pay-off the "goodness" of his position at the planning horizon. A comparable notion in economics is that of the depreciated value of an asset at the planning horizon. To compute such a value precisely would require the player actually to carry his strategy beyond the horizon. If there is time-discounting of pay-offs, this has the advantage of reducing the importance of errors in estimating these depreciated values. (Time-discounting may sometimes be essential in order to assure convergence of the summed pay-offs.)

It is easy to conjure up other dynamic complications, which may be of considerable practical importance. Two more may be mentioned — without attempting to incorporate them formally. The consequences that the organism experiences may change the pay-off function — it doesn't know how well it likes cheese until it has eaten cheese. Likewise, one method for refining the mapping of A on S may be to select a particular alternative and experience its consequences. In these cases, one of the elements of the pay-off associated with a particular alternative is the information that is gathered about the mapping or about the pay-off function.

V. Conclusion

The aim of this paper has been to construct definitions of "rational choice" that are modeled more closely upon the actual decision processes in the behavior of organisms than definitions heretofore proposed. We have outlined a fairly complete model for the static case, and have described one extension of this model into dynamics. As has been indicated in the last section, a great deal remains to be done before we can handle realistically a more completely dynamic system.

In the introduction, it was suggested that definitions of this kind might have normative as well as descriptive value. In particular, they may suggest approaches to rational choice in areas that appear to be far beyond the capacities of existing or prospective computing equipment. The comparison of the I.Q. of a computer with that of a human being is very difficult. If one were to factor the scores made by each on a comprehensive intelligence test, one would undoubtedly find that in those factors on which the one scored as a genius the other would appear a moron — and conversely. A survey of possible definitions of rationality might suggest directions for the design and use of computing equipment with reasonably good scores on some of the factors of intelligence in which present computers are moronic.

The broader aim, however, in constructing these definitions of "approximate" rationality is to provide some materials for the construction of a theory of the behavior of a human individual or of groups of individuals who are making decisions in an organizational context. The apparent paradox to be faced is that the economic theory of the firm and the theory of administration attempt to deal with human behavior in situations in which that behavior is at least "intendedly" rational; while, at the same time, it can be shown that if we assume the global kinds of rationality of the classical theory the problems of internal structure of the firm or other organization largely disappear.[8] The paradox vanishes, and the outlines of theory begin to emerge when we substitute for "economic man" or "administrative man" a choosing organism of limited knowledge and ability. This organism's simplifications of the real world for purposes of choice introduce discrepancies between the simplified model and the reality; and these discrepancies, in turn, serve to explain many of the phenomena of organizational behavior.

8. See Herbert A. Simon, *Administrative Behavior* (Macmillan, 1947), pp. 39–41, 80–84, 96–102, 240–44.

APPENDIX

Example of Rational Determination of an Acceptable Pay-Off

In the body of this paper, the notion is introduced that rational adjustment may operate at various "levels." That is, the organism may choose rationally within a given set of limits postulated by the model, but it may also undertake to set these limits rationally. The house-selling illustration of Section 2.1 provides an example of this.

We suppose that an individual is selling a house. Each day (or other unit of time) he sets an acceptance price: $d(k)$, say, for the kth day. If he receives one or more offers above this price on the day in question, he accepts the highest offer; if he does not receive an offer above $d(k)$, he retains the house until the next day, and sets a new acceptance price, $d(k+1)$.

Now, if he has certain information about the probability distribution of offers on each day, he can set the acceptance price so that it will be optimal in the sense that it will maximize the expected value, $V[d(k)]$, of the sales price.

To show this, we proceed as follows. Let $p_k(y)$ be the probability that y will be the highest price offered on the kth day. Then:

$$P_k(d) = \int_{d(k)}^{\infty} p_k\,(y)dy \tag{A.1}$$

is the probability that the house will be sold on the kth day if it has not been sold earlier.

$$\mathcal{E}_k(d) = \int_{d(k)}^{\infty} y\ p(y,k)dy \tag{A.2}$$

will be the expected value received by the seller on the kth day if the house has not been sold earlier. Taking into account the probability that the house will be sold before the kth day,

$$E_k(d) = \mathcal{E}_k(d) \prod_{j=1}^{k-1} (1 - P_j(d)) \tag{A.3}$$

will be the unconditional expected value of the seller's receipts on the kth day; and

(A.4) $$V\{d(k)\} = \sum_{k=1}^{\infty} E_k(d)$$

will be the expected value of the sales price.

Now we wish to set $d(k)$, for each k, at the level that will maximize (A.4). The k components of the function $d(k)$ are independent. Differentiating V partially with respect to each component, we get:

(A.5) $$\frac{\partial V}{\partial d(i)} = \sum_{k=1}^{\infty} \frac{\partial E_k(d)}{\partial d(i)} \qquad (i = 1, \ldots, n).$$

But:

(A.6) $$\frac{\partial E_i(d)}{\partial d(i)} = \frac{\partial \mathcal{E}_i(d)}{\partial d(i)} \prod_{j=1}^{i-1} (1 - P_j(d)), \quad \text{and}$$

(A.7) $$\frac{\partial E_k(d)}{\partial d(i)} = \mathcal{E}_k(d) \prod_{\substack{j \neq i \\ j=1}}^{k-1} (1 - P_j(d))\left(- \frac{\partial P_i(d)}{\partial d(i)}\right) \text{ for } i < k \text{ and}$$

(A.8) $$\frac{\partial E_k(d)}{\partial d(i)} = 0 \qquad \text{for } i > k.$$

Hence for a maximum:

(A.9) $$\frac{\partial V}{\partial d(i)} = -d(i)p_i(d) \prod_{j=1}^{i-1} (1 - P_j(d)) + \sum_{k=i+1}^{\infty} \mathcal{E}_k (d) \prod_{j \neq i}^{k-1} (1 - P_j(d))p_i(d) = 0.$$

Factoring out $p_i(d)$, we obtain, finally:

(A.10) $$d(i) = \frac{\sum_{k=i+1}^{\infty} \mathcal{E}_k(d) \prod_{j \neq i}^{k-1} (1 - P_j(d))}{\prod_{j=1}^{i-1} (1 - P_j(d))} = \sum_{k=i+1}^{\infty} \mathcal{E}_k(d) \prod_{j=i+1}^{k-1} (1 - P_j(d)).$$

For the answer to be meaningful, the infinite sum in (A.10) must converge. If we look at the definition (A.2) for $\mathcal{E}_k(d)$ we see this would come about if the probability distribution of offers shifts downward through time with sufficient rapidity. Such a shift might correspond to (a) expectations of falling prices, or (b) interpretation of y as the *present value* of the future price, discounted at a sufficiently high interest rate.

Alternatively, we can avoid the question of convergence by assuming a reservation price $a(n)$, for the nth day, which is low enough so that $P_n(d)$ is unity. We shall take this last alternative, but before proceeding, we wish to interpret the equation (A.10). Equation (A.10) says that the rational acceptance price on the ith day, $d(i)$, is equal to the expected value of the sales price if the house is not sold on the ith day and acceptance prices are set optimally for subsequent days. This can be seen by observing that the right-hand side of (A.10) is the same as the right-hand side of (A.4) but with the summation extending from $k = (i + 1)$ instead of from $(k = 1)$.[9]

Hence, in the case where the summation is terminated at period n — that is, the house will be sold with certainty in period n if it has not been sold previously — we can compute the optimal $d(i)$ by working backward from the terminal period, and without the necessity of solving simultaneously the equations (A.10).

It is interesting to observe what additional information the seller needs in order to determine the rational acceptance price, over and above the information he needs once the acceptance price is set. He needs, in fact, virtually complete information as to the probability distribution of offers for all relevant subsequent time periods.

Now the seller who does not have this information, and who will be satisfied with a more bumbling kind of rationality, will make approximations to avoid using the information he doesn't have. First, he will probably limit the planning horizon by assuming a price at which he can certainly sell and will be willing to sell in the nth time period. Second, he will set his initial acceptance price quite high, watch the distribution of offers he receives, and gradually and approximately adjust his acceptance price downward or upward until

9. Equation (A.10) appears to have been arrived at independently by D. A. Darling and W. M. Kincaid. See their abstract, "An Inventory Problem," in the *Journal of Operations Research Society of America*, I, 80 (Feb. 1953).

he receives an offer he accepts — without ever making probability calculations. This, I submit, is the kind of rational adjustment that humans find "good enough" and are capable of exercising in a wide range of practical circumstances.

HERBERT A. SIMON.

CARNEGIE INSTITUTE OF TECHNOLOGY

[2]

The American Economic Review

VOLUME XLIX JUNE 1959 NUMBER THREE

THEORIES OF DECISION-MAKING IN ECONOMICS AND BEHAVIORAL SCIENCE

By HERBERT A. SIMON*

[*Editor's note:* This is the first of eight survey articles on recent developments in economics scheduled for appearance in the *Review* over the next few years. Financial support of the series has been generously provided by the Rockefeller Foundation. The managing editor is particularly grateful for the personal interest which the late Dr. Norman S. Buchanan, Director for the Social Sciences at the Foundation, took in the planning of the project.]

Recent years have seen important new explorations along the boundaries between economics and psychology. For the economist, the immediate question about these developments is whether they include new advances in psychology that can fruitfully be applied to economics. But the psychologist will also raise the converse question—whether there are developments in economic theory and observation that have implications for the central core of psychology. If economics is able to find verifiable and verified generalizations about human economic behavior, then these generalizations must have a place in the more general theories of human behavior to which psychology and sociology aspire. Influence will run both ways.[1]

I. *How Much Psychology Does Economics Need?*

How have psychology and economics gotten along with little relation in the past? The explanation rests on an understanding of the goals toward which economics, viewed as a science and a discipline, has usually aimed.

Broadly speaking, economics can be defined as the science that

* The author is professor of administration at the Carnegie Institute of Technology. This paper draws heavily upon earlier investigations with his colleagues in the Graduate School of Industrial Administration, carried out in library, field, and laboratory, under several grants from the Ford Foundation for research on organizations. He is especially indebted to Julian Feldman, whose wide-ranging exploration of the so-called binary choice experiment [25] has provided an insightful set of examples of alternative approaches to a specific problem of choice.

[1] The influence of economics upon recent work in the psychology of higher mental processes is well illustrated by Bruner, Goodnow and Austin [14, Ch. 3 and 4]. In this work, game theory is used to throw light on the processes of concept formation.

describes and predicts the behavior of several kinds of economic man—notably the consumer and the entrepreneur. While perhaps literally correct, this definition does not reflect the principal focus in the literature of economics. We usually classify work in economics along two dimensions: (a) whether it is concerned with industries and the whole economy (macroeconomics) or with individual economic actors (microeconomics); and (b) whether it strives to describe and explain economic behavior (descriptive economics), or to guide decisions either at the level of public policy (normative macroeconomics) or at the level of the individual consumer or businessman (normative microeconomics).

The profession and literature of economics have been largely preoccupied with normative macroeconomics. Although descriptive macroeconomics provides the scientific base for policy prescription, research emphases have been determined in large part by relevance to policy (e.g., business cycle theory). Normative microeconomics, carried forward under such labels as "management science," "engineering economics," and "operations research," is now a flourishing area of work having an uneasy and ill-defined relation with the profession of economics, traditionally defined. Much of the work is being done by mathematicians, statisticians, engineers, and physical scientists (although many mathematical economists have also been active in it).[2]

This new area, like the old, is normative in orientation. Economists have been relatively uninterested in descriptive microeconomics—understanding the behavior of individual economic agents—except as this is necessary to provide a foundation for macroeconomics. The normative microeconomist "obviously" doesn't need a theory of human behavior: he wants to know how people *ought* to behave, not how they *do* behave. On the other hand, the macroeconomist's lack of concern with individual behavior stems from different considerations. First, he assumes that the economic actor is rational, and hence he makes strong predictions about human behavior without performing the hard work of observing people. Second, he often assumes competition, which carries with it the implication that only the rational survive. Thus, the classical economic theory of markets with perfect competition and rational agents is deductive theory that requires almost no contact with empirical data once its assumptions are accepted.[3]

Undoubtedly there is an area of human behavior that fits these assumptions to a reasonable approximation, where the classical theory

[2] The models of rational decision-making employed in operations research are surveyed in Churchman, Ackoff, and Arnoff [16]; Bowman and Fetter [11]; and Vazsonyi [69].

[3] As an example of what passes for empirical "evidence" in this literature, I cite pp. 22-23 of Friedman's *Essays in Positive Economics* [27], which will amaze anyone brought up in the empirical tradition of psychology and sociology, although it has apparently excited little adverse comment among economists.

with its assumptions of rationality is a powerful and useful tool. Without denying the existence of this area, or its importance, I may observe that it fails to include some of the central problems of conflict and dynamics with which economics has become more and more concerned. A metaphor will help to show the reason for this failure.

Suppose we were pouring some viscous liquid—molasses—into a bowl of very irregular shape. What would we need in order to make a theory of the form the molasses would take in the bowl? How much would we have to know about the properties of molasses to predict its behavior under the circumstances? If the bowl were held motionless, and if we wanted only to predict behavior in equilibrium, we would have to know little, indeed, about molasses. The single essential assumption would be that the molasses, under the force of gravity, would minimize the height of its center of gravity. With this assumption, which would apply as well to any other liquid, and a complete knowledge of the environment—in this case the shape of the bowl—the equilibrium is completely determined. Just so, the equilibrium behavior of a perfectly adapting organism depends only on its goal and its environment; it is otherwise completely independent of the internal properties of the organism.

If the bowl into which we were pouring the molasses were jiggled rapidly, or if we wanted to know about the behavior before equilibrium was reached, prediction would require much more information. It would require, in particular, more information about the properties of molasses: its viscosity, the rapidity with which it "adapted" itself to the containing vessel and moved towards its "goal" of lowering its center of gravity. Likewise, to predict the short-run behavior of an adaptive organism, or its behavior in a complex and rapidly changing environment, it is not enough to know its goals. We must know also a great deal about its internal structure and particularly its mechanisms of adaptation.

If, to carry the metaphor a step farther, new forces, in addition to gravitational force, were brought to bear on the liquid, we would have to know still more about it even to predict behavior in equilibrium. Now its tendency to lower its center of gravity might be countered by a force to minimize an electrical or magnetic potential operating in some lateral direction. We would have to know its relative susceptibility to gravitational and electrical or magnetic force to determine its equilibrium position. Similarly, in an organism having a multiplicity of goals, or afflicted with some kind of internal goal conflict, behavior could be predicted only from information about the relative strengths of the several goals and the ways in which the adaptive processes responded to them.

Economics has been moving steadily into new areas where the power of the classical equilibrium model has never been demonstrated, and where its adequacy must be considered anew. Labor economics is such an area, oligopoly or imperfect competition theory another, decision-making under uncertainty a third, and the theory of economic development a fourth. In all of these areas the complexity and instability of his environment becomes a central feature of the choices that economic man faces. To explain his behavior in the face of this complexity, the theory must describe him as something more than a featureless, adaptive organism; it must incorporate at least some description of the processes and mechanisms through which the adaptation takes place. Let us list a little more concretely some specific problems of this kind:

(a) The classical theory postulates that the consumer maximizes utility. Recent advances in the theory of rational consumer choice have shown that the existence of a utility function, and its characteristics, if it exists, can be studied empirically.

(b) The growing separation between ownership and management has directed attention to the motivations of managers and the adequacy of the profit-maximization assumption for business firms. So-called human relations research has raised a variety of issues about the motivation of both executives and employees.

(c) When, in extending the classical theory, the assumptions of perfect competition were removed, even the definition of rationality became ambiguous. New definitions had to be constructed, by no means as "obvious" intuitively as simple maximization, to extend the theory of rational behavior to bilateral monopoly and to other bargaining and outguessing situations.

(d) When the assumptions of perfect foresight were removed, to handle uncertainty about the environment, the definition of rationality had to be extended in another direction to take into account prediction and the formation of expectations.

(e) Broadening the definition of rationality to encompass goal conflict and uncertainty made it hard to ignore the distinction between the objective environment in which the economic actor "really" lives and the subjective environment that he perceives and to which he responds. When this distinction is made, we can no longer predict his behavior—even if he behaves rationally—from the characteristics of the objective environment; we also need to know something about his perceptual and cognitive processes.

We shall use these five problem areas as a basis for sorting out some recent explorations in theory, model building, and empirical testing. In Section II, we will examine developments in the theory of utility and consumer choice. In Section III, we will consider somewhat parallel issues relating to the motivation of managers. In Section IV, we will deal with conflict of goals and the phenomena of bargaining. In Section V, we will survey some of the work that has been done on uncertainty and the formation of expectations. In Section VI, we will explore recent developments in the theory of human problem-solving and other higher mental processes, and see what implications these have for economic decision-making.

II. *The Utility Function*

The story of the re-establishment of cardinal utility, as a consequence of the introduction of uncertainty into the theory of choice, is well known.[4] When Pareto and Slutsky had shown that the theory of consumer demand could be derived from the properties of indifference curves, without postulating a cardinal utility function underlying these curves, it became fashionable to regard utility as an ordinal measure—a ranking of alternatives by preference. Indeed, it could be shown that only ordinal utility had operational status—that the experiments that had been proposed, and even tried in a couple of instances, to measure an individual's utilities by asking him to choose among alternatives could never distinguish between two cardinal utility functions that were ordinally equivalent—that differed only by stretchings and contractions of the unit of measurement.

It was shown by von Neumann and Morgenstern, as a byproduct of their development of the theory of games, that if the choice situation were extended to include choices among uncertain prospects—among lottery tickets, say—cardinal utilities could be assigned to the outcomes in an unequivocal way.[5] Under these conditions, if the subject's behavior was consistent, it was possible to measure cardinally the utilities that different outcomes had for him.

A person who behaved in a manner consistent with the axioms of choice of von Neumann and Morgenstern would act so as to maximize the expected value—the average, weighted by the probabilities of the alternative outcomes of a choice—of his utility. The theory could be tested empirically, however, only on the assumption that the probabilities assigned to the alternatives by the subject were identical with the "objective" probabilities of these events as known to the experimenter. For example, if a subject believed in the gamblers' fallacy, that after a run of heads an unbiased coin would be more likely to fall tails, his choices might appear inconsistent with his utility function, while the real difficulty would lie in his method of assigning probabilities. This

[4] Ward Edwards [23] provides an account of these developments from the psychologist's point of view; Chapter 2 of Luce and Raiffa [43] is an excellent introduction to the "new" utility theory. Arrow [5] contains a nonmathematical survey of this and related topics.

[5] The second edition of von Neumann and Morgenstern [50] contains the first rigorous axiomatic demonstration of this point.

difficulty of "subjective" versus "objective" probability soon came to light when attempts were made to test experimentally whether people behaved in accordance with the predictions of the new utility theory. At the same time, it was discovered that the problem had been raised and solved thirty years earlier by the English philosopher and mathematician Frank Ramsey.[6] Ramsey had shown that, by an appropriate series of experiments, the utilities and subjective probabilities assigned by a subject to a set of uncertain alternatives could be measured simultaneously.

Empirical Studies

The new axiomatic foundations of the theory of utility, which show that it is possible at least in principle to determine empirically whether people "have" utility functions of the appropriate kind, have led to a rash of choice experiments. An experimenter who wants to measure utilities, not merely in principle but in fact, faces innumerable difficulties. Because of these difficulties, most experiments have been limited to confronting the subjects with alternative lottery tickets, at various odds, for small amounts of money. The weight of evidence is that, under these conditions, most persons choose in a way that is reasonably consistent with the axioms of the theory—they behave as though they were maximizing the expected value of utility and as though the utilities of the several alternatives can be measured.[7]

When these experiments are extended to more "realistic" choices—choices that are more obviously relevant to real-life situations—difficulties multiply. In the few extensions that have been made, it is not at all clear that the subjects behave in accordance with the utility axioms. There is some indication that when the situation is very simple and transparent, so that the subject can easily see and remember when he is being consistent, he behaves like a utility maximizer. But as the choices become a little more complicated—choices, for example, among phonograph records instead of sums of money—he becomes much less consistent [21, Ch. 3] [47].[8]

We can interpret these results in either of two ways. We can say that consumers "want" to maximize utility, and that if we present

[6] Ramsey's important essay [57] was sufficiently obscure that it was overlooked until the ideas were rediscovered independently by de Finetti [26]. Valuable notes on the history of the topic together with a thorough formal treatment will be found in the first five chapters of Savage [58].

[7] Some of the empirical evidence is reviewed in [23]. A series of more recent empirical studies is reported in Davidson and Suppes [21].

[8] Some more recent experiments [57a], show a relatively high degree of transitivity. A. G. Papandreou, in a publication I have not yet seen (University of California Publications in Economics) also reports a high degree of transitivity.

them with clear and simple choices that they understand they will do so. Or we can say that the real world is so complicated that the theory of utility maximization has little relevance to real choices. The former interpretation has generally appeared more attractive to economists trained in classical utility theory and to management scientists seeking rules of behavior for normative microeconomics; the latter to behavioral scientists interested in the description of behavior.

Normative Applications

The new utility theory has provided the formal framework for much recent work in mathematical statistics—i.e., statistical decision theory.[9] Similarly (it would be accurate to say "synonymously"), this framework provides the basis for most of the normative models of management science and operations research designed for actual application to the decision-making problems of the firm.[10] Except for some very recent developments, linear programming has been limited to decision-making under certainty, but there have been far-reaching developments of dynamic programming dealing with the maximization of expected values of outcomes (usually monetary outcomes) in situations where future events can be predicted only in terms of probability distributions.[11]

Again, there are at least two distinct interpretations that can be placed on these developments. On the one hand, it can be argued: "Firms would like to maximize profits if they could. They have been limited in doing so by the conceptual and computational difficulties of finding the optimal courses of action. By providing powerful new mathematical tools and computing machines, we now enable them to behave in the manner predicted by Alfred Marshall, even if they haven't been able to in the past." Nature will imitate art and economic man will become as real (and as artificial) as radios and atomic piles.

The alternative interpretation rests on the observation that, even with the powerful new tools and machines, most real-life choices still lie beyond the reach of maximizing techniques—unless the situations are heroically simplified by drastic approximations. If man, according to this interpretation, makes decisions and choices that have some ap-

[9] The systematic development of statistics as decision theory is due largely to A. Wald [70] on the basis of the earlier work of J. Neyman and E. Pearson. Savage [58] carries the development further, erecting the foundations of statistics solidly on utility and probability theory.

[10] This work relates, of course, to profit maximization and cost minimization rather than utility maximization, but it is convenient to mention it at this point. See [11] [16] [69].

[11] Arrow, Harris and Marschak [3] were among the first to treat inventory decisions dynamically. A general treatment of the theory of dynamic programming will be found in Bellman [9].

pearance of rationality, rationality in real life must involve something simpler than maximization of utility or profit. In Section VI, we will see where this alternative interpretation leads.

The Binary Choice Experiment

Much recent discussion about utility has centered around a particularly simple choice experiment. This experiment, in numerous variants, has been used by both economists and psychologists to test the most diverse kinds of hypotheses. We will describe it so that we can use it as a common standard of comparison for a whole range of theories and empirical studies.[12]

We will call the situation we are about to describe the *binary choice* experiment. It is better known to most game theorists—particularly those located not far from Nevada—as a two-armed bandit; and to most psychologists as a partial reinforcement experiment. The subject is required, in each of a series of trials, to choose one or the other of two symbols—say, plus or minus. When he has chosen, he is told whether his choice was "right" or "wrong," and he may also receive a reward (in psychologist's language, a reinforcement) for "right" choices. The experimenter can arrange the schedule of correct responses in a variety of ways. There may be a definite pattern, or they may be randomized. It is not essential that one and only one response be correct on a given trial: the experimenter may determine that both or neither will be correct. In the latter case the subject may or may not be informed whether the response he did not choose would have been correct.

How would a utility-maximizing subject behave in the binary choice experiment? Suppose that the experimenter rewarded "plus" on one-third of the trials, determined at random, and "minus" on the remaining two-thirds. Then a subject, provided that he believed the sequence was random and observed that minus was rewarded twice as often as plus, should always, rationally, choose minus. He would find the correct answer two-thirds of the time, and more often than with any other strategy.

Unfortunately for the classical theory of utility in its simplest form, few subjects behave in this way. The most commonly observed behavior is what is called *event matching*.[13] The subject chooses the two alternatives (not necessarily at random) with relative frequencies roughly proportional to the relative frequencies with which they are rewarded.

[12] My understanding of the implications of the binary choice experiment owes much to conversations with Julian Feldman, and to his unpublished work on the experiment. See also, Bush and Mosteller [15] particularly Chapter 13.

[13] An example of data consistent with event-matching behavior is given on page 283 of [15].

Thus, in the example given, two-thirds of the time he would choose minus, and as a result would make a correct response, on the average, in 5 trials out of 9 (on two-thirds of the trials in which he chooses minus, and one-third of those in which he chooses plus).[14]

All sorts of explanations have been offered for the event-matching behavior. The simplest is that the subject just doesn't understand what strategy would maximize his expected utility; but with adult subjects in a situation as transparent as this one, this explanation seems far-fetched. The alternative explanations imply either that the subject regards himself as being engaged in a competitive game with the experimenter (or with "nature" if he accepts the experimenter's explanation that the stimulus is random), or that his responses are the outcome of certain kinds of learning processes. We will examine these two types of explanation further in Sections IV and V respectively. The important conclusion at this point is that even in an extremely simple situation, subjects do not behave in the way predicted by a straightforward application of utility theory.

Probabilistic Preferences

Before we leave the subject of utility, we should mention one recent important development. In the formalizations mentioned up to this point, probabilities enter only into the estimation of the consequences that will follow one alternative or another. Given any two alternatives, the first is definitely preferable to the second (in terms of expected utility), or the second to the first, or they are strictly indifferent. If the same pair of alternatives is presented to the subject more than once, he should always prefer the same member of the pair.

One might think this requirement too strict—that, particularly if the utility attached to one alternative were only slightly greater or less than that attached to the other, the subject might vacillate in his choice. An empirical precedent for such vacillation comes not only from casual observation of indecision but from analogous phenomena in the psychophysical laboratory. When subjects are asked to decide which of two weights is heavier, the objectively heavier one is chosen more often than the lighter one, but the relative frequency of choosing the heavier approaches one-half as the two weights approach equality. The probability that a subject will choose the objectively heavier weight depends, in general, on the ratio of the two weights.

Following several earlier attempts, a rigorous and complete axiom system for a utility theory incorporating probabilistic preferences has been constructed recently by Duncan Luce [cf. 43, App. 1]. Although

[14] Subjects tend to choose the more highly rewarded alternative slightly more frequently than is called for by event matching. Hence, the actual behavior tends to be some kind of average between event matching and the optimal behavior. See [15, Ch. 13].

the theory weakens the requirements of consistency in preference, it is empirically testable, at least in principle. Conceptually, it provides a more plausible interpretation of the notion of "indifference" than does the classical theory.

III. *The Goals of Firms*

Just as the central assumption in the theory of consumption is that the consumer strives to maximize his utility, so the crucial assumption in the theory of the firm is that the entrepreneur strives to maximize his residual share—his profit. Attacks on this hypothesis have been frequent.[15] We may classify the most important of these as follows:

(a) The theory leaves ambiguous whether it is short-run or long-run profit that is to be maximized.

(b) The entrepreneur may obtain all kinds of "psychic income" from the firm, quite apart from monetary rewards. If he is to maximize his utility, then he will sometimes balance a loss of profits against an increase in psychic income. But if we allow "psychic income," the criterion of profit maximization loses all of its definiteness.

(c) The entrepreneur may not care to maximize, but may simply want to earn a return that he regards as satisfactory. By sophistry and and adept use of the concept of psychic income, the notion of seeking a satisfactory return can be translated into utility maximizing but not in any operational way. We shall see in a moment that "satisfactory profits" is a concept more meaningfully related to the psychological notion of aspiration levels than to maximization.

(d) It is often observed that under modern conditions the equity owners and the active managers of an enterprise are separate and distinct groups of people, so that the latter may not be motivated to maximize profits.

(e) Where there is imperfect competition among firms, maximizing is an ambiguous goal, for what action is optimal for one firm depends on the actions of the other firms.

In the present section we shall deal only with the third of these five issues. The fifth will be treated in the following section; the first, second, and fourth are purely empirical questions that have been discussed at length in the literature; they will be considered here only for their bearing on the question of satisfactory profits.

Satisficing versus Maximizing

The notion of satiation plays no role in classical economic theory, while it enters rather prominently into the treatment of motivation in psychology. In most psychological theories the motive to act stems from

[15] For a survey of recent discussions see Papandreou [55].

drives, and action terminates when the drive is satisfied. Moreover, the conditions for satisfying a drive are not necessarily fixed, but may be specified by an aspiration level that itself adjusts upward or downward on the basis of experience.

If we seek to explain business behavior in the terms of this theory, we must expect the firm's goals to be not maximizing profit, but attaining a certain level or rate of profit, holding a certain share of the market or a certain level of sales. Firms would try to "satisfice" rather than to maximize.[16]

It has sometimes been argued that the distinction between satisficing and maximizing is not important to economic theory. For in the first place, the psychological evidence on individual behavior shows that aspirations tend to adjust to the attainable. Hence in the long run, the argument runs, the level of aspiration and the attainable maximum will be very close together. Second, even if some firms satisficed, they would gradually lose out to the maximizing firms, which would make larger profits and grow more rapidly than the others.

These are, of course, precisely the arguments of our molasses metaphor, and we may answer them in the same way that we answered them earlier. The economic environment of the firm is complex, and it changes rapidly; there is no a priori reason to assume the attainment of long-run equilibrium. Indeed, the empirical evidence on the distribution of firms by size suggests that the observed regularities in size distribution stem from the statistical equilibrium of a population of adaptive systems rather than the static equilibrium of a population of maximizers.[17]

Models of satisficing behavior are richer than models of maximizing behavior, because they treat not only of equilibrium but of the method of reaching it as well. Psychological studies of the formation and change of aspiration levels support propositions of the following kinds.[18] (a) When performance falls short of the level of aspiration, search behavior (particularly search for new alternatives of action) is induced. (b) At the same time, the level of aspiration begins to adjust itself downward until goals reach levels that are practically attainable. (c) If the two mechanisms just listed operate too slowly to adapt aspirations to performance, emotional behavior—apathy or aggression, for example—will replace rational adaptive behavior.

[16] A comparison of satisficing with maximizing models of decision-making can be found in [64, Ch. 14]. Katona [40] has independently made similar comparisons of economic and psychological theories of decision.

[17] Simon and Bonini [66] have constructed a stochastic model that explains the observed data on the size distributions of business firms.

[18] A standard psychological reference on aspiration levels is [42]. For applications to economics, see [61] and [45] (in the latter, consult the index under "aspiration levels").

The aspiration level defines a natural zero point in the scale of utility—whereas in most classical theories the zero point is arbitrary. When the firm has alternatives open to it that are at or above its aspiration level, the theory predicts that it will choose the best of those known to be available. When none of the available alternatives satisfies current aspirations, the theory predicts qualitatively different behavior: in the short run, search behavior and the revision of targets; in the longer run, what we have called above emotional behavior, and what the psychologist would be inclined to call neurosis.[19]

Studies of Business Behavior

There is some empirical evidence that business goals are, in fact, stated in satisficing terms.[20] First, there is the series of studies stemming from the pioneering work of Hall and Hitch that indicates that businessmen often set prices by applying a standard markup to costs. Some economists have sought to refute this fact, others to reconcile it—if it is a fact—with marginalist principles. The study of Earley [22a, pp. 44-70] belongs to the former category, but its evidence is suspect because the questions asked of businessmen are leading ones—no one likes to admit that he would accept less profit if he could have more. Earley did not ask his respondents how they determined marginal cost and marginal revenue, how, for example, they estimated demand elasticities.

Another series of studies derived from the debate over the Keynesian doctrine that the amount of investment was insensitive to changes in the rate of interest. The general finding in these studies has been that the rate of interest is not an important factor in investment decisions [24] [39, Ch. 11] [71].

More recently, my colleagues Cyert and March, have attempted to test the satisficing model in a more direct way [19]. They found in one industry some evidence that firms with a declining share of market strove more vigorously to increase their sales than firms whose shares of the market were steady or increasing.

Aspirations in the Binary Choice Experiment

Although to my knowledge this has not been done, it would be easy to look for aspiration-level phenomena in the binary choice experiment.

[19] Lest this last term appear fanciful I should like to call attention to the phenomena of panic and broken morale, which are well known to observers of the stock market and of organizations but which have no reasonable interpretation in classical utility theory. I may also mention that psychologists use the theory described here in a straightforward way to produce experimental neurosis in animal and human subjects.

[20] A comprehensive bibliography of empirical work prior to 1950 will be found in [37]. Some of the more recent work is [19] [24] [39, Ch. 11].

By changing the probabilities of reward in different ways for different groups of subjects, we could measure the effects of these changes on search behavior—where amount of search would be measured by changes in the pattern of responses.

Economic Implications

It has sometimes been argued that, however realistic the classical theory of the firm as a profit maximizer, it is an adequate theory for purposes of normative macroeconomics. Mason, for example, in commenting on Papandreou's essay on "Problems in the Theory of the Firm" [55, pp. 183-222] says, "The writer of this critique must confess a lack of confidence in the marked superiority, *for purposes of economic analysis,* of this newer concept of the firm over the older conception of the entrepreneur." The italics are Mason's.

The theory of the firm is important for welfare economics—e.g., for determining under what circumstances the behavior of the firm will lead to efficient allocation of resources. The satisficing model vitiates all the conclusions about resource allocation that are derivable from the maximizing model when perfect competition is assumed. Similarly, a dynamic theory of firm sizes, like that mentioned above, has quite different implications for public policies dealing with concentration than a theory that assumes firms to be in static equilibrium. Hence, welfare economists are justified in adhering to the classical theory only if: (a) the theory is empirically correct as a description of the decision-making process; or (b) it is safe to assume that the system operates in the neighborhood of the static equilibrium. What evidence we have mostly contradicts both assumptions.

IV. *Conflict of Interest*

Leaving aside the problem of the motivations of hired managers, conflict of interest among economic actors creates no difficulty for classical economic theory—indeed, it lies at the very core of the theory —so long as each actor treats the other actors as parts of his "given" environment, and doesn't try to predict their behavior and anticipate it. But when this restriction is removed, when it is assumed that a seller takes into account the reactions of buyers to his actions, or that each manufacturer predicts the behaviors of his competitors—all the familiar difficulties of imperfect competition and oligopoly arise.[21]

The very assumptions of omniscient rationality that provide the basis for deductive prediction in economics when competition is present lead

[21] There is by now a voluminous literature on the problem. The difficulties in defining rationality in competitive situations are well stated in the first chapter of von Neumann and Morgenstern [50].

to ambiguity when they are applied to competition among the few. The central difficulty is that rationality requires one to outguess one's opponents, but not to be outguessed by them, and this is clearly not a consistent requirement if applied to all the actors.

Game Theory

Modern game theory is a vigorous and extensive exploration of ways of extending the concept of rational behavior to situations involving struggle, outguessing, and bargaining. Since Luce and Raiffa [43] have recently provided us with an excellent survey and evaluation of game theory, I shall not cover the same ground here.[22] I concur in their general evaluation that, while game theory has greatly clarified the issues involved, it has not provided satisfactory solutions. Not only does it leave the definition of rational conduct ambiguous in all cases save the zero-sum two-person game, but it requires of economic man even more fantastic reasoning powers than does classical economic theory.[23]

Power and Bargaining

A number of exploratory proposals have been put forth as alternatives to game theory—among them Galbraith's notion of countervailing power [30] and Schelling's bargaining theory [59] [60]. These analyses draw at least as heavily upon theories of power and bargaining developed initially to explain political phenomena as upon economic theory. They do not lead to any more specific predictions of behavior than do game-theoretic approaches, but place a greater emphasis upon description and actual observation, and are modest in their attempt to derive predictions by deductive reasoning from a few "plausible" premises about human behavior.

At least four important areas of social science and social policy, two of them in economics and two more closely related to political science, have as their central concern the phenomena of power and the processes of bargaining: the theory of political parties, labor-management relations, international politics, and oligopoly theory. Any progress in the basic theory applicable to one of these is certain to be of almost equal importance to the others. A growing recognition of their common concern is evidenced by the initiation of a new cross-disciplinary journal, *Journal of Conflict Resolution.*

[22] Chapters 5 and 6 of [43] provide an excellent survey of the attempts that have been made to extend the theory of games to the kinds of situations most relevant to economics.

[23] In a forthcoming volume on *Strategy and Market Structure,* Martin Shubik approaches the topics of imperfect competition and oligopoly from the standpoint of the theory of games.

Games against Nature

While the binary choice experiment is basically a one-person game, it is possible to interpret it as a "game against nature," and hence to try to explain it in game-theoretic terms. According to game theory, the subject, if he believes in a malevolent nature that manipulates the dice against him, should minimax his expected utility instead of maximizing it. That is, he should adopt the course of action that will maximize his expected utility under the assumption that nature will do her worst to him.

Minimaxing expected utility would lead the subject to call plus or minus at random and with equal probability, regardless of what the history of rewards has been. This is something that subjects demonstrably do not do.

However, it has been suggested by Savage [58] and others that people are not as interested in maximizing utility as they are in minimizing regret. "Regret" means the difference between the reward actually obtained and the reward that could have been obtained with perfect foresight (actually, with perfect hindsight!). It turns out that minimaxing regret in the binary choice experiment leads to event-matching behavior [64, Ch. 16]. Hence, the empirical evidence is at least crudely consistent with the hypothesis that people play against nature by minimaxing regret. We shall see, however, that event-matching is also consistent with a number of other rules of behavior that seem more plausible on their face; hence we need not take the present explanation too seriously—at least I am not inclined to do so.

V. *The Formation of Expectations*

While the future cannot enter into the determination of the present, expectations about the future can and do. In trying to gain an understanding of the saving, spending, and investment behavior of both consumers and firms, and to make short-term predictions of this behavior for purposes of policy-making, economists have done substantial empirical work as well as theorizing on the formation of expectations.

Empirical Studies

A considerable body of data has been accumulated on consumers' plans and expectations from the Survey of Consumer Finances, conducted for the Board of Governors of the Federal Reserve System by the Survey Research Center of the University of Michigan [39, Ch. 5]. These data, and similar data obtained by others, begin to give us some information on the expectations of consumers about their own incomes, and the predictive value of their expenditure plans for their actual subsequent behavior. Some large-scale attempts have been made, notably by Modigliani and Brumberg [48, pp. 388-436] and, a little later, by Friedman [28] to relate these empirical findings to classical utility theory. The current empirical research on businessmen's expectations is of two main kinds:

1. Surveys of businessmen's own forecasts of business and business conditions in the economy and in their own industries [24, pp. 165-88] [29, pp. 189-98]. These are obtained by straightforward questionnaire methods that assume, implicitly, that businessmen can and do make such forecasts. In some uses to which the data are put, it is also assumed that the forecasts are used as one basis for businessmen's actions.

2. Studies of business decisions and the role of expectations in these decisions—particularly investment and pricing decisions. We have already referred to studies of business decisions in our discussion of the goals of the firm.[24]

Expectations and Probability

The classical way to incorporate expectations into economic theory is to assume that the decision-maker estimates the joint probability distribution of future events.[25] He can then act so as to maximize the expected value of utility or profit, as the case may be. However satisfying this approach may be conceptually, it poses awkward problems when we ask how the decision-maker actually estimates the parameters of the joint probability distribution. Common sense tells us that people don't make such estimates, nor can we find evidence that they do by examining actual business forecasting methods. The surveys of businessmen's expectations have never attempted to secure such estimates, but have contented themselves with asking for point predictions—which, at best, might be interpreted as predictions of the means of the distributions.

It has been shown that under certain special circumstances the mean of the probability distribution is the only parameter that is relevant for decision—that even if the variance and higher moments were known to the rational decision-maker, he would have no use for them.[26] In these cases, the arithmetic mean is actually a certainty equivalent, the optimal decision turns out to be the same as if the future were known with certainty. But the situations where the mean is a certainty equival-

[24] See the references cited [12, p. 160].

[25] A general survey of approaches to decision-making under uncertainty will be found in [2] and in [43, Ch. 13].

[26] The special case in which mean expectations constitute a certainty equivalent is treated in [62]. An alternative derivation, and fuller discussion is given by Theil [67, Ch. 8, sect. 6].

ent are, as we have said, very special ones, and there is no indication that businessmen ever ask whether the necessary conditions for this equivalence are actually met in practice. They somehow make forecasts in the form of point predictions and act upon them in one way or another.

The "somehow" poses questions that are important for business cycle theory, and perhaps for other problems in economics. The way in which expectations are formed may affect the dynamic stability of the economy, and the extent to which cycles will be amplified or damped. Some light, both empirical and theoretical, has recently been cast on these questions. On the empirical side, attempts have been made: (a) to compare businessmen's forecasts with various "naïve" models that assume the future will be some simple function of the recent past, and (b) to use such naïve models themselves as forecasting devices.

The simplest naïve model is one that assumes the next period will be exactly like the present. Another assumes that the change from present to next period will equal the change from last period to present; a third, somewhat more general, assumes that the next period will be a weighted average of recent past periods. The term "naïve model" has been applied loosely to various forecasting formulae of these general kinds. There is some affirmative evidence that business forecasts fit such models. There is also evidence that elaboration of the models beyond the first few steps of refinement does not much improve prediction; see, for example, [20]. Arrow and his colleagues [4] have explored some of the conditions under which forecasting formulae will, and will not, introduce dynamic instability into an economic system that is otherwise stable. They have shown, for example, that if a system of multiple markets is stable under static expectations, it is stable when expectations are based on a moving average of past values.

The work on the formation of expectations represents a significant extension of classical theory. For, instead of taking the environment as a "given," known to the economic decision-maker, it incorporates in the theory the processes of acquiring knowledge about that environment. In doing so, it forces us to include in our model of economic man some of his properties as a learning, estimating, searching, information-processing organism [65].

The Cost of Information

There is one way in which the formation of expectations might be reincorporated in the body of economic theory: by treating information-gathering as one of the processes of production, so to speak, and applying to it the usual rules of marginal analysis. Information, says price theory, should be gathered up to the point where the incremental cost of additional information is equal to the incremental profit that can be earned by having it. Such an approach can lead to propositions about optimal amounts of information-gathering activity and about the relative merits of alternative information-gathering and estimating schemes.[27]

This line of investigation has, in fact, been followed in statistical decision theory. In sampling theory we are concerned with the optimal size of sample (and in the special and ingenious case of sequential sampling theory, with knowing when to stop sampling), and we wish to evaluate the efficiencies of alternative sampling procedures. The latter problem is the simpler, since it is possible to compare the relative costs of alternative schemes that have the same sampling error, and hence to avoid estimating the value of the information.[28] However, some progress has been made also toward estimating the value of improved forecast accuracy in situations where the forecasts are to be used in applying formal decision rules to choice situations.[29]

The theory of teams developed by Marschak and Radner is concerned with the same problem (see, e.g., [46]) It considers situations involving decentralized and interdependent decision-making by two or more persons who share a common goal and who, at a cost, can transmit information to each other about their own actions or about the parts of the environment with which they are in contact. The problem then is to discover the optimal communication strategy under specified assumptions about communication costs and payoffs.

The cost of communication in the theory of teams, like the cost of observations in sampling theory, is a parameter that characterizes the economic actor, or the relation of the actor to his environment. Hence, while these theories retain, in one sense, a classical picture of economic man as a maximizer, they clearly require considerable information about the characteristics of the actor, and not merely about his environment. They take a long stride toward bridging the gap between the traditional concerns of economics and the concerns of psychology.

Expections in the Binary Choice Experiment

I should like to return again to the binary choice experiment, to see what light it casts on the formation of expectations. If the subject is told by the experimenter that the rewards are assigned at random, if he

[27] Fundamental and applied research are examples of economically significant information-gathering activities. Griliches [34] has recently made an attempt to estimate the economic return from research on hybrid corn.

[28] Modern treatments of sampling theory, like Cochran [17] are based on the idea of minimizing the cost of obtaining a fixed amount of information.

[29] For the theory and an application to macroeconomics, see Theil [67, Ch. 8, sects. 5 and 6].

is told what the odds are for each alternative, ***and if he believes the experimenter,*** the situation poses no forecasting problem. We have seen, however, that the behavior of most subjects is not consistent with these assumptions.

How would sequential sampling theory handle the problem? Each choice the subject makes now has two consequences: the immediate reward he obtains from it, and the increment of information it provides for predicting the future rewards. If he thinks only of the latter consequences, he is faced with the classical problem of induction: to estimate the probability that an event will occur in the future on the basis of its frequency of occurrence in the past. Almost any rule of induction would require a rational (maximizing) subject to behave in the following general manner: to sample the two alternatives in some proportion to estimate the probability of reward associated with each; after the error of estimate had been reduced below some bound, always to choose the alternative with the higher probability of reward. Unfortunately, this does not appear to be what most subjects do.

If we give up the idea of maximization, we can make the weaker assumption that the subject is adaptive—or learns—but not necessarily in any optimal fashion. What do we mean by adaptation or learning? We mean, gradually and on the basis of experience responding more frequently with the choice that, in the past, has been most frequently rewarded. There is a whole host of rules of behavior possessing this characteristic. Postulate, for example, that at each trial the subject has a certain probability of responding "plus," and the complementary probability of responding "minus." Postulate further that when he makes a particular response the probability of making the same response on the next trial is increased if the response is rewarded and decreased if the response is not rewarded. The amount of increment in the response probability is a parameter characterizing the learning rate of the particular subject. Almost all schemes of this kind produce asymptotic behaviors, as the number of trials increases, that are approximately event-matching in character.

Stochastic learning models, as the processes just described are usually called, were introduced into psychology in the early 1950's by W. K. Estes and Bush and Mosteller [15] and have been investigated extensively since that time. The models fit some of the gross features of the observed behaviors—most strikingly the asymptotic probabilities—but do not explain very satisfactorily the fine structure of the observations.

Observation of subjects in the binary choice experiment reveals that usually they not only refuse to believe that (or even to act as if) the reward series were random, but in fact persist over many trials in searching for systematic patterns in the series. To account for such behavior, we might again postulate a learning model, but in this case a model in which the subject does not react probabilistically to his environment, but forms and tests definite hypotheses about systematic patterns in it. Man, in this view, is not only a learning animal; he is a pattern-finding and concept-forming animal. Julian Feldman [25] has constructed theories of this kind to explain the behavior of subjects in the binary choice experiment, and while the tests of the theories are not yet completed, his findings look exceedingly promising.

As we move from maximizing theories, through simple stochastic learning theories, to theories involving pattern recognition our model of the expectation-forming processes and the organism that performs it increases in complexity. If we follow this route, we reach a point where a theory of behavior requires a rather elaborate and detailed picture of the rational actor's cognitive processes.

VI. *Human Cognition and Economics*

All the developments we have examined in the preceding four sections have a common theme: they all involve important modifications in the concept of economic man and, for the reasons we have stated, modifications in the direction of providing a fuller description of his characteristics. The classical theory is a theory of a man choosing among fixed and known alternatives, to each of which is attached known consequences. But when perception and cognition intervene between the decision-maker and his objective environment, this model no longer proves adequate. We need a description of the choice process that recognizes that alternatives are not given but must be sought; and a description that takes into account the arduous task of determining what consequences will follow on each alternative [63, Ch. 5] [64, Part 4] [14].

The decision-maker's information about his environment is much less than an approximation to the real environment. The term "approximation" implies that the subjective world of the decision-maker resembles the external environment closely, but lacks, perhaps, some fineness of detail. In actual fact the perceived world is fantastically different from the "real" world. The differences involve both omissions and distortions, and arise in both perception and inference. The sins of omission in perception are more important than the sins of commission. The decision-maker's model of the world encompasses only a minute fraction of all the relevant characteristics of the real environment, and his inferences extract only a minute fraction of all the information that is present even in his model.

Perception is sometimes referred to as a "filter." This term is as misleading as "approximation," and for the same reason: it implies that what comes through into the central nervous system is really quite a bit like what is "out there." In fact, the filtering is not merely a passive selection of some part of a presented whole, but an active process involving attention to a very small part of the whole and exclusion, from the outset, of almost all that is not within the scope of attention.

Every human organism lives in an environment that generates millions of bits of new information each second, but the bottleneck of the perceptual apparatus certainly does not admit more than 1,000 bits per second, and probably much less. Equally significant omissions occur in the processing that takes place when information reaches the brain. As every mathematician knows, it is one thing to have a set of differential equations, and another thing to have their solutions. Yet the solutions are logically implied by the equations—they are "all there," if we only knew how to get to them! By the same token, there are hosts of inferences that *might* be drawn from the information stored in the brain that are not in fact drawn. The consequences implied by information in the memory become known only through active information-processing, and hence through active selection of particular problem-solving paths from the myriad that might have been followed.

In this section we shall examine some theories of decision-making that take the limitations of the decision-maker and the complexity of the environment as central concerns. These theories incorporate some mechanisms we have already discussed—for example, aspiration levels and forecasting processes—but go beyond them in providing a detailed picture of the choice process.

A real-life decision involves some goals or values, some facts about the environment, and some inferences drawn from the values and facts. The goals and values may be simple or complex, consistent or contradictory; the facts may be real or supposed, based on observation or the reports of others; the inferences may be valid or spurious. The whole process may be viewed, metaphorically, as a process of "reasoning," where the values and facts serve as premises, and the decision that is finally reached is inferred from these premises [63]. The resemblance of decision-making to logical reasoning is only metaphorical, because there are quite different rules in the two cases to determine what constitute "valid" premises and admissible modes of inference. The metaphor is useful because it leads us to take the individual *decision premise* as the unit of description, hence to deal with the whole interwoven fabric of influences that bear on a single decision—but without being bound by the assumptions of rationality that limit the classical theory of choice.

Rational Behavior and Role Theory

We can find common ground to relate the economist's theory of decision-making with that of the social psychologist. The latter is particularly interested, of course, in social influences on choice, which determine the *role* of the actor. In our present terms, a role is a social prescription of some, but not all, of the premises that enter into an individual's choices of behavior. Any particular concrete behavior is the resultant of a large number of premises, only some of which are prescribed by the role. In addition to role premises there will be premises about the state of the environment based directly on perception, premises representing beliefs and knowledge, and idiosyncratic premises that characterize the personality. Within this framework we can accommodate both the rational elements in choice, so much emphasized by economics, and the nonrational elements to which psychologists and sociologists often prefer to call attention.

Decision Premises and Computer Programs

The analysis of choice in terms of decision premises gives us a conceptual framework for describing and explaining the process of deciding. But so complex is the process that our explanations of it would have remained schematic and hypothetical for a long time to come had not the modern digital computer appeared on the scene. The notion of decision premise can be translated into computer terminology, and when this translation has been accomplished, the digital computer provides us with an instrument for simulating human decision processes—even very complex ones—and hence for testing empirically our explanations of those processes [53].

A fanciful (but only slightly fanciful) example will illustrate how this might be done. Some actual examples will be cited presently. Suppose we were to construct a robot incorporating a modern digital computer, and to program (i.e., to instruct) the robot to take the role of a business executive in a specified company. What would the program look like? Since no one has yet done this, we cannot say with certainty, but several points are fairly clear. The program would not consist of a list of prescribed and proscribed behaviors, since what an executive does is highly contingent on information about a wide variety of circumstances. Instead, the program would consist of a large number of *criteria* to be applied to possible and proposed courses of action, of routines for *generating* possible courses of action, of computational procedures for *assessing* the state of the environment and its implications for action, and the like. Hence, the program—in fact, a role prescription—would interact with information to produce concrete behavior adapted to the situation. The elements of such a program take the form of what we have called decision premises, and what the computer specialists would call instructions.

The promise of constructing actual detailed descriptions of concrete roles and decision processes is no longer, with the computer, a mere prospectus to be realized at some undefined future date. We can already provide actual examples, some of them in the area of economics.

1. *Management Science.* In the paragraphs on normative applications in Section II, we have already referred to the use of such mathematical techniques as linear programming and dynamic programming to construct formal decision processes for actual situations. The relevance of these decision models to the present discussion is that they are not merely abstract "theories" of the firm, but actual decision-making devices. We can think of any such device as a simulation of the corresponding human decision-maker, in which the equations and other assumptions that enter into the formal decision-making procedure correspond to the decision premises—including the role prescription—of the decision-maker.

The actual application of such models to concrete business situations brings to light the information-processing tasks that are concealed in the assumptions of the more abstract classical models [65, pp. 51-52]:

(1) The models must be formulated so as to require for their application only data that are obtainable. If one of the penalties, for example, of holding too small inventories is the loss of sales, a decision model that proposes to determine optimal inventory levels must incorporate a procedure for putting a dollar value on this loss.

(2) The models must call only for practicable computations. For example, several proposals for applying linear programming to certain factory scheduling problems have been shown to be impracticable because, even with computers, the computation time is too great. The task of decision theory (whether normative or descriptive) is to find alternative techniques—probably only approximate—that demand much less computation.

(3) The models must not demand unobtainable forecast information. A procedure that would require a sales department to estimate the third moment of next month's sales distribution would not have wide application, as either description or prescription, to business decision-making.

These models, then, provide us with concrete examples of roles for a decision-maker described in terms of the premises he is expected to apply to the decision—the data and the rules of computation.

2. *Engineering Design.* Computers have been used for some years to carry out some of the analytic computations required in engineering design—computing the stresses, for example, in a proposed bridge

design. Within the past two years, ways have been found to program computers to carry out synthesis as well as analysis—to evolve the design itself.[30] A number of companies in the electrical industry now use computers to design electric motors, transformers, and generators, going from customer specifications to factory design without human intervention. The significance of this for our purpose here is that the synthesis programs appear to simulate rather closely the processes that had previously been used by college-trained engineers in the same design work. It has proved possible to write down the engineers' decision premises and inference processes in sufficient detail to produce workable computer programs.

3. *Human Problem Solving.* The management science and engineering design programs already provide examples of simulation of human decision-making by computer. It may be thought that, since in both instances the processes are highly arithmetical, these examples are relevant to only a very narrow range of human problem-solving activity. We generally think of a digital computer as a device which, if instructed in painful detail by its operator, can be induced to perform rather complicated and tedious arithmetical operations. More recent developments require us to revise these conceptions of the computer, for they enable it to carry out tasks that, if performed by humans, we would certainly call "thinking" and "learning."

Discovering the proof of a theorem of Euclid—a task we all remember from our high school geometry course—requires thinking and usually insight and imagination. A computer is now being programmed to perform this task (in a manner closely simulating the human geometer), and another computer has been successfully performing a highly similar task in symbolic logic for the past two years.[31] The latter computer is programmed to learn—that is to improve its performance on the basis of successful problem-solving experience—to use something akin to imagery or metaphor in planning its proofs, and to transfer some of its skills to other tasks—for example, solving trigonometric identities—involving completely distinct subject matter. These programs, it should be observed, do not involve the computer in rapid arithmetic—or any arithmetic for that matter. They are basically nonnumerical, involving the manipulation of all kinds of symbolic material, including words.

Still other computer programs have been written to enable a computer to play chess.[32] Not all of these programs, or those previously

[30] A nontechnical description of such a program will be found in [33].

[31] The program for proving theorems in logic is discussed in [51] and [52], Gelernter and Rochester's geometry program in [31].

[32] A survey of computer chess programs can be found in [54].

mentioned, are close simulations of the processes humans use. However, in some direct attempts to investigate the human processes by thinking-aloud techniques and to reproduce in computer programs the processes observed in human subjects, several striking simulations have been achieved.[33] These experiments have been described elsewhere and can't be reviewed here in detail.

4. *Business Games.* Business games, like those developed by the American Management Association, International Business Machines Corporation, and several universities, represent a parallel development.[34] In the business game, the decisions of the business firms are still made by the human players, but the economic environment of these firms, including their markets, are represented by computer programs that calculate the environment's responses to the actions of the players. As the games develop in detail and realism, their programs will represent more and more concrete descriptions of the decision processes of various economic actors—for example, consumers.

The games that have been developed so far are restricted to numerical magnitudes like prices and quantities of goods, and hence resemble the management science and engineering design programs more closely than they do those we have described under the heading of human problem solving. There is no reason, however, to expect this restriction to remain very long.

Implications for Economics

Apart from normative applications (e.g., substituting computers for humans in certain decision-making tasks) we are not interested so much in the detailed descriptions of roles as in broader questions: (1) What general characteristics do the roles of economic actors have? (2) How do roles come to be structured in the particular ways they do? (3) What bearing does this version of role theory have for macroeconomics and other large-scale social phenomena?

Characterizing Role Structure. Here we are concerned with generalizations about thought processes, particularly those generalizations that are relatively independent of the substantive content of the role. A classical example is Dewey's description of stages in the problem-solving process. Another example, of particular interest to economics, is the hypothesis we have already discussed at length: that economic man is a *satisficing* animal whose problem solving is based on search activity to meet certain aspiration levels rather than a *maximizing* animal whose problem solving involves finding the best alternatives in terms of specified criteria [64]. A third hypothesis is that operative goals (those

[33] Much of this work is still unpublished, but see [53] and [54].

[34] Two business games are described by Andlinger [1].

associated with an observable criterion of success, and relatively definite means of attainment) play a much larger part in governing choice than nonoperative goals (those lacking a concrete measure of success or a program for attainment) [45, p. 156].

Understanding How Roles Emerge. Within almost any single business firm, certain characteristic types of roles will be represented: selling roles, production roles, accounting roles, and so on [22]. Partly, this consistency may be explained in functional terms—that a model that views the firm as producing a product, selling it, and accounting for its assets and liabilities is an effective simplification of the real world, and provides the members of the organization with a workable frame of reference. Imitation within the culture provides an alternative explanation. It is exceedingly difficult to test hypotheses as to the origins and causal conditions for roles as universal in the society as these, but the underlying mechanisms could probably be explored effectively by the study of less common roles—safety director, quality control inspector, or the like—that are to be found in some firms, but not in all.

With our present definition of role, we can also speak meaningfully of the role of an entire business firm—of decision premises that underlie its basic policies. In a particular industry we find some firms that specialize in adapting the product to individual customer's specifications; others that specialize in product innovation. The common interest of economics and psychology includes not only the study of individual roles, but also the explanation of organizational roles of these sorts.

Tracing the Implications for Macroeconomics. If basic professional goals remain as they are, the interest of the psychologist and the economist in role theory will stem from somewhat different ultimate aims. The former will use various economic and organizational phenomena as data for the study of the structure and determinants of roles; the latter will be primarily interested in the implications of role theory for the model of economic man, and indirectly, for macroeconomics.

The first applications will be to those topics in economics where the assumption of static equilibrium is least tenable. Innovation, technological change, and economic development are examples of areas to which a good empirically tested theory of the processes of human adaptation and problem solving could make a major contribution. For instance, we know very little at present about how the rate of innovation depends on the amounts of resources allocated to various kinds of research and development activity [34]. Nor do we understand very well the nature of "know how," the costs of transferring technology from one firm or economy to another, or the effects of various kinds and amounts of education upon national product. These are difficult questions to answer from aggregative data and gross observation, with the result that our views have been formed more by arm-chair theorizing than by testing hypotheses with solid facts.

VII. *Conclusion*

In exploring the areas in which economics has common interests with the other behavioral sciences, we have been guided by the metaphor we elaborated in Section I. In simple, slow-moving situations, where the actor has a single, operational goal, the assumption of maximization relieves us of any need to construct a detailed picture of economic man or his processes of adaptation. As the complexity of the environment increases, or its speed of change, we need to know more and more about the mechanisms and processes that economic man uses to relate himself to that environment and achieve his goals.

How closely we wish to interweave economics with psychology depends, then, both on the range of questions we wish to answer and on our assessment of how far we may trust the assumptions of static equilibrium as approximations. In considerable part, the demand for a fuller picture of economic man has been coming from the profession of economics itself, as new areas of theory and application have emerged in which complexity and change are central facts. The revived interest in the theory of utility, and its application to choice under uncertainty, and to consumer saving and spending is one such area. The needs of normative macroeconomics and management science for a fuller theory of the firm have led to a number of attempts to understand the actual processes of making business decisions. In both these areas, notions of adaptive and satisficing behavior, drawn largely from psychology, are challenging sharply the classical picture of the maximizing entrepreneur.

The area of imperfect competition and oligopoly has been equally active, although the activity has thus far perhaps raised more problems than it has solved. On the positive side, it has revealed a community of interest among a variety of social scientists concerned with bargaining as a part of political and economic processes. Prediction of the future is another element common to many decision processes, and particularly important to explaining business cycle phenomena. Psychologists and economists have been applying a wide variety of approaches, empirical and theoretical, to the study of the formation of expectations. Surveys of consumer and business behavior, theories of statistical induction, stochastic learning theories, and theories of concept formation have all been converging on this problem area.

The very complexity that has made a theory of the decision-making process essential has made its construction exceedingly difficult. Most approaches have been piecemeal—now focused on the criteria of choice, now on conflict of interest, now on the formation of expectations. It seemed almost utopian to suppose that we could put together a model of adaptive man that would compare in completeness with the simple model of classical economic man. The sketchiness and incompleteness of the newer proposals has been urged as a compelling reason for clinging to the older theories, however inadequate they are admitted to be.

The modern digital computer has changed the situation radically. It provides us with a tool of research—for formulating and testing theories—whose power is commensurate with the complexity of the phenomena we seek to understand. Although the use of computers to build theories of human behavior is very recent, it has already led to concrete results in the simulation of higher mental processes. As economics finds it more and more necessary to understand and explain disequilibrium as well as equilibrium, it will find an increasing use for this new tool and for communication with its sister sciences of psycology and sociology.

References

1. G. R. Andlinger, "Business Games—Play One," *Harvard Bus. Rev.*, Apr. 1958, *36*, 115-25.
2. K. J. Arrow, "Alternative Approaches to the Theory of Choice in Risk-Taking Situations," *Econometrica*, Oct. 1951, *19*, 404-37.
3. K. J. Arrow, T. E. Harris, and J. Marschak, "Optimal Inventory Policy," *Econometrica*, July 1951, *19*, 250-72.
4. K. J. Arrow and M. Nerlove, "A Note on Expectations and Stability," *Econometrica*, Apr. 1958, *26*, 297-305.
5. K. J. Arrow, "Utilities, Attitudes, Choices," *Econometrica*, Jan. 1958, *26*, 1-23.
6. D. Bakan, "Learning and the Principle of Inverse Probability," *Psych. Rev.*," Sept. 1953, *60*, 360-70.
7. A. Bavelas, "A Mathematical Model for Group Structures," *Applied Anthropology*, Summer 1948, *7*, 16-30.
8. M. Beckmann, "Decision and Team Problems in Airline Reservations," *Econometrica*, Jan. 1958, *26*, 134-45
9. R. Bellman, *Dynamic Programming*. Princeton 1957.
10. H. R. Bowen, *The Business Enterprise as a Subject for Research*. New York 1955.
11. E. H. Bowman and R. B. Fetter, *Analysis for Production Management*. Homewood, Ill., 1957.
12. M. J. Bowman, ed., *Expectations, Uncertainty, and Business Behavior*. New York 1958.
13. H. Brems, "Response Lags and Nonprice Competition," in Bowman [12], Ch. 10, pp. 134-43.

14. J. Bruner, J. J. Goodnow and G. A. Austin, *A Study of Thinking.* New York 1956.
15. R. R. Bush and F. Mosteller, *Stochastic Models for Learning.* New York 1955.
16. C. W. Churchman, R. L. Ackoff and E. L. Arnoff, *Introduction to Operations Research.* New York 1957.
17. W. G. Cochran, *Sampling Techniques.* New York 1953.
18. R. M. Cyert and J. G. March, "Organizational Structure and Pricing Behavior in an Oligopolistic Market," *Am. Econ. Rev.,* Mar. 1955, *45,* 129-39.
19. ——— and ———, "Organizational Factors in the Theory of Oligopoly," *Quart. Jour. Econ.,* Feb. 1956, *70,* 44-64.
20. W. Darcovich, "Evaluation of Some Naive Expectations Models for Agricultural Yields and Prices," in Bowman [12], Ch. 14, pp. 199-202.
21. D. Davidson and P. Suppes, *Decision Making: An Experimental Approach.* Stanford 1957.
22. D. C. Dearborn and H. A. Simon, "Selective Perception: A Note on the Departmental Identification of Executives," *Sociometry,* June 1958, *21,* 140-44.
22a. J. S. Earley, "Marginal Policies of 'Excellently Managed' Companies," *Am. Econ. Rev.,* Mar. 1956, *66,* 44-70.
23. W. Edwards, "The Theory of Decision Making," *Psych. Bull.,* Sept. 1954, *51,* 380-417.
24. R. Eisner, "Expectations, Plans, and Capital Expenditures," in Bowman [12], Ch. 12, 165-88.
25. J. Feldman, "A Theory of Binary Choice Behavior," Carnegie Inst. of Tech., Grad. Sch. Indus. Admin., Complex Information Processing Working Paper No. 12, rev., May 5, 1958. Unpublished ditto.
26. B. de Finetti "La prevision: ses lois logiques, ses sources subjectives," *Annales Inst. Henri Poincare,* 1937, *7,* 1-68.
27. M. Friedman, *Essays in Positive Economics.* Chicago 1953.
28. ———, *A Theory of the Consumption Function.* New York 1956.
29. I. Friend, "Critical Evaluation of Surveys of Expectations, Plans, and Investment Behavior," in Bowman [12], Ch. 13, pp. 189-98.
30. J. K. Galbraith, *American Capitalism: The Concept of Countervailing Power.* Boston 1952.
31. H. L. Gelernter and N. Rochester, "Intelligent Behavior in Problem-Solving Machines," *IBM Jour. Research and Develop.,* Oct. 1958, *2,* 336-45.
32. N. Georgescu-Roegen, "The Nature of Expectation and Uncertainty" in Bowman [12], Ch. 1, pp. 11-29.
33. G. L. Godwin, "Digital Computers Tap Out Designs for Large Motors—Fast," *Power,* Apr. 1958.
34. Z. Griliches, "Hybrid Corn: An Exploration in the Economics of Technological Change," *Econometrica,* Oct. 1957, *25,* 501-22.
35. H. Guetzkow and H. A. Simon, "The Impact of Certain Communication

Nets in Task Oriented Groups," *Management Sci.*, July 1955, *1*, 233-50.
36. B. F. HALEY, ed., *A Survey of Contemporary Economics*, Vol. II. Homewood, Ill. 1952.
37. S. P. HAYES, "Some Psychological Problems of Economics," *Psych. Bull.*, July 1950, *47*, 289-330.
38. C. C. HOLT, F. MODIGLIANI AND H. A. SIMON, "A Linear Decision Rule for Production and Employment Scheduling," *Management Sci.*, Oct. 1955, *2*, 1-30.
39. G. KATONA, *Psychological Analysis of Economic Behavior.* New York 1951.
40. ———, "Rational Behavior and Economic Behavior," *Psych. Rev.*, July 1953, *60*, 307-18.
41. H. J. LEAVITT, "Some Effects of Certain Communication Patterns on Group Performance," *Jour. Abnormal and Soc. Psych.*, Feb. 1951, *46*, 38-50.
42. K. LEWIN, AND OTHERS, "Level of Aspiration," in J. McV. Hunt, *Personality and the Behavior Disorders*, New York 1944, pp. 333-78.
43. R. D. LUCE AND H. RAIFFA, *Games and Decisions.* New York 1957.
44. R. MACK, "Business Expectations and the Buying of Materials," in Bowman [12], Ch. 8, pp. 106-18.
45. J. G. MARCH AND H. A. SIMON, *Organizations.* New York 1958.
46. J. MARSCHAK, "Elements for a Theory of Teams," *Management Sci.*, Jan. 1955, *1*, 127-37.
47. K. O. MAY, "Intransitivity, Utility, and the Aggregation of Preference Patterns," *Econometrica*, Jan. 1954, *22*, 1-13.
48. F. MODIGLIANI AND R. E. BRUMBERG, "Utility Analysis and the Consumption Function," in K. K. Kurihara, *Post Keynesian Economics*, New Brunswick, N.J., 1954, pp. 388-436.
49. F. MOSTELLER AND P. NOGEE, "An Experimental Measurement of Utility," *Jour. Pol. Econ.* Oct. 1951, *59*, 371-404.
50. J. VON NEUMANN AND O. MORGENSTERN, *Theory of Games and Economic Behavior.* Princeton 1947.
51. A. NEWELL AND H. A. SIMON, "The Logic Theory Machine," *IRE Transactions of Information Theory*, Sept. 1956, IT-*2*, 61-79.
52. A. NEWELL, J. C. SHAW AND H. A. SIMON, "Empirical Explorations of the Logic Theory Machine," *Proceedings of the Western Joint Computer Conference, Feb. 26-28, 1957*, pp. 218-30.
53. ———, ———, ———, "Elements of a Theory of Human Problem Solving," *Psych. Rev.* May 1958, *65*, 151-66.
54. ———, ———, ———, "Chess-Playing Programs and the Problem of Complexity," *IBM Jour. Research and Develop.*, Oct. 1958, *2*, 320-35.
55. A. G. PAPANDREOU, "Some Basic Problems in the Theory of the Firm," in Haley [36], Ch. 5, pp. 183-222.
56. M. J. PECK, "Marginal Analysis and the Explanation of Business Behavior Under Uncertainty," in Bowman [12], Ch. 9, pp. 119-33.
57. F. P. RAMSEY, "Truth and Probability," in the *Foundations of Mathematics and Other Logical Essays*, London 1931, pp. 156-98.

57a. A. M. Rose, "A Study of Irrational Judgments," *Jour. Pol. Econ.*, Oct. 1957, *65*, 394-402.
58. L. J. Savage, *The Foundations of Statistics*. New York 1954.
59. T. C. Schelling, "Bargaining, Communication, and Limited War," *Jour. Conflict Resolution*, Mar. 1957, *1*, 19-36.
60. ———, "An Essay on Bargaining," *Am. Econ. Rev.*, June 1956, *46*, 281-306.
61. S. Siegel, "Level of Aspiration and Decision Making," *Psych. Rev.*, July 1957, *64*, 253-62.
62. H. A. Simon, "Dynamic Programming Under Uncertainty with a Quadratic Criterion Function," *Econometrica*, Jan. 1956, *24*, 74-81.
63. ———, *Administrative Behavior*. New York 1957.
64. ———, *Models of Man*. New York 1957.
65. ———, "The Role of Expectations in an Adaptive or Behavioristic Model," in Bowman [12], Ch. 3, pp. 49-58.
66. H. A. Simon and C. P. Bonini, "The Size Distribution of Business Firms," *Am. Econ. Rev.*, Sept. 1958, *48*, 607-17.
67. H. Theil, *Economic Forecasts and Policy*. Amsterdam 1958.
68. L. L. Thurstone, "The Indifference Function," *Jour. Soc. Psych.* May 1931, *2*, 139-67.
69. A. Vazsonyi, *Scientific Programming in Business and Industry*. New York 1958.
70. A. Wald, *Statistical Decision Functions*. New York 1950.
71. T. Wilson and P. W. S. Andrews, *Oxford Studies in the Price Mechanism*. Oxford 1951.

[3]

THE ARCHITECTURE OF COMPLEXITY

HERBERT A. SIMON*

Professor of Administration, Carnegie Institute of Technology

(*Read April 26, 1962*)

A NUMBER of proposals have been advanced in recent years for the development of "general systems theory" which, abstracting from properties peculiar to physical, biological, or social systems, would be applicable to all of them.[1] We might well feel that, while the goal is laudable, systems of such diverse kinds could hardly be expected to have any nontrivial properties in common. Metaphor and analogy can be helpful, or they can be misleading. All depends on whether the similarities the metaphor captures are significant or superficial.

It may not be entirely vain, however, to search for common properties among diverse kinds of complex systems. The ideas that go by the name of cybernetics constitute, if not a theory, at least a point of view that has been proving fruitful over a wide range of applications.[2] It has been useful to look at the behavior of adaptive systems in terms of the concepts of feedback and homeostasis, and to analyze adaptiveness in terms of the theory of selective information.[3] The ideas of feedback and information provide a frame of reference for viewing a wide range of situations, just as do the ideas of evolution, of relativism, of axiomatic method, and of operationalism.

In this paper I should like to report on some things we have been learning about particular kinds of complex systems encountered in the behavioral sciences. The developments I shall discuss arose in the context of specific phenomena, but the theoretical formulations themselves make little reference to details of structure. Instead they refer primarily to the complexity of the systems under view without specifying the exact content of that complexity. Because of their abstractness, the theories may have relevance—application would be too strong a term—to other kinds of complex systems that are observed in the social, biological, and physical sciences.

In recounting these developments, I shall avoid technical detail, which can generally be found elsewhere. I shall describe each theory in the particular context in which it arose. Then, I shall cite some examples of complex systems, from areas of science other than the initial application, to which the theoretical framework appears relevant. In doing so, I shall make reference to areas of knowledge where I am not expert—perhaps not even literate. I feel quite comfortable in doing so before the members of this society, representing as it does the whole span of the scientific and scholarly endeavor. Collectively you will have little difficulty, I am sure, in distinguishing instances based on idle fancy or sheer ignorance from instances that cast some light on the ways in which complexity exhibits itself wherever it is found in nature. I shall leave to you the final judgment of relevance in your respective fields.

I shall not undertake a formal definition of

* The ideas in this paper have been the topic of many conversations with my colleague, Allen Newell. George W. Corner suggested important improvements in biological content as well as editorial form. I am also indebted, for valuable comments on the manuscript, to Richard H. Meier, John R. Platt, and Warren Weaver. Some of the conjectures about the nearly decomposable structure of the nucleus-atom-molecule hierarchy were checked against the available quantitative data by Andrew Schoene and William Wise. My work in this area has been supported by a Ford Foundation grant for research in organizations and a Carnegie Corporation grant for research on cognitive processes. To all of the above, my warm thanks, and the usual absolution.

[1] See especially the yearbooks of the Society for General Systems Research. Prominent among the exponents of general systems theory are L. von Bertalanffy, K. Boulding, R. W. Gerard, and J. G. Miller. For a more skeptical view—perhaps too skeptical in the light of the present discussion—see H. A. Simon and A. Newell, Models: their uses and limitations, *in* L. D. White, ed., *The state of the social sciences*, 66–83, Chicago, Univ. of Chicago Press, 1956.

[2] N. Wiener, *Cybernetics*, New York, John Wiley & Sons, 1948. For an imaginative forerunner, see A. J. Lotka, *Elements of mathematical biology*, New York, Dover Publications, 1951, first published in 1924 as *Elements of physical biology*.

[3] C. Shannon and W. Weaver, *The mathematical theory of communication*, Urbana, Univ. of Illinois Press, 1949; W. R. Ashby, *Design for a brain*, New York, John Wiley & Sons, 1952.

"complex systems."[4] Roughly, by a complex system I mean one made up of a large number of parts that interact in a nonsimple way. In such systems, the whole is more than the sum of the parts, not in an ultimate, metaphysical sense, but in the important pragmatic sense that, given the properties of the parts and the laws of their interaction, it is not a trivial matter to infer the properties of the whole. In the face of complexity, an in-principle reductionist may be at the same time a pragmatic holist.[5]

The four sections that follow discuss four aspects of complexity. The first offers some comments on the frequency with which complexity takes the form of hierarchy—the complex system being composed of subsystems that, in turn, have their own subsystems, and so on. The second section theorizes about the relation between the structure of a complex system and the time required for it to emerge through evolutionary processes: specifically, it argues that hierarchic systems will evolve far more quickly than non-hierarchic systems of comparable size. The third section explores the dynamic properties of hierarchically-organized systems, and shows how they can be decomposed into subsystems in order to analyze their behavior. The fourth section examines the relation between complex systems and their descriptions.

Thus, the central theme that runs through my remarks is that complexity frequently takes the form of hierarchy, and that hierarchic systems have some common properties that are independent of their specific content. Hierarchy, I shall argue, is one of the central structural schemes that the architect of complexity uses.

[4] W. Weaver, in: Science and complexity, *American Scientist* **36**: 536, 1948, has distinguished two kinds of complexity, disorganized and organized. We shall be primarily concerned with organized complexity.

[5] See also John R. Platt, Properties of large molecules that go beyond the properties of their chemical sub-groups, *Jour. Theoret. Biol.* **1**: 342–358, 1961. Since the reductionism-holism issue is a major *cause de guerre* between scientists and humanists, perhaps we might even hope that peace could be negotiated between the two cultures along the lines of the compromise just suggested. As I go along, I shall have a little to say about complexity in the arts as well as in the natural sciences. I must emphasize the pragmatism of my holism to distinguish it sharply from the position taken by W. M. Elsasser in *The physical foundation of biology*, New York, Pergamon Press, 1958.

HIERARCHIC SYSTEMS

By a ***hierarchic system***, or hierarchy, I mean a system that is composed of interrelated subsystems, each of the latter being, in turn, hierarchic in structure until we reach some lowest level of elementary subsystem. In most systems in nature, it is somewhat arbitrary as to where we leave off the partitioning, and what subsystems we take as elementary. Physics makes much use of the concept of "elementary particle" although particles have a disconcerting tendency not to remain elementary very long. Only a couple of generations ago, the atoms themselves were elementary particles; today, to the nuclear physicist they are complex systems. For certain purposes of astronomy, whole stars, or even galaxies, can be regarded as elementary subsystems. In one kind of biological research, a cell may be treated as an elementary subsystem; in another, a protein molecule; in still another, an amino acid residue.

Just why a scientist has a right to treat as elementary a subsystem that is in fact exceedingly complex is one of the questions we shall take up. For the moment, we shall accept the fact that scientists do this all the time, and that if they are careful scientists they usually get away with it.

Etymologically, the word "hierarchy" has had a narrower meaning than I am giving it here. The term has generally been used to refer to a complex system in which each of the subsystems is subordinated by an authority relation to the system it belongs to. More exactly, in a hierarchic formal organization, each system consists of a "boss" and a set of subordinate subsystems. Each of the subsystems has a "boss" who is the immediate subordinate of the boss of the system. We shall want to consider systems in which the relations among subsystems are more complex than in the formal organizational hierarchy just described. We shall want to include systems in which there is no relation of subordination among subsystems. (In fact, even in human organizations, the formal hierarchy exists only on paper; the real flesh-and-blood organization has many inter-part relations other than the lines of formal authority.) For lack of a better term, I shall use hierarchy in the broader sense introduced in the previous paragraphs, to refer to all complex systems analyzable into successive sets of subsystems, and speak of "formal hierarchy" when I want to refer to the more specialized concept.[6]

[6] The mathematical term "partitioning" will not do for what I call here a hierarchy; for the set of subsystems,

SOCIAL SYSTEMS

I have already given an example of one kind of hierarchy that is frequently encountered in the social sciences: a formal organization. Business firms, governments, universities all have a clearly visible parts-within-parts structure. But formal organizations are not the only, or even the most common, kind of social hierarchy. Almost all societies have elementary units called families, which may be grouped into villages or tribes, and these into larger groupings, and so on. If we make a chart of social interactions, of who talks to whom, the clusters of dense interaction in the chart will identify a rather well-defined hierarchic structure. The groupings in this structure may be defined operationally by some measure of frequency of interaction in this sociometric matrix.

BIOLOGICAL AND PHYSICAL SYSTEMS

The hierarchical structure of biological systems is a familiar fact. Taking the cell as the building block, we find cells organized into tissues, tissues into organs, organs into systems. Moving downward from the cell, well-defined subsystems—for example, nucleus, cell membrane, microsomes, mitochondria, and so on—have been identified in animal cells.

The hierarchic structure of many physical systems is equally clear-cut. I have already mentioned the two main series. At the microscopic level we have elementary particles, atoms, molecules, macromolecules. At the macroscopic level we have satellite systems, planetary systems, galaxies. Matter is distributed throughout space in a strikingly non-uniform fashion. The most nearly random distributions we find, gases, are not random distributions of elementary particles but random distributions of complex systems, i.e. molecules.

A considerable range of structural types is subsumed under the term hierarchy as I have defined it. By this definition, a diamond is hierarchic, for it is a crystal structure of carbon atoms that can be further decomposed into protons, neutrons, and electrons. However, it is a very "flat" hierarchy, in which the number of first-order subsystems belonging to the crystal can be indefinitely large. A volume of molecular gas is a flat hierarchy in the same sense. In ordinary usage, we tend to reserve the word hierarchy for a system that is divided into a ***small or moderate number*** of subsystems, each of which may be further subdivided. Hence, we do not ordinarily think of or refer to a diamond or a gas as a hierarchic structure. Similarly, a linear polymer is simply a chain, which may be very long, of identical subparts, the monomers. At the molecular level it is a very flat hierarchy.

In discussing formal organizations, the number of subordinates who report directly to a single boss is called his *span of control*. I will speak analogously of the *span* of a system, by which I shall mean the number of subsystems into which it is partitioned. Thus, a hierarchic system is flat at a given level if it has a wide span at that level. A diamond has a wide span at the crystal level, but not at the next level down, the molecular level.

In most of our theory construction in the following sections we shall focus our attention on hierarchies of moderate span, but from time to time I shall comment on the extent to which the theories might or might not be expected to apply to very flat hierarchies.

There is one important difference between the physical and biological hierarchies, on the one hand, and social hierarchies, on the other. Most physical and biological hierarchies are described in spatial terms. We detect the organelles in a cell in the way we detect the raisins in a cake—they are "visibly" differentiated substructures localized spatially in the larger structure. On the other hand, we propose to identify social hierarchies not by observing who lives close to whom but by observing who interacts with whom. These two points of view can be reconciled by defining hierarchy in terms of intensity of interaction, but observing that in most biological and physical systems relatively intense interaction implies relative spatial propinquity. One of the interesting characteristics of nerve cells and telephone wires is that they permit very specific strong interactions at great distances. To the extent that interactions are channeled through specialized communications and transportation systems, spatial propinquity becomes less determinative of structure.

SYMBOLIC SYSTEMS

One very important class of systems has been omitted from my examples thus far: systems of human symbolic production. A book is a hierarchy in the sense in which I am using that term. It is generally divided into chapters, the chapters

and the successive subsets in each of these defines the partitioning, independently of any systems of relations among the subsets. By hierarchy I mean the partitioning in conjunction with the relations that hold among its parts.

into sections, the sections into paragraphs, the paragraphs into sentences, the sentences into clauses and phrases, the clauses and phrases into words. We may take the words as our elementary units, or further subdivide them, as the linguist often does, into smaller units. If the book is narrative in character, it may divide into "episodes" instead of sections, but divisions there will be.

The hierarchic structure of music, based on such units as movements, parts, themes, phrases, is well known. The hierarchic structure of products of the pictorial arts is more difficult to characterize, but I shall have something to say about it later.

THE EVOLUTION OF COMPLEX SYSTEMS

Let me introduce the topic of evolution with a parable. There once were two watchmakers, named Hora and Tempus, who manufactured very fine watches. Both of them were highly regarded, and the phones in their workshops rang frequently —new customers were constantly calling them. However, Hora prospered, while Tempus became poorer and poorer and finally lost his shop. What was the reason?

The watches the men made consisted of about 1,000 parts each. Tempus had so constructed his that if he had one partly assembled and had to put it down—to answer the phone say—it immediately fell to pieces and had to be reassembled from the elements. The better the customers liked his watches, the more they phoned him, the more difficult it became for him to find enough uninterrupted time to finish a watch.

The watches that Hora made were no less complex than those of Tempus. But he had designed them so that he could put together subassemblies of about ten elements each. Ten of these subassemblies, again, could be put together into a larger subassembly; and a system of ten of the latter subassemblies constituted the whole watch. Hence, when Hora had to put down a partly assembled watch in order to answer the phone, he lost only a small part of his work, and he assembled his watches in only a fraction of the man-hours it took Tempus.

It is rather easy to make a quantitative analysis of the relative difficulty of the tasks of Tempus and Hora: Suppose the probability that an interruption will occur while a part is being added to an incomplete assembly is p. Then the probability that Tempus can complete a watch he has started without interruption is $(1-p)^{1000}$—a very small number unless p is .001 or less. Each interruption will cost, on the average, the time to assemble $1/p$ parts (the expected number assembled before interruption). On the other hand, Hora has to complete one hundred eleven sub-assemblies of ten parts each. The probability that he will not be interrupted while completing any one of these is $(1-p)^{10}$, and each interruption will cost only about the time required to assemble five parts.[7]

Now if p is about .01—that is, there is one chance in a hundred that either watchmaker will be interrupted while adding any one part to an assembly—then a straightforward calculation shows that it will take Tempus, on the average, about four thousand times as long to assemble a watch as Hora.

We arrive at the estimate as follows:

1. Hora must make 111 times as many complete assemblies per watch as Tempus; but,
2. Tempus will lose on the average 20 times as much work for each interrupted assembly as Hora [100 parts, on the average, as against 5];and,
3. Tempus will complete an assembly only 44 times per million attempts ($.99^{1000} = 44 \times 10^{-6}$), while Hora will complete nine out of ten ($.99^{10} = 9 \times 10^{-1}$). Hence Tempus will have to make 20,000 as many attempts per completed assembly as Hora. $(9 \times 10^{-1})/(44 \times 10^{-6}) = 2 \times 10^{4}$. Multiplying these three ratios, we get:

$$1/111 \times 100/5 \times .99^{10}/.99^{1000}$$
$$= 1/111 \times 20 \times 20{,}000 \sim 4{,}000.$$

[7] The speculations on speed of evolution were first suggested by H. Jacobson's application of information theory to estimating the time required for biological evolution. See his paper, Information, reproduction, and the origin of life, in *American Scientist* **43**: 119–127, January, 1955. From thermodynamic considerations it is possible to estimate the amount of increase in entropy that occurs when a complex system decomposes into its elements. (See, for example, R. B. Setlow and E. C. Pollard, *Molecular biophysics*, 63–65, Reading, Mass., Addison-Wesley Publishing Co., 1962, and references cited there.) But entropy is the logarithm of a probability, hence information, the negative of entropy, can be interpreted as the logarithm of the reciprocal of the probability—the "improbability," so to speak. The essential idea in Jacobson's model is that the expected time required for the system to reach a particular state is inversely proportional to the probability of the state—hence increases exponentially with the amount of information (negentropy) of the state.

Following this line of argument, but not introducing the notion of levels and stable subassemblies, Jacobson arrived at estimates of the time required for evolution so large as to make the event rather improbable. Our analysis, carried through in the same way, but with attention to the stable intermediate forms, produces very much smaller estimates.

BIOLOGICAL EVOLUTION

What lessons can we draw from our parable for biological evolution? Let us interpret a partially completed subassembly of k elementary parts as the coexistence of k parts in a small volume—ignoring their relative orientations. The model assumes that parts are entering the volume at a constant rate, but that there is a constant probability, p, that the part will be dispersed before another is added, unless the assembly reaches a stable state. These assumptions are not particularly realistic. They undoubtedly underestimate the decrease in probability of achieving the assembly with increase in the size of the assembly. Hence the assumptions understate—probably by a large factor—the relative advantage of a hierarchic structure.

Although we cannot, therefore, take the numerical estimate seriously the lesson for biological evolution is quite clear and direct. The time required for the evolution of a complex form from simple elements depends critically on the numbers and distribution of potential intermediate stable forms. In particular, if there exists a hierarchy of potential stable "subassemblies," with about the same span, s, at each level of the hierarchy, then the time required for a subassembly can be expected to be about the same at each level—that is proportional to $1/(1\text{-}p)^s$. The time required for the assembly of a system of n elements will be proportional to $\log_s n$, that is, to the number of levels in the system. One would say—with more illustrative than literal intent—that the time required for the evolution of multi-celled organisms from single-celled organisms might be of the same order of magnitude as the time required for the evolution of single-celled organisms from macromolecules. The same argument could be applied to the evolution of proteins from amino acids, of molecules from atoms, of atoms from elementary particles.

A whole host of objections to this oversimplified scheme will occur, I am sure, to every working biologist, chemist, and physicist. Before turning to matters I know more about, I shall mention three of these problems, leaving the rest to the attention of the specialists.

First, in spite of the overtones of the watchmaker parable, the theory assumes no teleological mechanism. The complex forms can arise from the simple ones by purely random processes. (I shall propose another model in a moment that shows this clearly.) Direction is provided to the scheme by the stability of the complex forms, once these come into existence. But this is nothing more than survival of the fittest—i.e., of the stable.

Second, not all large systems appear hierarchical. For example, most polymers—e.g., nylon—are simply linear chains of large numbers of identical components, the monomers. However, for present purposes we can simply regard such a structure as a hierarchy with a span of one—the limiting case. For a chain of any length represents a state of relative equilibrium.[8]

Third, the evolution of complex systems from simple elements implies nothing, one way or the other, about the change in entropy of the entire system. If the process absorbs free energy, the complex system will have a smaller entropy than the elements; if it releases free energy, the opposite will be true. The former alternative is the one that holds for most biological systems, and the net inflow of free energy has to be supplied from the sun or some other source if the second law of thermodynamics is not to be violated. For the evolutionary process we are describing, the equilibria of the intermediate states need have only local and not global stability, and they may be stable only in the steady state—that is, as long as there is an external source of free energy that may be drawn upon.[9]

Because organisms are not energetically closed systems, there is no way to deduce the direction, much less the rate, of evolution from classical thermodynamic considerations. All estimates indicate that the amount of entropy, measured in physical units, involved in the formation of a one-celled biological organism is trivially small—about -10^{-11} cal/degree.[10] The "improbability" of evolution has nothing to do with this quantity of entropy, which is produced by every bacterial cell every generation. The irrelevance of quantity of

[8] There is a well-developed theory of polymer size, based on models of random assembly. See for example P. J. Flory, *Principles of polymer chemistry*, ch. 8, Ithaca, Cornell Univ. Press, 1953. Since *all* subassemblies in the polymerization theory are stable, limitation of molecular growth depends on "poisoning" of terminal groups by impurities or formation of cycles rather than upon disruption of partially-formed chains.

[9] This point has been made many times before, but it cannot be emphasized too strongly. For further discussion, see Setlow and Pollard, *op. cit.*, 49–64; E. Schrodinger, *What is life?* Cambridge Univ. Press, 1945; and H. Linschitz, The information content of a bacterial cell, in H. Questler, ed., *Information theory in biology*, 251–262, Urbana, Univ. of Illinois Press, 1953.

[10] See Linschitz, *op. cit.* This quantity, 10^{-11} cal/degree, corresponds to obout 10^{13} bits of information.

information, in this sense, to speed of evolution can also be seen from the fact that exactly as much information is required to "copy" a cell through the reproductive process as to produce the first cell through evolution.

The effect of the existence of stable intermediate forms exercises a powerful effect on the evolution of complex forms that may be likened to the dramatic effect of catalysts upon reaction rates and steady state distribution of reaction products in open systems.[11] In neither case does the entropy change provide us with a guide to system behavior.

PROBLEM SOLVING AS NATURAL SELECTION

Let us turn now to some phenomena that have no obvious connection with biological evolution: human problem-solving processes. Consider, for example, the task of discovering the proof for a difficult theorem. The process can be—and often has been—described as a search through a maze. Starting with the axioms and previously proved theorems, various transformations allowed by the rules of the mathematical systems are attempted, to obtain new expressions. These are modified in turn until, with persistence and good fortune, a sequence or path of transformations is discovered that leads to the goal.

The process usually involves a great deal of trial and error. Various paths are tried; some are abandoned, others are pushed further. Before a solution is found, a great many paths of the maze may be explored. The more difficult and novel the problem, the greater is likely to be the amount of trial and error required to find a solution. At the same time, the trial and error is not completely random or blind; it is, in fact, rather highly selective. The new expressions that are obtained by transforming given ones are examined to see whether they represent progress toward the goal. Indications of progress spur further search in the same direction; lack of progress signals the abandonment of a line of search. Problem solving requires *selective* trial and error.[12]

A little reflection reveals that cues signaling progress play the same role in the problem-solving process that stable intermediate forms play in the biological evolutionary process. In fact, we can take over the watchmaker parable and apply it also to problem solving. In problem solving, a partial result that represents recognizable progress toward the goal plays the role of a stable subassembly.

Suppose that the task is to open a safe whose lock has ten dials, each with one hundred possible settings, numbered from 0 to 99. How long will it take to open the safe by a blind trial-and-error search for the correct setting? Since there are 100^{10} possible settings, we may expect to examine about one-half of these, on the average, before finding the correct one—that is, fifty billion billion settings. Suppose, however, that the safe is defective, so that a click can be heard when any one dial is turned to the correct setting. Now each dial can be adjusted independently, and does not need to be touched again while the others are being set. The total number of settings that has to be tried is only 10×50, or five hundred. The task of opening the safe has been altered, by the cues the clicks provide, from a practically impossible one to a trivial one.[13]

A considerable amount has been learned in the past five years about the nature of the mazes that represent common human problem-solving tasks—proving theorems, solving puzzles, playing chess, making investments, balancing assembly lines, to mention a few. All that we have learned about these mazes points to the same conclusion: that human problem solving, from the most blundering to the most insightful, involves nothing more than varying mixtures of trial and error and selectivity. The selectivity derives from various rules of

[11] See H. Kacser, Some physico-chemical aspects of biological organization, Appendix, pp. 191–249 in C. H. Waddington, *The strategy of the genes*, London, George Allen & Unwin, 1957.

[12] See A. Newell, J. C. Shaw, and H. A. Simon, Empirical explorations of the logic theory machine, *Proceedings of the 1957 Western Joint Computer Conference*, February, 1957, New York: Institute of Radio Engineers; Chess-playing programs and the problem of complexity, *IBM Journal of Research and Development* 2: 320–335, October, 1958; and for a similar view of problem solving, W. R. Ashby, Design for an intelligence amplifier, 215–233 in C. E. Shannon and J. McCarthy, *Automata studies*, Princeton, Princeton Univ. Press, 1956.

[13] The clicking safe example was supplied by D. P. Simon. Ashby, *op. cit.*, 230, has called the selectivity involved in situations of this kind "selection by components." The even greater reduction in time produced by hierarchization in the clicking safe example, as compared with the watchmaker's metaphor, is due to the fact that a random *search* for the correct combination is involved in the former case, while in the latter the parts come together in the right order. It is not clear which of these metaphors provides the better model for biological evolution, but we may be sure that the watchmaker's metaphor gives an exceedingly conservative estimate of the savings due to hierarchization. The safe may give an excessively high estimate because it assumes all possible arrangements of the elements to be equally probable.

thumb, or heuristics, that suggest which paths should be tried first and which leads are promising. We do not need to postulate processes more sophisticated than those involved in organic evolution to explain how enormous problem mazes are cut down to quite reasonable size.[14]

THE SOURCES OF SELECTIVITY

When we examine the sources from which the problem-solving system, or the evolving system, as the case may be, derives its selectivity, we discover that selectivity can always be equated with some kind of feedback of information from the environment.

Let us consider the case of problem solving first. There are two basic kinds of selectivity. One we have already noted: various paths are tried out, the consequences of following them are noted, and this information is used to guide further search. In the same way, in organic evolution, various complexes come into being, at least evanescently, and those that are stable provide new building blocks for further construction. It is this information about stable configurations, and not free energy or negentropy from the sun, that guides the process of evolution and provides the selectivity that is essential to account for its rapidity.

The second source of selectivity in problem solving is previous experience. We see this particularly clearly when the problem to be solved is similar to one that has been solved before. Then, by simply trying again the paths that led to the earlier solution, or their analogues, trial-and-error search is greatly reduced or altogether eliminated.

What corresponds to this latter kind of information in organic evolution? The closest analogue is reproduction. Once we reach the level of self-reproducing systems, a complex system, when it has once been achieved, can be multiplied indefinitely. Reproduction in fact allows the inheritance of acquired characteristics, but at the level of genetic material, of course; i.e., only characteristics acquired by the genes can be inherited. We shall return to the topic of reproduction in the final section of this paper.

ON EMPIRES AND EMPIRE-BUILDING

We have not exhausted the categories of complex systems to which the watchmaker argument can reasonably be applied. Philip assembled his Macedonian empire and gave it to his son, to be later combined with the Persian subassembly and others into Alexander's greater system. On Alexander's death, his empire did not crumble to dust, but fragmented into some of the major subsystems that had composed it.

The watchmaker argument implies that if one would be Alexander, one should be born into a world where large stable political systems already exist. Where this condition was not fulfilled, as on the Scythian and Indian frontiers, Alexander found empire building a slippery business. So too, T. E. Lawrence's organizing of the Arabian revolt against the Turks was limited by the character of his largest stable building blocks, the separate, suspicious desert tribes.

The profession of history places a greater value upon the validated particular fact than upon tendentious generalization. I shall not elaborate upon my fancy, therefore, but will leave it to historians to decide whether anything can be learned for the interpretation of history from an abstract theory of hierarchic complex systems.

CONCLUSION: THE EVOLUTIONARY EXPLANATION OF HIERARCHY

We have shown thus far that complex systems will evolve from simple systems much more rapidly if there are stable intermediate forms than if there are not. The resulting complex forms in the former case will be hierarchic. We have only to turn the argument around to explain the observed predominance of hierarchies among the complex systems nature presents to us. Among possible complex forms, hierarchies are the ones that have the time to evolve. The hypothesis that complexity will be hierarchic makes no distinction among very flat hierarchies, like crystals, and tissues, and polymers, and the intermediate forms. Indeed, in the complex systems we encounter in nature, examples of both forms are prominent. A more complete theory than the one we have developed here would presumably have something to say about the determinants of width of span in these systems.

NEARLY DECOMPOSABLE SYSTEMS

In hierarchic systems, we can distinguish between the interactions *among* subsystems, on the one hand, and the interactions *within* subsystems —i.e., among the parts of those subsystems—on the other. The interactions at the different levels may be, and often will be, of different orders of

[14] A. Newell and H. A. Simon, Computer simulation of human thinking, *Science* 134: 2011–2017, December 22, 1961.

	A1	A2	A3	B1	B2	C1	C2	C3
A1	—	100	—	2	—	—	—	—
A2	100	—	100	1	1	—	—	—
A3	—	100	—	—	2	—	—	—
B1	2	1	—	—	100	2	1	—
B2	—	1	2	100	—	—	1	2
C1	—	—	—	2	—	—	100	—
C2	—	—	—	1	—	100	—	100
C3	—	—	—	—	2	—	100	—

FIG. 1. A hypothetical nearly-decomposable system. In terms of the heat-exchange example of the text, A1, A2, and A3 may be interpreted as cubicles in one room, B1 and B2 as cubicles in a second room, and C1, C2, and C3 as cubicles in a third. The matrix entries then are the heat diffusion coefficients between cubicles.

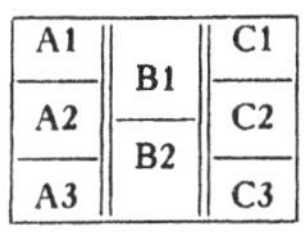

magnitude. In a formal organization there will generally be more interaction, on the average, between two employees who are members of the same department than between two employees from different departments. In organic substances, intermolecular forces will generally be weaker than molecular forces, and molecular forces than nuclear forces.

In a rare gas, the intermolecular forces will be negligible compared to those binding the molecules—we can treat the individual particles, for many purposes, as if they were independent of each other. We can describe such a system as *decomposable* into the subsystems comprised of the individual particles. As the gas becomes denser, molecular interactions become more significant. But over some range, we can treat the decomposable case as a limit, and as a first approximation. We can use a theory of perfect gases, for example, to describe approximately the behavior of actual gases if they are not too dense. As a second approximation, we may move to a theory of *nearly decomposable* systems, in which the interactions among the subsystems are weak, but not negligible.

At least some kinds of hierarchic systems can be approximated successfully as nearly decomposable systems. The main theoretical findings from the approach can be summed up in two propositions: (*a*) in a nearly decomposable system, the short-run behavior of each of the component subsystems is approximately independent of the short-run behavior of the other components; (*b*) in the long run, the behavior of any one of the components depends in only an aggregate way on the behavior of the other components.

Let me provide a very concrete simple example of a nearly decomposable system.[15] Consider a building whose outside walls provide perfect thermal insulation from the environment. We shall take these walls as the boundary of our system. The building is divided into a large number of rooms, the walls between them being good, but not perfect, insulators. The walls between rooms are the boundaries of our major subsystems. Each room is divided by partitions into a number of cubicles, but the partitions are poor insulators. A thermometer hangs in each cubicle. Suppose that at the time of our first observation of the system there is a wide variation in temperature from cubicle to cubicle and from room to room—the various cubicles within the building are in a state of thermal disequilibrium. When we take new temperature readings several hours later, what shall we find? There will be very little variation in temperature among the cubicles within each single room, but there may still be large temperature variations *among* rooms. When we take readings again several days later, we find an almost uniform temperature throughout the building; the temperature differences among rooms have virtually disappeared.

We can describe the process of equilibration formally by setting up the usual equations of heat flow. The equations can be represented by the matrix of their coefficients, r_{ij}, where r_{ij} is the rate at which heat flows from the ith cubicle to the jth cubicle per degree difference in their temperatures. If cubicles i and j do not have a common wall, r_{ij} will be zero. If cubicles i and j have a common wall, and are in the same room, r_{ij} will be large. If cubicles i and j are separated by the wall of a

[15] This discussion of near-decomposability is based upon H. A. Simon and A. Ando, Aggregation of variables in dynamic systems, *Econometrica* **29**: 111–138, April, 1961. The example is drawn from the same source, 117–118. The theory has been further developed and applied to a variety of economic and political phenomena by Ando and F. M. Fisher. See F. M. Fisher, On the cost of approximate specification in simultaneous equation estimation, *Econometrica* **29**: 139–170, April, 1961, and F. M. Fisher and A. Ando, Two theorems on *Ceteris Paribus* in the analysis of dynamic systems, *American Political Science Review* **61**: 103–113, March, 1962.

room, r_{ij} will be nonzero but small. Hence, by grouping all the cubicles together that are in the same room, we can arrange the matrix of coefficients so that all its large elements lie inside a string of square submatrices along the main diagonal. All the elements outside these diagonal squares will be either zero or small (see figure 1). We may take some small number, ϵ, as the upper bound of the extradiagonal elements. We shall call a matrix having these properties a *nearly decomposable matrix*.

Now it has been proved that a dynamic system that can be described by a nearly decomposable matrix has the properties, stated above, of a nearly decomposable system. In our simple example of heat flow this means that in the short run each room will reach an equilibrium temperature (an average of the initial temperatures of its offices) nearly independently of the others; and that each room will remain approximately in a state of equilibrium over the longer period during which an over-all temperature equilibrium is being established throughout the building. After the intraroom short-run equilibria have been reached, a single thermometer in each room will be adequate to describe the dynamic behavior of the entire system—separate thermometers in each cubicle will be superfluous.

NEAR DECOMPOSABILITY OF SOCIAL SYSTEMS

As a glance at figure 1 shows, near decomposability is a rather strong property for a matrix to possess, and the matrices that have this property will describe very special dynamic systems—vanishingly few systems out of all those that are thinkable. How few they will be depends, of course, on how good an approximation we insist upon. If we demand that epsilon be very small, correspondingly few dynamic systems will fit the definition. But we have already seen that in the natural world nearly decomposable systems are far from rare. On the contrary, systems in which each variable is linked with almost equal strength with almost all other parts of the system are far rarer and less typical.

In economic dynamics, the main variables are the prices and quantities of commodities. It is empirically true that the price of any given commodity and the rate at which it is exchanged depend to a significant extent only on the prices and quantities of a few other commodities, together with a few other aggregate magnitudes, like the average price level or some over-all measure of economic activity. The large linkage coefficients are associated, in general, with the main flows of raw materials and semi-finished products within and between industries. An input-output matrix of the economy, giving the magnitudes of these flows, reveals the nearly decomposable structure of the system—with one qualification. There is a consumption subsystem of the economy that is linked strongly to variables in most of the other subsystems. Hence, we have to modify our notions of decomposability slightly to accommodate the special role of the consumption subsystem in our analysis of the dynamic behavior of the economy.

In the dynamics of social systems, where members of a system communicate with and influence other members, near decomposability is generally very prominent. This is most obvious in formal organizations, where the formal authority relation connects each member of the organization with one immediate superior and with a small number of subordinates. Of course many communications in organizations follow other channels than the lines of formal authority. But most of these channels lead from any particular individual to a very limited number of his superiors, subordinates, and associates. Hence, departmental boundaries play very much the same role as the walls in our heat example.

PHYSICO-CHEMICAL SYSTEMS

In the complex systems familiar in biological chemistry, a similar structure is clearly visible. Take the atomic nuclei in such a system as the elementary parts of the system, and construct a matrix of bond strengths between elements. There will be matrix elements of quite different orders of magnitude. The largest will generally correspond to the covalent bonds, the next to the ionic bonds, the third group to hydrogen bonds, still smaller linkages to van der Waals forces.[16] If we select an epsilon just a little smaller than the magnitude of a covalent bond, the system will decompose into subsystems—the constituent molecules. The smaller linkages will correspond to the intermolecular bonds.

It is well known that high-energy, high-fre-

[16] For a survey of the several classes of molecular and inter-molecular forces, and their dissociation energies. see Setlow and Pollard, *op. cit.*, chapter 6. The energies of typical covalent bonds are of the order of 80–100 k cal/mole, of the hydrogen bonds, 10 k cal/mole. Ionic bonds generally lie between these two levels, the bonds due to van der Waals forces are lower in energy.

quency vibrations are associated with the smaller physical subsystems, low-frequency vibrations with the larger systems into which the subsystems are assembled. For example, the radiation frequencies associated with molecular vibrations are much lower than those associated with the vibrations of the planetary electrons of the atoms; the latter, in turn, are lower than those associated with nuclear processes.[17] Molecular systems are nearly decomposable systems, the short-run dynamics relating to the internal structures of the subsystems; the long-run dynamics to the interactions of these subsystems.

A number of the important approximations employed in physics depend for their validity on the near-decomposability of the systems studied. The theory of the thermodynamics of irreversible processes, for example, requires the assumption of macroscopic disequilibrium but microscopic equilibrium,[18] exactly the situation described in our heat-exchange example. Similarly computations in quantum mechanics are often handled by treating weak interactions as producing perturbations on a system of strong interactions.

SOME OBSERVATIONS ON HIERARCHIC SPAN

To understand why the span of hierarchies is sometimes very broad—as in crystals—sometimes narrow, we need to examine more detail of the interactions. In general, the critical consideration is the extent to which interaction between two (or a few) subsystems excludes interaction of these subsystems with the others. Let us examine first some physical examples.

Consider a gas of identical molecules, each of which can form covalent bonds, in certain ways, with others. Let us suppose that we can associate with each atom a specific number of bonds that it is capable of maintaining simultaneously. (This number is obviously related to the number we usually call its valence.) Now suppose that two atoms join, and that we can also associate with the combination a specific number of external bonds it is capable of maintaining. If this number is the same as the number associated with the individual atoms, the bonding process can go on indefinitely—the atoms can form crystals or polymers of indefinite extent. If the number of bonds of which the composite is capable is less than the number associated with each of the parts, then the process of agglomeration must come to a halt.

We need only mention some elementary examples. Ordinary gases show no tendency to agglomerate because the multiple bonding of atoms "uses up" their capacity to interact. While each oxygen atom has a valence of two, the O_2 molecules have a zero valence. Contrariwise, indefinite chains of single-bonded carbon atoms can be built up because a chain of any number of such atoms, each with two side groups, has a valence of exactly two.

Now what happens if we have a system of elements that possess both strong and weak interaction capacities, and whose strong bonds are exhaustible through combination? Subsystems will form, until all the capacity for strong interaction is utilized in their construction. Then these subsystems will be linked by the weaker second-order bonds into larger systems. For example, a water molecule has essentially a valence of zero—all the potential covalent bonds are fully occupied by the interaction of hydrogen and oxygen molecules. But the geometry of the molecule creates an electric dipole that permits weak interaction between the water and salts dissolved in it—whence such phenomena as its electrolytic conductivity.[19]

Similarly, it has been observed that, although electrical forces are much stronger than gravitational forces, the latter are far more important than the former for systems on an astronomical scale. The explanation, of course, is that the electrical forces, being bipolar, are all "used up" in the linkages of the smaller subsystems, and that significant net balances of positive or negative charges are not generally found in regions of macroscopic size.

In social as in physical systems there are generally limits on the simultaneous interaction of large numbers of subsystems. In the social case, these limits are related to the fact that a human being is more nearly a serial than a parallel information-processing system. He can carry on only one conversation at a time, and although this does not limit the size of the audience to which a mass communication can be addressed, it does

[17] Typical wave numbers for vibrations associated with various systems (the wave number is the reciprocal of wave length hence proportional to frequency):

steel wire under tension—10^{-10} to 10^{-9} cm^{-1}
molecular rotations—10^{0} to 10^{2} cm^{-1}
molecular vibrations—10^{2} to 10^{3} cm^{-1}
planetary electrons—10^{4} to 10^{5} cm^{-1}
nuclear rotations—10^{9} to 10^{10} cm^{-1}
nuclear surface vibrations—10^{11} to 10^{12} cm^{-1}.

[18] S. R. de Groot, *Thermodynamics of irreversible processes,* 11–12, New York, Interscience Publishers, 1951.

[19] See, for example, L. Pauling, *General chemistry,* ch. 15.

limit the number of people simultaneously involved in most other forms of social interaction. Apart from requirements of direct interaction, most roles impose tasks and responsibilities that are time consuming. One cannot, for example, enact the role of "friend" with large numbers of other people.

It is probably true that in social as in physical systems, the higher frequency dynamics are associated with the subsystems, the lower frequency dynamics with the larger systems. It is generally believed, for example, that the relevant planning horizon of executives is longer the higher their location in the organizational hierarchy. It is probably also true that both the average duration of an interaction between executives and the average interval between interactions is greater at higher than at lower levels.

SUMMARY: NEAR DECOMPOSABILITY

We have seen that hierarchies have the property of near-decomposability. Intra-component linkages are generally stronger than intercomponent linkages. This fact has the effect of separating the high-frequency dynamics of a hierarchy—involving the internal structure of the components—from the low frequency dynamics—involving interaction among components. We shall turn next to some important consequences of this separation for the description and comprehension of complex systems.

THE DESCRIPTION OF COMPLEXITY

If you ask a person to draw a complex object—e.g., a human face—he will almost always proceed in a hierarchic fashion.[20] First he will outline the face. Then he will add or insert features: eyes, nose, mouth, ears, hair. If asked to elaborate, he will begin to develop details for each of the features—pupils, eyelids, lashes for the eyes, and so on—until he reaches the limits of his anatomical knowledge. His information about the object is arranged hierarchicly in memory, like a topical outline.

When information is put in outline form, it is easy to include information about the relations among the major parts and information about the internal relations of parts in each of the suboutlines. Detailed information about the relations of subparts belonging to different parts has no place in the outline and is likely to be lost. The loss of such information and the preservation mainly of information about hierarchic order is a salient characteristic that distinguishes the drawings of a child or someone untrained in representation from the drawing of a trained artist. (I am speaking of an artist who is striving for representation.)

NEAR DECOMPOSABILITY AND COMPREHENSIBILITY

From our discussion of the dynamic properties of nearly decomposable systems, we have seen that comparatively little information is lost by representing them as hierarchies. Subparts belonging to different parts only interact in an aggregative fashion—the detail of their interaction can be ignored. In studying the interaction of two large molecules, generally we do not need to consider in detail the interactions of nuclei of the atoms belonging to the one molecule with the nuclei of the atoms belonging to the other. In studying the interaction of two nations, we do not need to study in detail the interactions of each citizen of the first with each citizen of the second.

The fact, then, that many complex systems have a nearly decomposable, hierarchic structure is a major facilitating factor enabling us to understand, to describe, and even to "see" such systems and their parts. Or perhaps the proposition should be put the other way round. If there are important systems in the world that are complex without being hierarchic, they may to a considerable extent escape our observation and our understanding. Analysis of their behavior would involve such detailed knowledge and calculation of the interactions of their elementary parts that it would be beyond our capacities of memory or computation.[21]

[20] George A. Miller has collected protocols from subjects who were given the task of drawing faces, and finds that they behave in the manner described here (private communication). See also E. H. Gombrich, *Art and illusion*, 291-296, New York, Pantheon Books, 1960.

[21] I believe the fallacy in the central thesis of W. M. Elsasser's *The physical foundation of biology*, mentioned earlier, lies in his ignoring the simplification in description of complex systems that derives from their hierarchic structure. Thus (p. 155): "If we now apply similar arguments to the coupling of enzymatic reactions with the substratum of protein molecules, we see that over a sufficient period of time, the information corresponding to the structural details of these molecules will be communicated to the dynamics of the cell, to higher levels of organization as it were, and may influence such dynamics. While this reasoning is only qualitative, it lends credence to the assumption that in the living organism, unlike the inorganic crystal, the effects of microscopic structure cannot be simply averaged out; as time goes on this influence will pervade the behavior of the cell 'at all levels.'"

But from our discussion of near-decomposability it would appear that those aspects of microstructure that control the slow developmental aspects of organismic

I shall not try to settle which is chicken and which is egg: whether we are able to understand the world because it is hierarchic, or whether it appears hierarchic because those aspects of it which are not elude our understanding and observation. I have already given some reasons for supposing that the former is at least half the truth—that evolving complexity would tend to be hierarchic—but it may not be the whole truth.

SIMPLE DESCRIPTIONS OF COMPLEX SYSTEMS

One might suppose that the description of a complex system would itself be a complex structure of symbols—and indeed, it may be just that. But there is no conservation law that requires that the description be as cumbersome as the object described. A trivial example will show how a system can be described economically. Suppose the system is a two-dimensional array like this:

$$\begin{array}{cccccccc} A & B & M & N & R & S & H & I \\ C & D & O & P & T & U & J & K \\ M & N & A & B & H & I & R & S \\ O & P & C & D & J & K & T & U \\ R & S & H & I & A & B & M & N \\ T & U & J & K & C & D & O & P \\ H & I & R & S & M & N & A & B \\ J & K & T & U & O & P & C & D \end{array}$$

Let us call the array $\begin{vmatrix} AB \\ CD \end{vmatrix}$ a, the array $\begin{vmatrix} MN \\ OP \end{vmatrix}$ m, the array $\begin{vmatrix} RS \\ TU \end{vmatrix}$ r, and the array $\begin{vmatrix} HI \\ JK \end{vmatrix}$ h. Let us call the array $\begin{vmatrix} am \\ ma \end{vmatrix}$ w, and the array $\begin{vmatrix} rh \\ hr \end{vmatrix}$ x. Then the entire array is simply $\begin{vmatrix} wx \\ xw \end{vmatrix}$. While the original structure consisted of 64 symbols, it requires only 35 to write down its description:

$$S = \frac{wx}{xw}$$

$$w = \frac{am}{ma} \qquad x = \frac{rh}{hr}$$

$$a = \frac{AB}{CD} \qquad m = \frac{MN}{OP} \qquad r = \frac{RS}{TU} \qquad h = \frac{HI}{JK}$$

We achieve the abbreviation by making use of the redundancy in the original structure. Since the pattern $\frac{AB}{CD}$, for example, occurs four times in the total pattern, it is economical to represent it by the single symbol, a.

If a complex structure is completely unredundant—if no aspect of its structure can be inferred from any other—then it is its own simplest description. We can exhibit it, but we cannot describe it by a simpler structure. The hierarchic structures we have been discussing have a high degree of redundancy, hence can often be described in economical terms. The redundancy takes a number of forms, of which I shall mention three:

1. Hierarchic systems are usually composed of only a few different kinds of subsystems, in various combinations and arrangements. A familiar example is the proteins, their multitudinous variety arising from arrangements of only twenty different amino acids. Similarly, the ninety-odd elements provide all the kinds of building blocks needed for an infinite variety of molecules. Hence, we can construct our description from a restricted alphabet of elementary terms corresponding to the basic set of elementary subsystems from which the complex system is generated.

2. Hierarchic systems are, as we have seen, often nearly decomposable. Hence only aggregative properties of their parts enter into the description of the interactions of those parts. A generalization of the notion of near-decomposability might be called the "empty world hypothesis" —most things are only weakly connected with most other things; for a tolerable description of reality only a tiny fraction of all possible interactions needs to be taken into account. By adopting a descriptive language that allows the absence of something to go unmentioned, a nearly empty world can be described quite concisely. Mother Hubbard did not have to check off the list of possible contents to say that her cupboard was bare.

3. By appropriate "recoding," the redundancy that is present but unobvious in the structure of a complex system can often be made patent. The most common recoding of descriptions of dynamic systems consists in replacing a description of the time path with a description of a differential law that generates that path. The simplicity, that is, resides in a constant relation between the state of the system at any given time and the state of the system a short time later. Thus, the structure of the sequence, 1 3 5 7 9 11 . . ., is most simply expressed by observing that each member is obtained by adding 2 to the previous one. But

dynamics can be separated out from the aspects that control the more rapid cellular metabolic processes. For this reason we should not despair of unravelling the web of causes. See also J. R. Platt's review of Elsasser's book in *Perspectives in biology and medicine* 2: 243–245, 1959.

this is the sequence that Galileo found to describe the velocity at the end of successive time intervals of a ball rolling down an inclined plane.

It is a familiar proposition that the task of science is to make use of the world's redundancy to describe that world simply. I shall not pursue the general methodological point here, but shall instead take a closer look at two main types of description that seem to be available to us in seeking an understanding of complex systems. I shall call these *state description* and *process description*, respectively.

STATE DESCRIPTIONS AND PROCESS DESCRIPTIONS

"A circle is the locus of all points equidistant from a given point." "To construct a circle, rotate a compass with one arm fixed until the other arm has returned to its starting point." It is implicit in Euclid that if you carry out the process specified in the second sentence, you will produce an object that satisfies the definition of the first. The first sentence is a state description of a circle, the second a process description.

These two modes of apprehending structure are the warp and weft of our experience. Pictures, blueprints, most diagrams, chemical structural formulae are state descriptions. Recipes, differential equations, equations for chemical reactions are process descriptions. The former characterize the world as sensed; they provide the criteria for identifying objects, often by modeling the objects themselves. The latter characterize the world as acted upon; they provide the means for producing or generating objects having the desired characteristics.

The distinction between the world as sensed and the world as acted upon defines the basic condition for the survival of adaptive organisms. The organism must develop correlations between goals in the sensed world and actions in the world of process. When they are made conscious and verbalized, these correlations correspond to what we usually call means-end analysis. Given a desired state of affairs and an existing state of affairs, the task of an adaptive organism is to find the difference between these two states, and then to find the correlating process that will erase the difference.[22]

Thus, problem solving requires continual translation between the state and process descriptions of the same complex reality. Plato, in the *Meno*, argued that all learning is remembering. He could not otherwise explain how we can discover or recognize the answer to a problem unless we already know the answer.[23] Our dual relation to the world is the source and solution of the paradox. We pose a problem by giving the state description of the solution. The task is to discover a sequence of processes that will produce the goal state from an initial state. Translation from the process description to the state description enables us to recognize when we have succeeded. The solution is genuinely new to us—and we do not need Plato's theory of remembering to explain how we recognize it.

There is now a growing body of evidence that the activity called human problem solving is basically a form of means-end analysis that aims at discovering a process description of the path that leads to a desired goal. The general paradigm is: given a blueprint, to find the corresponding recipe. Much of the activity of science is an application of that paradigm: given the description of some natural phenomena, to find the differential equations for processes that will produce the phenomena.

THE DESCRIPTION OF COMPLEXITY IN SELF-REPRODUCING SYSTEMS

The problem of finding relatively simple descriptions for complex systems is of interest not only for an understanding of human knowledge of the world but also for an explanation of how a complex system can reproduce itself. In my discussion of the evolution of complex systems, I touched only briefly on the role of self-reproduction.

Atoms of high atomic weight and complex inorganic molecules are witnesses to the fact that the evolution of complexity does not imply self-reproduction. If evolution of complexity from simplicity is sufficiently probable, it will occur repeatedly; the statistical equilibrium of the system will find a large fraction of the elementary particles participating in complex systems.

If, however, the existence of a particular complex form increased the probability of the creation of another form just like it, the equilibrium between complexes and components could be greatly altered in favor of the former. If we have a description of an object that is sufficiently clear and

[22] See H. A. Simon and A. Newell, Simulation of human thinking, *in* M. Greenberger (ed.), *Management and the computer of the future*, 95–114, esp. pp 110 ff., New York, Wiley, 1962.

[23] *The works of Plato*, B. Jowett, trans., 3: 26–35, New York, Dial Press.

complete, we can reproduce the object from the description. Whatever the exact mechanism of reproduction, the description provides us with the necessary information.

Now we have seen that the descriptions of complex systems can take many forms. In particular, we can have state descriptions or we can have process descriptions; blueprints or recipes. Reproductive processes could be built around either of these sources of information. Perhaps the simplest possibility is for the complex system to serve as a description of itself—a template on which a copy can be formed. One of the most plausible current theories, for example, of the reproduction of deoxyribonucleic acid (DNA) proposes that a DNA molecule, in the form of a double helix of matching parts (each essentially a "negative" of the other), unwinds to allow each half of the helix to serve as a template on which a new matching half can form.

On the other hand, our current knowledge of how DNA controls the metabolism of the organism suggests that reproduction by template is only one of the processes involved. According to the prevailing theory, DNA serves as a template both for itself and for the related substance ribonucleic acid (RNA). RNA, in turn, serves as a template for protein. But proteins—according to current knowledge—guide the organism's metabolism not by the template method but by serving as catalysts to govern reaction rates in the cell. While RNA is a blueprint for protein, protein is a recipe for metabolism.[24]

ONTOGENY RECAPITULATES PHYLOGENY

The DNA in the chromosomes of an organism contains some, and perhaps most, of the information that is needed to determine its development and activity. We have seen that, if current theories are even approximately correct, the information is recorded not as a state description of the organism but as a series of "instructions" for the construction and maintenance of the organism from nutrient materials. I have already used the metaphor of a recipe; I could equally well compare it with a computer program, which is also a sequence of instructions, governing the construction of symbolic structures. Let me spin out some of the consequences of the latter comparison.

If genetic material is a program—viewed in its relation to the organism—it is a program with special and peculiar properties. First, it is a self-reproducing program; we have already considered its possible copying mechanism. Second, it is a program that has developed by Darwinian evolution. On the basis of our watchmaker's argument, we may assert that many of its ancestors were also viable programs—programs for the subassemblies.

Are there any other conjectures we can make about the structure of this program? There is a well-known generalization in biology that is verbally so neat that we would be reluctant to give it up even if the facts did not support it: ontogeny recapitulates phylogeny. The individual organism, in its development, goes through stages that resemble some of its ancestral forms. The fact that the human embryo develops gill bars and then modifies them for other purposes is a familiar particular belonging to the generalization. Biologists today like to emphasize the qualifications of the principle—that ontogeny recapitulates only the grossest aspects of phylogeny, and these only crudely. These qualifications should not make us lose sight of the fact that the generalization does hold in rough approximation—it does summarize a very significant set of facts about the organism's development. How can we interpret these facts?

One way to solve a complex problem is to reduce it to a problem previously solved—to show what steps lead from the earlier solution to a solution of the new problem. If, around the turn of the century, we wanted to instruct a workman to make an automobile, perhaps the simplest way would have been to tell him how to modify a wagon by removing the singletree and adding a motor and transmission. Similarly, a genetic program could be altered in the course of evolution by adding new processes that would modify a simpler form into a more complex one—to construct a gastrula, take a blastula and alter it!

The genetic description of a single cell may, therefore, take a quite different form from the genetic description that assembles cells into a multi-celled organism. Multiplication by cell division would require, as a minimum, a state description (the DNA, say), and a simple "interpretive process"—to use the term from computer language—that copies this description as a part of the larger copying process of cell division. But such a mechanism clearly would not suffice for the

[24] C. B. Anfinsen, *The molecular basis of evolution*, chs. 3 and 10, New York, Wiley, 1959, will qualify this sketchy, oversimplified account. For an imaginative discussion of some mechanisms of process description that could govern molecular structure, see H. H. Pattee, On the origin of macromolecular sequences, *Biophysical Journal* 1: 683–710, 1961.

differentiation of cells in development. It appears more natural to conceptualize that mechanism as based on a process description, and a somewhat more complex interpretive process that produces the adult organism in a sequence of stages, each new stage in development representing the effect of an operator upon the previous one.

It is harder to conceptualize the interrelation of these two descriptions. Interrelated they must be, for enough has been learned of gene-enzyme mechanisms to show that these play a major role in development as in cell metabolism. The single clue we obtain from our earlier discussion is that the description may itself be hierarchical, or nearly decomposable, in structure, the lower levels governing the fast, "high-frequency" dynamics of the individual cell, the higher level interactions governing the slow, "low-frequency" dynamics of the developing multi-cellular organism.

There are only bits of evidence, apart from the facts of recapitulation, that the genetic program is organized in this way, but such evidence as exists is compatible with this notion.[25] To the extent that we can differentiate the genetic information that governs cell metabolism from the genetic information that governs the development of differentiated cells in the multi-cellular organization, we simplify enormously—as we have already seen—our task of theoretical description. But I have perhaps pressed this speculation far enough.

The generalization that in evolving systems whose descriptions are stored in a process language, we might expect ontogeny partially to recapitulate phylogeny has applications outside the realm of biology. It can be applied as readily, for example, to the transmission of knowledge in the educational process. In most subjects, particularly in the rapidly advancing sciences, the progress from elementary to advanced courses is to a considerable extent a progress through the conceptual history of the science itself. Fortunately, the recapitulation is seldom literal—any more than it is in the biological case. We do not teach the phlogiston theory in chemistry in order later to correct it. (I am not sure I could not cite examples in other subjects where we do exactly that.) But curriculum revisions that rid us of the accumulations of the past are infrequent and painful. Nor are they always desirable—partial recapitulation may, in many instances, provide the most expeditious route to advanced knowledge.

[25] There is considerable evidence that successive genes along a chromosome often determine enzymes controlling successive stages of protein syntheses. For a review of some of this evidence, see P. E. Hartman, Transduction: a comparative review, *in* W. D. McElroy and B. Glass (eds.), *The chemical basis of heredity*, Baltimore, Johns Hopkins Press, 1957, at pp. 442–454. Evidence for differential activity of genes in different tissues and at different stages of development is discussed by J. G. Gall, Chromosomal Differentiation, *in* W. D. McElroy and B. Glass (eds.), *The chemical basis of development*, Baltimore, Johns Hopkins Press, 1958, at pp. 103–135. Finally, a model very like that proposed here has been independently, and far more fully, outlined by J. R. Platt, A 'book model' of genetic information transfer in cells and tissues, *in* Kasha and Pullman (eds.), *Horizons in biochemistry*, New York, Academic Press, forthcoming. Of course, this kind of mechanism is not the only one in which development could be controlled by a process description. Induction, in the form envisaged in Spemann's organizer theory, is based on process description, in which metabolites in already formed tissue control the next stages of development.

SUMMARY: THE DESCRIPTION OF COMPLEXITY

How complex or simple a structure is depends critically upon the way in which we describe it. Most of the complex structures found in the world are enormously redundant, and we can use this redundancy to simplify their description. But to use it, to achieve the simplification, we must find the right representation.

The notion of substituting a process description for a state description of nature has played a central role in the development of modern science. Dynamic laws, expressed in the form of systems of differential or difference equations, have in a large number of cases provided the clue for the simple description of the complex. In the preceding paragraphs I have tried to show that this characteristic of scientific inquiry is not accidental or superficial. The correlation between state description and process description is basic to the functioning of any adaptive organism, to its capacity for acting purposefully upon its environment. Our present-day understanding of genetic mechanisms suggests that even in describing itself the multi-cellular organism finds a process description—a genetically encoded program—to be the parsimonious and useful representation.

CONCLUSION

Our speculations have carried us over a rather alarming array of topics, but that is the price we must pay if we wish to seek properties common to many sorts of complex systems. My thesis has been that one path to the construction of a nontrivial theory of complex systems is by way of a theory of hierarchy. Empirically, a large proportion of the complex systems we observe in nature exhibit hierarchic structure. On theoretical grounds we could expect complex systems to be hierarchies in a world in which complexity had to evolve from simplicity. In their dynamics, hierarchies have a property, near-decomposability, that greatly simplifies their behavior. Near-decomposability also simplifies the description of a complex system, and makes it easier to understand how the information needed for the development or reproduction of the system can be stored in reasonable compass.

In both science and engineering, the study of "systems" is an increasingly popular activity. Its popularity is more a response to a pressing need for synthesizing and analyzing complexity than it is to any large development of a body of knowledge and technique for dealing with complexity. If this popularity is to be more than a fad, necessity will have to mother invention and provide substance to go with the name. The explorations reviewed here represent one particular direction of search for such substance.

[4]

THEORIES OF BOUNDED RATIONALITY

HERBERT A. SIMON

1. Introduction

Rationality denotes a style of behavior that is appropriate to the achievement of given goals, within the limits imposed by given conditions and constraints. Theories of rational behavior may be normative or descriptive – that is, they may prescribe how people or organizations should behave in order to achieve certain goals under certain conditions, or they may purport to describe how people or organizations do, in fact, behave. This essay will be concerned with the structure of theories of rational behavior, whether they are intended prescriptively or descriptively.

Individual and organizational rationality. A theory of rational behavior may be concerned with the rationality of individuals or the rationality of organizations. In fact, the two bodies of theory are not wholly distinct.[1] One plausible distinction between them is that a theory of organizational rationality must treat the phenomena of goal conflict, while a theory of individual rationality need not. This is only partly correct, for goal conflict may be important in individual as in group behavior – it is a major theme of so-called "dissonance theory" in psychology. (See N. P. CHAPANIS and J. A. CHAPANIS (1964).) A theory of individual behavior microscopic enough to concern itself with the internal organization (neurological or functional) of the central nervous system will have a significant organizational component. A theory of organizational behavior macroscopic enough to treat the organization as a monolith will be a theory of an "individual." Although this chapter will be aimed primarily at understanding individual rationality, I shall not hesitate to use the theory of the firm – classically, the theory of a

---

[1] This point was made by J. MARSCHAK (1955) in his first paper on teams, "Elements for a Theory of Teams." I shall follow his good precedent.

monolithic entrepreneur – as a convenient and enlightening illustrative example.

From the standpoint of this chapter, then, the distinction between individual and organization will not be very important. A more significant taxonomy of theories of rational behavior, for our purposes, differentiates them by the assumptions they make about the "givens" – the given goals and given conditions. Particularly important is the distinction between those theories that locate all the conditions and constraints in the environment, outside the skin of the rational actor, and those theories that postulate important constraints arising from the limitations of the actor himself as an information processor. Theories that incorporate constraints on the information-processing capacities of the actor may be called *theories of bounded rationality*.

Rationality in the classical theory of the firm. The classical theory of the firm in its simplest form provides a useful standard for comparing and differentiating theories of rationality. In the theory of the firm, the given objective is to maximize profits, where profit is defined as the difference between gross receipts from sales and cost of production. The given conditions are two in number:

(I) *the demand function*: the quantity demanded is a function of price:

(1) $$q_d = D(p), \text{ or } p = D^{-1}(q_d).$$

Since gross receipts equal price times quantity, the demand function determines gross receipts:

(2) $$R = pq_d.$$

(II) *the cost function*: the cost of production is a function of the quantity produced:

(3) $$C = C(q_s).$$

If the quantity produced equals the quantity demanded,

(4) $$q_s = q_d,$$

then the profit, to be maximized, is simply the difference between gross receipts and the cost of production:

(5) $$\text{Profit} = R - C = pq - C(q),$$

and, under appropriate assumptions regarding differentiability, we will have for the maximum profit:

$$d(R-C)/dq = p + q d(D^{-1}(q))/dq - dC(q)/dq = 0. \tag{6}$$

The constraints in this theory, the demand and cost functions, D and C, are both located in the actor's environment. He is assumed to find the solution of equation (6). To do this, he must have perfect knowledge of these constraints, and must be able to perform the necessary calculations – to set the derivative of profit with respect to quantity equal to zero and to solve the resulting algebraic equation.

The limits of rationality. Theories of bounded rationality can be constructed by modifying these assumptions in a variety of ways. *Risk and uncertainty* can be introduced into the demand function, the cost function, or both. For example, certain parameters of one or both of these functions can be assumed to be random variables with known distributions. Then the assumption of the actor's perfect knowledge of these functions has been replaced by the assumption that he has perfect knowledge of their distributions. This change in assumptions may, in turn, make it easier or more difficult to carry out the calculations for finding the optimum – usually it becomes much more difficult than in the corresponding case of certainty.

Another way in which rationality can be bounded is by assuming that the actor has only *incomplete information about alternatives.* Fewer models have been constructed to deal with this situation than with the situation in which he has incomplete information about consequences. However, in certain search models it is assumed that the actor knows the probability distribution of profits in a population of possible alternative actions. Specific actions become available to him – say, by random sampling from this population – as a function of the amount of resources he devotes to search. His task is to find the alternative that maximizes his expected profit net of the search cost. In this class of models, selecting the best alternative from among those already discovered is assumed to be a trivial problem; the decision question has been switched to the question of how much of the actor's resources should be allocated to search.[2]

---

[2] For an example, see STIGLER (1961). Theories of the allocation of resources to search can also be constructed to deal with incomplete information about consequences. Sequential sampling theory falls into this category, for it answers the question: shall I make a decision now, or wait until I have gathered additional information? The question is answered by comparing the incremental cost of enlarging the sample with the expected gain through the resulting average improvement in the decision.

Finally, rationality can be bounded by assuming *complexity* in the cost function or other environmental constraints so great as to prevent the actor from calculating the best course of action. Limits on rationality stemming from this source have not been prominent in classical theories of rational behavior. However, in numerical analysis, the theory of approximation provides analogues, for it is concerned with the rate at which an approximation can be expected to improve as a function of amount of computational effort. By introducing explicitly into that theory the cost of computational effort, it can be transformed into a theory of optimal approximation.

Alternatives to the classical goals. The classical theory can be modified not only by altering the nature of the conditions and constraints, but also by altering the nature of the given goals. Some modern theories of the firm depart from the classical theory, not along any of the dimensions mentioned above, but by postulating different goals from the classical goal of profit maximization.

BAUMOL (1959, pp. 45–53), for example, has developed a model in which the firm maximizes sales subject to the constraint that profit should not be less than a specified "satisfactory" level. According to this theory of Baumol, equation (6) in the classical model should be replaced by:

$$\mathrm{d}R/\mathrm{d}q = p + q\mathrm{d}(D^{-1}(q))/\mathrm{d}q = 0\,, \tag{6'}$$

subject to the constraint that

$$P = R - C \geq P^*\,. \tag{7}$$

It may be observed that the informational and computational requirements for applying Baumol's theory to concrete situations are not very different from the requirements of the classical model.

This essay will not be concerned with variants of the theory of rationality that assume goals different from profit or utility maximization, except to the extent that there is significant interaction between the assumptions about goals and the assumptions about conditions and constraints. We shall see, however, that this is a very important exception. In actual fact, most of the variants of the theory that make significant modifications in the assumptions about conditions and constraints also call for assumptions about goals that are different from the classical assumptions of profit or utility maximization. The reasons for this interaction will appear as we proceed.

2. Approaches to Rational Choice in Chess

A number of the persons who have engaged in research on rational decision-making have taken the game of chess as a microcosm that mirrors interesting properties of decision-making situations in the real world. The research on rational choice in chess provides some useful illustrations of alternative approaches to rationality.

The problem confronting a chess player whose turn it is to move can be interpreted in either of two ways. First, it can be interpreted as a problem of finding a good (or the best) strategy – where "strategy" means a conditional sequence of moves, defining what move will be made at each successive stage after each possible response of the opponent.

Second, the problem can be interpreted as one of finding a set of accurate evaluations for the alternative moves immediately before the player.

From a classical standpoint, these two problems are not distinguishable. If the player has unlimited computational power, it does not matter whether he selects a complete strategy for his future behavior in the game, or selects each of his moves, one at a time, when it is his turn to play. For the way in which he goes about evaluating the next move is by constructing alternative complete strategies for the entire future play of the game, and selecting the one that promises the best return (i.e., the best return under the assumption that the opponent will also do *his* best to win). This is the approach taken in the von Neumann-Morgenstern theory of games (VON NEUMANN and MORGENSTERN (1953)).

The game-theoretical definition of rationality in chess. As von Neumann and Morgenstern observed, chess is a trivial game. "... if the theory of Chess (i.e., the complete tree of possible games) were really fully known there would be nothing left to play" (*ibid.*, p. 125). Each terminus of the tree of possible games represents a win, loss, or draw for White. Moving backward one branch on the tree, the player whose move it is at that branch can examine the termini to which it could lead by his choice of move, and can choose the move having the preferred terminus. The value of that terminus becomes, then, the value of the branch that leads to it. Working backward in this way, a value – win, lose, or draw for White – can be assigned to each position, and ultimately to each of the initial legal moves for White. Now each player can specify an optimal strategy – a strategy that will guarantee him at least as good an outcome as any other – by specifying which move he would select at each branch point in the tree whenever it is his move.

Unfortunately, as von Neumann and Morgenstern also observed, the triviality of chess offers no practical help to a player in actually choosing a move. "But our proof, which guarantees the validity of one (and only one) of these three alternatives [that the game must have the value of win lose or draw for White], gives no practically usable method to determine the true one. This relative, human difficulty necessitates the use of those incomplete, heuristic methods of playing, which constitute 'good' Chess; and without it there would be no element of 'struggle' and 'surprise' in that game" (*ibid.*).

What "impracticality" means becomes more vivid when we calculate how much search would be involved in finding the game-theoretically correct strategy in chess. On the average, at any given position in a game of chess, there are about 30 legal moves – in round numbers, for a move and its replies, an average of about 10^3 continuations. Forty moves would be a not unreasonable estimate of the average length of a game. Then there would be perhaps 10^{120} possible games of chess. Obviously the exact number does not matter: a number like 10^{40} would be less spectacular, but quite large enough to support the conclusions of the present argument.

Studies of the decision-making of chess players indicate strongly that strong players seldom look at as many as one hundred possibilities – that is one hundred continuations from the given position – in selecting a move or strategy. One hundred is a reasonably large number, by some standards, but somewhat smaller than 10^{120}! Chess players do not consider all possible strategies and pick the best, but generate and examine a rather small number, making a choice as soon as they discover one that they regard as satisfactory (see DE GROOT (1965)).

Before we consider in detail how they do it, let us return to the classical model and ask whether there is any way in which we could make it relevant to the practical choice problem, taking account of the size of the problem space, in a game like chess. One possible way would be to replace the actual problem space with a very much smaller space that approximates the actual one in some appropriate sense, and then apply the classical theory to the smaller approximate space.

This approach was taken in some of the early computer programs for playing chess and checkers. In the Los Alamos program, for example, the computer generated all legal moves, all legal replies to each, and so on, two moves deep. Each of the terminal positions thus generated (about a million in a two-move analysis) was evaluated, and the minimax procedure applied, working backwards, to find the best first move. Thus, a space of about

10^6 elements was substituted for the space of 10^{120} elements that represents the "real" world of chess.

The scheme was approximate, because the actual chess values of the million terminal positions were not known, and could not be known accurately without returning to the space of 10^{120} elements – that is, returning to the game-theoretical analysis of the full game. In place of these unknown true values, approximate values were computed, using rules of thumb that are commonly employed by chess players – conventional numerical values for the pieces, and measures of mobility. Thus, the approximate scheme was not guaranteed to select the objectively best move, but only the move leading to the positions that appeared best, in terms of these heuristic criteria, after an analysis two moves deep. Experience indicates that it is not possible to make such approximate evaluations accurately enough to enable the program to play good chess. The optimal decision in the approximated world is not necessarily even a good decision in the real world.

Satisficing processes in chess thinking. Chess programs now exist that take the alternative course, trying to emulate the human chess player in looking at only a very few continuations. The effectiveness of such a scheme depends critically on three components: the *move generators*, processes that select the continuations to be explored; the *evaluators*, processes that determine how good each continuation is; and the *stop rules*, criteria that determine when the search should be terminated and a move selected.

By scanning a chess position, features of the position can be detected that suggest appropriate moves. To take an extreme case, suppose a chess player discovers, when it is his move, that one of his Pawns attacks the opponent's Queen. Obviously, the capture of the Queen by the Pawn is one move that deserves consideration. It may turn out to be a poor move – another piece will checkmate him, say, if he captures the Queen – but its superficial merits are obvious, and its deficiencies can only be detected by considering it and evaluating it dynamically. A simple process that would generate this move, and others like it, would consist in determining which of the opponent's pieces were attacked by a piece of lesser value, or were undefended and attacked by any piece. Thus, a suitable set of move-generating processes might identify for further analysis all or most of the moves deserving serious consideration. If the generators were ordered appropriately, they might usually identify first the most promising moves, then the ones slightly less promising, and so on.

Possible moves, produced by the move generators, can be evaluated by a combination of static and dynamic criteria. Static criteria are features of the position, or differences between successive positions. Thus, one of the important static evaluators used by all chess players is the piece count: each piece is assigned a conventional value (say, Pawn = 1, Knight and Bishop = 3, Rook = 5, Queen = 9), and the sums of the values for the two players are compared. In general, if the piece count of one player exceeds that of the other by more than one point (or even, in many cases, by a single point), the player with the higher count can find a winning continuation *unless* the balance is very quickly redressed by a sequence of forceful moves. (Thus, it does not matter being 5 points down if you can capture the opponent's Queen on the next move without further reprisals.)

The short-run tactical considerations are handled by carrying out dynamic analysis of plausible continuations until a position is reached that is sufficiently quiet or "dead" that it can safely be evaluated by means of the static evaluators. These static evaluators are then propagated backwards to the move under consideration by the familiar minimax procedure.

Two kinds of stop rules are needed in a program having this structure: rules to stop exploration at dead positions that can be evaluated statically, and rules to stop the entire process and select a move when a satisfactory one has been found. The former class of stop rules has already been discussed; the latter needs to be examined more closely. If the alternatives in a choice situation are not given, but have to be discovered or invented, and if the number of possible alternatives is very large, then a choice has to be made before all or most of them have been looked at. It was precisely this difficulty in the classical requirement of comparing all alternatives that led to the approach described here. But if all alternatives are not to be examined, some criterion must be used to determine that an adequate, or satisfactory, one has been found. In the psychological literature, criteria that perform this function in decision processes are called *aspiration levels*. The Scottish word "satisficing" (= satisfying) has been revived to denote problem solving and decision making that sets an aspiration level, searches until an alternative is found that is satisfactory by the aspiration level criterion, and selects that alternative (SIMON (1957), Part IV).

In satisficing procedures, the existence of a satisfactory alternative is made likely by dynamic mechanisms that adjust the aspiration levels to reality on the basis of information about the environment. Thus, in a chess-playing program, the initial aspiration level can be set (preferably with a little upward bias) on the basis of a static evaluation of the position. As alternative moves are considered and evaluated by dynamic and static analysis, the evaluation of the position can gradually be reduced until the best move discovered so far reaches or exceeds in value the aspiration level.

The limits of rationality in chess. In the introductory section of this paper, three limits on perfect rationality were listed: uncertainty about the consequences that would follow from each alternative, incomplete information about the set of alternatives, and complexity preventing the necessary computations from being carried out. Chess illustrates how, in real world problem-solving situations, these three categories tend to merge.

If we describe the chess player as choosing a *strategy*, then his difficulty in behaving rationally – and the impossibility of his behaving as game theory says he should – resides in the fact that he has incomplete information as to what alternatives (strategies) are open to him. He has time to discover only a minute fraction of these strategies, and to specify the ones he discovers only incompletely.

Alternatively, if we describe the chess player as choosing a *move*, his difficulty in behaving rationally lies in the fact that he has only rough information about the consequences of adopting each of the alternatives (moves) that is open to him. It would not be impossible for him to generate the whole set of his legal moves, for they seldom number more than about thirty. However, he can evaluate them, even approximately, only by carrying out further analysis through the immense, branching, move tree. Since only a limited amount of processing time is available for the evaluation, he must allocate the time among the alternative moves. The practical facts of the matter are that it is usually better to generate only a few of the entire set of legal moves, evaluating these rather thoroughly, than it is to generate all of them, evaluating them superficially. Hence the good chess player does not examine all the moves open to him, but only a small fraction of them. (Data presented by DE GROOT (1965) suggest that typically a half dozen to a dozen of a set of thirty legal moves may be generated and explored by the chess player.)

From still a third standpoint, the chess player's difficulty in behaving rationally has nothing to do with uncertainty – whether of consequences or alternatives – but is a matter of complexity. For there is no risk or uncertainty, in the sense in which those terms are used in economics or statistical decision theory, in the game of chess. As von Neumann and Morgenstern observe, it is a game of perfect information. No probabilities of future events need enter the calculations, and no contingencies, in a statistical sense, arise.

From a game-theoretical standpoint, the presence of the opponent does not introduce contingencies. The opponent can always be counted on to do his worst. The point becomes clear if we replace the task of playing chess with the task of proving theorems. In the latter task, there is no opponent. Nor are there contingencies: the true and the derivable theorems reside eternally in Plato's heaven. Rationality in theorem proving is a problem only because the maze of possible proof paths is vast and complex.

What we refer to as "uncertainty" in chess or theorem proving, therefore, is uncertainty introduced into a perfectly certain environment by inability – computational inability – to ascertain the structure of that environment. But the result of the uncertainty, whatever its source, is the same: approximation must replace exactness in reaching a decision. In particular, when the uncertainty takes the form of an unwieldy problem space to be explored, the problem-solving process must incorporate mechanisms for determining when the search or evaluation will stop and an alternative will be chosen.

Satisficing and optimizing. The terms satisficing and optimizing, which we have already introduced, are labels for two broad approaches to rational behavior in situations where complexity and uncertainty make global rationality impossible. In these situations, optimization becomes approximate optimization – the description of the real-world situation is radically simplified until reduced to a degree of complication that the decision maker can handle. Satisficing approaches seek this simplification in a somewhat different direction, retaining more of the detail of the real-world situation, but settling for a satisfactory, rather than an approximate-best, decision. One cannot predict in general which approach will lead to the better decisions as measured by their real-world consequences. In chess at least, good players have clearly found satisficing more useful than approximating-and-optimizing.

A satisficing decision procedure can often be turned into a procedure for optimizing by introducing a rule for optimal amount of search, or, what amounts to the same thing, a rule for fixing the aspiration level optimally. Thus, the aspiration level in chess might be adjusted, dynamically, to such a level that the expected improvement in the move chosen, per minute of additional search, would just balance the incremental cost of the search.

Although such a translation is formally possible, to carry it out in practice requires additional information and assumptions beyond those needed for satisficing. First, the values of alternatives must be measured in units comparable with the units for measuring search cost, in order to permit comparison at the margins. Second, the marginal productivity of search – the expected increase in the value per unit of search time – must be estimated on some basis or other. If one were designing a chess-playing program, it is doubtful whether effort spent in attempting to imbed the program in such a dynamic optimizing framework would be nearly as worthwhile as equivalent effort spent in improving the selectivity of the program's move-generating and move-evaluating heuristics.

Another quite different translation between optimizing and satisficing schemes has also been suggested from time to time. A chess program of the "classical" type, which makes optimal decisions in an approximated world, can be regarded as a particular kind of satisficing program, in which "satisfactory" is defined by the approximating procedure that is used. Hence, it is difficult to draw a formal distinction between optimizing and satisficing procedures that is so iron-clad as to prevent either from being reinterpreted in the frame of the other. The practical difference, however – the difference in emphasis that results from adopting one viewpoint or the other – is often very great.

In research on optimizing procedures, considerable attention has been paid to the formal properties of the evaluation functions, to the existence and efficiency of procedures for computing the optimum, and to procedures for reducing uncertainty (e.g., forecasting methods). The nature of the approximations that are necessary to cast real-world problems into forms suitable for optimization, and the means for choosing among alternative approximations, have been less fully and less systematically studied. Much effort, for example, has gone into the discovery of efficient algorithms for solving linear programming problems. Finding an appropriate way of formulating a concrete real-world decision problem as a linear-programming problem remains largely an art.[3]

Research on satisficing procedures has focussed primarily on the efficiency of search – on the nature of the heuristic methods that enable the rare solutions in enormous spaces of possibilities to be sought and found with moderate amounts of search effort. Since moderate changes in heuristics often make order-of-magnitude changes in search effectiveness, highly accurate means for assessing the quality of solutions or the effort required to find them may be relatively unimportant. It probably does not require delicate evaluation functions or stop rules to change a duffer's chess play to a reasonably effective move-choosing program.

[3] The work of A. Charnes and W. W. Cooper (1961) is full of sophisticated examples of this art. See, for instances, Appendix B and Chapter 11 of Volume I.

3. Bounded Rationality in Design

The engineering activities usually called "design" have not been much discussed under the heading of rational decision-making. The reason for this should be clear from the foregoing discussion: classical decision theory has been concerned with choice among *given* alternatives; design is concerned with the discovery and elaboration of alternatives. Our exploration of the microcosm of chess has indicated, however, how the theory of design can be assimilated to a satisficing theory of rational choice. Let me spell the point out a little more fully.

Consider that interpretation of chess which views the task as one of choosing a strategy, and not just a single move. Specifically, consider a situation where a player is searching for a combination (a strategy) that will definitely checkmate his opponent, even though it may require sacrifices of pieces along the way. A chess player will ordinarily not enter into such a course of action unless he can see it through to the end – unless he can *design*, that is, a water-tight mating combination.

As we have seen already, the evaluations and comparisons that take place during this design process are not, in general, comparisons among complete designs. Evaluations take place, first of all, to guide the search – the elaboration of the design itself. They provide the basis for decisions that the design should be elaborated in one direction rather than another. Complete designs (in this case, mating combinations), when they are finally arrived at, are not generally evaluated by comparing them with alternative designs, but by comparing them with standards defined by aspiration levels. In the chess situation, as soon as the player discovers a strategy that guarantees a checkmate, he adopts it. He does not look for all possible checkmating strategies and adopt the best (H. A. SIMON and P. A. SIMON (1962)).

In the design of complex objects – a bridge, say, or an airplane – the process has an even more involved search structure. Here, the early stages of search take place in highly simplified spaces that abstract most of the detail from the real-world problem, leaving only its most important elements in summarized form. When a plan, a schematized and aggregated design, has been elaborated in the planning space, the detail of the problem can be reintroduced, and the plan used as a guide in the search for a complete design.

More than two spaces may be used, of course; there may be a whole hierarchy of planning spaces, leading from a highly abstract and global design to successive specification of detail. At each of these levels of abstraction, the design process, too, may be differently structured. Since the more abstract spaces tend to be "smoother," it is often possible to use optimization models for planning purposes, reverting to satisficing search models to fill in the detail of the design. Thus, linear programming or dynamic programming may be used for general planning of factory operations, while more heuristic techniques are used for scheduling of individual jobs. In other situations, the overall design process may employ satisficing search procedures, while optimizing techniques may be used to set parameters once the general design has been fixed.[4]

4. Bounded Rationality in Management Science

Most of the formal techniques that constitute the technical backbone of management science and operations research are procedures for finding the best of a set of alternatives in terms of some criterion – that is, they fall in our category of "classical" procedures. Linear and dynamic programming are among the most powerful of these techniques. The dominant approach to problems in this sphere has been to simplify the real-world problems to the point where the formal optimizing models can be used as approximations.

Some industrial problems of a combinatorial sort have not yielded easily to this approach. Typically, the recalcitrant problems involve integer solutions, or, what usually amounts to the same thing, the consideration of possible permutations and combinations of a substantial number of elements. Warehouse location is a problem of this kind. The task is to "determine the geographical pattern of warehouse locations which will be most profitable to the company by equating the marginal cost of warehouse operation with the transportation cost savings and incremental profits resulting from more rapid delivery" (KUEHN and HAMBURGER (1963), p. 643).

A heuristic program devised by KUEHN and HAMBURGER (1963) for locating warehouses has two parts: "(1) the main program, which locates warehouses one at a time until no additional warehouses can be added to the distribution network without increasing total costs, and (2) the bump and shift routine, ..., which attempts to modify solutions ... by evaluating the profit implications of dropping individual warehouses or of shifting them from one location to another" (*ibid.*, p. 645).

[4] Some modern semi-automated procedures for the design of chemical processing plants proceed from heuristic techniques for selecting the unit operations and their flow, then employ linear programming to determine the parameters of the system so specified.

This program fits our earlier characterization of design procedures. A possible plan is gradually built up, step by step, through a search procedure, and then possible local modifications are investigated before the final plan is settled upon. In building up the initial plan, locations are tried that are near concentrations of demand, adding at each step the warehouse that produces the greatest cost savings for the entire system. Only a fraction of the possible warehouse sites, which preliminary screening selects as "promising," are evaluated in detail at each stage. Finally, a so-called "bump-shift" routine modifies the programs tentatively arrived at by (1) eliminating warehouses no longer economical because new warehouses have been introduced at later steps of the program, (2) considering shifting warehouses to alternative sites within their territories. The flow diagram of the warehouse location programs, which will serve to illustrate the typical structure of heuristic programs when they are formalized, is shown in Fig. 1.

Kuehn and Hamburger have carried out some detailed comparisons of the heuristic program with optimizing techniques. They conclude that "in theory, a linear programming approach ... could be used to solve the problem. In practice, however, the size and nonlinearities involved in many problems are such that application is not currently feasible" (*ibid.*, p. 658). They attribute the superior performance of the heuristic program to two main causes: "(1) computational simplicity, which results in substantial reductions in solution times and permits the treatment of large-scale problems, and (2) flexibility with respect to the underlying cost functions, eliminating the need for restrictive assumptions" (*ibid.*, p. 656).

Perhaps the technique most widely used in management science to deal with situations too complex for the application of known optimization methods is simulation. The amount of detail incorporated in the simulation of a large system is limited only by computational feasibility. On the other hand, simulation, unaided by other formal tools of analysis, provides no direct means for discovering and evaluating alternative plans of action. In simulation, the trial and error is supplied by the human investigators rather than by the technique of analysis itself (see FORRESTER (1961)).

5. Conclusion

The theory of rational decision has undergone extremely rapid development in the past thirty years. A considerable part of the impetus for this development came, during and since World War II, from the attempt to use formal decision procedures in actual real-world situations of considerable

A HEURISTIC PROGRAM FOR LOCATING WAREHOUSES

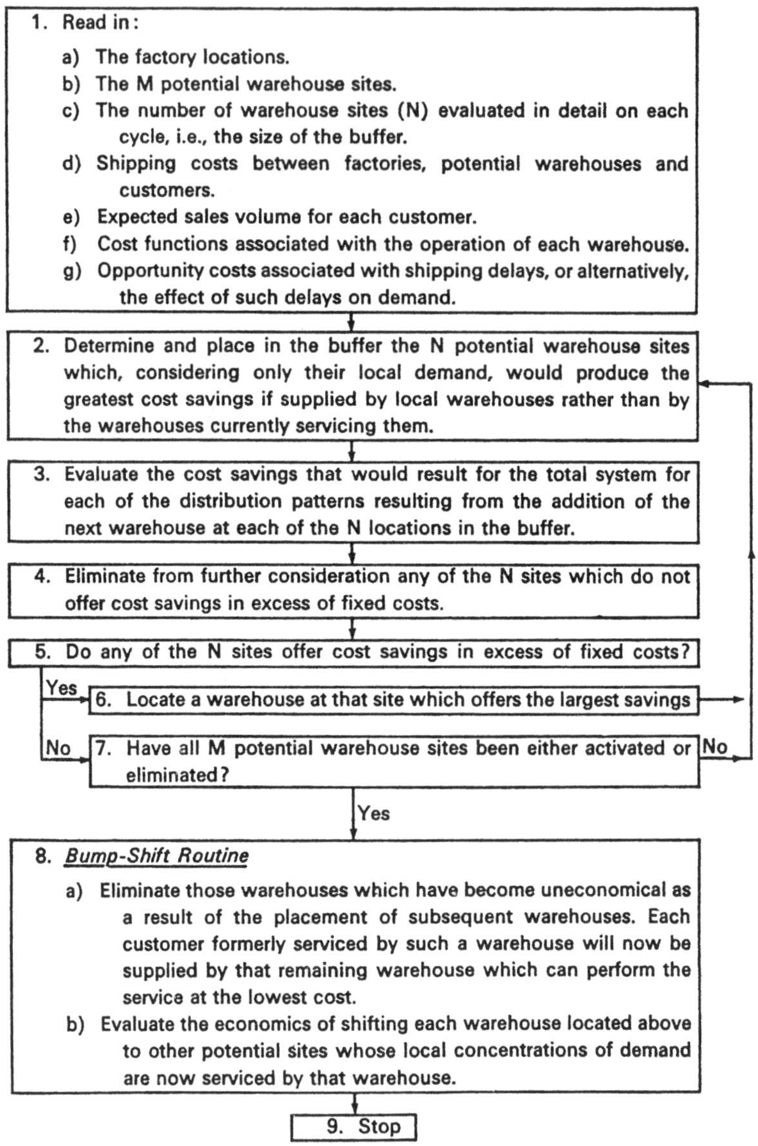

Fig. 1. Flow diagram

complexity. To deal with this complexity the formal models have grown in power and sophistication. But complexity has also stimulated the development of new kinds of models of rational decision that take special account of the very limited information-gathering and computing capacity of human beings and their associated computers.

One response to the concern with uncertainty, with the difficulties of discovering or designing alternatives, and with computational complexity has been to introduce search and information transmission processes explicitly into the models. Another (not exclusive) response has been to replace optimization criteria with criteria of satisfactory performance. The satisficing approach has been most often employed in models where "heuristic" or trial-and-error methods are used to aid the search for plausible alternatives.

As a result of all these developments, the decision maker today, in business, government, universities, has available to him an unprecedented collection of models and computational tools to aid him in his decision-making processes. Whatever the compromises he must make with reality in order to comprehend and cope with it, these tools make substantially more tractable the task of matching man's bounded capabilities with the difficulty of his problems.

References

BAUMOL, W. J. (1959), *Business Behavior, Value and Growth*, Macmillan, New York, pp. 45–53.

CHAPANIS, N. P. and J. A. CHAPANIS (1964), "Cognitive Dissonance: Five Years Later," *Psychological Bulletin*, *61*, 1023.

CHARNES, A. and W. W. COOPER (1961), *Management Models and Industrial Applications of Linear Programming*, Wiley, New York, (2 volumes).

DE GROOT, A. (1965), *Thought and Choice in Chess*, Mouton, The Hague.

FORRESTER, J. W. (1961), *Industrial Dynamics*, M.I.T. Press, Cambridge.

KUEHN, A. A. and M. J. HAMBURGER (1963), "A Heuristic Program for Locating Warehouses," *Management Science*, *9*, 643-666.

MARSCHAK, J. (1955), "Elements for a Theory of Teams," *Management Science*, *1*, 127–137

SIMON, H. A. (1957), Part IV in *Models of Man*, Wiley, New York, pp. 196–279.

SIMON, H. A. and P. A. SIMON (1962), "Trial and Error Search in Solving Difficult Problems," *Behavioral Science*, *7*, 425–429.

STIGLER, G. J. (1961), "The Economics of Information," *Journal of Political Economy*, *69*, 213–225.

VON NEUMANN, J. and O. MORGENSTERN (1953), *Theory of Games and Economic Behavior*, (3rd ed.), Princeton University Press, Princeton, pp. 125.

[5]

RICHARD T. ELY LECTURE

Rationality as Process and as Product of Thought

By HERBERT A. SIMON*

This opportunity to deliver the Richard T. Ely Lecture affords me some very personal satisfactions. Ely, unbeknownst to him, bore a great responsibility for my economic education, and even for my choice of profession. The example of my uncle, Harold Merkel, who was a student of Commons and Ely at Wisconsin before World War I, taught me that human behavior was a fit subject for scientific study, and directed me to economics and political science instead of high energy physics or molecular biology. Some would refer to this as satisficing, for I had never heard of high energy physics or molecular biology, and hence was spared an agonizing weighing of alternative utiles. I simply picked the first profession that sounded fascinating.

Ely's influence went much further than that. My older brother's copy of his *Outlines of Economics*—the 1930 edition—was on our bookshelves when I prepared for high school debates on tariffs versus free trade, and on the Single Tax of Henry George. It provided me with a sufficiently good grounding in principles that I was later able to take Henry Simons' intermediate theory course at the University of Chicago, and the graduate courses of Frank Knight and Henry Schultz without additional preparation.

The Ely textbook, in its generation, held the place of Samuelson or Bach in ours. If it would not sound as though I were denying any progress in economics over the past half century, I might suggest that Ely's textbook could be substituted for any of our current ones at a substantial reduction in weight, and without students or teacher being more than dimly aware of the replacement. Of course they would not hear from Ely about marginal propensities to do this or that, nor about the late lamented Phillips curve. But monetarists could rejoice in Ely's uncompromising statement of the quantity theory (p. 298, italics), and in his assertion that "the solution of the problem of unemployment depends largely upon indirect measures, such as monetary and banking reform"—Ely does go on to say, however, that "we shall recognize that society must offer a willing and able man an opportunity to work" (p. 528).

*Carnegie-Mellon University.

I. Rationality in and out of Economics

I have more than personal reasons for directing your attention to Ely's textbook. On page 4, we find a definition of economics that is, I think, wholly characteristic of books contemporary with his. "Economics," he says, "is the science which treats of those social phenomena that are due to the wealth-getting and wealth-using activities of man." Economics, that is to say, concerns itself with a particular subset of man's behaviors—those having to do with the production, exchange, and consumption of goods and services.

Many, perhaps most, economists today would regard that view as too limiting. They would prefer the definition proposed in the *International Encyclopedia of the Social Sciences*: "Economics . . . is the study of the allocation of scarce resources among unlimited and competing uses" (vol. 4, p. 472). If beefsteak is scarce, they would say, so are votes, and the tools of economic analysis can be used as readily to analyze the allocation of the one as of the other. This point of view has launched economics into many excursions and incursions into political science and her other sister social sciences, and has generated a certain amount of hubris in the profession with respect to its broader civilizing mission. I would suppose that the program of this meeting, with its emphasis upon the relations between economics and the other social sciences, is at least partly a reflection of that hubris.

A. *Rationality in Economics*

The topic of allocating scarce resources can be approached from either its normative or its positive side. Fundamental to the approach from either side are assumptions about the adaptation of means to ends, of actions to goals and situations. Economics, whether normative or positive, has not simply been the study of the allocation of scarce resources, it has been the study of the *rational* allocation of scarce resources.

Moreover, the term "rational" has long had in economics a much more specific meaning than its general dictionary signification of "agreeable to reason; not absurd, preposterous, extravagant, foolish, fanciful, or the like; intelligent, sensible." As is well known, the rational man of economics is a maximizer, who will settle for nothing less than the best. Even his expectations, we have learned in the past few years, are rational (see John Muth, 1961).[1] And his rationality extends as far as the bedroom for, as Gary Becker tells us, "he would read in bed at night only if the value of reading exceeded the value (to him) of the loss in sleep suffered by his wife" (1974, p. 1078).

It is this concept of rationality that is economics' main export commodity in its trade with the other social sciences. It is no novelty in those sciences to propose that people behave rationally—if that term is taken in its broader dictionary sense. Assumptions of rationality are essential components of virtually all the sociological, psychological, political, and anthropological theories with which I am familiar. What economics has to export, then, is not rationality, but a very particular and special form of it—the rationality of the utility maximizer, and a pretty smart one at that. But international flows have to be balanced. If the program of this meeting aims at more active intercourse between economics and her sister social sciences, then we must ask not only what economics will export, but also what she will receive in payment. An economist might well be tempted to murmur the lines of the tentmaker: "I wonder often what the Vintners buy—One half as precious as the stuff they sell."

My paper will be much concerned with that question, and before I proceed, it may be well to sketch in outline the path I propose to follow in answering it. The argument has three major steps.

First, I would like to expand on the theme that almost all human behavior has a large rational component, but only in terms of the broader everyday sense of rationality, not the economists' more specialized sense of maximization.

Second, I should like to show that economics itself has not by any means limited itself to the narrower definition of rationality. Much economic literature (for example, the literature of comparative institutional analysis) uses weaker definitions of rationality extensively; and that literature would not be greatly, if at all, improved by substituting the stronger definition for the weaker one.[2] To the extent that the weaker definition is adequate for purposes of analysis, economics will find that there is indeed much that is importable from the other social sciences.

Third, economics has largely been preoccupied with the *results* of rational choice rather than the *process* of choice. Yet as economic analysis acquires a broader concern with the dynamics of choice under uncertainty, it will become more and more essential to consider choice processes. In the past twenty years, there have been im-

[1]The term is ill-chosen, for rational expectations in the sense of Muth are profit-maximizing expectations only under very special circumstances (see below). Perhaps we would mislead ourselves and others less if we called them by the less alluring phrase, "consistent expectations."

[2]For an interesting argument in support of this proposition from a surprising source, see Becker (1962). What Becker calls "irrationality" in his article would be called "bounded rationality" here.

portant advances in our understanding of procedural rationality, particularly as a result of research in artificial intelligence and cognitive psychology. The importation of these theories of the processes of choice into economics could provide immense help in deepening our understanding of the dynamics of rationality, and of the influences upon choice of the institutional structure within which it takes place.

We begin, then, by looking at the broader concept of rationality to which I have referred, and its social science applications.

B. *Rationality in the Other Social Sciences: Functional Analysis*

Let me provide some examples how rationality typically enters into social science theories. Consider first so-called "social exchange" theories (see, for example, George Homans). The central idea here is that when two or more people interact, each expects to get something from the interaction that is valuable to him, and is thereby motivated to give something up that is valuable to the others. Social exchange, in the form of the "inducements-contributions balance" of Chester I. Barnard and the author (1947), has played an important role in organization theory, and in even earlier times (see, for example, George Simmel) was a central ingredient in sociological theories. Much of the theorizing and empirical work on the topic has been concerned with determining what constitutes a significant inducement or contribution in particular classes of exchange situations—that is, with the actual shape and substance of the "utility function." Clearly, the man of social exchange theory is a rational man, even if he is never asked to equate things at the margin.

It is perhaps more surprising to discover how pervasive assumptions of rationality are in psychoanalytic theory—confirming the suspicion that there is indeed method in madness. In his *Five Lectures* Sigmund Freud has this to say about neurotic illnesses:

> We see that human beings fall ill when, as a result of external obstacles or of an internal lack of adaptation, the satisfaction of their erotic needs *in reality* is frustrated. We see that they then take flight into *illness* in order that by its help they may find a satisfaction to take the place of what has been frustrated . . . We suspect that our patients' resistance to recovery is no simple one, but compounded of several motives. Not only does the patient's ego rebel against giving up the repressions by means of which it has risen above its original disposition, but the sexual instincts are unwilling to renounce their substitutive satisfaction so long as it is uncertain whether reality will offer them anything better.

Almost all explanations of pathological behavior in the psychoanalytic literature take this form: they explain the patient's illness in terms of the functions it performs for him.

The quotation from Freud is illustrative of a kind of functional reasoning that goes far beyond psychoanalysis and is widely used throughout the social sciences, and especially anthropology and sociology. Behaviors are functional if they contribute to certain goals, where these goals may be the pleasure or satisfaction of an individual or the guarantee of food or shelter for the members of a society. Functional analysis in this sense is concerned with explaining how "major social patterns operate to maintain the integration or adaptation of the larger system" (see Frank Cancian). Institutions are functional if reasonable men might create and maintain them in order to meet social needs or achieve social goals.

It is not necessary or implied that the adaptation of institutions or behavior patterns to goals be conscious or intended. When awareness and intention are present, the function is usually called *manifest*, otherwise it is a *latent* function. The function, whether it be manifest or latent, provides the grounds for the reasonableness or rationality of the institution or behavior pattern. As in economics, evolutionary arguments are often adduced to explain the persistence and survival of functional patterns, and to avoid assumptions of deliberate calculation in explaining them.

In practice, it is very rarely that the existence or character of institutions are *deduced* from the functions that must be performed for system survival. In almost all cases it is the other way round; it is empirical observation of the behavior pattern that raises the question of why it persists—what function it performs. Perhaps, in an appropriate axiomatic formulation, it would be possible to *deduce* that every society must have food-gathering institutions. In point of fact, such institutions can be *observed* in every society, and their existence is then rationalized by the argument that obtaining food is a functional requisite for all societies. This kind of argument may demonstrate the sufficiency of a particular pattern for performing an essential function, but cannot demonstrate its necessity—cannot show that there may not be alternative, functionally equivalent, behavior patterns that would satisfy the same need.

The point may be stated more formally. Functional arguments are arguments about the movements of systems toward stable self-maintaining equilibria. But without further specification, there is no reason to suppose that the attained equilibria that are reached will be global maxima or minima of some function rather than local, relative maxima or minima. In fact, we know that the conditions that every local maximum of a system be a global maximum are very strong (usually some kind of "convexity" conditions).

Further, when the system is complex and its environment continually changing (that is, in the conditions under which biological and social evolution actually take place), there is no assurance that the system's momentary position will lie anywhere near a point of equilibrium, whether local or global. Hence, all that can be concluded from a functional argument is that certain characteristics (the satisfaction of certain functional requirements in a particular way) are consistent with the survival and further development of the system, not that these same requirements could not be satisfied in some other way. Thus, for example, societies can satisfy their functional needs for food by hunting or fishing activities, by agriculture, or by predatory exploitation of other societies.

C. *Functional Analysis in Economics*

Functional analysis of exactly this kind, though with a different vocabulary, is commonly employed by economists, especially when they seek to use economic tools to "explain" institutions and behaviors that lie outside the traditional domains of production and distribution. Moreover, it occurs within those domains. As an example, the fact is observed that individuals frequently insure against certain kinds of contingencies. Attitudes are then postulated (for example, risk aversion) for which buying insurance is a functional and reasonable action. If some people are observed to insure, and others not, then this difference in behavior can be explained by a difference between them in risk aversion.

To take a second example, George Stigler and Becker wish to explain the fact (if it is a fact—their empiricism is very casual) that as people hear more music, they want to hear still more. They invent a commodity, "music appreciation" (not to be confused with time spent in listening to music), and suggest that listening to music might produce not only immediate enjoyment but also an investment in *capacity* for appreciating music (i.e., in amount of enjoyment produced per listening hour). Once these assumptions are granted, various conclusions can be drawn about the demand for music appreciation. However, only weak conclusions follow about listening time unless additional strong postulates are introduced about the elasticity of demand for appreciation.

A rough "sociological" translation of the Stigler-Becker argument would be that listening to music is functional both in producing pleasure and in enhancing the pleasure of subsequent listening—a typical functional argument. It is quite unclear what is gained by dressing it in the garb of marginalism. We might be willing to grant that people would be inclined to invest more in musical appreciation early in life than later in life (because they would have a longer time in which to amortize the investment) without insisting that costs and returns were being equated at the margin, and without gaining any new insights into the situation from making the latter assumption.

A sense of fairness compels me to take a third example from my own work. In my 1951 paper, I defined the characteristics of an employment contract that distinguish it from an ordinary sales contract, and then showed why reasonable men might prefer the former to the latter as the basis for establishing an employment relation. My argument requires a theorem and fifteen numbered equations, and assumes that both employer and employee maximize their utilities. Actually, the underlying functional argument is very simple. An employee who didn't care very much which of several alternative tasks he performed would not require a large inducement to accept the authority of an employer—that is, to permit the employer to make the choice among them. The employer in turn would be willing to provide the necessary inducement in order to acquire the right to postpone his decisions about the employee's agenda, and in this way to postpone some of his decisions whose outcomes are contingent on future uncertain events.[3] The rigorous economic argument, involving the idea of maximizing behavior by employer and employee, is readily translatable into a simple qualitative argument that an employment contract may be a functional ("reasonable") way of dealing with certain kinds of uncertainty. The argument then explains why employment relations are so widely used in our society.

The translation of these examples of economic reasoning into the language of functional analysis could be paralleled by examples of translation scholarship which run in the opposite direction. Political scientists, for example, long ago observed that under certain circumstances institutions of representative democracy spawned a multiplicity of political parties, while under other circumstances, the votes were divided in equilibrium between two major parties. These contrasting equilibria could readily be shown by functional arguments to result from rational voting decisions under different rules of the electoral game, as was observed by Maurice Duverger, in his classic work on political parties, as well as by a number of political scientists who preceded him. In recent years, these same results have been rederived more rigorously by economists and game theorists, employing much stronger assumptions of utility maximization by the voters; it was hard to see that the maximization assumptions have produced any new predictions of behavior.[4]

D. *Summary*

Perhaps these examples suffice to show that there is no such gap as is commonly supposed between the view of man espoused by economics and the view found in the other social sciences. The view of man as rational is not peculiar to economics, but is endemic, and even ubiquitous, throughout the social sciences. Economics tends to emphasize a particular

[3]Recently, Oliver Williamson has pointed out that I would have to introduce slightly stronger assumptions to justify the employment contract as rational if one of the alternatives to it were what he calls a "contingent claims" contract, but the point of my example is not affected. To exclude the contingent claims contract as a viable alternative, we need merely take account of the large transaction costs it would entail under real world conditions.

[4]For an introduction to this literature, see William H. Riker and Peter C. Ordeshook, and Riker. Anthony Downs' book belongs to an intermediate genre. While it employs the language of economics, it limits itself to verbal, nonrigorous reasoning which certainly does not make any essential use of maximizing assumptions (as contrasted with rationality assumptions in the broader sense), and which largely translates into the economic vocabulary generalizations that were already part of the science and folklore of politics. In the next section, other examples of this kind of informal use of rationality principles are examined to analyze institutions and their behavior.

form of rationality—maximizing behavior—as its preferred engine of explanation, but the differences are often differences in vocabulary more than in substance. We shall see in a moment that in much economic discussion the notion of maximization is used in a loose sense that is very close to the common sense notions of rationality used elsewhere in the social sciences.

One conclusion we may draw is that economists might well exercise a certain amount of circumspection in their endeavors to export economic analysis to the other social sciences. They may discover that they are sometimes offering commodities that are already in generous supply, and which can therefore be disposed of only at a ruinously low price. On the other side of the trade, they may find that there is more of interest in the modes and results of inquiry of their fellow social scientists than they have generally been aware.

II. On Applying the Principle of Rationality

What is characteristic of the examples of functional analysis cited in the last section, whether they be drawn from economics or from the other social sciences, is that they are not focused on, or even much concerned with, how variables are equated at the margin, or how equilibrium is altered by marginal shifts in conditions (for example, shifts in a supply or demand schedule). Rather, they are focused on qualitative and structural questions, typically, on the choice among a small number of discrete institutional alternatives:

Not "how much flood insurance will a man buy?" but "what are the structural conditions that make buying insurance rational or attractive?"

Not "at what levels will wages be fixed?" but "when will work be performed under an employment contract rather than a sales contract?"

If we want a natural science analogy to this kind of theorizing, we can find it in geology. A geologist notices deep scratches in rock; he notices that certain hills of gravel are elongated along a north-south axis, and that the boulders embedded in them are not as smooth as those usually found on beaches. To explain these facts, he evokes a structural, and not at all quantitative, hypothesis: that these phenomena were produced by the process of glaciation.

In the first instance, he does not try to explain the depth of the glacial till, or estimate the weight of the ice that produced it, but simply to identify the basic causative process. He wants to explain the role of glaciation, of erosion, of vulcanization, of sedimentation in producing the land forms that he observes. His explanations, morever, are after-the-fact, and not predictive.

A. *Toward Qualitative Analysis*

As economics expands beyond its central core of price theory, and its central concern with quantities of commodities and money, we observe in it this same shift from a highly quantitative analysis, in which equilibration at the margin plays a central role, to a much more qualitative institutional analysis, in which discrete structural alternatives are compared.

In these analyses aimed at explaining institutional structure, maximizing assumptions play a much less significant role than they typically do in the analysis of market equilibria. The rational man who sometimes prefers an employment contract to a sales contract need not be a maximizer. Even a satisficer will exhibit such a preference whenever the difference in rewards between the two arrangements is sufficiently large and evident.

For this same reason, such analyses can often be carried out without elaborate mathematical apparatus or marginal calculation. In general, much cruder and simpler arguments will suffice to demonstrate an inequality between two quantities than are required to show the conditions under which these quantities are equated at the margin. Thus, in the recent works of Janos Kornai, Williamson, and John Montias on economic organization, we find only rather modest and simple applications of mathematical analysis. In the ways in which they involve principles of rationality, the arguments of these authors resemble James March and the author's *Organizations* more closely than Paul Samuelson's *Foundations*.[5]

What is the predominant form of reasoning that we encounter in these theoretical treatments of social institutions? Do they contain arguments based on maximizing assumptions? Basically, they rest upon a very simple form of causal analysis. Particular institutional structures or practices are seen to entail certain undesirable (for example, costly) or desirable (for example, value-producing) consequences. *Ceteris paribus*, situations and practices will be preferred when important favorable consequences are associated with them, and avoided when important unfavorable consequences are associated with them. A shift in the balance of consequences, or in awareness of them, may motivate a change in institutional arrangements.

Consider the following argument from Montias typical of this genre of analysis, which relates to the balance in organizations between centralization and decentralization.

> Decentralizing measures are generally aimed at remedying two shortcomings of an 'overcentralized' system structure. (1) Superordinates are overburdened with responsibility for the detailed direction and coordination of their subordinates' activities. (2) This 'petty tutelage' deprives subordinates of the opportunity to make decisions that might increase the payoff of the organization of which they are a part. . . . Why not loosen controls . . . ? . . . When controls are loosened, unless the incentive system is modified to bring about greater harmony between the goals of supervisors and supervisees, it may induce producers to shift their input and output mix in directions that . . . vitiate any benefits that might be reaped by the organization as a whole from the exercise of greater initiative at lower tiers. [p. 215]

Here two costs or disadvantages of centralization (burden on supervisors, restriction of choice-set of subordinates) are set off against a disadvantage of decentralization (goals of subordinates divergent from organization goals).

What can we learn about organization from an argument like this? Certainly little or nothing about the optimal balance point between centralization and decentralization in any particular organization. Rather, we might derive conclusions of these kinds:

1. That increasing awareness of one of the predicted consequences may cause an organization to move in the direction of centralization or decentralization. (For example, an egregious case of "suboptimizing" by a subordinate may cause additional centralized controls to be instituted.)

2. That new technical devices may tilt the balance between centralization and decentralization. For example, invention and adoption of divisionalized profit and loss statements led toward decentralization of many large American business firms in the 1950's; while reduction in information costs through computerization led at a later date to centralization of inventory control decisions in those same firms.

Of course Montias' conclusions could also be derived from a more formal optimization analysis—in fact he presents

[5]A notable exception to this generalization about the economic literature on organizations is the work of Jacob Marschak and Roy Radner on the theory of teams. These authors chose the strategy of detailed, precise analysis of the implications of maximizing assumptions for the transmission of information in organizations. The price they paid for this rigor was to find themselves limited to the highly simplified situations where solutions could be found for the mathematical problems they posed. We need not, of course, make an either-or choice between these two modes of inquiry. While it may be difficult or impossible to extend the formal analysis of the theory of teams to problems of real world complexity, the rigorous microtheory may illuminate the workings of important component mechanisms in the complex macrosituations. The methodological issues in choosing between analytic tractability and realism are quite parallel to those involved in the choice between laboratory and field methods for gathering empirical information about social phenomena. Neither one by itself marks the exclusive path toward truth.

such an analysis on the two pages following the passage quoted above. But it is not clear that anything new is added by the formalization, since the parameters imputed to the system are largely unmeasured and unmeasurable.

There is something to be said for an Ockham's Razor that, eschewing assumptions of optimization, provides an explanation of behavior that is consistent with *either* optimizing or satisficing procedures on the part of the human agents. Parsimony recommends that we prefer the postulate that men are reasonable to the postulate that they are supremely rational when either one of the two assumptions will do our work of inference as well as the other.[6]

B. *Procedural Rationality*

The kind of qualitative analysis I have been describing has another virtue. In complex situations there is likely to be a considerable gap between the real environment of a decision (the world as God or some other omniscient observer sees it) and the environment as the actors perceive it. The analysis can then address itself either to normative questions—the whole range of consequences that *should* enter into decisions in such situations—or descriptive questions, including the questions of which components of the situation are likely to be taken into account by the actors, and how the actors are likely to represent the situation as a whole.

In the precomputer era, for example, it was very difficult for managers in business organizations to pay attention to all the major variables affected by their decisions. Company treasurers frequently made decisions about working capital with little or no attention to their impact on inventory levels, while production and marketing executives made decisions about inventory without taking into account impacts on liquidity. The introduction of computers changed the ways in which executives were able to reach decisions; they could now view them in terms of a much wider set of interrelated consequences than before. The perception of the environment of a decision is a function of—among other things—the information sources and computational capabilities of the executives who make it.

Learning phenomena are also readily handled within this framework. A number of the changes introduced into planning and control procedures in eastern European countries during the 1960's were instituted when the governments in question learned by experience of some of the dysfunctional consequences of trying to control production by means of crude aggregates of physical quantities. An initial distrust of prices and market mechanisms was gradually and partially overcome after direct experience of the disadvantages of some of the alternative mechanisms. These learning experiences could be paralleled with experiences of American steel companies, for example, that experimented with tonnage incentives for mill department superintendents.

A general proposition that might be asserted about organizations is that the number of considerations that are potentially relevant to the effectiveness of an organization design is so large that only a few of the more salient of these lie within the circle of awareness at any given time, that the membership of this subset changes continually as new situations (produced by external or internal events) arise, and that "learning" in the form of reaction to perceived consequences is the dominant way in which rationality exhibits itself.

In a world where these kinds of adjustments are prominent, a theory of rational behavior must be quite as much concerned with the characteristics of the rational actors—the means they use to cope with uncertainty and cognitive complexity—as

[6]Ockham is usually invoked on behalf of the parsimony of optimizing assumptions, and against the additional *ad hoc* postulates that satisficing models are thought to require in order to guarantee uniqueness of solutions. But that argument only applies when we are trying to deduce unique equilibria, a task quite different from the one most institutional writers set for themselves. However, I have no urge to enlarge on this point. My intent here is not polemical, on behalf of satisficing postulates, but rather to show how large a plot of common ground is shared by optimizing and satisficing analysis. Again, compare Becker (1962).

with the characteristics of the objective environment in which they make their decisions. In such a world, we must give an account not only of *substantive rationality*—the extent to which appropriate courses of action are chosen—but also *procedural rationality*—the effectiveness, in light of human cognitive powers and limitations, of the *procedures* used to choose actions. As economics moves out toward situations of increasing cognitive complexity, it becomes increasingly concerned with the ability of actors to cope with the complexity, and hence with the procedural aspects of rationality. In the remainder of my talk, I would like to develop this concept of procedural rationality, and its implications for economic analysis.

III. Mind as the Scarce Resource

Until rather recently, such limited attention as was paid by economists to procedural, as distinct from substantive, rationality was mainly motivated by the problems of uncertainty and expectations. The simple notion of maximizing utility or profit could not be applied to situations where the optimum action depended on uncertain environmental events, or upon the actions of other rational agents (for example, imperfect competition).

The former difficulty was removed to some degree by replacing utility maximization with the maximization of subjective expected utility (*SEU*) as the criterion of rationality. In spite of its conceptual elegance, however, the *SEU* solution has some grave defects as either a normative or a descriptive formulation. In general, the optimal solution depends upon all of the moments of the frequency distributions of uncertain events. The exceptions are a small but important class of cases where the utility or profit function is quadratic and all constraints are in the form of equations rather than inequalities.[7] The empirical defect of the *SEU* formulation is that when it has been subjected to test in the laboratory or the real world, even in relatively simple situations, the behavior of human subjects has generally departed widely from it.

Some of the evidence has been surveyed by Ward Edwards, and more recently by Daniel Kahneman and Amos Tversky. They describe experimental situations in which estimates formed on the basis of initial information are not revised nearly as much by subsequent information as would be required by Bayes' Theorem. In other situations, subjects respond largely to the information received most recently, and take inadequate account of prior information.

Behavior that is radically inconsistent with the *SEU* framework occurs also in naturalistic settings. Howard Kunreuther et al. have recently carried out extensive studies of behavior and attitudes relating to the purchase of flood insurance by persons owning property in low-lying areas. They found that knowledge of the availability of insurance, or rates, and of objective risks was very imperfect, and that the actual decisions whether or not to insure were related much more to personal experience with floods than to any objective facts about the situation—or even to personal subjective beliefs about those facts. In the face of this evidence, it is hard to take *SEU* seriously as a theory of actual human behavior in the face of uncertainty.[8]

For situations where the rationality of an action depends upon what others (who are also striving to be rational) do again, no consensus has been reached as to what constitutes optimal behavior. This is one of the reasons I have elsewhere called imperfect competition "the permanent and ineradicable scandal of economic theory" (1976b, p. 140). The most imaginative and

[7]In this case the expected values of the environmental variables serve as certainty equivalents, so that *SEU* maximization requires only replacing the unknown true values by these expected values. See the author (1957).

[8]Kunreuther et al. point out that the theory cannot be "saved" by assuming utility to be radically nonlinear in money. In the flood insurance case, that interpretation of the data would work only if we were willing to assume that money has strongly *increasing* marginal utility, not a very plausible escape route for the theory.

ambitious attempt to resolve the difficulty was the von Neumann-Morgenstern theory of games, which is embarrassing in the wealth of alternative solutions it offers. While the theory of games reveals the potential richness of behavior when rational individuals are faced with conflict of interest, the capability of reacting to each other's actions (or expected actions), and possibilities for coalition, it has provided no unique and universally accepted criterion of rationality to generalize the *SEU* criterion and extend it to this broader range of situations.

The so-called "rational expectations" models, currently so popular (and due originally to Muth), pass over these problems rather than solving them. They ignore potential coalitions and attempted mutual outguessing behavior, and correspond to optimal solutions only when the losses are quadratic functions of the errors of estimate.[9] Hence they do not correspond to any classical criterion of rationality, and labeling them with that term, rather than the more neutral "consistent expectations," provides them with a rather unwarranted legitimation.

Finally, it should be remarked that the main motivation in economics for developing theories of uncertainty and mutual expectations has not been to replace substantive criteria of rationality with procedural criteria, but rather to find substantive criteria broad enough to extend the concept of rationality beyond the boundaries of static optimization under certainty. As with classical decision theory, the interest lies not in *how* decisions are made but in *what* decisions are made. (But see, contra, such analyses as Richard Cyert and Morris DeGroot.)

[9]That is, only under the conditions where the uncertainty equivalents of fn. 8 exist. Under other circumstances, a "rational" person would be well advised, if he knew that all others were following the "rational expectations" or "consistent expectations" rule, to recalculate his own optimal behavior on that assumption. Of course if others followed the same course, we would be back in the "outguessing" situation.

A. *Search and Teams*

Decision procedures have been treated more explicitly in the small bodies of work that have grown up in economics on the theory of search and on the theory of teams. Both these bodies of theory are specifically concerned with the limits on the ability of the economic actor to discover or compute what behavior is optimal for him. Both aspire not only to *take account* of human bounded rationality, but to *bring it within the compass* of the rational calculus. Let me explain what I mean by that distinction.

Problems of search arise when not all the alternatives of action are presented to the rational actor *ab initio*, but must be sought through some kind of costly activity. In general, an action will be chosen before the search has revealed all possible alternatives. One example of this kind of problem is the sale of a house, or some other asset, when offers are received sequentially and remain open for only a limited time (see the author, 1955). Another example which has been widely cited is the purchase of an automobile involving travel to dealers' lots (see Stigler, 1961). In both these examples, the question is not how the search is carried out, but how it is decided when to terminate it—that is, the amount of search. The question is answered by postulating a cost that increases with the total amount of search. In an optimizing model, the correct point of termination is found by equating the marginal cost of search with the (expected) marginal improvement in the set of alternatives. In a satisficing model, search terminates when the best offer exceeds an aspiration level that itself adjusts gradually to the value of the offers received so far. In both cases, search becomes just another factor of production, and investment in search is determined by the same marginal principle as investment in any other factor. However cavalierly these theories treat the actual search process, they do recognize explicitly that information gathering is not a free activity, and that unlimited amounts of it are not available.

The theory of teams, as developed by Marschak and Radner, goes a step farther in specifying the procedure of decision. That theory, as is well known, is concerned with the improvement that may be realized in a team's decisions by interchange of information among the team members. But here the theory does not limit itself to determining the aggregate amount of information that should be transmitted, but seeks to calculate what messages should be exchanged, under what conditions, and at what cost. The content of the communication as well as the total amount of information becomes relevant to the theory.

In its attitude toward rationality, the theory of teams is as "classical," however, as is search theory. The bounds on the rationality of the team members are "externalized" and represented as costs of communication, so that they can be folded into the economic calculation along with the costs and benefits of outcomes.

B. *Rational Search Procedures*

To find theories that compare the merits of alternative search procedures, we must look largely outside the domain of economics. A number of such theories have been developed in the past thirty years, mainly by management scientists and researchers in the field of artificial intelligence. An important example is the body of work that has been done on integer programming.

Integer programming problems resemble linear programming problems (to maximize some quantity, subject to constraints in the form of linear equations and inequalities), with the added condition that certain variables can only take whole numbers as their values. The integer constraint makes inapplicable most of the powerful computational methods available for solving linear programming problems, with the result that integer programming problems are far less tractable, computationally, than linear programming problems having comparable numbers of variables.

Solution methods for integer programming problems use various forms of highly selective search—for example branch-and-bound methods that establish successively narrower limits for the value of the optimum, and hence permit a corresponding narrowing of search to promising regions of the space. It becomes a matter of considerable practical and theoretical interest to evaluate the relative computational efficiency of competing search procedures, and also to estimate how the cost of search will grow with the size of the problem posed. Until recently, most evaluation of search algorithms has been empirical: they have been tested on sample problems. Recently, however, a body of theory—called theory of computational complexity—has grown up that begins to answer some of these questions in a more systematic way.

I cannot give here an account of the theory of computational complexity, or all of its implications for procedural rationality. A good introduction will be found in Alfred Aho et al. One important set of results that comes out of the theory does require at least brief mention. These results have to do with the way in which the amount of computation required to solve problems of a given class grows with the size of the problems—with the number of variables, say.[10]

In a domain where computational requirements grow rapidly with problem size, we will be able to solve only small problems; in domains where the requirements grow slowly, we will be able to solve much larger problems. The problems that the real world presents to us are generally enormous compared with the problems that we can solve on even our largest computers. Hence, our computational models are always rough approximations to the reality, and we must hope that the approximation will not be too inexact to be useful.

[10]Most of the theorems in computational complexity have to do with the "worst case," that is, with the maximum amount of computation required to solve *any* problem of the given class. Very few results are available for the expected cost, averaged over all problems of the class.

We will be particularly concerned that computational costs not increase rapidly with problem size.

It is customary in the theory of computational complexity to regard problems of a given size as "tractable" if computations do not grow faster than at some fixed power of problem size. Such classes of problems are known as "polynomial complex." Problems that grow exponentially in complexity with size are not polynomial complex, since the rate of growth of computation comes to exceed any fixed power of their size.

A large and important class of problems which includes the general integer programming problem, as well as standard scheduling problems, all have been shown to have the same level of complexity—if one is polynomial complex, then all are; if one is not polynomial complex, then none are. These problems have been labeled "*NP*-complete." It is conjectured, but not yet proven, that the class of *NP*-complete problems is not polynomially complex, but probably exponentially complex.

The significance of these findings and conjectures is in showing that computational difficulties, and the need to approximate, are not just a minor annoying feature of our world to be dealt with by manufacturing larger computers or breeding smarter people. Complexity is deep in the nature of things, and discovering tolerable approximation procedures and heuristics that permit huge spaces to be searched very selectively lies at the heart of intelligence, whether human or artificial. A theory of rationality that does not give an account of problem solving in the face of complexity is sadly incomplete. It is worse than incomplete; it can be seriously misleading by providing "solutions" to economic questions that are without operational significance.

One interesting and important direction of research in computational complexity lies in showing how the complexity of problems might be decreased by weakening the requirements for solution—by requiring solutions only to approximate the optimum, or by replacing an optimality criterion by a satisficing criterion. Results are still fragmentary, but it is already known that there are some cases where such modifications reduce exponential or *NP*-complete problem classes to polynomial-complete classes.

The theory of heuristic search, cultivated in artificial intelligence and information processing psychology, is concerned with devising or identifying search procedures that will permit systems of limited computational capacity to make complex decisions and solve difficult problems. (For a general survey of the theory, see Nils Nilsson.) When a task environment has patterned structure, so that solutions to a search problem are not scattered randomly throughout it, but are located in ways related to the structure, then an intelligent system capable of detecting the pattern can exploit it in order to search for solutions in a highly selective way.

One form, for example, of selective heuristic search, called best-first search, assigns to each node in the search space an estimate of the distance of that node from a solution. At each stage, the next increment of effort is expended in searching from the node, among those already reached, that has the smallest distance estimate (see, for example, the author and J.B. Kadane). As another example, when the task is to find a good or best solution, it may be possible to assign upper and lower bounds on the values of the solutions that can be obtained by searching a particular part of the space. If the upper bound on region *A* is lower than the lower bound on some other region, then region *A* does not need to be searched at all.

I will leave the topics of computational complexity and heuristic search with these sketchy remarks. What implications these developments in the theory of procedural rationality will have for economics defined as "the science which treats of the wealth-getting and wealth-using activities of man" remain to be seen. That they are an integral part of economics defined as "the science which treats of the allocation of scarce resources" is obvious. The scarce resource is computational capacity—the mind. The ability of man to solve complex problems, and the magnitude of the resources that have to be allocated to solving them, depend on the efficiency with which this resource, mind, is deployed.

C. *Attention as the Scarce Resource*

Finally, I would like to turn from the rather highly developed approaches to procedural rationality that I have been discussing back to the more qualitative kinds of institutional issues that were considered in the previous section of this paper. Many of the central issues of our time are questions of how we use limited information and limited computational capacity to deal with enormous problems whose shape we barely grasp.

For many purposes, a modern government can be regarded as a parallel computing device. While one part of its capability for rational problem solving is directed to fire protection, another is directed to paving highways, and another to collecting refuse. For other important purposes, a government, like a human being, is a serial processing system, capable of attending to only one thing at a time. When important new policies must be formulated, public and official attention must be focused on one or a few matters. Other concerns, no matter how pressing, must wait their turn on the agenda. When the agenda becomes crowded, public life begins to appear more and more as a succession of crises. When problems become interrelated, as energy and pollution problems have become, there is the constant danger that attention directed to a single facet of the web will spawn solutions that disregard vital consequences for the other facets. When oil is scarce, we return to coal, but forget that we must then deal with vastly increased quantities of sulfur oxides in our urban air. Or we outlaw nuclear power stations because of radiation hazards, but fail to make alternative provision to meet our energy needs. It is futile to talk of substantive rationality in public affairs without considering what procedural means are available to order issues on the public agenda in a rational way, and to insure attention to the indirect consequences of actions taken to reach specific goals or solve specific problems.

In a world where information is relatively scarce, and where problems for decision are few and simple, information is almost always a positive good. In a world where attention is a major scarce resource, information may be an expensive luxury, for it may turn our attention from what is important to what is unimportant. We cannot afford to attend to information simply because it is there. I am not aware that there has been any systematic development of a theory of information and communication that treats attention rather than information as the scarce resource.[11] Some of the practical consequences of attention scarcity have already been noticed in business and government, where early designs of so-called "management information systems" flooded executives with trivial data and, until they learned to ignore them, distracted their attention from more important matters. It is probably true of contemporary organizations that an automated information system that does not consume and digest vastly more information than it produces and distributes harms the performance of the organization in which it is incorporated.

The management of attention and tracing indirect consequences of action are two of the basic issues of procedural rationality that confront a modern society. There are others of comparable importance: what decision-making procedure is rational when the basic quantities for making marginal comparisons are simply not known? A few years ago, I served as chairman of a National Academy of Sciences (*NAS*) committee whose job it was to advise the Congress on the control of automobile emissions (see *NAS*, Coordinating Committee on Air Quality Studies). It is easy to formulate an *SEU* model to conceptualize the problem. There is a production function for automobiles that associates different costs with different levels of emissions. The laws govern-

[11] Some unsystematic remarks on the subject will be found in the author (1976a, chs. 13, 14).

ing the chemistry of the atmosphere determine the concentrations of polluting substances in the air as a function of the levels of emissions. Biomedical science tells us what effects on life and health can be expected from various concentrations of pollutants. All we need do is to attach a price tag to life and health, and we can calculate the optimum level of pollution control.

There is only one hitch—which will be apparent to all of you. None of the relevant parameters of the various "production functions" are known—except, within half an order of magnitude, the cost of reducing the emissions themselves. The physics and chemistry of the atmosphere presents a series of unsolved problems—particularly relating to the photochemical reactions affecting the oxides of nitrogen and ozone. Medical science is barely able to detect that there *are* health effects from pollutants, much less measure how large these effects are. The committee's deliberations led immediately to one conclusion—one that congressmen are accustomed to hearing from such committees: We need more research. But while the research is being done, what provisions should be incorporated in the Clean Air Act of 1977 (or the Acts of 1978 through 2000, for that matter)? For research won't give us clear answers then either. What constitutes procedural rationality in such circumstances?

"Reasonable men" reach "reasonable" conclusions in circumstances where they have no prospect of applying classical models of substantive rationality. We know only imperfectly how they do it. We know even less whether the procedures they use in place of the inapplicable models have any merit—although most of us would choose them in preference to drawing lots. The study of procedural rationality in circumstances where attention is scarce, where problems are immensely complex, and where crucial information is absent presents a host of challenging and fundamental research problems to anyone who is interested in the rational allocation of scarce resources.

IV. Conclusion

In histories of human civilization, the invention of writing and the invention of printing are always treated as key events. Perhaps in future histories the invention of electrical communication and the invention of the computer will receive comparable emphasis. What all of these developments have in common, and what makes them so important, is that they represent basic changes in man's equipment for making rational choices—in his computational capabilities. Problems that are impossible to handle with the head alone (multiplying large numbers together, for example) become trivial when they can be written down on paper. Interactions of energy and environment that almost defy conceptualization lend themselves to at least approximate modeling with modern computers.

The advances in man's capacity for procedural rationality are not limited to these obvious examples. The invention of algebra, of analytic geometry, of the calculus were such advances. So was the invention, if we may call it that, of the modern organization, which greatly increased man's capacity for coordinated parallel activity. Changes in the production function for information and decisions are central to any account of changes over the centuries of the human condition.

In the past, economics has largely ignored the processes that rational man uses in reaching his resource allocation decisions. This was possibly an acceptable strategy for explaining rational decision in static, relatively simple problem situations where it might be assumed that additional computational time or power could not change the outcome. The strategy does not work, however, when we are seeking to explain the decision maker's behavior in complex, dynamic circumstances that involve a great deal of uncertainty, and that make severe demands upon his attention.

As economics acquires aspirations to explain behavior under these typical conditions of modern organizational and public life, it will have to devote major energy to building a theory of procedural rationality to complement existing theories of substantive rationality. Some elements of such a theory can be borrowed from the neighboring disciplines of operations research, artificial intelligence, and cognitive psychology; but an enormous job remains to be done to extend this work and to apply it to specifically economic problems.

Jacob Marschak, throughout his long career, had a deep belief in and commitment to the interdependencies and complementarity of the several social sciences. I have shared that belief and commitment, without always agreeing with him in detail as to the precise route for exploiting it. The developments I have been describing strengthen greatly, it seems to me, the rational grounds for both belief and commitment. Whether we accept the more restricted definition of economics that I quoted from Ely's textbook, or the wider definition that is widely accepted today, we have every reason to try to communicate with the other social sciences, both to find out what we have to say that may be of interest to them, and to discover what they can teach us about the nature of procedural rationality.

REFERENCES

Alfred V. Aho et al., *The Design and Analysis of Computer Algorithms*, Reading 1974.

Chester I. Barnard, *The Functions of the Executive*, Cambridge 1938.

G. S. Becker, "Irrational Behavior and Economic Theory," *J. Polit. Econ.*, Feb. 1962, *70*, 1–13.

———, "A Theory of Social Interations," *J. Polit. Econ.*, Nov./Dec. 1974, *82*, 1063 93.

F. M. Cancian, "Functional Analysis," in *International Encyclopedia of the Social Sciences*, 1968, *6*, 29–42.

R. M. Cyert and M. H. Degrott, "Sequential Strategies in Dual Control," *Theory Decn.*, Apr. 1977, *8*, 173–92.

Anthony Downs, *An Economic Theory of Democracy*, New York 1957.

Maurice Duverger, *Political Parties*, rev. ed., New York 1959, (*Les Partis Politiques*, Paris 1951).

W. Edwards, "Conservation in Human Information Processing," in Benjamin Kleinmuntz, ed., *Formal Representation of Human Thought*, New York 1968.

Richard T. Ely, *Outlines of Economics*, rev. ed., New York 1930.

S. Freud, "Five Lectures on Psychoanalysis" (originally "The Origin and Development of Psychoanalysis" 1910) in *The Complete Psychological Works of Sigmund Freud*, Vol. 11, London 1957.

George Homans, *Social Behavior: Its Elementary Forms*, New York 1961.

D. Kahneman and A. Tversky, "On the Psychology of Prediction," *Psychol. Rev.*, July 1973, *80*, 237–51.

Janos Kornai, *Anti-Equilibrium*, Amsterdam 1971.

Howard Kunreuther et al., *Protecting Against High-Risk Hazards: Public Policy Lessons*, New York 1978.

James G. March and Herbert A. Simon, *Organizations*, New York 1958.

Jacob Marschak and Roy Radner, *Economic Theory of Teams*, New Haven 1972.

John M. Montias, *The Structure of Economic Systems*, New Haven 1976.

J. F. Muth, "Rational Expectations and the Theory of Price Movements," *Econometrica*, July 1961, *29*, 315–35.

Nils Nilsson, *Problem-Solving Methods in Artificial Intelligence*, New York 1971.

A. Rees, "Economics," in *International Encyclopedia of the Social Sciences*, 1968, *4*, 472.

William H. Riker, *The Theory of Political Coalitions*, New Haven 1962.

——— **and Peter C. Ordeshook**, *An Introduction to Positive Political Theory*, New Jersey 1973.

Paul Samuelson, *Foundations of Economic Analysis*, Cambridge 1947.

George Simmel, *Soziologie*, Berlin 1908.

Herbert A. Simon, "A Formal Theory of the Employment Relation," *Enconometrica*, July 1951, *19*, 293–305.

———, "A Behavioral Model of Rational

Choice," *Quart. J. Econ.*, Feb. 1955, *69*, 99–118.

———, "Dynamic Programming Under Uncertainty with a Quadratic Criterion Function," *Econometrica*, Jan. 1956, *24*, 74–81.

———, (1976a) *Administrative Behavior*, 3d ed., New York 1976.

———, (1976b) "From Substantive to Procedural Rationality," in Spiro J. Latsis, ed., *Method and Appraisal in Economics*, Cambridge 1976.

——— **and J. B. Kadane,** "Optimal Problem-Solving Search: All-or-None Solutions," *Artificial Intel.*, Fall 1975, *6*, 235–48.

G. J. Stigler, "The Economics of Information," *J. Polit. Econ.*, June 1961, *69*, 213–15.

——— **and G. S. Becker,** "De Gustibus non est Disputandum," *Amer. Econ. Rev.*, Mar. 1977, *67*, 76–90.

Oliver E. Williamson, *Markets and Hierarchies*, New York 1975.

National Academy of Sciences, (*NAS*) Coordinating Committee on Air Quality Studies, *Air Quality and Automobile Emission Control*, Vol. 1 summary rep., Washington 1974.

[6]

Rational Decision Making in Business Organizations

By HERBERT A. SIMON*

In the opening words of his *Principles*, Alfred Marshall proclaimed economics to be a psychological science:

> Political Economy or Economics is a study of mankind in the ordinary business of life; it examines that part of individual and social action which is most closely connected with the attainment and with the use of the material requisites of wellbeing.
>
> Thus it is on the one side a study of wealth; and on the other, and more important side, a part of the study of man. For man's character has been moulded by his every-day work, and the material resources which he thereby procures, more than by any other influence unless it be that of his religious ideals.

In its actual development, however, economic science has focused on just one aspect of man's character, his reason, and particularly on the application of that reason to problems of allocation in the face of scarcity. Still, modern definitions of the economic sciences, whether phrased in terms of allocating scarce resources or in terms of rational decision making, mark out a vast domain for conquest and settlement. In recent years there has been considerable exploration by economists even of parts of this domain that were thought traditionally to belong to the disciplines of political science, sociology, and psychology.

I. Decision Theory as Economic Science

The density of settlement of economists over the whole empire of economic science is very uneven, with a few areas of modest size holding the bulk of the population. The economic Heartland is the normative study of the international and national economies and their markets, with its triple main concerns of full employment of resources, the efficient allocation of resources, and equity in distribution of the economic product. Instead of the ambiguous and over-general term "economics," I will use "political economy" to designate this Heartland, and "economic sciences" to denote the whole empire, including its most remote colonies. Our principal concern in this paper will be with the important colonial territory known as decision theory. I will have something to say about its normative and descriptive aspects, and particularly about its applications to the theory of the firm. It is through the latter topic that the discussion will be linked back to the Heartland of political economy.

Underpinning the corpus of policy-oriented normative economics, there is, of course, an impressive body of descriptive or "positive" theory which rivals in its mathematical beauty and elegance some of the finest theories in the physical sciences. As examples I need only remind you of Walrasian general equilibrium theories and their modern descendants in the works of Henry Schultz, Samuelson, Hicks, and others; or the subtle and impressive body of theory created by Arrow, Hurwicz, Debreu, Malinvaud, and their colleagues showing the equivalence, under certain conditions, of competitive equilibrium with Pareto optimality.

The relevance of some of the more refined parts of this work to the real world can be, and has been, questioned. Perhaps some of these intellectual mountains have been

*Carnegie-Mellon University. This article is the lecture Herbert Simon delivered in Stockholm, Sweden, December 8, 1978, when he received the Nobel Prize in Economic Science.

The author is indebted to Albert Ando, Otto A. Davis, and Benjamin M. Friedman for valuable comments on an earlier draft of this paper.

climbed simply because they were there—because of the sheer challenge and joy of scaling them. That is as it should be in any human scientific or artistic effort. But regardless of the motives of the climbers, regardless of real world veridicality, there is no question but that positive political economy has been strongly shaped by the demands of economic policy for advice on basic public issues.

This too is as it should be. It is a vulgar fallacy to suppose that scientific inquiry cannot be fundamental if it threatens to become useful, or if it arises in response to problems posed by the everyday world. The real world, in fact, is perhaps the most fertile of all sources of good research questions calling for basic scientific inquiry.

A. *Decision Theory in the Service of Political Economy*

There is, however, a converse fallacy that deserves equal condemnation: the fallacy of supposing that fundamental inquiry is worth pursuing only if its relevance to questions of policy is immediate and obvious. In the contemporary world, this fallacy is perhaps not widely accepted, at least as far as the natural sciences are concerned. We have now lived through three centuries or more of vigorous and highly successful inquiry into the laws of nature. Much of that inquiry has been driven by the simple urge to understand, to find the beauty of order hidden in complexity. Time and again, we have found the "idle" truths arrived at through the process of inquiry to be of the greatest moment for practical human affairs. I need not take time here to argue the point. Scientists know it, engineers and physicians know it, congressmen and members of parliaments know it, the man on the street knows it.

But I am not sure that this truth is as widely known in economics as it ought to be. I cannot otherwise explain the rather weak and backward development of the descriptive theory of decision making including the theory of the firm, the sparse and scattered settlement of its terrain, and the fact that many, if not most, of its investigators are drawn from outside economics—from sociology, from psychology, and from political science. Respected and distinguished figures in economics—Edward Mason, Fritz Machlup, and Milton Friedman, for example—have placed it outside the Pale (more accurately, have placed economics outside *its* Pale), and have offered it full autonomy provided that it did not claim close kinship with genuine economic inquiry.

Thus, Mason, commenting on Papandreou's 1952 survey of research on the behavioral theory of the firm, mused aloud:

> ... has the contribution of this literature to economic analysis really been a large one? ... The writer of this critique must confess a lack of confidence in the marked superiority, *for purposes of economic analysis*, of this newer concept of the firm, over the older conception of the entrepreneur. [pp. 221–22]

And, in a similar vein, Friedman sums up his celebrated polemic against realism in theory:

> Complete "realism" is clearly unattainable, and the question whether a theory is realistic "enough" can be settled only by seeing whether it yields predictions that are good enough *for the purpose in hand* or that are better than predictions from alternative theories. [p. 41, emphasis added]

The "purpose in hand" that is implicit in both of these quotations is providing decision-theoretic foundations for positive, and then for normative, political economy. In the views of Mason and Friedman, fundamental inquiry into rational human behavior in the context of business organizations is simply not (by definition) economics—that is to say, political economy—unless it contributes in a major way to that purpose. This is sometimes even interpreted to mean that economic theories of decision making are not falsified in any interesting or relevant sense when their empirical predictions of *microphenomena* are found to be grossly incompatible with the observed data. Such theories, we are told, are still realistic "enough" provided that they do not contradict aggregate observations of concern to political economy. Thus economists who are zealous in insisting that economic actors maximize turn around and become satisficers when the evaluation of their own theories is concerned. They believe that businessmen maximize, but they know that economic theorists satisfice.

The application of the principle of satisficing to theories is sometimes defended as an application of Occam's Razor: accept the simplest theory that works.[1] But Occam's Razor has a double edge. Succinctness of statement is not the only measure of a theory's simplicity. Occam understood his rule as recommending theories that make no more assumptions than necessary to account for the phenomena (*Essentia non sunt multiplicanda praeter necessitatem*). A theory of profit or utility maximization can be stated more briefly than a satisficing theory of the sort I shall discuss later. But the former makes much stronger assumptions than the latter about the human cognitive system. Hence, in the case before us, the two edges of the razor cut in opposite directions.

In whichever way we interpret Occam's principle, parsimony can be only a secondary consideration in choosing between theories, unless those theories make identical predictions. Hence, we must come back to a consideration of the phenomena that positive decision theory is supposed to handle. These may include both phenomena at the microscopic level of the decision-making agents, or aggregative phenomena of concern to political economy.

[1]The phrase "that works" refutes, out of hand, Friedman's celebrated paean of praise for lack of realism in assumptions. Consider his example of falling bodies (pp. 16–19). His valid point is that it is advantageous to use the simple law, ignoring air resistance, when it gives a "good enough" approximation. But of course the conditions under which it gives a good approximation are not at all the conditions under which it is unrealistic or a "wildly inaccurate descriptive representation of reality." We can use it to predict the path of a body falling in a vacuum, but not the path of one falling through the Earth's atmosphere. I cannot in this brief space mention, much less discuss, all of the numerous logical fallacies that can be found in Friedman's 40-page essay. For additional criticism, see Simon (1963) and Samuelson (1963).

B. *Decision Theory Pursued for its Intrinsic Interest*

Of course the definition of the word "economics" is not important. Like Humpty Dumpty, we can make words mean anything we want them to mean. But the professional training and range of concern of economists does have importance. Acceptance of the narrow view that economics is concerned only with the aggregative phenomena of political economy defines away a whole rich domain of rational human behavior as inappropriate for economic research.

I do not wish to appear to be admitting that the behavioral theory of the firm *has been* irrelevant to the construction of political economy. I will have more to say about its relevance in a moment. My present argument is counterfactual in form: *even if* there were no present evidence of such relevance, human behavior in business firms constitutes a highly interesting body of empirical phenomena that calls out for explanation as do all bodies of phenomena. And if we may extrapolate from the history of the other sciences, there is every reason to expect that as explanations emerge, relevance for important areas of practical application will not be long delayed.

It has sometimes been implied (Friedman, p. 14) that the correctness of the assumptions of rational behavior underlying the classical theory of the firm is not merely irrelevant, but is not even empirically testable in any direct way, the only valid test being whether these assumptions lead to tolerably correct predictions at the macroscopic level. That would be true, of course, if we had no microscopes, so that the micro-level behavior was not directly observable. But we do have microscopes. There are many techniques for observing decision-making behavior, even at second-by-second intervals if that is wanted. In testing our economic theories, we do not have to depend on the rough aggregate time-series that are the main grist for the econometric mill, or even upon company financial statements.

The classical theories of economic decision making and of the business firm make very specific testable predictions about the concrete behavior of decision-making agents. Behavioral theories make quite different predictions. Since these predictions can be tested directly by observation, either theory (or both) may be falsified as readily when such predictions fail as when predictions about aggregate phenomena are in error.

C. *Aggregative Tests of Decision Theory: Marginalism*

If some economists have erroneously supposed that micro-economic theory can only be tested by its predictions of aggregate phenomena, we should avoid the converse error of supposing that aggregate phenomena are irrelevant to testing decision theory. In particular, are there important, *empirically verified*, aggregate predictions that follow from the theory of perfect rationality but that do not follow from behavioral theories of rationality?

The classical theory of omniscient rationality is strikingly simple and beautiful. Moreover, it allows us to predict (correctly or not) human behavior without stirring out of our armchairs to observe what such behavior is like. All the predictive power comes from characterizing the shape of the environment in which the behavior takes place. The environment, combined with the assumptions of perfect rationality, fully determines the behavior. Behavioral theories of rational choice—theories of bounded rationality—do not have this kind of simplicity. But, by way of compensation, their assumptions about human capabilities are far weaker than those of the classical theory. Thus, they make modest and realistic demands on the knowledge and computational abilities of the human agents, but they also fail to predict that those agents will equate costs and returns at the margin.

D. *Have the Marginalist Predictions Been Tested?*

A number of empirical phenomena have been cited as providing more or less conclusive support for the classical theory of the firm as against its behavioral competitors (see Dale Jorgensen and Calvin Siebert). But there are no direct observations that individuals or firms do actually equate marginal costs and revenues. The empirically verified consequences of the classical theory are almost always weaker than this. Let us look at four of the most important of them: the fact that demand curves generally have negative slopes; the fact that fitted Cobb-Douglas functions are approximately homogeneous of the first degree; the fact of decreasing returns to scale; and the fact that executive salaries vary with the logarithm of company size. Are these indeed facts? And does the evidence support a maximizing theory against a satisficing theory?

Negatively Sloping Demand Curves. Evidence that consumers actually distribute their purchases in such a way as to maximize their utilities, and hence to equate marginal utilities, is nonexistent. What the empirical data do confirm is that demand curves generally have negative slopes. (Even this "obvious" fact is tricky to verify, as Henry Schultz showed long years ago.) But negatively sloping demand curves could result from a wide range of behaviors satisfying the assumptions of bounded rationality rather than those of utility maximization. Gary Becker, who can scarcely be regarded as a hostile witness for the classical theory, states the case very well:

> Economists have long been aware that some changes in the feasible or opportunity sets of households would lead to the same response *regardless of the decision rule used*. For example, a decrease in real income necessarily decreases the amount spent on at least one commodity... It has seldom been realized, however, that the change in opportunities resulting from a change in relative prices also tends to produce a systematic response, regardless of the decision rule. In particular, the fundamental theorem of traditional theory—that demand curves are negatively inclined—largely results from the change in opportunities alone and is largely independent of the decision rule. [p. 4]

Later, Becker is even more explicit, saying, "Not only utility maximization but also many other decision rules, incorporating a wide variety of irrational behavior, lead to negatively inclined demand curves because of the effect of a change in prices on opportunities" (p. 5).[2]

First-Degree Homogeneity of Production Functions. Another example of an observed phenomenon for which the classical assumptions provide sufficient, but not necessary, conditions is the equality between labor's share of product and the exponent of the labor factor in fitted Cobb-Douglas production functions (see Simon and Ferdinand Levy). Fitted Cobb-Douglas functions are homogeneous, generally of degree close to unity and with a labor exponent of about the right magnitude. These findings, however, cannot be taken as strong evidence for the classical theory, for the identical results can readily be produced by mistakenly fitting a Cobb-Douglas function to data that were in fact generated by a linear accounting identity (value of goods equals labor cost plus capital cost), (see E. H. Phelps-Brown). The same comment applies to the SMAC production function (see Richard Cyert and Simon). Hence, the empirical findings do not allow us to draw any particular conclusions about the relative plausibility of classical and behavioral theories, both of which are equally compatible with the data.

The Long-Run Cost Curve. Somewhat different is the case of the firm's long-run cost curve, which classical theory requires to be U shaped if competitive equilibrium is to be stable. Theories of bounded rationality do not predict this—fortunately, for the observed data make it exceedingly doubtful that the cost curves are in fact generally U shaped. The evidence for many industries shows costs at the high-scale ends of the curves to be essentially constant or even declining (see Alan Walters). This finding is compatible with stochastic models of business firm growth and size (see Y. Ijiri and Simon), but not with the static equilibrium model of classical theory.

Executive Salaries. Average salaries of top corporate executives grow with the logarithm of corporate size (see David Roberts). This finding has been derived from the assumptions of the classical theory of profit maximization only with the help of very particular *ad hoc* assumptions about the distribution of managerial ability (see Robert Lucas, 1978). The observed relation is implied by a simple behavioral theory that assumes only that there is a single, culturally determined, parameter which fixes the average ratio of the salaries of managers to the salaries of their immediate subordinates (see Simon, 1957). In the case of the executive salary data, the behavioral model that explains the observations is substantially more parsimonious (in terms of assumptions about exogenous variables) than the classical model that explains the same observations.

Summary: Phenomena that Fail to Discriminate. It would take a much more extensive review than is provided here to establish the point conclusively, but I believe it is the case that specific phenomena requiring a theory of utility or profit maximization for their explanation rather than a theory of bounded rationality simply have not been observed in aggregate data. In fact, as my last two examples indicate, it is the classical rather than the behavioral form of the theory that faces real difficulties in handling some of the empirical observations.

Failures of Classical Theory. It may well be that classical theory can be patched up sufficiently to handle a wide range of situations where uncertainty and outguessing phenomena do not play a central role—that is, to handle the behavior of economies that are relatively stable and not too distant from a competitive equilibrium. However, a strong positive case for replacing the classical theory by a model of bounded rationality begins to emerge when we examine situations involving decision making under uncertainty and imperfect competition. These situations the classical theory was never designed to handle, and has never handled satisfactorily. Statistical decision theory employing the idea of subjective expected utility, on the one hand, and game theory, on the other, have contributed enormous conceptual clarification to these kinds of situations without providing

[2]In a footnote, Becker indicates that he denotes as irrational "[A]ny deviation from utility maximization." Thus, what I have called "bounded rationality" is "irrationality" in Becker's terminology.

satisfactory descriptions of actual human behavior, or even, for most cases, normative theories that are actually usable in the face of the limited computational powers of men and computers.

I shall have more to say later about the positive case for a descriptive theory of bounded rationality, but I would like to turn first to another territory within economic science that has gained rapidly in population since World War II, the domain of normative decision theory.

E. *Normative Decision Theory*

Decision theory can be pursued not only for the purposes of building foundations for political economy, or of understanding and explaining phenomena that are in themselves intrinsically interesting, but also for the purpose of offering direct advice to business and governmental decision makers. For reasons not clear to me, this territory was very sparsely settled prior to World War II. Such inhabitants as it had were mainly industrial engineers, students of public administration, and specialists in business functions, none of whom especially identified themselves with the economic sciences. Prominent pioneers included the mathematician, Charles Babbage, inventor of the digital computer, the engineer, Frederick Taylor, and the administrator, Henri Fayol.

During World War II, this territory, almost abandoned, was rediscovered by scientists, mathematicians, and statisticians concerned with military management and logistics, and was renamed "operations research" or "operations analysis." So remote were the operations researchers from the social science community that economists wishing to enter the territory had to establish their own colony, which they called "management science." The two professional organizations thus engendered still retain their separate identities, though they are now amicably federated in a number of common endeavors.

Optimization techniques were transported into management science from economics, and new optimization techniques, notably linear programming, were invented and developed, the names of Dantzig, Kantorovich, and Koopmans being prominent in the early development of that tool.

Now the salient characteristic of the decision tools employed in management science is that they have to be capable of actually making or recommending decisions, taking as their inputs the kinds of empirical data that are available in the real world, and performing only such computations as can reasonably be performed by existing desk calculators or, a little later, electronic computers. For these domains, idealized models of optimizing entrepreneurs, equipped with complete certainty about the world—or, at worst, having full probability distributions for uncertain events—are of little use. Models have to be fashioned with an eye to practical computability, no matter how severe the approximations and simplifications that are thereby imposed on them.

Model construction under these stringent conditions has taken two directions. The first is to retain optimization, but to simplify sufficiently so that the optimum (in the simplified world!) is computable. The second is to construct satisficing models that provide good enough decisions with reasonable costs of computation. By giving up optimization, a richer set of properties of the real world can be retained in the models. Stated otherwise, decision makers can satisfice either by finding optimum solutions for a simplified world, or by finding satisfactory solutions for a more realistic world. Neither approach, in general, dominates the other, and both have continued to co-exist in the world of management science.

Thus, the body of theory that has developed in management science shares with the body of theory in descriptive decision theory a central concern with the *ways* in which decisions are made, and not just with the decision outcomes. As I have suggested elsewhere (1978b), these are theories of *how* to decide rather than theories of *what* to decide.

Let me cite one example, from work in which I participated, of how model building in normative economics is shaped by computational considerations (see Charles Holt, Franco Modigliani, John Muth, and Simon).

In face of uncertain and fluctuating production demands, a company can smooth and stabilize its production and employment levels at the cost of holding buffer inventories. What kind of decision rule will secure a reasonable balance of costs? Formally, we are faced with a dynamic programming problem, and these generally pose formidable and often intolerable computational burdens for their solution.

One way out of this difficulty is to seek a special case of the problem that will be computationally tractable. If we assume the cost functions facing the company all to be quadratic in form, the optimal decision rule will then be a linear function of the decision variables, which can readily be computed in terms of the cost parameters. Equally important, under uncertainty about future sales, only the expected values, and not the higher moments, of the probability distributions enter into the decision rule (Simon, 1956b). Hence the assumption of quadratic costs reduces the original problem to one that is readily solved. Of course the solution, though it provides optimal decisions for the simplified world of our assumptions, provides, at best, satisfactory solutions for the real-world decision problem that the quadratic function approximates. In-principle, unattainable optimization is sacrificed for in-practice, attainable satisfaction.

If human decision makers are as rational as their limited computational capabilities and their incomplete information permit them to be, then there will be a close relation between normative and descriptive decision theory. Both areas of inquiry are concerned primarily with procedural rather than substantive rationality (Simon, 1978a). As new mathematical tools for computing optimal and satisfactory decisions are discovered, and as computers become more and more powerful, the recommendations of normative decision theory will change. But as the new recommendations are diffused, the actual, observed, practice of decision making in business firms will change also. And these changes may have macro-economic consequences. For example, there is some agreement that average inventory holdings of American firms have been reduced significantly by the introduction of formal procedures for calculating reorder points and quantities.

II. Characterizing Bounded Rationality

The principal forerunner of a behavioral theory of the firm is the tradition usually called Institutionalism. It is not clear that all of the writings, European and American, usually lumped under this rubric have much in common, or that their authors would agree with each other's views. At best, they share a conviction that economic theory must be reformulated to take account of the social and legal structures amidst which market transactions are carried out. Today, we even find a vigorous development within economics that seeks to achieve institutionalist goals within the context of neoclassical price theory. I will have more to say about that a little later.

The name of John R. Commons is prominent—perhaps the most prominent—among American Institutionalists. Commons' difficult writings (for example, *Institutional Economics*) borrow their language heavily from the law, and seek to use the *transaction* as their basic unit of behavior. I will not undertake to review Commons' ideas here, but simply remark that they provided me with many insights in my initial studies of organizational decision making (see my *Administrative Behavior,* p. 136).

Commons also had a substantial influence on the thinking of Chester I. Barnard, an intellectually curious business executive who distilled from his experience as president of the New Jersey Bell Telephone Company, and as executive of other business, governmental, and nonprofit organizations, a profound book on decision making titled *The Functions of the Executive.* Barnard proposed original theories, which have stood up well under empirical scrutiny, of the nature of the authority mechanism in organizations, and of the motivational bases for employee acceptance of organizational goals (the so-called "inducements-contributions" theory); and he provided a realistic description of organizational decision making, which he characterized as "opportunistic." The numerous references to Barnard's work in *Administrative Behavior* attest, though inadequately, to the impact he had on my own thinking about organizations.

A. *In Search of a Descriptive Theory*

In 1934–35, in the course of a field study of the administration of public recreational facilities in Milwaukee, which were managed jointly by the school board and the city public works department, I encountered a puzzling phenomenon. Although the heads of the two agencies appeared to agree as to the objectives of the recreation program, and did not appear to be competing for empire, there was continual disagreement and tension between them with respect to the allocation of funds between physical maintenance, on the one hand, and play supervision on the other. Why did they not, as my economics books suggested, simply balance off the marginal return of the one activity against that of the other?

Further exploration made it apparent that they didn't equate expenditures at the margin because, intellectually, they couldn't. There was no measurable production function from which quantitative inferences about marginal productivities could be drawn; and such qualitative notions of a production function as the two managers possessed were mutually incompatible. To the public works administrator, a playground was a physical facility, serving as a green oasis in the crowded gray city. To the recreation administrator, a playground was a social facility, where children could play together with adult help and guidance.

How can human beings make rational decisions in circumstances like these? How are they to apply the marginal calculus? Or, if it does not apply, what do they substitute for it?

The phenomenon observed in Milwaukee is ubiquitous in human decision making. In organization theory it is usually referred to as *subgoal identification*. When the goals of an organization cannot be connected operationally with actions (when the production function can't be formulated in concrete terms), then decisions will be judged against subordinate goals that can be so connected. There is no unique determination of these subordinate goals. Their formulation will depend on the knowledge, experience, and organizational environment of the decision maker. In the face of this ambiguity, the formulation can also be influenced in subtle, and not so subtle, ways by his self-interest and power drives.

The phenomenon arises as frequently in individual as in social decision making and problem solving. Today, under the rubric of *problem representation*, it is a central research interest of cognitive psychology. Given a particular environment of stimuli, and a particular background of previous knowledge, how will a person organize this complex mass of information into a problem formulation that will facilitate his solution efforts? How did Newton's experience of the apple, if he had one, get represented as an instance of attraction of apple by Earth?

Phenomena like these provided the central theme for *Administrative Behavior*. That study represented "an attempt to construct tools useful in my own research in the field of public administration." The product was actually not so much a theory as prolegomena to a theory, stemming from the conviction "that decision making is the heart of administration, and that the vocabulary of administrative theory must be derived from the logic and psychology of human choice." It was, if you please, an exercise in problem representation.

On examination, the phenomenon of subgoal identification proved to be the visible tip of a very large iceberg. The shape of the iceberg is best appreciated by contrasting it with classical models of rational choice. The classical model calls for knowledge of all the alternatives that are open to choice. It calls for complete knowledge of, or ability to compute, the consequences that will follow on each of the alternatives. It calls for certainty in the decision maker's present and future evaluation of these consequences. It calls for the ability to compare consequences, no matter how diverse and heterogeneous, in terms of some consistent measure of utility. The task, then, was to replace the classical model with one that would describe how decisions could be (and probably actually were) made when the alternatives of search had to be sought out, the consequences of choosing particular alternatives were only very imperfectly known both because of limited computational power and because of uncertainty in the external world, and the decision maker did not possess a general and consistent utility function for comparing heterogeneous alternatives.

Several procedures of rather general applicability and wide use have been discovered that transform intractable decision problems into tractable ones. One procedure already mentioned is to look for satisfactory choices instead of optimal ones. Another is to replace abstract, global goals with tangible subgoals, whose achievement can be observed and measured. A third is to divide up the decision-making task among many specialists, coordinating their work by means of a structure of communications and authority relations. All of these, and others, fit the general rubric of "bounded rationality," and it is now clear that the elaborate organizations that human beings have constructed in the modern world to carry out the work of production and government can only be understood as machinery for coping with the limits of man's abilities to comprehend and compute in the face of complexity and uncertainty.

This rather vague and general initial formulation of the idea of bounded rationality called for elaboration in two directions: greater formalization of the theory, and empirical verification of its main claims. During the decade that followed the publication of *Administrative Behavior*, substantial progress was made in both directions, some of it through the efforts of my colleagues and myself, much of it by other research groups that shared the same Zeitgeist.

B. *Empirical Studies*

The principal source of empirical data about organizational decision making has been straightforward "anthropological" field study, eliciting descriptions of decision-making procedures and observing the course of specific decision-making episodes. Examples are my study, with Guetzkow, Kozmetsky, and Tyndall (1954), of the ways in which accounting data were used in decision making in large corporations; and a series of studies, with Richard Cyert, James March, and others, of specific nonprogrammed policy decisions in a number of different companies (see Cyert, Simon, and Donald Trow). The latter line of work was greatly developed and expanded by Cyert and March and its theoretical implications for economics explored in their important work, *A Behavioral Theory of the Firm*.

At about the same time, the fortuitous availability of some data on businessmen's perceptions of a problem situation described in a business policy casebook enabled DeWitt Dearborn and me to demonstrate empirically the cognitive basis for identification with subgoals, the phenomenon that had so impressed me in the Milwaukee recreation study. The businessmen's perceptions of the principal problems facing the company described in the case were mostly determined by their own business experiences—sales and accounting executives identified a sales problem, manufacturing executives, a problem of internal organization.

Of course there is vastly more to be learned and tested about organizational decision making than can be dealt with in a handful of studies. Although many subsequent studies have been carried out in Europe and the United States, this domain is still grossly undercultivated (for references, see March, 1965; E. Johnsen, 1968; G. Eliasson, 1976). Among the reasons for the relative neglect of such studies, as contrasted, say, with laboratory experiments in social psychology, is that they are extremely costly and time consuming, with a high grist-to-grain ratio, the methodology for carrying them out is primitive, and satisfactory access to decision-making behavior is hard to secure. This part of economics has not yet acquired the habits of patience and persistence in the pursuit of facts that is exemplified in other domains by the work, say, of Simon Kuznets or of the architects of the MIT-SSRC-Penn econometric models.

C. *Theoretical Inquiries*

On the theoretical side, three questions seemed especially to call for clarification: what are the circumstances under which an employment relation will be preferred to some other form of contract as the arrangement for securing the performance of work; what is the relation between the classical theory of the firm and theories of organizational equilibrium first proposed by Chester Barnard; and what are the main characteristics of human rational choice in situations where complexity precludes omniscience?

The Employment Relation. A fundamental characteristic of modern industrial society is that most work is performed, not by individuals who produce products for sale, nor by individual contractors, but by persons who have accepted employment in a business firm and the authority relation with the employer that employment entails. Acceptance of authority means willingness to permit one's behavior to be determined by the employer, at least within some zone of indifference or acceptance. What is the advantage of this arrangement over a contract for specified goods or services? Why is so much of the world's work performed in large, hierarchic organizations?

Analysis showed (Simon, 1951) that a combination of two factors could account for preference for the employment contract over other forms of contracts: uncertainty as to which future behaviors would be advantageous to the employer, and a greater indifference of the employee as compared with the employer (within the former's area of acceptance) as to which of these behaviors he carried out. When the secretary is hired, the employer does not know what letters he will want her to type, and the secretary has no great preference for typing one letter rather than another. The employment contract permits the choice to be postponed until the uncertainty is resolved, with little cost to the employee and great advantage to the employer. The explanation is closely analogous to one Jacob Marschak had proposed for liquidity preference. Under conditions of uncertainty it is advantageous to hold resources in liquid, flexible form.

Organizational Equilibrium. Barnard had described the survival of organizations in terms of the motivations that make their participants (employees, investors, customers, suppliers) willing to remain in the system. In *Administrative Behavior*, I had developed this notion further into a motivational theory of the balance between the inducements that were provided by organizations to their participants, and the contributions those participants made to the organizations' resources.

A formalization of this theory (Simon, 1952; 1953) showed its close affinity to the classical theory of the firm, but with an important and instructive difference. In comparing the two theories, each inducement-contribution relation became a supply schedule for the firm. The survival conditions became the conditions for positive profit. But while the classical theory of the firm assumes that all profits accrue to a particular set of participants, the owners, the organization theory treats the surplus more symmetrically, and does not predict how it will be distributed. Hence the latter theory leaves room, under conditions of monopoly and imperfect competition, for bargaining among the participants (for example, between labor and owners) for the surplus. The survival conditions—positive profits rather than maximum profits—also permit a departure from the assumptions of perfect rationality.

Mechanisms of Bounded Rationality. In *Administrative Behavior*, bounded rationality is largely characterized as a residual category—rationality is bounded when it falls short of omniscience. And the failures of omniscience are largely failures of knowing all the alternatives, uncertainty about relevant exogenous events, and inability to calculate consequences. There was needed a more positive and formal characterization of the mechanisms of choice under conditions of bounded rationality. Two papers (Simon, 1955; 1956a) undertook first steps in that direction.

Two concepts are central to the characterization: *search* and *satisficing*. If the alternatives for choice are not given initially to the decision maker, then he must search for them. Hence, a theory of bounded rationality must incorporate a theory of search. This idea was later developed independently by George Stigler in a very influential paper that took as its example of a decision situation the purchase of a second-hand automobile. Stigler poured the search theory back into the old bottle of classical utility maximization, the cost of search being equated with its marginal return. In my 1956 paper, I had demonstrated the same formal equivalence, using as my example a dynamic programming formulation of the process of selling a house.

But utility maximization, as I showed, was not essential to the search scheme—fortunately, for it would have required the decision maker to be able to estimate the marginal costs and returns of search in a decision situation that was already too complex for the exercise of global rationality. As an alternative, one could postulate that the decision maker had formed some *aspiration* as to how good an alternative he should find. As soon as he discovered an alternative for choice meeting his level of aspiration, he would terminate the search and choose that alternative. I called this mode of selection *satisficing*. It had its roots in the empirically based psychological theories, due to Lewin and others, of aspiration levels. As psychological inquiry had shown, aspiration levels are not static, but tend to rise and fall in consonance with changing experiences. In a benign environment that provides many good alternatives, aspirations rise; in a harsher enviornment, they fall.

In long-run equilibrium it might even be the case that choice with dynamically adapting aspiration levels would be equivalent to optimal choice, taking the costs of search into account. But the important thing about the search and satisficing theory is that it showed how choice could actually be made with reasonable amounts of calculation, and using very incomplete information, without the need of performing the impossible—of carrying out this optimizing procedure.

D. *Summary*

Thus, by the middle 1950's, a theory of bounded rationality had been proposed as an alternative to classical omniscient rationality, a significant number of empirical studies had been carried out that showed actual business decision making to conform reasonably well with the assumptions of bounded rationality but not with the assumptions of perfect rationality, and key components of the theory—the nature of the authority and employment relations, organizational equilibrium, and the mechanisms of search and satisficing—had been elucidated formally. In the remaining parts of this paper, I should like to trace subsequent developments of decision-making theory, including developments competitive with the theory of bounded rationality, and then to comment on the implications (and potential implications) of the new descriptive theory of decision for political economy.

III. The Neoclassical Revival

Peering forward from the late 1950's, it would not have been unreasonable to predict that theories of bounded rationality would soon find a large place in the mainstream of economic thought. Substantial progress had been made in providing the theories with some formal structure, and an increasing body of empirical evidence showed them to provide a far more veridical picture of decision making in business organizations than did the classical concepts of perfect rationality.

History has not followed any such simple course, even though many aspects of the Zeitgeist were favorable to movement in this direction. During and after World War II, a large number of academic economists were exposed directly to business life, and had more or less extensive opportunities to observe how decisions were actually made in business organizations. Moreover, those who became active in the development of the new management science were faced with the necessity of developing decision-making procedures that could actually be applied in practical situations. Surely these trends would be conducive to moving the basic assumptions of economic rationality in the direction of greater realism.

But these were not the only things that were happening in economics in the postwar period. First, there was a vigorous reaction that sought to defend classical theory from behavioralism on methodological grounds. I have already commented on these methodological arguments in the first part of my talk. However deeply one may disagree with them, they were stated persuasively and are still influential among academic economists.

Second, the rapid spread of mathematical knowledge and competence in the economics profession permitted the classical theory, especially when combined with statistical decision theory and the theory of games due to von Neumann and Morgenstern, to develop to new heights of sophistication and elegance, and to expand to embrace, albeit in highly stylized form, some of the phenomena of uncertainty and imperfect information. The flowering of mathematical economics and econometrics has provided two generations of economic theorists with a vast garden of formal and technical problems that have absorbed their energies and postponed encounters with the inelegancies of the real world.

If I sound mildly critical of these developments, I should confess that I have also been a part of them, admire them, and would be decidedly unhappy to return to the premathematical world they have replaced. My concern is that the economics profession has exhibited some of the serial one-thing-at-a-time character of human rationality, and has seemed sometimes to be unable to distribute its attention in a balanced fashion among neoclassical theory, macroeconometrics, and descriptive decision theory. As a result, not as much professional effort has been devoted to the latter two, and especially the third, as one might have hoped and expected. The Heartland is more overpopulated than ever, while rich lands in other parts of the empire go untilled.

A. *Search and Information Transfer*

Let me allude to just three of the ways in which classical theory has sought to cope with some of its traditional limitations, and has even sought to make the development of a behavioral theory, incorporating psychological assumptions, unnecessary. The first was to introduce search and information transfer explicitly as economic activities, with associated costs and outputs, that could be inserted into the classical production function. I have already referred to Stigler's 1961 paper on the economics of information, and my own venture in the same direction in the 1956 essay cited earlier.

In theory of this genre, the decision maker is still an individual. A very important new direction, in which decisions are made by groups of individuals, in teams or organizations, is the economic theory of teams developed by Jacob Marschak and Roy Radner. Here we see genuine organizational phenomena—specialization of decision making as a consequence of the costs of transmitting information—emerge from the rational calculus. Because the mathematical difficulties are formidable, the theory remains largely illustrative and limited to very simple situations in miniature organizations. Nevertheless, it has greatly broadened our understanding of the economics of information.

In none of these theories—any more than in statistical decision theory or the theory of games—is the assumption of perfect maximization abandoned. Limits and costs of information are introduced, not as psychological characteristics of the decision maker, but as part of his technological environment. Hence, the new theories do nothing to alleviate the computational complexities facing the decision maker—do not see him coping with them by heroic approximation, simplifying and satisficing, but simply magnify and multiply them. Now he needs to compute not merely the shapes of his supply and demand curves, but, in addition, the costs and benefits of computing those shapes to greater accuracy as well. Hence, to some extent, the impression that these new theories deal with the hitherto ignored phenomena of uncertainty and information transmission is illusory. For many economists, however, the illusion has been persuasive.

B. *Rational Expectations Theory*

A second development in neoclassical theory on which I wish to comment is the so-called "rational expectations" theory.

There is a bit of historical irony surrounding its origins. I have already described the management science inquiry of Holt, Modigliani, Muth, and myself that developed a dynamic programming algorithm for the special (and easily computed) case of quadratic cost functions. In this case, the decision rules are linear, and the probability distributions of future events can be replaced by their expected values, which serve as certainty equivalents (see Simon, 1956; Henri Theil, 1957).

Muth imaginatively saw in this special case a paradigm for rational behavior under uncertainty. What to some of us in the HMMS research team was an approximating, satisficing simplification, served for him as a major line of defense for perfect rationality. He said in his seminal 1961 *Econometrica* article, "It is sometimes argued that the assumption of rationality in economics leads to theories inconsistent with, or inadequate to explain, observed phenomena, especially changes over time... Our hypothesis is based on exactly the opposite point of view: that dynamic economic models do not assume enough rationality" (p. 316).

The new increment of rationality that Muth proposed was that "expectations, since they are informed predictions of future events, are essentially the same as the predictions of the relevant economic theory" (p. 316). He would cut the Gordian knot. Instead of dealing with uncertainty by elaborating the model of the decision process, he would once and for all—if his hypothesis were correct—make process irrelevant. The subsequent vigorous development of rational expectations theory, in the hands of Sargent, Lucas, Prescott, and others, is well known to most readers (see, for example, Lucas, 1975).

It is too early to render a final verdict on the rational expectations theory. The issue will ultimately be decided, as all scientific debates should be, by a gradual winnowing of the empirical evidence, and that winnowing process has just begun. Meanwhile, certain grave theoretical difficulties have already been noticed. As Muth himself has pointed out, it is rational (i.e., profit maximizing) to use the "rational expectations" decision rule if the relevant cost equations are in fact quadratic. I have suggested elsewhere (1978a) that it might therefore be less misleading to call the rule a "consistent expectations" rule.

Perhaps even more important, Albert Ando and Benjamin Friedman (1978, 1979) have shown that the policy implications of the rational expectations rule are quite different under conditions where new information continually becomes available to the system, structural changes occur, and the decision maker learns, than they are under steady-state conditions. For example, under the more dynamic conditions, monetary neutrality—which in general holds for the static consistent expectations models—is no longer guaranteed for any finite time horizon.

In the recent "revisionist" versions of consistent expectations theory, moreover, where account is taken of a changing environment of information, various behavioral assumptions reappear to explain how expectations are formed—what information decision makers will consider, and what they will ignore. But unless these assumptions are to be made on a wholly *ad hoc* and arbitrary basis, they create again the need for an explicit and valid theory of the decision-making *process* (see Simon, 1958a; B. Friedman, 1979).

C. *Statistical Decision Theory and Game Theory*

Statistical decision theory and game theory are two other important components of the neoclassical revival. The former addresses itself to the question of incorporating uncertainty (or more properly, risk) into the decision-making models. It requires heroic assumptions about the information the decision maker has concerning the probability distributions of the relevant variables, and simply increases by orders of magnitude the computational problems he faces.

Game theory addresses itself to the "outguessing" problem that arises whenever an economic actor takes into account the possible reactions to his own decisions of the other actors. To my mind, the main product of the very elegant apparatus of game theory has been to demonstrate quite clearly that it is virtually impossible to define an unambiguous criterion of rationality for this class of situations (or, what amounts to the same thing, a definitive definition of the "solution" of a game). Hence, game theory has not brought to the theories of oligopoly and imperfect competition the relief from their contradictions and complexities that was originally hoped for it. Rather, it has shown that these difficulties are ineradicable. We may be able to reach consensus that a certain criterion of rationality is appropriate to a particular game, but if someone challenges the consensus, preferring a different criterion, we will have no logical basis for persuading him that he is wrong.

D. *Conclusion*

Perhaps I have said enough about the neoclassical revival to suggest why it has been a highly attractive commodity in competition with the behavioral theories. To some economists at least, it has held open the possibility and hope that important questions that had been troublesome for classical economics could now be addressed without sacrifice of the central assumption of perfect rationality, and hence also with a maximum of a priori inference and a minimum of tiresome grubbing with empirical data. I have perhaps said enough also with respect to the limitations of these new constructs to indicate why I do not believe that they solve the problems that motivated their development.

IV. Advances in the Behavioral Theory

Although they have played a muted role in the total economic research activity during the past two decades, theories of bounded rationality and the behavioral theory of the business firm have undergone steady development during that period. Since surveying the whole body of work would be a major undertaking, I shall have to be satisfied here with suggesting the flavor of the whole by citing a few samples of different kinds of important research falling in this domain. Where surveys on particular topics have been published, I will limit myself to references to them.

First, there has been work in the psychological laboratory and the field to test whether people in relatively simple choice situations behave as statistical decision theory (maximization of expected utilities) say they do. Second, there has been extensive psychological research, in which Allen Newell and I have been heavily involved, to discover the actual microprocesses of human decision making and problem solving. Third, there have been numerous empirical observations—most of them in the form of "case studies"—of the actual processes of decision making in organizational and business contexts. Fourth, there have been reformulations and extensions of the theory of the firm replacing classical maximization with behavioral decision postulates.

A. *Utility Theory and Human Choice*

The axiomatization of utility and probability after World War II and the revival of Bayesian statistics opened the way to testing empirically whether people behaved in choice situations so as to maximize subjective expected utility (*SEU*). In early studies, using extremely simple choice situations, it appeared that perhaps they did. When even small complications were introduced into the situations, wide departures of behavior from the predictions of *SEU* theory soon became evident. Some of the most dramatic and convincing empirical refutations of the theory have been reported by D. Kahneman and A. Tversky, who showed that under one set of circumstances, decision makers gave far too little weight to prior knowledge and based their choices almost entirely on new evidence, while in other circumstances new evidence had little influence on opinions already formed. Equally large and striking departures from the behavior predicted by the *SEU* theories were found by Howard Kunreuther and his colleagues in their studies of individual decisions to purchase or not to purchase flood insurance. On the basis of these and other pieces of evidence, the conclusion seems unavoidable that the *SEU* theory does not provide a good prediction—not even a good approximation—of actual behavior.

Notice that the refutation of the theory has to do with the *substance* of the decisions, and not just the process by which they are reached. It is not that people do not go through the calculations that would be required to reach the *SEU* decision—neoclassical thought has never claimed that they did. What has been shown is that they do not even behave *as if* they had carried out those calculations, and that result is a direct refutation of the neoclassical assumptions.

B. *Psychology of Problem Solving*

The evidence on rational decision making is largely negative evidence, evidence of what people do *not* do. In the past twenty years a large body of positive evidence has also accumulated about the processes that people use to make difficult decisions and solve complex problems. The body of theory that has been built up around this evidence is called information processing psychology, and is usually expressed formally in computer programming languages. Newell and I have summed up our own version of this theory in our book, *Human Problem Solving*, which is part of a large and rapidly growing literature that assumes an information processing framework and makes use of computer simulation as a central tool for expressing and testing theories.

Information processing theories envisage problem solving as involving very selective search through problem spaces that are often immense. Selectivity, based on rules of thumb or "heuristics," tends to guide the search into promising regions, so that solutions will generally be found after search of only a tiny part of the total space. Satisficing criteria terminate search when satisfactory problem solutions have been found. Thus, these theories of problem solving clearly fit within the framework of bounded rationality that I have been expounding here.

By now the empirical evidence for this general picture of the problem solving process is extensive. Most of the evidence pertains to relatively simple, puzzle-like situations of the sort that can be brought into the psychological laboratory for controlled study, but a great deal has been learned, also, about professional level human tasks like making medical diagnoses, investing in portfolios of stocks and bonds, and playing chess. In tasks of these kinds, the general search mechanisms operate in a rich context of information stored in human long-term memory, but the general organization of the process is substantially the same as for the simpler, more specific tasks.

At the present time, research in information processing psychology is proceeding in several directions. Exploration of professional level skills continues. A good deal of effort is now being devoted also to determining how initial representations for new problems are acquired. Even in simple problem domains, the problem solver has much latitude in the way he formulates the problem space in which he will search, a finding that underlines again how far the actual process is from a search for a uniquely determined optimum (see J. R. Hayes and Simon).

The main import for economic theory of the research in information processing psychology is to provide rather conclusive empirical evidence that the decision-making process in problem situations conforms closely to the models of bounded rationality described earlier. This finding implies, in turn, that choice is not determined uniquely by the objective characteristics of the problem situation, but depends also on the particular heuristic process that is used to reach the decision. It would appear, therefore, that a model of process is an essential component in any positive theory of decision making that purports to describe the real world, and that the neoclassical ambition of avoiding the necessity for such a model is unrealizable (Simon, 1978a).

C. *Organizational Decision Making*

It would be desirable to have, in addition to the evidence from the psychological research just described, empirical studies of the process of decision making in organizational contexts. The studies of individual problem solving and decision making do not touch on the many social-psychological factors that enter into the decision process in organizations. A substantial number of investigations have been carried out in the past twenty years of the decision-making process in organizations, but they are not easily summarized. The difficulty is that most of these investigations have taken the form of case studies of specific decisions or particular classes of decisions in individual organizations. To the best of my knowledge, no good review of this literature has been published, so that it is difficult even to locate and identify the studies that have been carried out.[3] Nor have any systematic methods been developed and tested for distilling out from these individual case studies their implications for the general theory of the decision-making process.

The case studies of organizational decision making, therefore, represent the natural history stage of scientific inquiry. They provide us with a multitude of facts about the decision-making process—facts that are almost uniformly consistent with the kind of behavioral model that has been proposed here. But we do not yet know how to use these facts to test the model in any formal way. Nor do we quite know what to do with the observation that the specific decision-making procedures used by organizations differ from one organization to another, and within each organization, even from one situation to another. We must not expect from these data generalizations as neat and precise as those incorporated in neoclassical theory.

Perhaps the closest approach to a method for extracting theoretically relevant information from case studies is computer simulation. By converting empirical evidence about a decision-making process into a computer program, a path is opened both for testing the adequacy of the program mechanisms for explaining the data, and for discovering the key features of the program that account, qualitatively, for the interesting and important characteristics of its behavior. Examples of the use of this technique are G.P.E. Clarkson's simulation of the decision making of an investment trust officer, Cyert, E. A. Feigenbaum, and March's simulation of the history of a duopoly, and C. P. Bonini's model of the effects of accounting information and supervisory pressures in altering employee motivations in a business firm. The simulation methodology is discussed from a variety of viewpoints in Dutton and Starbuck.[4]

D. *Theories of the Business Firm*

The general features of bounded rationality—selective search, satisficing, and so on—have been taken as the starting points for a number of attempts to build theories of the business firm incorporating behavioral assumptions. Examples of such theories would include the theory of Cyert and March, already mentioned; William Baumol's theory of sales maximization subject to minimum profit constraints; Robin Marris' models of firms whose goals are stated in terms of rates of growth; Harvey Leibenstein's theory of "X-inefficiency" that depresses production below the theoretically attainable; Janos Kornai's dichotomy between supply-driven and demand-driven management; Oliver Williamson's theory of transactional costs; the evolutionary models of Richard Nelson and Sidney Winter (1973); Cyert and Morris DeGroot's (1974) models incorporating adaptive learning; Radner's (1975a,b) explicit satisficing models; and others.

Characterized in this way, there seems to be little commonality among all of these theories and models, except that they depart in one way or another from the classical assumption of perfect rationality in firm decision making. A closer look, however, and a more abstract description of their assumptions, shows that they share several basic characteristics. Most of them depart from the assumption of profit maximization in the short run, and replace it with an assumption

[3]For leads into the literature, see March and Simon; March; Johnsen; J. M. Dutton and W. H. Starbuck. However, there are large numbers of specific case studies, some of them carried out as thesis projects, some concerned with particular fields of business application, which have never been recorded in these reference sources (for example, Eliasson, 1976).

[4]In addition to simulations of the firm, there are very interesting and potentially important efforts to use simulation to build bridges directly from decision theory to political economy. See G. Orcutt and R. Caldwell-Wertheimer, and Eliasson (1978).

of goals defined in terms of targets—that is, they are to greater or lesser degree satisficing theories. If they do retain maximizing assumptions, they contain some kind of mechanism that prevents the maximum from being attained, at least in the short run. In the Cyert-March theory, and that of Leibenstein, this mechanism can be viewed as producing "organizational slack," the magnitude of which may itself be a function of motivational and environmental variables.

Finally, a number of these theories assume that organizational learning takes place, so that if the environment were stationary for a sufficient length of time, the system equilibrium would approach closer and closer to the classical profit-maximizing equilibrium. Of course they generally also assume that the environmental disturbances will generally be large enough to prevent the classical solution from being an adequate approximation to the actual behavior.

The presence of something like organizational slack in a model of the business firm introduces complexity in the firm's behavior in the short run. Since the firm may operate very far from any optimum, the slack serves as a buffer between the environment and the firm's decisions. Responses to environmental events can no longer be predicted simply by analyzing the "requirements of the situation," but depend on the specific decision processes that the firm employs. However well this characteristic of a business firm model corresponds to reality, it reduces the attractiveness of the model for many economists, who are reluctant to give up the process-independent predictions of classical theory, and who do not feel at home with the kind of empirical investigation that is required for disclosing actual real world decision processes.

But there is another side to the matter. If, in the face of identical environmental conditions, different decision mechanisms can produce different firm behaviors, this sensitivity of outcomes to process can have important consequences for analysis at the level of markets and the economy. Political economy, whether descriptive or normative, cannot remain indifferent to this source of variability in response. At the very least it demands that—before we draw policy conclusions from our theories, and particularly before we act on those policy conclusions—we carry out sensitivity analyses to test how far our conclusions would be changed if we made different assumptions about the decision mechanisms at the micro level.

If our conclusions are robust—if they are not changed materially by substituting one or another variant of the behavioral model for the classical model—we will gain confidence in our predictions and recommendations; if the conclusions are sensitive to such substitutions, we will use them warily until we can determine which micro theory is the correct one.

As reference to the literature cited earlier in this section will verify, our predictions of the operations of markets and of the economy *are* sensitive to our assumptions about mechanisms at the level of decision processes. Moreover, the assumptions of the behavioral theories are almost certainly closer to reality than those of the classical theory. These two facts, in combination, constitute a direct refutation of the argument that the unrealism of the assumptions of the classical theory is harmless. We cannot use the *in vacua* version of the law of falling bodies to predict the sinking of a heavy body in molasses. The predictions of the classical and neoclassical theories and the policy recommendations derived from them must be treated with the greatest caution.

V. Conclusion

There is a saying in politics that "you can't beat something with nothing." You can't defeat a measure or a candidate simply by pointing to defects and inadequacies. You must offer an alternative.

The same principle applies to scientific theory. Once a theory is well entrenched, it will survive many assaults of empirical evidence that purports to refute it unless an alternative theory, consistent with the evidence, stands ready to replace it. Such conservative protectiveness of established beliefs is, indeed, not unreasonable. In the first place, in empirical science we aspire only to approximate truths; we are under no illusion that we can find a single formula, or even a moderately complex one, that captures the whole truth and nothing else. We are committed to a strategy of successive approximations, and when we find discrepancies between theory and data, our first impulse is to patch rather than to rebuild from the foundations.

In the second place, when discrepancies appear, it is seldom immediately obvious where the trouble lies. It may be located in the fundamental assumptions of the theory, but it may as well be merely a defect in the auxiliary hypotheses and measurement postulates we have had to assume in order to connect theory with observations. Revisions in these latter parts of the structure may be sufficient to save the remainder.

What then is the present status of the classical theory of the firm? There can no longer be any doubt that the micro assumptions of the theory—the assumptions of perfect rationality—are contrary to fact. It is not a question of approximation; they do not even remotely describe the processes that human beings use for making decisions in complex situations.

Moreover, there is an alternative. If anything, there is an embarrassing richness of alternatives. Today, we have a large mass of descriptive data, from both laboratory and field, that show how human problem solving and decision making actually take place in a wide variety of situations. A number of theories have been constructed to account for these data, and while these theories certainly do not yet constitute a single coherent whole, there is much in common among them. In one way or another, they incorporate the notions of bounded rationality: the need to search for decision alternatives, the replacement of optimization by targets and satisficing goals, and mechanisms of learning and adaptation. If our interest lies in descriptive decision theory (or even normative decision theory), it is now entirely clear that the classical and neoclassical theories have been replaced by a superior alternative that provides us with a much closer approximation to what is actually going on.

But what if our interest lies primarily in normative political economy rather than in the more remote regions of the economic sciences? Is there then any reason why we should give up the familiar theories? Have the newer concepts of decision making and the firm shown their superiority "for purposes of economic analysis"?

If the classical and neoclassical theories were, as is sometimes argued, simply powerful tools for deriving aggregative consequences that held alike for both perfect and bounded rationality, we would have every reason to retain them for this purpose. But we have seen, on the contrary, that neoclassical theory does not always lead to the same conclusions at the level of aggregate phenomena and policy as are implied by the postulate of bounded rationality, in any of its variants. Hence, we cannot defend an uncritical use of these contrary-to-fact assumptions by the argument that their veridicality is unimportant. In many cases, in fact, this veridicality may be crucial to reaching correct conclusions about the central questions of political economy. Only a comparison of predictions can tell us whether a case before us is one of these.

The social sciences have been accustomed to look for models in the most spectacular successes of the natural sciences. There is no harm in that, provided that it is not done in a spirit of slavish imitation. In economics, it has been common enough to admire Newtonian mechanics (or, as we have seen, the Law of Falling Bodies), and to search for the economic equivalent of the laws of motion. But this is not the only model for a science, and it seems, indeed, not to be the right one for our purposes.

Human behavior, even rational human behavior, is not to be accounted for by a handful of invariants. It is certainly not to be accounted for by assuming perfect adaptation to the environment. Its basic mechanisms may be relatively simple, and I believe they are, but that simplicity operates in interaction with extremely complex boundary conditions imposed by the environment and by the very facts of human long-term memory and of the capacity of human beings, individually and collectively, to learn.

If we wish to be guided by a natural science metaphor, I suggest one drawn from biology rather than physics (see Newell and Simon, 1976). Obvious lessons are to be learned from evolutionary biology, and rather less obvious ones from molecular biology. From molecular biology, in particular, we can glimpse a picture of how a few basic mechanisms—the DNA of the Double Helix, for example, or the energy transfer mechanisms elucidated so elegantly by Peter Mitchell—can account for a wide range of complex phenomena. We can see the role in science of laws of qualitative structure, and the power of qualitative as well as quantitative explanation.

I am always reluctant to end a talk about the sciences of man in the future tense. It conveys too much the impression that these are potential sciences which may some day be actualized, but that do not really exist at the present time. Of course that is not the case at all. However much our knowledge of human behavior falls short of our need for such knowledge, still it is enormous. Sometimes we tend to discount it because so many of the phenomena are accessible to us in the very activity of living as human beings among human beings that it seems commonplace to us. Moreover, it does not always answer the questions for which we need answers. We cannot predict very well the course of the business cycle nor manage the employment rate. (We cannot, it might be added, predict very well the time of the next thunderstorm in Stockholm, or manage the earth's climates.)

With all these qualifications and reservations, we do understand today many of the mechanisms of human rational choice. We do know how the information processing system called Man, faced with complexity beyond his ken, uses his information processing capacities to seek out alternatives, to calculate consequences, to resolve uncertainties, and thereby—sometimes, not always—to find ways of action that are sufficient unto the day, that satisfice.

REFERENCES

A. A. Alchian, "Uncertainty, Evolution, and Economic Theory," *J. Polit. Econ.*, June 1950, *58*, 211-21.

A. Ando, "On a Theoretical and Empirical Basis of Macroeconometric Models," paper presented to the NSF-NBER Conference on Macroeconomic Modeling, Ann Arbor, Oct. 1978.

Chester I. Barnard, *The Functions of the Executive*, Cambridge, Mass. 1938.

William Baumol, *Business Behavior, Value and Growth*, New York 1959.

G. S. Becker, "Irrational Behavior and Economic Theory," *J. Polit. Econ.*, Feb. 1962, *70*, 1–13.

Charles P. Bonini, *Simulation of Information and Decision Systems in the Firm*, Englewood Cliffs 1963.

Alfred Chandler, *Strategy and Structure*, Cambridge, Mass. 1962.

N. C. Churchill, W. W. Cooper, and T. Sainsbury, "Laboratory and Field Studies of the Behavioral Effects of Audits," in C. P. Bonini et al., eds., *Management Controls*, New York 1964.

G. P. E. Clarkson, "A Model of the Trust Investment Process," in E. A. Feigenbaum and J. Feldman, eds., *Computers and Thought*, New York 1963.

John R. Commons, *Institutional Economics*, Madison 1934.

R. M. Cyert, E. A. Feigenbaum, and J. G. March, "Models in a Behavioral Theory of the Firm," *Behav. Sci.*, Apr. 1959, *4*, 81–95.

———**and M. H. DeGroot,** "Rational Expectations and Bayesian Analysis," *J. Polit. Econ.*, May/June 1974, *82*, 521–36.

——— **and** ——— "Adaptive Utility," in R. H. Day and T. Groves, eds., *Adaptive Economic Models*, New York 1975, 233–46.

———**and James G. March,** *A Behavioral Theory of the Firm*, Englewood Cliffs 1963.

——— **and H. A. Simon,** "Theory of the Firm: Behavioralism and Marginalism," unpublished work. paper, Carnegie-Mellon Univ. 1971.

———, ———**, and D. B. Trow,** "Observation of a Business Decision," *J. Bus., Univ. Chicago*, Oct. 1956, *29*, 237–48.

D. C. Dearborn and H. A. Simon, "Selective Perception: The Identifications of Executives," *Sociometry*, 1958, *21*, 140–144; reprinted in *Administrative Behavior*, ch. 15, 3d ed., New York 1976.

J. M. Dutton and W. H. Starbuck, *Computer Simulation of Human Behavior*, New York 1971.

G. Eliasson, *Business Economic Planning*, New York 1976.

———, *A Micro-to-Macro Model of the Swedish Economy*, Stockholm 1978.

B. M. Friedman, "Optimal Expectations and the Extreme Information Assumptions of 'Rational Expectations' Macromodels," *J. Monet. Econ.*, Jan. 1979 *5*, 23–41.

———, "A Discussion of the Methodological Premises of Professors Lucas and Sargent," in *After the Phillips Curve: The Persistence of High Inflation and High Unemployment*, Boston 1978.

Milton Friedman, *Essays in Positive Economics*, Chicago 1953.

J. R. Hayes and H. A. Simon, "Understanding Written Problem Instructions," in W. Gregg, ed., *Knowledge and Cognition*, Potomac 1974, 167–200.

A. O. Hirschman, *Exit, Voice and Loyalty*, Cambridge, Mass. 1970.

Charles C. Holt, Franco Modigliani, John F. Muth, and Herbert A. Simon, *Planning Production, Inventories and Work Force*, Englewood Cliffs 1960.

Y. Ijiri and H. A. Simon, *Skew Distributions and the Sizes of Business Firms*, Amsterdam 1977.

E. Johnsen, *Studies in Multiobjective Decision Models*, Lund 1968.

D. W. Jorgenson and C. D. Siebert, "A Comparison of Alternative Theories of Corporate Investment Behavior," *Amer. Econ. Rev.*, Sept. 1968, *58*, 681–712.

D. Kahneman and A. Tversky, "On the Psychology of Prediction," *Psychol. Rev.*, July 1973, *80*, 237–51.

Janos Kornai, *Anti-Equilibrium*, Amsterdam 1971.

Howard Kunreuther et al., *Disaster Insurance Protection: Public Policy Lessons*, New York 1978.

Harvey Leibenstein, *Beyond Economic Man*, Cambridge, Mass. 1976.

J. Lesourne, *A Theory of the Individual for Economic Analysis*, Vol. 1, Amsterdam 1977.

R. E. Lucas, Jr., "An Equilibrium Model of the Business Cycle," *J. Polit. Econ.*, Dec. 1975, *83*, 1113–44.

———, "On the Size Distribution of Business Firms," *Bell J. Econ.*, Autumn 1978, *9*, 508–23.

James G. March, *Handbook of Organizations*, Chicago 1965.

——— **and H. A. Simon,** *Organizations*, New York 1958.

Robin Marris, *The Economic Theory of "Managerial" Capitalism*, London 1964.

Jacob Marschak, "Role of Liquidity under Complete and Incomplete Information," *Amer. Econ. Rev. Proc.*, May 1949, *39*, 182–95.

——— **and Roy Radner,** *Economic Theory of Teams*, New Haven 1972.

Alfred Marshall, *Principles of Economics*, 8th ed., New York 1920.

E. S. Mason, "Comment," in Bernard T. Haley, ed., *A Survey of Contemporary Economics*, Vol. II, Homewood 1952, 221–22.

J. M. Montias, *The Structure of Economic Systems*, New Haven 1976.

J. F. Muth, "Rational Expectations and the Theory of Price Movements," *Econometrica*, July 1961, *29*, 315–53.

———, "Optimal Properties of Exponentially Weighted Forecasts," *J. Amer. Statist. Assn.*, June 1960, *55*, 299–306.

R. R. Nelson, and S. Winter, "Toward an Evolutionary Theory of Economic Capabilities," *Amer. Econ. Rev. Proc.*, May 1973, *63*, 440–49.

——— **and** ———, "Neoclassical vs. Evolutionary Theories of Economic Growth," *Econ. J.*, Dec. 1974, *84*, 886–905.

Allen Newell and Herbert A. Simon, *Human Problem Solving*, Englewood Cliffs, 1972.

——— **and** ———, "Computer Science as Empirical Inquiry: Symbols and Search," *Communications of the ACM*, Mar. 1976, *19*,113–26.

G. Orcutt, and R. Caldwells-Wertheimer II, *Policy Exploration through Microanalytic Simulation*, Washington 1976.

A. Papandreou, "Some Basic Problems in the Theory of the Firm," in Bernard F. Haley, ed., *A Survey of Contemporary Economics*, Vol. II, Homewood 1952.

E. H. Phelps-Brown, "The Meaning of the Fitted Cobb-Douglas Function," *Quart. J. Econ.*, Nov. 1957, *71*, 546–60.

R. Radner, (1975a) "A Behavioral Model of Cost Reduction," *Bell J. Econ.*, Spring 1975, *6*, 196–215.

———, (1975b) "Satisficing," *J. Math. Econ.*, June–Sept. 1975, *2*, 253–62.

David R. Roberts, *Executive Compensation*, Glencoe 1959.

P. A. Samuelson, "Discussion: Problems of Methodology," *Amer. Econ. Rev. Proc.*, May 1963, *53*, 231–36.

Henry Schultz, *The Theory and Measurement of Demand*, Chicago 1938.

Herbert A. Simon, *Administrative Behavior*, New York 1947; 3d ed. 1976.

———, "A Formal Theory of the Employment Relation," *Econometrica*, July 1951, *19*, 293–305

———, "A Comparison of Organization Theories," *Rev. Econ. Stud.*, No. 1, 1952, *20*, 40–48.

———, "A Behavioral Model of Rational Choice," *Quart. J. Econ.*, Feb. 1955, *69*, 99–118.

———, "Rational Choice and the Structure of the Environment," *Psychol. Rev.*, Mar. 1956, *63*, 129–38.

———, "Dynamic Programming under Uncertainty with a Quadratic Criterion Function," *Econometrica*, Jan. 1956, *24*, 74–81.

———, *Models of Man*, New York 1957.

———, "The Compensation of Executives," *Sociometry*, 1957, *20*, 32–35.

———, "Theories of Decision Making in Economics and Behavioral Science," *Amer. Econ. Rev.*, June 1959, *49*, 223–83.

———, "Discussion: Problems of Methodology," *Amer. Econ. Rev. Proc.*, May 1963, *53*, 229–31.

———, "From Substantive to Procedural Rationality," in Spiro J. Latsis, ed., *Methodological Appraisal in Economics*, Cambridge 1976.

———, (1978a) "Rationality as Process and as Product of Thought," *Amer. Econ. Rev. Proc.*, May 1978, *68*, 1–16.

———, (1978b) "On How to Decide What to Do," *Bell J. Econ.*, Autumn 1978, *9*, 494–507.

———, **G. Kozmetsky, H. Guetzkow, and G. Tyndall,** *Centralization vs. Decentralization in Organizing the Controller's Department*, New York 1954; reprinted Houston 1978.

——— **and F. K. Levy,** "A Note on the Cobb-Douglas Function," *Rev. Econ. Stud.*, June 1963, *30*, 93–94.

G. J. Stigler, "The Economics of Information," *J. Polit. Econ.*, June 1961, *69*, 213–15.

H. Theil, "A Note on Certainty Equivalence in Dynamic Planning," *Econometrica*, Apr. 1957, *25*, 346–49.

John von Neumann and Oscar Morgenstern, *Theory of Games and Economic Behavior*, Princeton 1944.

A. A. Walters, "Production and Cost Functions: An Econometric Survey," *Econometrica*, Jan.–Apr. 1963, *31*, 1–66.

Oliver Williamson, *Markets and Hierarchies: Analysis and Antitrust Implications*, New York 1975.

S. Winter, "Satisficing, Selection, and the Innovating Remnant," *Quart. J. Econ.*, May 1971, *85*, 237–61.

Part II
George J. Stigler

Introduction to Part II: George J. Stigler (1911–91)

George Stigler was born in Renton (a suburb of Seattle), Washington, USA in 1911. He obtained a BA from the University of Washington in 1931, an MBA from Northwestern University in 1932, and a PhD from the University of Chicago in 1938. A graduate student under Frank Knight at Chicago, his doctoral thesis on the history of production and distribution theories was subsequently published by Macmillan (Stigler, 1941). He was appointed assistant professor at Iowa State College in 1936, a post he held before moving to the University of Minnesota in 1938. Working in the faculty at Minnesota, he was promoted from assistant and associate to full professor over the period from 1938 to 1946. In 1942 Stigler went on leave, first to work at the National Bureau of Economic Research (NBER) (where he was a research staff member until 1976), and then to the Statistical Research Group at Columbia University before returning to Minnesota in 1945. In 1946 he accepted the offer of a professorship at Brown University but after a year moved to Columbia University, where he was professor from 1947 to 1958. In 1958 Stigler returned to the University of Chicago where he remained until he retired in 1981. From 1981 to 1991 he was the Charles R. Walgreen Distinguished Service Professor, Emeritus, at the University of Chicago. At Chicago he established the Industrial Organization Workshop, founded the Center for the Study of the Economy and the State in 1977, and was an editor of the *Journal of Political Economy* from 1974 until his death in 1991.

Among his many offices and honours, Stigler was president of each of the American Economic Association in 1964, the History of Economics Society in 1977 and the Mont Pelerin Society from 1976 to 1978, and was awarded the National Medal of Science in 1987. In 1982 he was awarded the Nobel Memorial Prize in Economics 'for his seminal studies of industrial structures, functioning of markets and causes and effects of public regulation' (Nobel Foundation, 2010).

Stigler's published work covers four main areas: the history of economic thought, microeconomic theory, industrial organization and economic regulation. In the field of the history of economic thought the publication of his doctoral thesis, *Production and Distribution Theories*, in 1941, marked the first major attempt to survey the neoclassical theories of production and distribution over the period from 1870 to 1895. This landmark book covers the work of such influential economists as Eugen von Böhm-Bawerk (1851–1914), John Bates Clark (1847–1938), Francis Ysidro Edgeworth (1845–1926), William Stanley Jevons (1835–82), Alfred Marshall (1842–1924), Carl Menger (1840–1921), Léon Walras (1834–1910) and Knut Wicksell (1851–1926). In addition to this definitive study he also wrote numerous articles on the history of economic ideas and the contributions of a number of great economists of the past. Some of his most important articles – including 'The Development of Utility Theory', 'Perfect Competition, Historically Contemplated', 'The Nature and Role of Originality in

Scientific Progress', 'The Influence of Events and Politics on Economic Theory' and 'Ricardo and the 93 Per Cent Labour Theory of Value' – have been gathered together in *Essays in the History of Economics* (Stigler, 1965).

Stigler made a number of important contributions both to microeconomic theory (including contributions to the theory of costs and production) and to industrial organization. Rather than attempt to survey the entire breadth of these contributions, in what follows we merely highlight, in approximate chronological order, some of his most important and influential published works. His paper on the diet problem entitled 'The Cost of Subsistence' (Stigler, 1945 – paper 7) played an important role in the subsequent development of the technique of linear programming. The year 1946 marked the publication of the first edition of his intermediate textbook, *The Theory of Price* – an earlier version of the book had been published by Macmillan in 1942 entitled *The Theory of Competitive Price*. One important feature of this influential textbook, which characterized his approach to economics, is the way theory is illustrated with real-world phenomena. Much of his subsequent published work involved the use of empirical evidence to test theories of industrial organization. In a paper published in 1947 in the *Journal of Political Economy* (Stigler, 1947c – paper 8) he uncovered the theoretical inadequacy and predictive failures of the kinked demand curve in oligopoly. On the basis of empirical tests he emphasized the frequency of price changes in oligopolistic industries against the traditional prediction that industries containing only a few firms rarely engage in price changes (see also Stigler and Kindahl, 1970).

His 1961 article, 'The Economics of Information' (paper 9), acknowledges that information is imperfect and can only be acquired at a cost. Furthermore, rational economic agents will have an incentive to search for and acquire information only up to the point where the benefit from additional information is equal to the costs incurred. In other words, Stigler recognized that the same considerations, involving a comparison between benefits and costs, apply to the acquisition of information as they do to the consumption and production of other goods and services. This seminal article, together with 'Information in the Labour Market' (Stigler, 1962a – paper 10), inspired much subsequent work in such fields of study as macroeconomics and labour economics, most notably on search models of unemployment. In another very influential paper published in the *Journal of Political Economy* in 1964 on the theory of oligopoly (Stigler, 1964a – paper 11) he argued that the stability of collusive behaviour in oligopolistic markets depends on the costs of detecting and enforcing significant movements away from price agreements. Those industries that are more successful than others at price collusion have lower costs of policing the price agreement. Many of his most important papers, which have had such a marked impact on the development of industrial economics since the 1970s, can be found in *The Organization of Industry* (Stigler, 1968).

In addition to these main published works, mention should also be made of some of Stigler's important empirical work, which he undertook over the period from 1947 to 1976 as a senior research staff member of the NBER. This work includes NBER monographs on domestic servants, trends in output and employment, employment trends in the service industries, scientific personnel, capital and rates of return in manufacturing industries and the behaviour of industrial prices (Stigler, 1947a; 1947b; 1956; 1963; Blank and Stigler, 1957; Stigler and Kindahl, 1970).

In the early 1960s, Stigler started detailed research into the practice and theory of economic regulation. A 1962 article, co-authored with Claire Friedland (Stigler and Friedland, 1962b), challenged the then-traditional view that public regulation achieves its stated objectives. In examining the case of electricity, Stigler and Friedland concluded that regulation had no significant effect on electricity prices in the USA. In a subsequent study, 'Public Regulation of the Securities Market', Stigler (1964b) concluded that regulation had not benefited investors buying new stock issues. These studies acted as a catalyst for economists in other countries to undertake research into the actual effects of economic regulation. In a seminal article, 'The Theory of Economic Regulation', published in 1971 (paper 12), he argued that 'as a rule, regulation is acquired by the industry and is designed and operated primarily for its benefit' rather than 'for the protection and benefit of the public' (Stigler, 1971, p. 3). Stigler's studies of the 'causes and effects of public regulation' led to a new area of study known as the economics of regulation. One important aspect of his work is the way he integrated the economics of regulation with the economics of politics. For Stigler, participants in the political market, as in the economic market, display self-interested rational behaviour and should therefore be subject to the same tools of analysis. His studies also helped open up another new area of research between economics and law. Some of his most important essays on regulation, including the three papers noted above, have been gathered together in *The Citizen and the State* (Stigler, 1975).

George Stigler will be remembered first and foremost for his pioneering work in industrial organization and economic regulation. His groundbreaking contributions (most notably Stigler, 1961; 1971) gave birth to two new areas of research on the 'economics of information' and the 'economics of regulation'. He has also been credited by the 1991 Nobel Memorial Laureate, Ronald Coase, with naming and formulating the Coase theorem (see entry on Coase in this volume and Stigler, 1989). A much-admired economist known for his clear, creative and insightful style of writing, Stigler's work is also often laced with humour (see, for example, Stigler, 1982).

Main Published Works

(1941), *Production and Distribution Theories*, New York: Macmillan.

(1945), 'The Cost of Subsistence', *Journal of Farm Economics*, **27**, May, pp. 303–14.

(1946), *The Theory of Price*, New York: Macmillan; 2nd edn 1952, 3rd edn 1966; 4th edn 1987.

(1947a), *Domestic Servants in the United States*, New York: National Bureau of Economic Research.

(1947b), *Trends in Output and Employment*, New York: National Bureau of Economic Research.

(1947c), 'The Kinky Oligopoly Demand Curve and Rigid Prices', *Journal of Political Economy*, **55**, October, pp. 432–49; reprinted in *The Organization of Industry*, Homewood, IL: Richard D. Irwin, 1968.

(1956), *Trends in Employment in the Service Industries*, New York: National Bureau of Economic Research.

(1957), *The Demand and Supply of Scientific Personnel* (with D.M. Blank), New York: National Bureau of Economic Research.

(1961), 'The Economics of Information', *Journal of Political Economy*, **69**, June, pp. 213–25; reprinted in *The Organization of Industry*, Homewood, IL: Richard D. Irwin, 1968.

(1962a), 'Information in the Labour Market', *Journal of Political Economy*, **70**, October, pp. 94–105; reprinted in *The Organization of Industry*, Homewood, IL: Richard D. Irwin, 1968.

(1962b), 'What Can Regulators Regulate? The Case of Electricity' (with C. Friedland), *Journal of Law and Economics*, **5**, October, pp. 1–16; reprinted in *The Citizen and the State: Essays on Regulation*, Chicago, IL: University of Chicago Press, 1975.

(1963), *Capital and Rates of Return in Manufacturing Industries*, Princeton, NJ: Princeton University Press.
(1964a), 'A Theory of Oligopoly', *Journal of Political Economy*, **72**, February, pp. 44–61; reprinted in *The Organization of Industry*, Homewood, IL: Richard D. Irwin, 1968.
(1964b), 'Public Regulation of the Securities Markets', *Journal of Business*, **37**, April, pp. 117–42; reprinted in *The Citizen and the State: Essays on Regulation*, Chicago, IL: University of Chicago Press, 1975.
(1965), *Essays in the History of Economics*, Chicago, IL: University of Chicago Press.
(1968), *The Organization of Industry*, Homewood, IL: Richard D. Irwin.
(1970), *The Behaviour of Industrial Prices* (with J.K. Kindahl), New York: National Bureau of Economic Research.
(1971), 'The Theory of Economic Regulation', *Bell Journal of Economics and Management Science*, **2**, Spring, pp. 3–21; reprinted in *The Citizen and the State: Essays on Regulation*, Chicago, IL: University of Chicago Press, 1975.
(1975), *The Citizen and the State: Essays on Regulation*, Chicago, IL: University of Chicago Press.
(1982), *The Economist as Preacher and Other Essays*, Chicago, IL: University of Chicago Press; Oxford: Basil Blackwell.
(1989), 'Two Notes on the Coase Theorem', *Yale Law Journal*, **99**, December, pp. 631–3.

Secondary Literature

Friedman, M. (1999), 'George Joseph Stigler', in *Biographical Memoirs, Volume 76*, Washington, DC: National Academy Press, pp. 340–59.
Mincer, J. (1983), 'George Stigler's Contributions to Economics', *Scandinavian Journal of Economics*, **85** (1), pp. 65–75.
Nobel Foundation (2010), Official Web Site, www.nobelprize.org.
Schmalensee, R. (1983), 'George Stigler's Contributions to Economics', *Scandinavian Journal of Economics*, **85** (1), pp. 77–86.

[7]

THE COST OF SUBSISTENCE

GEORGE J. STIGLER
University of Minnesota

ELABORATE investigations have been made of the adequacy of diets at various income levels, and a considerable number of "low-cost," "moderate," and "expensive" diets have been recommended to consumers. Yet, so far as I know, no one has determined the minimum cost of obtaining the amounts of calories, protein, minerals, and vitamins which these studies accept as adequate or optimum. This will be done in the present paper, not only for its own interest but because it sheds much light on the meaning of conventional "low-cost" diets.

This paper is organized under five headings, devoted to

1. The quantities of the various nutrients which should be contained in an average person's diet.
2. The quantities of these nutrients which are found in certain common foods.
3. The methodology of finding the minimum cost diet.
4. The minimum cost diet in August 1939 and August 1944.
5. Comparison with conventional low-cost diets.

The curious may wish to turn first to Table 2, which gives the composition and cost of the most economical diets in August 1939 and 1944 for an active economist (weighing 70 kilograms) who lives in a large city.

Nutritive Requirements

The economist uses a production function to describe the relationship between the quantities of the productive services and the quantity of product. The product derived from an increment of productive service A is usually assumed (1) to diminish as the quantity of A increases, and (2) to depend upon the quantities of the other productive services used with A.

This approach can be applied also to the relationship between quantities of nutrients and "health" (used here generically to describe strength, vigor, avoidance of disease, etc.). The findings of nutrition studies clearly indicate:

1. After certain minimum values of the nutrients are secured, additional quantities yield decreasing (and in some cases eventually negative) returns to health.
2. The optimum quantity of any nutrient depends upon the quantities of the other nutrients available.

A few of the many illustrations of these findings may be given.

Diminishing returns is illustrated by the facts that the amount of calcium in the body increases much more slowly than the input of calcium, and that increases of longevity are not proportional to increases of calcium inputs.[1] The incidence of goiter was found to vary in inverse proportion to the amount of iodine in the water in Michigan localities.[2] An example of substitution is the recommendation of 30 micrograms of thiamine per 100 calories not derived from fats,[3] and one of complementarity is the loss of riboflavin which accompanies a deficiency of thiamine.[4]

The science of nutrition is much too young to have attained even an approximate measurement of the "health" function for representative individuals, or to determine the extent of individual variation. The optimum quantity of calories is known fairly accurately, but the requirements of other nutrients are known only roughly or not at all. Many minima (to which 50 percent is usually added as a safety factor) are found by determining the lowest level of input compatible with a stable rate of loss of the nutrient through excreta. It is probable that nutrient requirements have been overstated; for example, a 5 month experiment on young men with riboflavin held at less than two-thirds of the recommended level led to the conclusion that they did not suffer any clinical or physiological defects.[5] The interrelationships among the various nutrients are even more obscure, and they are virtually ignored in dietary recommendations.

The ultimate health function will doubtless be very complex. In addition to calories, the body requires about thirteen minerals (some in very minute quantities), and perhaps half as many vitamins. Protein contains two dozen amino acids, of which almost

[1] Sherman, H. C., H. L. Campbell, and C. S. Lanford, "Experiments on the Relation of Nutrition to the Composition of the Body and the Length of Life," *Proceedings of the National Academy of Science*, XXV (1939), 16–20.

[2] Curtis, G. M. and M. B. Fertman, "Iodine in Nutrition," *Journal of the American Medical Association*, Vol. 121 (February 6, 1943), p. 423.

[3] Sherman, H. C., *Chemistry of Food and Nutrition* (6th ed., 1941), p. 360.

[4] Sure, B., "Vitamin Interrelationships, III," *Journal of Nutrition*, XXVII (1944), 447–52.

[5] The tests were made on conscientious objectors; see A. Keys, A. F. Henschel, O. Mickelsen, J. M. Brozek, and J. H. Crawford, "Physiological and Biochemical Functions in Normal Young Men on a Diet restricted in Riboflavin," *Journal of Nutrition*, XXVII (1944), 165–78. Similar results were found for thiamine when the daily output was .9 mg.; see A. Keys, A. F. Henschel, O. Mickelsen, and J. M. Brozek, "The Performance of Normal Young Men on Controlled Thiamine Intakes," *Journal of Nutrition*, XXVI (1943), 399–415.

half are necessary to human beings.[6] The precise determination of our needs for these—and no doubt other yet undiscovered—nutrients lies far in the future.

Nevertheless standards of dietary adequacy have been established, perhaps prematurely and certainly very tentatively. The "allowances" (a term used to indicate their preliminary nature) of the National Research Council embody what is presumably the 1943 consensus of the experts; they are given in Table 1. Other minerals and vitamins are believed to be supplied in adequate quantities if these nutrients are secured from natural foods. The requirements are net of losses in the preparation of food. These standards are met by the minimum cost diets derived subsequently.

TABLE 1. DAILY ALLOWANCES OF NUTRIENTS FOR A MODERATELY ACTIVE MAN (weighing 154 pounds)*

Nutrient	Allowance
Calories	3,000 calories
Protein	70 grams
Calcium	.8 grams
Iron	12 milligrams
Vitamin A	5,000 International Units
Thiamine (B_1)	1.8 milligrams
Riboflavin (B_2 or G)	2.7 milligrams
Niacin (Nicotinic Acid)	18 milligrams
Ascorbic Acid (C)	75 milligrams

* National Research Council, *Recommended Dietary Allowances*, Reprint and Circular Series No. 115, January, 1943.

Nutritive Values of Foods

The minimum cost of an adequate diet is obviously governed by the nutritive values and costs of the foods eligible for inclusion. The very restricted list of foods considered in this study is discussed in Section 3 and the foods are listed in Tables A and B. It may be mentioned here that only natural foods are included; vitamin pills are excluded because they do not contain all of the nutrients (known and unknown) which are necessary to good health.[7]

The nutritive values of common foods are known only roughly,

[6] For summaries of the present knowledge, see *Yearbook of Agriculture*, 1939, Food and Life; H. C. Sherman, *Chemistry of Food and Nutrition* (6th ed., 1941).

[7] Puppies put on a diet in which the vitamins were provided from synthetic sources lived only 100 to 150 days; see J. P. Lambooy and E. S. Nasset, "The Inadequacy of Eight Synthetic B Vitamins for the Nutrition of Puppies," *Journal of Nutrition*, XXVI (1943), 293–302.

TABLE A. NUTRITIVE VALUES OF COMMON FOODS PER DOLLAR OF EXPENDITURE, AUGUST 15, 1939

Commodity	Unit	Price Aug. 15, 1939 (cents)	Edible Weight per $1.00 (grams)	Calories (1,000)	Protein (grams)	Calcium (grams)	Iron (mg.)	Vitamin A (1,000 I.U.)	Thiamine (mg.)	Ribo-flavin (mg.)	Niacin (mg.)	Ascorbic Acid (mg.)
**1. Wheat Flour (Enriched)	10 lb.	36.0	12,600	44.7	1,411	2.0	365		55.4	33.3	441	
2. Macaroni	1 lb.	14.1	3,217	11.6	418	.7	54		3.2	1.9	68	
3. Wheat Cereal (Enriched)	28 oz.	24.2	3,280	11.8	377	14.4	175		14.4	8.8	114	
4. Corn Flakes	8 oz.	7.1	3,194	11.4	252	.1	56		13.5	2.3	68	
5. Corn Meal	1 lb.	4.6	9,861	36.0	897	1.7	99	30.9	17.4	7.9	106	
6. Hominy Grits	24 oz.	8.5	8,005	28.6	680	.8	80		10.6	1.6	110	
7. Rice	1 lb.	7.5	6,048	21.2	460	.6	41		2.0	4.8	60	
8. Rolled Oats	1 lb.	7.1	6,389	25.3	907	5.1	341		37.1	8.9	64	
9. White Bread (Enriched)	1 lb.	7.9	5,742	15.0	488	2.5	115		13.8	8.5	126	
10. Whole Wheat Bread	1 lb.	9.1	4,985	12.2	484	2.7	125		13.9	6.4	160	
11. Rye Bread	1 lb.	9.2	4,930	12.4	439	1.1	82		9.9	3.0	66	
12. Pound Cake	1 lb.	24.8	1,829	8.0	130	.4	31	18.9	2.8	3.0	17	
13. Soda Crackers	1 lb.	15.1	3,004	12.5	288	.5	50					
14. Milk	1 qt.	11.0	8,867	6.1	310	10.5	18	16.8	4.0	16.0	7	177
**15. Evaporated Milk (can)	14½ oz.	6.7	6,035	8.4	422	15.1	9	26.0	3.0	23.5	11	60
16. Butter	1 lb.	30.8	1,473	10.8	9	.2	3	44.2		.2	2	
*17. Oleomargarine	1 lb.	16.1	2,817	20.6	17	.6	6	55.8	.2			
18. Eggs	1 doz.	32.6	1,857	2.9	238	1.0	52	18.6	2.8	6.5	1	
**19. Cheese (Cheddar)	1 lb.	24.2	1,874	7.4	448	16.4	19	28.1	.8	10.3	4	
20. Cream	½ pt.	14.1	1,689	3.5	49	1.7	3	16.9	.6	2.5		17
21. Peanut Butter	1 lb.	17.9	2,534	15.7	661	1.0	48		9.6	8.1	471	
22. Mayonnaise	½ pt.	16.7	1,198	8.6	18	.2	8	2.7	.4	.5		
23. Crisco	1 lb.	20.3	2,234	20.1								
24. Lard	1 lb.	9.8	4,628	41.7				.2		.5	5	
25. Sirloin Steak	1 lb.	39.6	1,145*	2.9	166	.1	34	.2	2.1	2.9	69	
26. Round Steak	1 lb.	36.4	1,246*	2.2	214	.1	32	.4	2.5	2.4	87	
27. Rib Roast	1 lb.	29.2	1,553*	3.4	213	.1	33			2.0		
28. Chuck Roast	1 lb.	22.6	2,007*	3.6	309	.2	46	.4	1.0	4.0	120	
29. Plate	1 lb.	14.6	3,107*	8.5	404	.2	62		.9			
**30. Liver (Beef)	1 lb.	26.8	1,692*	2.2	333	.2	139	169.2	6.4	50.8	316	525
31. Leg of Lamb	1 lb.	27.6	1,643*	3.1	245	.1	20		2.8	3.9	86	
32. Lamb Chops (Rib)	1 lb.	36.6	1,239*	3.3	140	.1	15		1.7	2.7	54	
33. Pork Chops	1 lb.	30.7	1,477*	3.5	196	.2	30		17.4	2.7	60	
34. Pork Loin Roast	1 lb.	24.2	1,874*	4.4	249	.3	37		18.2	3.6	79	
35. Bacon	1 lb.	25.6	1,772*	10.4	152	.2	23		1.8	1.8	71	
36. Ham—smoked	1 lb.	27.4	1,655*	6.7	212	.2	31		9.9	3.3	50	
37. Salt Pork	1 lb.	16.0	2,835*	18.8	164	.1	26		1.4	1.8		
38. Roasting Chicken	1 lb.	30.3	1,497*	1.8	184	.1	30	.1	.9	1.8	68	46
39. Veal Cutlets	1 lb.	42.3	1,072*	1.7	156	.1	24		1.4	2.4	57	
40. Salmon, Pink (can)	16 oz.	13.0	3,489	5.8	705	6.8	45	3.5	1.0	4.9	209	
41. Apples	1 lb.	4.4	9,072	5.8	27	.5	36	7.3	3.6	2.7	5	544
42. Bananas	1 lb.	6.1	4,982	4.9	60	.4	30	17.4	2.5	3.5	28	498
43. Lemons	1 doz.	26.0	2,380	1.0	21	.5	14		.5		4	952
44. Oranges	1 doz.	30.9	4,439	2.2	40	1.1	18	11.1	3.6	1.3	10	1,998
*45. Green Beans	1 lb.	7.1	5,750	2.4	138	3.7	80	69.0	4.3	5.8	37	862
**46. Cabbage	1 lb.	3.7	8,949	2.6	125	4.0	36	7.2	9.0	4.5	26	5,369
47. Carrots	1 bunch	4.7	6,080	2.7	73	2.8	43	188.5	6.1	4.3	89	608
48. Celery	1 stalk	7.3	3,915	.9	51	3.0	23	.9	1.4	1.4	9	313
49. Lettuce	1 head	8.2	2,247	.4	27	1.1	22	112.4	1.8	3.4	11	449
*50. Onions	1 lb.	3.6	11,844	5.8	166	3.8	59	16.6	4.7	5.9	21	1,184

*51. Potatoes	15 lb.	34.0	16,810	14.3	336	1.8	118	6.7	29.4	7.1	198	2,522
**52. Spinach	1 lb.	8.1	4,592	1.1	106	—	138	918.4	5.7	13.8	33	2,755
**53. Sweet Potatoes	1 lb.	5.1	7,649	9.6	138	2.7	54	290.7	8.4	5.4	83	1,912
54. Peaches (can)	No. 2½	16.8	4,894	3.7	20	.4	10	21.5	.5	1.0	31	196
55. Pears (can)	No. 2½	20.4	4,030	3.0	8	.3	8	.8	.8	.8	5	81
56. Pineapple (can)	No. 2½	21.3	3,993	2.4	16	.4	8	2.0	2.8	.8	7	399
57. Asparagus (can)	No. 2	27.7	1,945	.4	33	.3	12	16.3	1.4	2.1	17	272
58. Green Beans (can)	No. 2	10.0	5,386	1.0	54	2.0	65	53.9	1.6	4.3	32	431
59. Pork and Beans (can)	16 oz.	7.1	6,389	7.5	364	4.0	134	3.5	8.3	7.7	56	
60. Corn (can)	No. 2	10.4	5,452	5.2	136	.2	16	12.0	1.6	2.7	42	218
61. Peas (can)	No. 2	13.8	4,109	2.3	136	.6	45	34.9	4.9	2.5	37	370
62. Tomatoes (can)	No. 2	8.6	6,263	1.3	63	.7	38	53.2	3.4	2.5	36	1,253
63. Tomato Soup (can)	10½ oz.	7.6	3,917	1.6	71	.6	43	57.9	3.5	2.4	67	862
*64. Peaches, Dried	1 lb.	15.7	2,889	8.5	87	1.7	173	86.8	1.2	4.3	55	57
*65. Prunes, Dried	1 lb.	9.0	4,284	12.8	99	2.5	154	85.7	3.9	4.3	65	257
66. Raisins, Dried	15 oz.	9.4	4,524	13.5	104	2.5	136	4.5	6.3	1.4	24	136
67. Peas, Dried	1 lb.	7.9	5,742	20.0	1,367	4.2	345	2.9	28.7	18.4	162	
**68. Lima Beans, Dried	1 lb.	8.9	5,097	17.4	1,055	3.7	459	5.1	26.9	38.2	93	
**69. Navy Beans, Dried	1 lb.	5.9	7,688	26.9	1,691	11.4	792		38.4	24.6	217	
70. Coffee	1 lb.	22.4	2,025	—	—	—	—		4.0	5.1	50	
71. Tea	¼ lb.	17.4	652	—	—	—	—			2.3	42	
72. Cocoa	8 oz.	8.6	2,637	8.7	237	3.0	72		2.0	11.9	40	
73. Chocolate	8 oz.	16.2	1,400	8.0	77	1.3	39		.9	3.4	14	
74. Sugar	10 lb.	51.7	8,773	34.9	—	—	—					
75. Corn Sirup	24 oz.	13.7	4,966	14.7	—	.5	74				5	
76. Molasses	18 oz.	13.6	3,752	9.0	—	10.3	244		1.9	7.5	146	
77. Strawberry Preserves	1 lb.	20.5	2,213	6.4	11	.4	7	.2	.2	.4	3	

* Quantities including inedible portions.

TABLE B. NUTRITIVE VALUES OF COMMON FOODS PER DOLLAR OF EXPENDITURE, AUGUST 15, 1944

Commodity	Price Aug. 15, 1944 (cents)	Calories (1,000)	Protein (grams)	Calcium (grams)	Iron (mg.)	Vitamin A (1,000 I.U.)	Thiamine (mg.)	Riboflavin (mg.)	Niacin (mg.)	Ascorbic Acid (mg.)
1. Wheat Flour	64.6	24.9	786	1.1	203		30.9	18.6	246	
3. Wheat Cereal	23.2	12.3	398	15.0	183		15.0	9.2	119	
5. Corn Meal	6.3	26.3	655	1.2	72	22.6	12.7	5.8	77	
8. Rolled Oats	9.9	18.1	651	3.7	245		26.6	6.4	46	
15. Evaporated Milk	10.0	5.6	283	10.1	6	17.4	2.0	15.7	7	40
46. Cabbage	4.9	2.0	94	3.0	27	5.4	6.8	3.4	20	4,054
51. Potatoes	80.1	6.1	143	.8	50	2.8	12.5	3.0	84	1,071
52. Spinach	11.6	.8	74	—	96	641.3	4.0	9.6	23	1,924
53. Sweet Potatoes	12.3	4.0	57	1.1	22	120.5	3.5	2.2	34	793
69. Navy Beans	10.8	14.7	924	6.2	433		21.0	13.4	119	
74. Sugar	67.0	26.9	—	—	—					
78. Pancake Flour[1]	12.2	16.0	479	18.1	46		3.7	1.9	41	
79. Beets[2]	7.3	2.2	85	1.1	70	132.3	2.9	6.3	29	895
80. Liver (Pork)[3]	21.9	2.7	408	.2	518	145.0	10.4	51.8	472	580

[1] Unit: 20 oz.; edible weight: 4,647 g. [2] Unit: 1 bunch; edible weight: 4,971 g. [3] Unit: 1 lb.; edible weight: 2,071 g.

and indeed they *can* be known only roughly. A large margin of uncertainty arises on several scores:

1. Many nutritive values have not been established quantitatively, or have been determined by obsolete and inaccurate techniques, or the determinations have large standard errors. Beef flank is known to contain the B complex, but the quantities are unknown. Vitamin A is measured by the rate of growth of rats, with standard errors averaging 10 or 15 percent of the mean values.
2. Most foods are not even approximately homogeneous, and wide ranges of nutritive values are found. For example, the milligrams of ascorbic acid in 100 grams of apples varies as follows with variety:[8]

Jonathan	4.4
McIntosh	2.0
Northern Spy	11.0
Ontario	20.8
Winesap	5.8
Winter Banana	6.6

   Again, the ascorbic acid in milk varies with the season.
3. The maturity of the product, the length and conditions of storage, temperature, and similar factors are important. The ascorbic acid decreases with the maturing of corn, but the vitamin A content increases. Vitamin A, thiamine, and ascorbic acid are often lost during storage.
4. Even when the nutritive values of the food are known, they are much affected by the way the food is prepared. Well-done rib roasts of beef have 69 percent of the thiamine, 77 percent of the riboflavin, and 79 percent of the niacin present in the raw cuts. Cabbage has a high ascorbic acid content, but if it is boiled for several hours and the liquid discarded, virtually none of the vitamin survives. On the other hand the vitamin A in turnip greens is increased by cooking.
5. The proportion of food wasted is an additional unknown in the evaluation of ordinary diets.[9]
6. The nutrients in foods cannot be wholly extracted. Spinach contains much calcium but it is not nutritionally available because of the presence of oxalic acid.

Enough difficulties have been indicated to suggest the almost infinite complexity of a refined and accurate assessment of nutritive value of a diet.

[8] On this and subsequent points, see L. E. Booher, E. R. Hartzler, and E. M. Hewston, *A Compilation of the Vitamin Values of Foods in Relation to Processing and Other Variants*, Department of Agriculture, Circular 638 (May 1942); and G. Adams and S. L. Smith, *The Vitamin Content and the Preservation of Foods*, Department of Agriculture, Miscell. Public. No. 536 (1944).

[9] Another difficulty that may be mentioned in this connection is the variation in the quantity of food received for a given price, as when oranges are purchased by the dozen and celery by the stalk.

In the subsequent work, I use C. Chatfield and G. Adams' *Proximate Composition of American Food Materials* for estimates of inedible refuse, calories, and protein.[10] The data on minerals and vitamins are from the unusually complete summary by A. D. Bowes and C. F. Church, *Food Values of Portions Commonly Used.*[11] In light of the foregoing remarks it should not be necessary to belabor the tentativeness of the figures.

The average nutritive values used are those of the foods as purchased. The losses due to waste and faulty preparation are ignored, as in most diet appraisals,[12] in part for the common reason that virtually nothing is known about the extent of these losses. But there is also the reason that these losses are largely avoidable, and a person who wished to minimize the cost of his food could reduce them to inappreciable amounts.

Methodology

The first step is to select a list of potential commodities; obviously the wider this list the lower the cost of the "adequate" diet will probably be. The list here chosen consists of the commodities for which retail prices are reported by the Bureau of Labor Statistics.[13] The list is reproduced in Table A, along with the nutritive values of one dollar's expenditures on each commodity.

The BLS list is a short one, and it excludes almost all fresh fruits, nuts, many cheap vegetables rich in nutrients, and fresh fish. It is beyond question that with a fuller list the minimum cost of meeting the National Research Council's allowances could be reduced, possibly by a substantial amount.[14]

Since the prices are averages of many (large) cities, the minimum cost diet will in principle be affected by seasonal price patterns and should be computed separately for each month. This effect will not prove to be great because seasonal foods play little

---

[10] Department of Agriculture, Circular 549, June 1940.

[11] Privately printed, Philadelphia (5th ed., 1944).

[12] *Diets of Families of Employed Wage Earners and Clerical Workers in Cities*, Department of Agriculture, Circular 507, January 1939; *Family Food Consumption and Dietary Levels*, Department of Agriculture, Miscellaneous Publication 405, 1941.

[13] The commodities are described in *Retail Prices of Food*, 1923–36, Bureau of Labor Statistics, Bulletin 635, October 1937. The price quotations are averages of 51 large cities in 1939 and 56 cities in 1944; they were taken from the *Monthly Labor Review*, October 1939 and December 1944.

[14] A physiological chemist to whom I showed the diets recommended in turn a mixture he fed to rats, which would (in 1945) cost a man about $27 a year.

part in the minimum cost diet.[15] It may be noted also that since the prices are averages, they overstate the cost for a representative city because a food with lower-than-average price can be exploited and a food with higher-than-average price curtailed.

As a first step in finding the minimum cost diet, one may exclude any commodity all of whose nutritive values (per dollar of expenditure) are less than those of some other commodity. This procedure is carried a trifle farther in practice, by excluding also a commodity which is definitely inferior to another in its important nutrients and only slightly superior in others. For example, white bread (commodity no. 9) has less than half the nutrients (per dollar) of white flour (commodity no. 1) except for calcium, for which neither commodity is an economical source. This preliminary weeding reduces the list of eligible foods from 77 to 15, and excludes all meats except liver, all sugars, beverages, and patented cereals. The survivors are starred in Table A.

Thereafter the procedure is experimental because there does not appear to be any direct method of finding the minimum of a linear function subject to linear conditions. By making linear combinations of various commodities it is possible to construct a composite commodity which is superior in all respects to some survivor, and by this process the list of eligible commodities can be reduced at least to 9 (which are double starred in Table A). The nutritive values of each of these commodities is then expressed in terms of days' supply of requirements. Various combinations of commodities were used to fulfill certain nutrient requirements,[16] and the one finally chosen is presented in Section 4. There is no reason to believe that the cheapest combination was found, for only a handful of the 510 possible combinations of commodities were examined.[17] On the other hand the annual cost could not have been reduced by more than a few dollars by a better selection from these commodities.[18]

---

[15] Although it is possible that if the diets had been constructed with prices for some other month, other foods would have been chosen.

[16] An excess of calories is objectionable, but there is no reason to expect ill effects of moderately excessive intakes of the other nutrients. In the test of various combinations of foods, those nutrients (in addition to calories) which would, if fulfilled, necessarily imply fulfillment of other nutrient conditions were used in the algebraic solution.

[17] As a matter of fact, each of these combinations will have a different cost with each set of linear (nutrient) conditions, and there are many such nutrient conditions because excesses are in general unobjectionable.

[18] The nutrient with the highest cost (when secured from its most economical

The derivation of the minimum cost budget for 1944 follows the same procedure.[19] The surviving commodities surviving the first test are reproduced in Table B.[20] Because of computational limitations, fewer trial combinations were investigated but again no large reduction in cost is possible by further search.

It should be added that the content of a diet can be altered substantially without affecting its cost appreciably. In the process of finding the 1939 minimum cost budget several alternative budgets of only slightly higher costs were found among the most preferable commodities.[21] It also appears reasonable to suppose that the number of commodities could be increased materially without increasing much the cost of the diet, although the laborious calculations necessary to illustrate this were not undertaken.

The Minimum Cost Diets

The minimum cost diets for August 1939 and August 1944 are given in Table 2, and their nutritive values are compared with the National Research Council's allowances in Table 3. Consideration

TABLE 2. MINIMUM COST ANNUAL DIETS, AUGUST 1939 AND 1944

Commodity	August 1939		August 1944	
	Quantity	Cost	Quantity	Cost
Wheat Flour	370 lb.	$13.33	535 lb.	$34.53
Evaporated Milk	57 cans	3.84	—	—
Cabbage	111 lb.	4.11	107 lb.	5.23
Spinach	23 lb.	1.85	13 lb.	1.56
Dried Navy Beans	285 lb.	16.80	—	—
Pancake Flour	—	—	134 lb.	13.08
Pork Liver	—	—	25 lb.	5.48
Total Cost		$39.93		$59.88

source) is calories; it would require $24.50 to supply for a year the calories from flour (commodity no. 1). But then only 61 days' calcium would be provided, and the most efficient source (cheese, no. 19) could meet the deficiency only at a cost of $14.90, and the contribution to calories would be relatively small. The requirements for vitamin A and ascorbic acid would still be unfilled. Use of other commodities for calories yields a similar conclusion.

[19] The corresponding table of nutritive values can of course be secured simply by multiplying the entries in Table A by the ratio of 1939 to 1944 prices.

[20] It will be observed that three new commodities are added to the list. The BLS abandoned price quotations on 19 commodities in Table A (including one starred commodity, dried lima beans), and 12 new commodities were examined in making Table B.

[21] The minimum cost diet for 1939, which differs greatly from that for 1944, would have cost only 13 percent more than the latter in 1944.

of the lists in Table 2 will suggest reasons in addition to those given in the preceding sections for not recommending the diets.

The cost of the minimum cost diet rose exactly 50 percent from 1939 to 1944; the cost of food in the BLS index of retail prices of food rose 47 percent in the same period. The fact that the minimum cost diet, with its variable composition, increased slightly more than the (relatively) fixed-composition index of the BLS, is indicative of the fact (which the detailed data confirm) that the more efficient food sources rose relatively more in price.

TABLE 3. ADEQUACY OF MINIMUM COST DIETS, AUGUST 1939 AND 1944

Nutrient	Percent of Year's Allowance*	
	August 1939	August 1944
Calories	100	100
Protein	194	141
Calcium	100	100
Iron	425	245
Vitamin A	100	100
Thiamine	220	185
Riboflavin	100	100
Niacin	148	179
Ascorbic Acid	100	100

* The allowances are given in Table 1.

In this connection it is interesting to notice that the quantity of wheat flour is increased substantially between the two dates, although its price rose more than other eligible cereals. This is an artificial example of the Giffen paradox, that

a rise in the price of bread makes so large a drain on the resources of the poorer labouring families and raises so much the marginal utility of money to them, that they are forced to curtail their consumption of meat and the more expensive farinaceous foods; . . .[22]

The purpose of the determination of the minimum cost diet will be explained in the next section, but in the light of comments of friends a few remarks (which are really a digression) may be added here. It is usually objected that relative prices would change if the commodities in Table 2 became the sole objects of demand. No one recommends these diets for anyone, let alone everyone; it would be the height of absurdity to practice extreme economy at the dinner table in order to have an excess of housing or recreation or

[22] Marshall, A., *Principles of Economics* (8th ed.), p. 132.

leisure. Waiving this point, all dietary studies accept the prices paid by consumers since these are the conditions of purchase which face the individual buyer. Moreover, any sensible system of prices will lead to similar results. If a society were so misguided as to adopt a minimum diet, it cannot be doubted that the prices of the commodities would fall once agriculture, transportation, food processing, and distributive industries were readjusted to this reduced task.

Comparison with Other Diets

It would no doubt be possible to cull from the literature a very large number of absurd estimates of the minimum cost of subsistence. Instead, I shall list a few restrained estimates by competent dieticians:

1. In 1936 Carpenter and Stiebeling described a minimum cost diet which "gives the cheapest combination of foods that it is desirable to use for an indefinite period," which cost (in 1935) about $125 a person.[23] (It would have cost about $100 in 1939.) A restricted diet for emergency use was also given; it cost $83 in 1935.
2. In 1939 Stiebeling and Clark estimated the cost of an "economical fair diet," as they unenthusiastically described it, at $78 to $104 per person in villages and cities. If the recommended classes of commodities are chosen from the BLS list, the 1939 cost would be about $94 and the 1944 cost about $138. This was explicitly stated not to be a minimum diet, but it was implied that much less was not tolerable.[24]
3. M. S. Rose presented an unqualifiedly minimum diet which would have cost about $115 in 1939.[25]

These low-cost diets of the professional dieticians thus cost about two or three times as much as a minimum cost diet.

Why do these conventional diets cost so much? The answer is evident from their composition. The dieticians take account of the palatability of foods, variety of diet, prestige of various foods, and other cultural facets of consumption. Primarily on such grounds

[23] *Diets to Fit the Family Income*, Department of Agriculture, Farmer's Bulletin No. 1757 (1936), p. 10.

[24] *Yearbook of Agriculture*, 1939, p. 333: The diet is for families "in straightened circumstances"; it covers "average minimum requirements but does not afford as wide a margin of safety as desirable. . . . "

[25] *Foundations of Nutrition* (1935), p. 472.

can one explain their emphasis on meats and the inclusion of sugar.[26]

There are two fundamental objections to so merging the physiological and the cultural components of diet. The first is that the particular judgments of the dieticians as to minimum palatability, variety, and prestige are at present highly personal and non-scientific, and should not be presented in the guise of being parts of a scientifically-determined budget. The second reason is that these cultural judgments, while they appear modest enough to government employees and even to college professors, can never be valid in such a general form. No one can now say with any certainty what the cultural requirements of a particular person may be, and on its face it will always be impossible to determine a unique cultural minimum diet for 140 million Americans of transcendental variety of background, social position, and cultural values. If the dieticians persist in presenting minimum diets, they should at least report separately the physical and cultural components of these diets.

---

[26] Tax-supported bureaucrats and professors may also have another reason for certain of their practices.

[8]

THE KINKY OLIGOPOLY DEMAND CURVE AND RIGID PRICES

GEORGE J. STIGLER

JUST before World War II, the theory was advanced that there exists a kink in the demand curve for the product of an oligopolist and that this kink goes far to explain observed price rigidities in oligopolistic industries. The theory has rapidly gained wide acceptance: many economists give it some place in their theoretical system, and some economists make it *the* theory of oligopoly price.

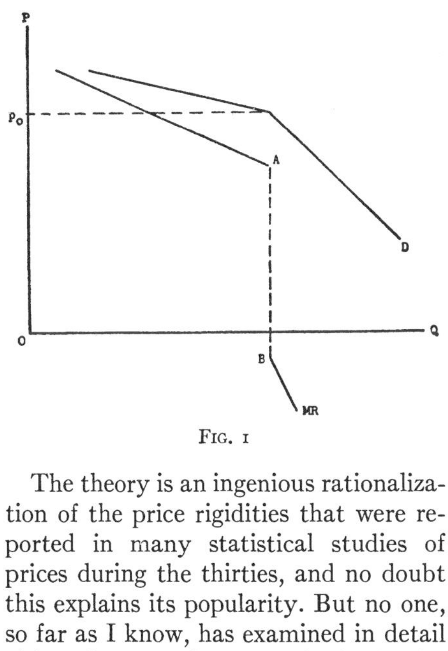

FIG. 1

The theory is an ingenious rationalization of the price rigidities that were reported in many statistical studies of prices during the thirties, and no doubt this explains its popularity. But no one, so far as I know, has examined in detail either the pure theory of the kinky demand curve or the degree of correspondence between the price patterns implied by the theory and the observed price patterns in oligopolistic industries. These two tasks will be undertaken in Parts I and II, respectively, of this paper.

I. THE FORMAL THEORY

1. THE RECEIVED THEORY

The theory of the kinky demand curve was advanced independently and almost simultaneously by R. L. Hall and C. J. Hitch in England and Paul M. Sweezy in America.[1] The latter's version will be summarized first.

THE SWEEZY VERSION

The market situation contemplated by Sweezy is one in which rivals will quickly match price reductions but only hesitantly and incompletely (if at all) follow price increases. This pattern of expected behavior produces a kink at the existing price (= p_0 in Fig. 1) in the demand curve for the product of an oligopolist,[2] and the corresponding marginal revenue curve will possess a discontinuity the length of which is proportional to the difference between the slopes of the upper and lower segments of the demand curve

[1] Hall and Hitch, "Price Theory and Business Behavior," *Oxford Economic Papers*, No. 2 (May, 1939), pp. 12–45; and Sweezy, "Demand under Conditions of Oligopoly," *Journal of Political Economy*, XLVII (August, 1939), 568–73.

[2] The demand curve for the product of an oligopolist can be defined only if the reactions of rivals to price changes are known. The upper branch of the demand curve in Fig. 1 represents the quantities that consumers will buy from one oligopolist at various prices if rival producers set a price of p_0; the lower branch represents the quantities that consumers will buy if the rivals charge identical prices. This demand curve is objective in the sense that it is consistent with the facts of the market if rivals behave in the specified manner. Sweezy appears to view it as subjective because it is based upon beliefs concerning rivals' price reactions which may have to be revised (although no occasions for revision of beliefs are treated in his article).

at the kink.[3] Sweezy assumes that "the marginal cost curve passes between the two parts of the marginal revenue curve," so that fluctuations in marginal cost are not likely to affect output and price.

He considers also two other possibilities. An oligopolist may believe that secret price cuts will remain secret, in which case the demand curve becomes elastic throughout and the kink disappears. Or the oligopolist may be a price leader, so that price increases will be followed and the kink again disappears.[4]

Sweezy assumes that shifts in demand will not affect the price at which the kink occurs and argues that the results of increases and decreases of demand are asymmetrical:

1. An increase of demand will make the demand curve less elastic in its upper branch, since rivals are operating closer to capacity,[5] and more elastic in the lower branch because rivals "are less worried about losses in [of?] business." If marginal costs are also shifting upward as demand increases, "an increase in demand is more likely to lead to a price increase than to a price cut."

2. A decrease in demand will have the converse effects—increased elasticity of the upper branch and decreased elasticity of the lower branch—so the discontinuity of marginal revenue will be increased and the oligopolists will be "more anxious than ever" to hold to the existing price.

Except where price leaders exist or secret price concessions are possible, therefore, oligopoly price may rise in good times and will not be reduced in bad times.[6]

THE OXFORD VERSION

Hall and Hitch conclude, after reporting interviews with some thirty-eight entrepreneurs on price policy, that businessmen seek prices that cover average cost, regardless of marginal revenue and marginal cost (which they seldom know).[7] This "full-cost" principle is apparently the result of tacit or open collusion, consideration of long-run demand and costs, moral conviction of fairness, and uncertainty of effects of price increases and decreases.[8] The particular results of the interviews need not be discussed here.[9]

[3] With reference to Fig. 1, if $f(x)$ is the demand curve, x_0 the output at the kink, and subscripts 1 and 2 refer to the upper and lower segments of the demand curve respectively,

$$A - B = x_0[f'(x_0 - O) - f'(x_0 + O)]$$
$$= p_0\left(\frac{1}{\eta_1} - \frac{1}{\eta_2}\right).$$

[4] These possibilities, which are obviously mutually exclusive, are illustrated in the same diagram (Sweezy, *op. cit.*, p. 571, Fig. 2). If the upper branch (for the price leader) and the lower branch (for the secret price cutter) were nevertheless joined, the resulting marginal revenue curve would again be discontinuous, but then maximum profits would never be secured at the price at which the kink arises.

[5] *Ibid.*, p. 571. Presumably the rivals' higher rates of production lead them to follow the price increase (although this reaction causes trouble; see below), or, if they maintain prices, the buyers are rationed.

[6] The implications of Sweezy's theory for price rigidity were emphasized by M. Bronfenbrenner in "Applications of the Discontinuous Oligopoly Demand Curve," *Journal of Political Economy*, XLVIII (1940), 420–27.

[7] The treatment of entrepreneurial knowledge is contradictory. On the one hand, Hall and Hitch state that "most of our informants were vague about anything so precise as elasticity. . . . . In addition, many, perhaps most, apparently made no effort, even implicitly, to estimate elasticities of demand . . . . and of those who do, the majority considered the information of little or no relevance to the pricing process save perhaps in very exceptional conditions" (Hall and Hitch, *op. cit.*, p. 18). But, on the other hand, a majority of the entrepreneurs believed that price cuts would be matched and price increases would not be matched by rivals (*ibid.*, p. 21, Tables 3 and 4) so they did act rationally on marginal principles (within a certain framework).

[8] Several of these factors contradict the existence of a kink in the demand curve.

[9] The questioning was not persistent and resourceful, nor were ambiguous answers clarified;

The entrepreneur therefore sets a price that covers average cost (including "profits") at the expected or some conventional output (see Fig. 2). Increases or decreases of demand will usually shift the kink to the right or left and leave price unchanged, but there are two exceptions to this rule:

1. If the demand decreases greatly and remains small for some time, the price is likely to be cut in the hope of maintaining output. The chief explanation for this

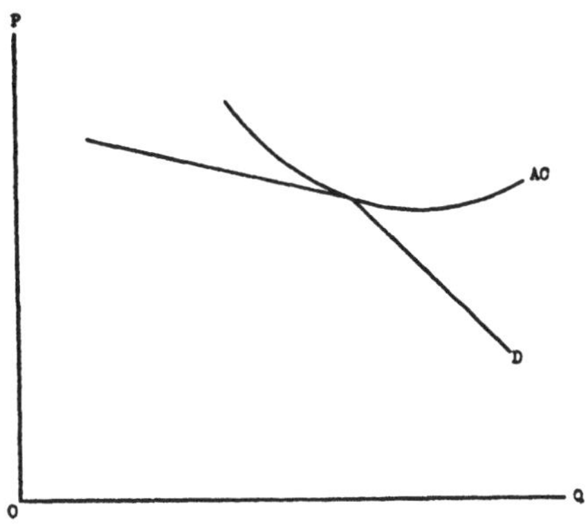

Fig. 2

price cut is that one rival becomes panicky and his irrational behavior forces the others to cut prices.

2. If the average cost curves of all firms shift by similar amounts, due perhaps to changes in factor prices or technology, this is "likely to lead to a revaluation of the 'full cost' price" (*ibid.*, p. 25). However, ". . . . there will be no tendency for [prices] to fall or rise more than the wage and raw material costs" (*ibid.*, p. 32).

The full-cost principle would suggest also that prices will vary inversely with output, i.e., that high prices are necessary to cover the high average costs of small outputs. This price pattern is not followed, apparently, because the oligopolists (1) place a value on price stability, (2) are influenced by the kink, and (3) wish to "keep plant running as full as possible, giving rise to a general feeling in favour of price concessions."[10]

for example, three entrepreneurs did not charge more than average cost because "buyers technically informed about costs" (*ibid.*, p. 21). Does this mean that buyers would otherwise enter into production of the article? Why was the same answer not given for unwillingness to sell below cost?

COMPARISON OF THE VERSIONS

The Sweezy version is a consistent application of the kinky demand curve to price determination, without conflicting principles to modify its workings. The Oxford version embraces also the "full-cost" principle (and apparently also the "large-output" principle), although the possibilities of conflict between the two are manifold. Hall and Hitch resolve some of the conflicts by abandoning the kink (e.g., when prices follow production costs) and some by abandoning the "full-cost" principle (e.g., when entrepreneurs do not raise prices in depression). They take no account of the difficulties raised by differences among the average costs of various oligopolists or of many other troublesome features of the "full-cost" principle. Their thesis that the kink follows changes in wage rates and material prices implies a degree of collusion—or at least such beautiful rapport—among the oligopolists that it is hard to see why a kink should appear at all (see below). Their fluid version can explain any pattern of prices, and therefore forecast none, and accordingly I shall henceforth devote primary attention to the Sweezy version.

2. ELABORATION OF THE THEORY

The discussions of the kinky demand curve have been rather laconic. Certain implications of the theory must be elaborated in order to derive specific price patterns for the subsequent empirical tests.

[10] *Ibid.*, p. 28.

THE LENGTH OF THE DISCONTINUITY IN MARGINAL REVENUE

The length of the discontinuity in marginal revenue is proportional to the difference between the slopes of the demand curve on the two sides of the kink. The longer this discontinuity, the greater the fluctuations in marginal cost (and in demand, if the kink stays at the same price) that are compatible with price stability and therefore the greater the probability of rigid prices in any interval of time. Some of the factors that affect the length of this discontinuity are:

a) The number of rivals (of a given degree of closeness, measured by the cross-elasticity of demand).—We should expect that a price increase is more likely to be followed if there are few rivals than if there are many, because the rivals will realize that the temporary gains from holding down their prices will soon be erased. If this is so, the discontinuity will be short (in time) or nonexistent when there are few rivals. The larger the number of rivals, the less likely are they to follow one oligopolist's price increases; on the other hand, the less likely are they also to match his price reductions, at least immediately. It seems probable, therefore, that the discontinuity is longest with an intermediate number of rivals, say, five to ten.

b) The relative size of rivals (of a given degree of closeness).—When one firm (or an inner clique) is dominant in size, it will presumably be the price leader. When this firm increases its price, rivals are likely to follow (for individually they can sell as much as they wish at the ruling price); when the firm cuts prices the rivals must follow. Hence the dominant firm will have no kink in its demand curve. The smaller firms cannot raise their prices above the leader's unless he is rationing buyers but can shade prices without being followed immediately or perhaps at all.[11] Again there will be no kink.

c) The differences among the rivals' products.—The discontinuity will be longer, the more homogeneous the products, because customers will shift more rapidly to the low-price firm.

d) The extent of collusion.—Should explicit collusion replace the stand-offish attitude visualized by the theory, the kink will vanish; there is no kink in a monopolist's demand curve.

Other factors affecting the length of the discontinuity in marginal revenue could be mentioned, for example, the number of buyers.[12] But these factors do

[11] These conclusions can also be reached by a more mechanical application of kink theory. A rise of the dominant firm's price will so increase the demand of each small firm that marginal cost will intersect marginal revenue at an output less than that at which the kink occurs, so the small firm will also increase price. A reduction in price by a small firm will decrease the demand for the output of the dominant firm by so small an amount that probably no price change will be induced.

[12] Fewness of buyers is difficult to fit into the kink theory. If few buyers face a competitive supply, each will presumably believe that, if he raises his buying price, rivals will follow and the quantity supplied to him will not increase much; and, if he lowers his buying price, rivals will not follow and the quantity supplied to him will decrease greatly. Hence there will be a kink in the supply curve to the firm (which is illustrated by Bronfenbrenner, *op. cit.*). Combining this with oligopoly of sellers, presumably both supply and demand curves have a kink at the same price, which will be especially rigid.

But the whole argument is very elusive. If one buyer offered a higher price to a seller who assumed that his rivals would not follow a price increase, the seller would of course offer his entire output to the buyer, whose supply curve might therefore be extremely elastic for higher prices—the opposite of the above argument. And, conversely, if one seller offered a lower price to one buyer, who assumed that his rivals would be unwilling to reduce their buying prices, the buyer would snatch at the bargain so the seller's demand curve would be elastic for lower prices—again the opposite of the above argument. The difficulty is that the assumptions are inconsistent: if sellers believe that price reductions will be matched but price increases will not be matched and buyers believe the opposite, someone is likely to be wrong.

not lend themselves to the type of empirical tests that will be employed in Part II and will not be discussed.

THE WORKINGS OF THE KINK

In order to study the workings of the kinky demand curve, let us consider two producers (of equal size) of similar, but not identical, commodities. The initial demand and marginal revenue curves of duopolist A are given in Figure 3; they are denoted by the subscript 1. Assume now that the aggregate demand for the two commodities increases so that A's demand curve shifts to D_2, but marginal

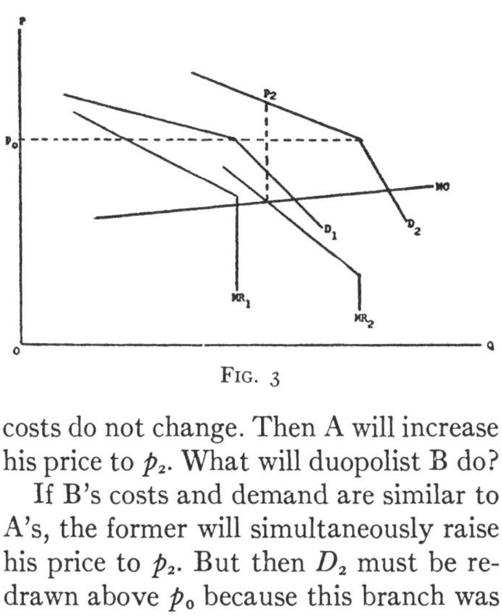

FIG. 3

costs do not change. Then A will increase his price to p_2. What will duopolist B do?

If B's costs and demand are similar to A's, the former will simultaneously raise his price to p_2. But then D_2 must be redrawn above p_0 because this branch was drawn on the assumption that the rival's price was p_0. The situation becomes classical duopoly—with the usual wide range of possible patterns of behavior. It would be foolish to put a new kink in D_2 (as redrawn) at the level p_2. Experience has shown that the rival will follow a price increase, and businessmen will learn from this experience that there is no kink.

On the other hand, B may still find it profitable to stay at price p_0. But then his demand curve must shift to the right, for it was drawn on the assumption that A set a price of p_0 or less. If this demand shift leads B to set a new price, then A's demand curve must be redrawn. Again the existence of the kink is contradicted by experience.

The theory of the kinky demand curve explains why prices that have been stable should continue to be stable despite certain changes in demand or costs. But the theory does not explain why prices that have once changed should settle down, again acquire stability, and gradually produce a new kink. One possible explanation might be that a period of stability of demand and costs has created a tradition of stable prices, so that, when demand or cost conditions change materially, the kink has emerged to preserve price stability.

OTHER KINKS AND DISCONTINUITIES

For present purposes it is not necessary to discuss additional implications of the theory of kinky demand curves, but two are of sufficient interest to deserve brief mention.

The pattern of oligopolistic behavior underlying the kinky demand curve will also produce a discontinuous marginal cost curve. If one firm reduces its wage rate, for example, other firms will not follow, but these other firms will match wage increases. At the output corresponding to this input kink, there will be a discontinuity in marginal cost. A good part of the appeal of the kinky demand curve theory is that it is easy to draw demand and cost curves that lead to price stability. This appeal is definitely weakened if the marginal cost curve is also discontinuous, as the reader can readily verify.

The same general line of reasoning leads to kinks in the curves of other variables of policy—advertising, quality changes, etc. Indeed, the logic of the theory requires only that there be one variable—output—against which the discontinuities in the other variables may be displayed.

3. ALTERNATIVE THEORIES OF PRICE STABILITY

Explanations of price stability are not common or prominent in the neoclassical price theory of Marshall's era. (Part II of this paper contains some evidence that bears on the question whether this is a cause for commendation or condemnation.) Of course it would be a grotesque caricature to describe this theory as requiring a change of price in response to every quiver of the demand or the cost curve. Three factors making for price stability were generally incorporated (without emphasis) into the neoclassical theory.

LONG-RUN CONSIDERATIONS

In the long run the demand curve is usually more elastic because buyers can make changes in technology, commitments, and habits that permit use of substitutes and because new rivals will be attracted at certain prices. Therefore an exorbitant current price may lose more (discounted) revenue in the future than it adds in the present. This type of consideration argues against raising prices greatly in short-run periods of inelastic demand but does not imply price rigidity.[13]

ADMINISTRATIVE WEAKNESSES IN COLLUSION

When a group of producers arrives at a mutually agreeable or tolerable price by collusion, this price will have a strong tendency to persist. When some of the firms will be injured by a price change (which must often occur when their costs, market areas, and product structures differ), they will naturally oppose change. When all will gain from a price change, they will usually wish different amounts of change. Opening the question of prices may therefore lead to a pitched battle, and one can seldom be sure that things will stay in hand. Frequent resort to this area of political-economic determination must be avoided, so changes are postponed as long as possible. If they are postponed long enough, the need for them will pass.

COST OF PRICE CHANGES

The nature of the product and market may be such that small or frequent price changes cost more than they yield. There are costs of informing buyers of price changes: new lists, advertising, etc. If long-term contracts contain provisions that the buyer will receive any price reductions during the life of the contract, the short-run marginal revenue from a price reduction may be small or negative. Even when there are no contracts, price reductions may incur the ill will of early buyers of a "style" good.

4. A COMPARISON OF THE IMPLICATIONS OF THE THEORIES OF PRICE STABILITY

There is no reason why the kinky demand curve cannot be joined with the other explanations of price stability. But there is also no purpose in adding it to the neoclassical theory unless it explains price behavior in areas where the other explanation is silent or contradicts the implications of the neoclassical theory in areas where both apply. For the empirical tests in Part II, the following differences between the implications of the kinky demand curve and the neoclassical theory will be used:

a) The kinky demand curve theory is silent on monopolies, for the essential

[13] Marshall also had the doctrine that prices will not fall to prime costs in depression because of a fear of "spoiling the market" (*Principles of Economics* [8th ed.; London: Macmillan & Co., 1920], pp. 374–76). He apparently assumed, in addition to oligopoly, that the long-run demand curve was inelastic for price reductions.

feature of retaliation by rivals is absent. Should monopoly prices be rigid, the forces that explain this rigidity (say cost of price changes) may suffice to explain an equal amount of price rigidity under oligopoly. Unless the factors making for monopoly price rigidity do not operate under oligopoly, we can dispense with the kink unless greater rigidity is found in the oligopolistic industries.

b) The discontinuity in marginal revenue will disappear, and with it the reason for price rigidity, if formerly independent firms enter into collusion. The neoclassical theory emphasizes the administrative weaknesses in collusion, on the other hand, and this argues for greater price rigidity.

c) Prices will be relatively flexible with very few and with many firms in the industry, and relatively rigid with a moderate number of firms (say, five to ten), according to the kink theory. The neoclassical theories of oligopoly are neither outspoken nor unanimous on this question, but there is a general suggestion that price flexibility increases continuously with the number of firms.

d) When there is a dominant firm or set of firms (acting together) in the role of price leader, prices should be more flexible than if there is no price leader, on the kink theory. The neoclassical theory is silent on this point.

e) Given the number and size configuration of firms, prices should be more flexible the more heterogeneous the products, under the kinky demand curve theory. The neoclassical theory has no such implication.

II. Empirical Tests of the Theory

One may submit to empirical tests either the assumption of entrepreneurial behavior underlying the theory of the kinky demand curve or the implications of the kink for price behavior. The former alternative requires an analysis of the sequence of price changes made by oligopolists in an industry; the latter alternative can be developed by a comparison of observed price rigidity with that prophesied by the theory.

1. THE VALIDITY OF THE ASSUMPTION

If price increases of one firm are not followed by rivals, but price reductions are followed, the oligopolists have a basis in experience for believing that there is a kink in their demand curves. If price reductions are not followed by rivals, or price increases are as closely followed, no such objective basis for a kink exists.

The cigarette industry (with three large firms) offers a good example of the type of experience that would create a belief in the existence of a kink. On September 28, 1918, the American Tobacco Company raised the list price of Lucky Strikes from $6.00 to $7.50 per thousand, but the rivals continued to charge the lower price. The sales of Lucky Strikes fell 31 per cent from September to November, when the price was reduced to $6.00, and continued to decline for several months.[14] The later price history in this industry, however, is not such as to create a belief in the existence of a kink:

April 20, 1928: Reynolds (Camels) announced a reduction from $6.40 to $6 per thousand, effective April 21. American Tobacco followed on April 21 and Liggett and Myers on April 23.

October 4, 1929: Reynolds announced an increase to $6.40, effective October 5, and both rivals followed on that day.

June 23, 1931: Reynolds announced an increase to $6.85, effective June 24, and both rivals followed that day.

January 1, 1933: American Tobacco reduced its price to $6, effective January 3, and both rivals followed that day.

February 11, 1933: American Tobacco re-

[14] This episode is reported in detail in the forthcoming study of the American tobacco industry by William H. Nicholls.

duced its price to $5.50, and both rivals followed the same day.

January 9, 1934: Reynolds increased its price to $6.10, and both rivals followed the same day.[15]

These price changes, incidentally, were relatively larger than they appear: the manufacturer's net was smaller by a three-dollar tax and trade discounts.

The more complicated pattern of price changes for automobiles is illustrated for two leading firms in Figure 4. The prices of the two firms changed at different dates and by different amounts, and price increases were more nearly simultaneous than price reductions. Price experience in this field should not lead a firm to believe that price reductions will be matched immediately or wholly nor that in a period of business recovery rivals will fail to increase prices.

[15] Federal Trade Commission, *Agricultural Income Inquiry* (Washington, 1937), I, 448. The history of prices after 1934 follows essentially the same pattern, although Nicholls reports an unmatched and unsuccessful price increase by Liggett and Myers on July 30, 1946—followed by a general increase on October 14, 1946, with American Tobacco the price leader.

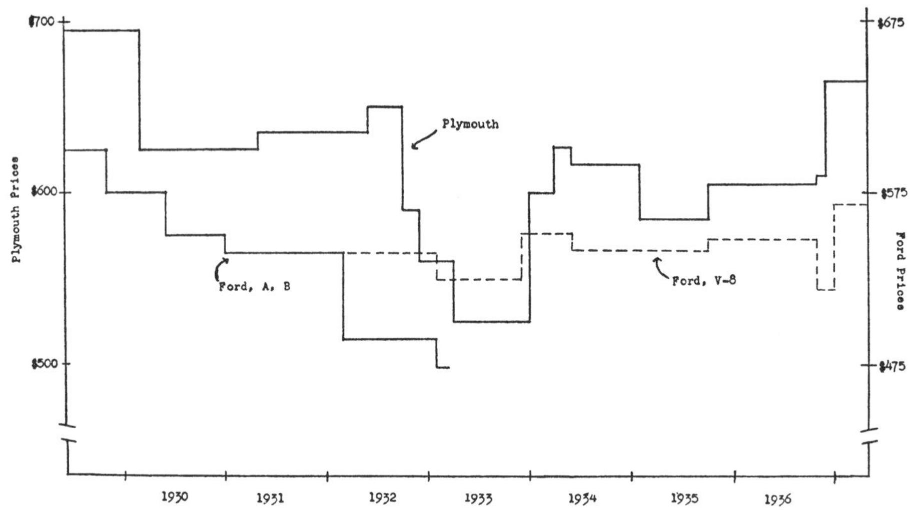

FIG. 4.—Factory prices of Plymouth and Ford four-door sedans, June, 1929—May, 1937. Source: Federal Trade Commission, *Report on Motor Vehicle Industry* (76th Cong., 1st sess., House Doc. 468 [Washington, 1940]), pp. 894–95, 896.

Six anthracite companies produced 62.5 per cent of the aggregate output in 1930, and eight companies usually produce 70 to 80 per cent of aggregate output.[16] The prices of seven companies, for each size of coal, are listed (in very large type) every week in the *Coal and Coal Trade Journal*. These prices are identical and they almost invariably change on the same day.[17] There is no evidence of a kink: prices change often in a marked, but by no means rigid, seasonal pattern.

Some direct evidence argues against the existence of a kink in the demand curve for steel produced by United States Steel: Bethlehem, for example, has faithfully followed the price increases.[18] But

[16] C. E. Fraser and G. F. Doriot, *Analysing Our Industries* (New York: McGraw-Hill Book Co., 1932), pp. 400, 401.

[17] Occasionally there is a temporary discrepancy. For example, six companies announced prices of $4.70 per ton for pea-size coal in the July 4, 1929, issue; one company retained the previous price of $4.60. A week later the exception disappeared.

[18] Temporary National Economic Committee, *Hearings*, Part 19: *Iron and Steel Industry* (Washington, 1940), pp. 10587 ff.

the important evidence is indirect: there is no evidence of price rigidity within this industry. The official price lists and trade-journal quotations have been honored almost exclusively in the breach, and the transactions take place at prices that appear to be fairly sensitive to demand conditions.[19] It is debatable whether the steel industry, with its price leader, should have rigid prices on the kinky demand curve theory, and it is also debatable whether the price leader often leads the industry in lowering prices.

Three firms produce most of the dynamite used in mining, quarrying, and construction in the United States. The wholesale prices for 40 per cent ammonium dynamite, per 50-pound bag, moved as follows during the thirties:

February 27, 1933: All firms reduced the price from $12.25 to $10.50.
March 12, 1934: Du Pont and Hercules reduced the price to $10; Atlas followed 17 days later.
January 14, 1935: All firms increased the price to $10.50.
May 7, 1936: Du Pont and Hercules reduced the price to $9.50; Atlas followed the next day.
May 8, 1937: Du Pont and Atlas increased the price to $10.50; Hercules followed 3 days later.[20]

Again there is no empirical basis for believing the kink exists.

Socony-Vacuum and Atlantic Refining are two important sellers of gasoline in the Boston area. Aside from three periods in 1934 and 1935 when Socony-Vacuum's price was less than Atlantic's, the prices of the two firms changed as shown in the accompanying list in the period 1929–37.

Simultaneous price changes		40
Increases	22	
Opposite	1	
Decreases	17	
Delay in following price increases		12
Days		
1	9	
2	1	
3	1	
4	1	
Delay in following price decreases		10
Days		
1	1	
2	3	
3	1	
10	1	
21	1	
23	1	
28	1	
47	1	

It appears, then, that price increases are more nearly simultaneous than price decreases—the opposite of the kinky demand curve assumption.[21]

The most striking case of contradiction of the assumption of the theory, however, is provided by potash. On June 1, 1934, the American Potash and Chemical Corporation issued a price list that carried about 26 per cent reductions from the prices in the previous year. The other firms failed to follow. On June 26 the lower prices were withdrawn, and the company lamented: "It was expected that other potash producers would like-

[19] See especially the study made by the Bureau of Labor Statistics, "Labor Department Examines Consumers' Prices of Steel Products," *Iron Age*, April 25, 1946. United States Steel officials testified before the T.N.E.C. that the Birmingham quotation had not been realized between 1932 and 1939 and that the general reduction in 1938 was merely a formal recognition of ruling prices (*Hearings*, Part 19, pp. 10546, 10505 ff.). See also *Hearings*, Part 27: *Iron and Steel Industry* (Washington, 1940), pp. 14141 f., 14172 f.

[20] I am indebted to Mr. Edward W. Proctor of Brown University for the information in this paragraph, which was secured by correspondence with Du Pont, Atlas Powder, and Hercules Powder. The three companies have headquarters in Wilmington; the latter two were created in 1912 by an antitrust action.

[21] I am indebted to Mr. Melvin D. Sargent of Brown University for the information on gasoline prices. The price quotations are from *Oil Price Handbook, 1929–37* (Cleveland: National Petroleum News, 1938).

wise announce their prices in accordance with long prevailing custom. No such announcements have been forthcoming. Under the circumstances this Company is compelled to withdraw the schedule of prices and terms referred to."[22]

In these seven industries there is little historical basis for a firm to believe that price increases will not be matched by rivals and that price decreases will be matched. This indicates only that not every oligopoly has reason to believe that it has a kinky demand curve, and most adherents of the theory would readily concede this.[23] On the other hand, here are seven industries in which the existence of the kinky demand curve is questionable—a list that is longer by seven than the list of industries for which a prima facie case has been made for the existence of the kink.[24]

2. THE VALIDITY OF THE IMPLICATIONS

The kinky demand curve would prove to be an incorrect or unimportant construction if oligopoly prices were as flexible as monopoly and/or competitive prices. It is not possible to make a direct test for price rigidity, in part, because the prices at which the products of oligopolists sell are not generally known. For the purpose of such a test we need transaction prices; instead, we have quoted prices on a temporal basis, and they are deficient in two respects.

The first deficiency is notorious: Nominal price quotations may be stable although the prices at which sales are taking place fluctuate often and widely. The disparity may be due to a failure to take account of quality, "extras," freight, guaranties, discounts, etc.; or the price collector may be deceived merely to strengthen morale within the industry. The various studies of steel prices, already referred to, contain striking examples of this disparity, and others can be cited.[25] We cannot infer that all nominally rigid prices are really flexible, but there is also very little evidence that they are really rigid.

The second deficiency is that published prices are on a temporal basis. If nine-tenths of annual sales occur at fluctuating prices within a month (as is true of some types of tobacco), and the remainder at a fixed price during the rest of the year, the nominal price rigidity for eleven months is trivial. With each price we ought to have the corresponding quantities sold: for a study of price rigidity, "April" would better be the fourth one-twelfth of the year's sales than the fourth month of the year.

Despite these shortcomings, a comparison of the implications of the kinky demand curve for price behavior with observable behavior (even if observable only in bulletins of the Bureau of Labor Statistics) has some value. If the theory

[22] *Chemical Industries* (July, 1934), p. 49.

[23] But apparently not all. O. Lange treats only of kinky demand curves in his theory of oligopoly (see *Price Flexibility and Employment* [Bloomington: Principia Press, 1944], chap. vii); and L. Tarshis has recently done the same in his *The Elements of Economics* (New York: Houghton Mifflin Co., 1947), pp. 139 ff.

[24] In the Conference on Price Research study, *Cost Behavior and Price Policy* (New York: National Bureau of Economic Research, 1943), it is stated: "There is rather strong reason for believing that leading firms in the automobile, steel, agricultural implement, and many other industries act upon approximately this view of the situation [i.e., that there is a kink in the demand curve]" (*ibid.*, p. 278). The reason is not given. We have discussed automobiles and steel; agricultural implements will be taken up subsequently.

[25] See the industry studies of the Division of Research of N.R.A.; the prices revealed in prosecutions under the Robinson-Patman Act; Saul Nelson, "A Consideration of the Validity of the Bureau of Labor Statistics Price Indexes," in *The Structure of the American Economy* (Washington: National Resources Committee, 1939), pp. 173–84.

cannot explain the pattern of rigidity of quoted prices among industries, there is no presumption that it would explain the pattern of transaction price rigidity among industries.

Our tests are made by comparing observed price rigidity in a group of industries with the relative rigidities forecast by the theory for industries with these market structures. We choose the period, June, 1929, through May, 1937, which embraces both a complete business cycle and the periods used in most empirical studies of price rigidity. We require three types of information:

a) *A list of oligopolistic industries.*—The two basic criteria are (1) a fairly precise knowledge of the industry structure, and (2) continuous price and output series. The industries are described briefly in the Appendix.[26]

b) *Some measure of expected price changes in the absence of restrictions on price changes.*—Shifts in demand are of primary (although far from exclusive) importance, and we measure them roughly by the coefficient of variation of production (or some related series) in 1929, 1931, 1933, 1935, and 1937.

c) *A measure of price rigidity.*—The basic test used is frequency of change in the monthly price quotations; for the theory under examination implies that there will be *no* changes—not merely that the price changes will be small. This test is supplemented by the coefficient of variation of monthly prices for two reasons. First, the price series have technical features that lead to more numerous price changes than actually occur. They are often averages of weekly quotations, and hence show two changes in the monthly averages when a price change occurs within a month.[27] They are often averages of prices of several firms, and if each firm makes one price change the average can display as many changes as there are firms. Second, it can be argued that the kink is an exaggeration—that actually there is a sharp bend in the demand curve of the firm so that small price changes are what the theory prophesies.[28] But frequent small price changes would still be improbable because of the cost of making price changes.

The basic data that are used in the tests are summarized in Table 1; fuller information is given in the Appendix. It will be observed that the two tests of price rigidity differ substantially: the coefficient of rank correlation between number of price changes and coefficient of variation of prices is +.69 for the nineteen oligopolies listed in Table 1.

MONOPOLIES VERSUS OLIGOPOLIES

The monopolies listed in Table 1 are unsurpassed for price rigidity, despite the fact that their outputs varied more than those of most oligopolistic industries. This finding, which could be supported by more cases,[29] suggests the possibility that the forces that make for price rigidity in monopolies are sufficiently strong to account for the lesser rigidity in

[26] More specifically, the oligopolies discussed by Clair Wilcox in *Competition and Monopoly in American Industry* ("T.N.E.C. Monographs," No. 21 [Washington, 1940]) formed the basic list. An industry was excluded if (1) necessary information was not available, (2) the industry was analyzed in the preceding section, or (3) the firms were in known collusion throughout the period. In addition, many chemicals were excluded because of ignorance of substitution relationships.

[27] Thus the B.L.S. reports as eight changes the six changes made by Pittsburgh Plate Glass during the period.

[28] To secure a sharp bend, we must assume that rivals will partly follow price increases and decreases that are small but fail to follow large increases and completely follow large decreases.

[29] Thus, the price of magnesium was very rigid; the rentals of the International Business Machines Corporation have not varied (Wilcox, *op. cit.*, p. 106); the retail price of incandescent lamps of

oligopolies. One might argue that special factors are at work in monopoly, but the only two that come to mind are fear of governmental attention or action and the conservatism that comes with size. The former, however, is even more effective against oligopolies because of the importance of conspiracy in the antitrust laws, and the latter is presumably also a function of absolute size. It should be added that the neoclassical theory does not provide a satisfactory explanation for this extraordinary rigidity of monopoly prices.

According to the kink theory, there will be no kink when the oligopolists enter into explicit collusion; and hence prices would be expected to become more flexible. All empirical evidence contradicts this implication. Of our industries, at least two had periods of collusion. There was a combination of rayon producers to fix prices between October 21, 1931, and May 23, 1932:[30] There were no price changes during this period, none in the preceding period of equal length, and four in the subsequent period of equal length. There are only two periods of protracted rigidity in the price series for copper: the first occurs under Copper Exporters (a Webb-Pomerene cartel), the second under N.R.A.

A number of examples are also provided by other industries. On August 30, 1932, the six important growers and canners of pineapple entered a ten-year agreement to restrict output and market through the Pineapple Producers Cooperative Association.[31] In the thirty-nine months preceding this date there were seventeen price changes in canned pineapples; in the subsequent fifty-seven months, eight changes. Prices of typewriters were very rigid during a period when the four important producers were charged with colluding.[32] During the period of operation of the midwestern oil pool (Madison Oil Case), prices "displayed a rigidity without parallel in the history of the industry."[33]

If the disappearance of the kink through collusion has a tendency to in-

TABLE 1

MEASURES OF MARKET STRUCTURE FOR TWENTY-ONE PRODUCTS AND OF THEIR PRICE FLEXIBILITY AND OUTPUT VARIABILITY JUNE, 1929—MAY, 1937

Product	Number of Firms in Industry	Price Leader	Price Flexibility: Number of Price Changes	Price Flexibility: Coefficient of Variation	Coefficient of Variation of Output
Oligopolies:					
Bananas	2	Yes	46	16	17
Boric acid	3	No	7	17	16
Cans	4	Yes	6	5	27
Cement	12	No	14	11	41
Copper	4	No	63	37	43
Gasoline*	11	No	84	22	16
Grain-binder	2	Yes	5	3	63
Linoleum	2	No?	12	9	30
Newsprint	9	No	6	16	16
Plaster	3	Yes	4	5	29
Plate glass	2	No	8	13	34
Plows	6	No	25	6	50
Rayon	8	No	26	30	34
Soap	3	No	9	12	7
Starch	4	Yes	20	12	13
Sulphur	2	Yes	0	0	24
Tires	8	No	36	9	16
Tractors	4	Yes	6	6	76
Window glass	3	No	20	21	24
Monopolies:					
Aluminum	1	....	2	6	47
Nickel	1	....	0	0	35

* In Pennsylvania and Delaware.

common sizes changed once or twice (United States Tariff Commission, *Incandescent Electric Lamps* [Report No. 133 (2d ser., Washington, 1939)], p. 47); this was virtually a General Electric monopoly because of its licensing provisions.

30 "Viscose Company *et al.*," *Federal Trade Commission Decisions*, XXV (Washington, 1939). 425.

31 "The move brought all the island packers into complete accord and cooperation for the first time in history" (*New York Times*, August 31, 1932, p. 10); see also J. A. Shoemaker, "Labor Conditions in Hawaii," *Monthly Labor Review*, January, 1941, pp. 30 ff.

32 Wilcox, *op. cit.*, p. 140.

33 *Ibid.*, p. 136.

crease price flexibility, this tendency is completely submerged by the opposite effects of administrative limitations on cartel price policy.

THE NUMBER OF FIRMS

The number of firms that enters into the formation of price policy is difficult to determine; a completely satisfactory determination would require knowledge of cross-elasticities of demand, the entrepreneur's knowledge and objectives, and similar data. As an unsatisfactory substitute for this information, we have been guided by two criteria: that sufficient firms be included to account for two-thirds to three-quarters of the output of the product and that the largest firm omitted from the count sell less than a tenth of the amount sold by the largest firm in the industry. Although these rules are arbitrary, they focus attention on relevant variables: if we do not include enough firms to account for a predominant share of output, the firms will not be able to control prices (attenuated oligopoly); and if we exclude firms large relative to those that are included, we may be omitting firms that are in the oligopolistic relationship. The precise number of firms, even by these arbitrary criteria, is in doubt in more than half the industries listed in Table 1, but it was thought better to give a single number than a range that invites mechanical averaging to secure a single number.

TABLE 2

Number of Firms in Industry	Number of Industries in Sample	Price Flexibility		Average of Coefficients of Variation of Outputs
		Number of Price Changes	Coefficient of Variation	
2	5	14.2	8.2	33.6
3, 4	8	16.8	14.4	29.4
6, 8	3	29.0	15.0	33.3
9, 11, 12	3	34.7	16.3	24.3

Our expectation, on the kink theory, is that a very few rivals will have relatively flexible prices because the impossibility of maintaining a price lower than a rival's will be evident. On the other hand, with many rivals the fear that price cuts will be matched is reduced, and again the kink disappears. We do not test this latter implication because it is identical with that of the neoclassical theory.

If the data in Table 1 are summarized by number of firms, we find a definite tendency for price flexibility to increase with the number of firms in the industry (Table 2). The coefficient of rank correlation between number of firms and number of price changes is +.41, that between number of firms and coefficient of variation of prices is +.31. There is virtually no relationship between fluctuations of output and number of firms, nor is the strength or direction of relationship between number of firms and price flexibility affected if industries with price leaders are segregated.[34] Thus there is a weak tendency for a greater number of firms to be associated with a greater frequency and amplitude of price changes, the contrary of the implications of the kinky demand curve.

PRICE LEADERSHIP

The term, "price leadership," is used in two very different senses in economic literature. In the one sense it refers to a dominant firm that sets the price, allows the minor firms to sell what they wish at this price (subject perhaps to nonprice competition), and supplies the remainder of the quantity demanded. In the other

[34] The coefficient of rank correlation between number of firms and number of price changes is .37 for seven products with price leaders and .39 for twelve products without price leaders.

sense, price leadership refers to the existence of a firm that conventionally first announces price changes that are usually followed by the remainder of the industry, even though this firm may not occupy a dominant position. For example, International Paper was for a long period the price leader in newsprint although it produced less than one-seventh of the output, and it was succeeded in this role by Great Northern, a smaller firm. This latter type of price leadership has been illuminatingly described by S. A. Swensrud of Standard Oil of Ohio:

In any territory all suppliers are watching the same things. They watch the statistical position of the industry as a whole, that is, production of crude oil and gasoline, sales of petroleum products, and stocks of crude oil and gasoline. . . . . They watch the ambitions of competitors to increase their share of the business in the territory. They gage these ambitions by reports of salesmen on price concessions to commercial customers, by observations of the amount of business done by trackside operators and sellers of unbranded and locally branded gasoline, by the reports of salesmen as to competitive offers being made to dealers, and by reports of salesmen as to the extent of secret price cuts, discounts, and the like being offered by retailers. All these facts are constantly before local managers and central organizations.

Now suppose that secret price cutting by dealers in some particular area breaks out into the open in the form of a cut in the posted price because some dealer becomes disgusted with the uncertainty as to how much business he is losing to competitors granting secret discounts. As the openly admitted price reduction operates, the local officers of all suppliers are assailed with demands from dealers, relayed and in some instances emphasized by salesmen, for a reduction in the tank-wagon price. . . . . The local manager of the leading marketer of course faces more demands than any other manager. He attempts to gage the permanence of the retail cut. Frequently local managers elect to make no change in the tank-wagon price. Ordinarily this decision springs from the conclusion that the local price war will soon run its course because it is not supported by weakness in basic markets. On other occasions the local manager concludes that the causes of the retail price cutting rest primarily on the availability of sufficient low-price gasoline so that the condition may be considered deep-seated, and he therefore authorizes or recommends a local reduction in the tank-wagon price. . . . . Thus the particular local territory becomes a subnormal territory, that is, one in which prices are out of line with those generally prevailing in the marketing area.

The major sales executives of all companies watch carefully the number and size of subnormal markets. . . . . If the number of local price cuts increases, if the number and amount of secret concessions to commercial consumers increase, if the secret unpublicized concessions to dealers increase, it becomes more and more difficult to maintain the higher prices. . . . . Finally, some company, usually the largest marketer in the territory, recognizes that the subnormal price has become the normal price and announces a general price reduction throughout the territory. . . . .

In summary, therefore, the so-called price leadership in the petroleum industry boils down to the fact that some company in each territory most of the time bears the onus of formally reconizing current conditions. . . . . In short, unless the so-called price leader accurately interprets basic conditions and local conditions, it soon will not be the leading marketer. Price leadership does not mean that the price leader can set prices to get the maximum profit and force other marketers to conform.[35]

The difference between these two types of price leadership from the viewpoint of the theory of kinky demand curves is basic. The dominant firm has no kink in its demand curve because rivals have no reason for charging a lower price: they are permitted to sell as much as they wish at the leader's price.[36] The second type of leader, the baromet-

[35] W. S. Farish and J. H. Pew, *Review and Criticism . . . . of Monograph No. 39* ("T.N.E.C. Monographs," No. 39A [Washington, 1941]), pp. 47–49.

[36] For the details of price determination in this situation see my "Notes on the Theory of Duopoly," *Journal of Political Economy*, XLVIII (1940), 523 ff.

ric firm, commands adherence of rivals to his price only because, and to the extent that, his price reflects market conditions with tolerable promptness. The widespread development of barometric firms is therefore explicitly a device to insure that there will be no kink, or that the kink will not prevent readjustment of price to important changes in cost or demand conditions.

TABLE 3

	Industries with Leader	Industries without Leader
Two-firm industries:		
Number in sample	3	2
Average number of price changes	17	10
Average coefficient of variation of prices	6.3	11.0
Average coefficient of variation of outputs	34.7	32.0
Three- and four-firm industries:		
Number in sample	4	4
Average number of price changes	9	24.8
Average coefficient of variation of prices	7.0	21.8
Average coefficient of variation of outputs	36.2	22.5

Only the price leadership exercised by dominant firms, therefore, is relevant in testing the implication of the kinky demand curve theory that there will be no kink when there is price leadership. Accordingly, we classify as industries with price leaders only those in which there is a relatively large firm, producing, say, 40 per cent of the output of the industry at a minimum, and more if the second largest firm is large (because otherwise the situation approaches classical duopoly). On this basis there are seven leaders among our nineteen industries (see Table 1), and they are compared with the remaining twelve industries in Table 3. Except for the number of price changes of two-firm industries (where bananas dominates the result), the prices of industries with price leaders are less flexible than those of industries without price leaders, despite the larger fluctuations of output of the former group. This is contrary to Sweezy's conjecture and is in keeping with the price rigidity found in monopolistic industries.

GOODNESS OF SUBSTITUTES

It is almost inherent in the methods of quotation of price statistics that most of the commodities examined in this article are nearly homogeneous. If products are rather heterogeneous, the significance of an average price becomes doubtful and the B.L.S. does not report it. Of our nineteen industries, only six have products whose prices appear to differ significantly and persistently among firms: soap, tractors, grain-binders, plows, tires, and linoleum. Their prices appear to change less often and less widely, on average, than those of homogeneous products as shown in Table 4. It should be noted that we might, with some justification, have designated our monopolies (aluminum and nickel) as oligopolies with differentiated products.

TABLE 4

	Homogeneous Products	Heterogeneous Products
Number of products	13	6
Average number of price changes	23.4	15.5
Average coefficient of variation of prices	15.8	7.5
Average coefficient of variation of outputs	25.7	40.3

3. CONCLUSION

The empirical evidence reveals neither price experiences that would lead oligopolists to believe in the existence of a kink nor the pattern of changes of price quotations that the theory leads us to expect. The industries included in these tests are not very numerous, but they are sufficiently varied and important to suggest that similar adverse results would be secured from a larger sample.

But is this adverse conclusion really surprising? The kink is a barrier to changes in prices that will increase profits, and business is the collection of devices for circumventing barriers to profits. That this barrier should thwart businessmen—especially when it is wholly of their own fabrication—is unbelievable. There are many ways in which it can be circumvented. We have had occasion to notice the development of price leadership of the barometric variety as one device, and the old-fashioned solution of collusion is not always overlooked. In addition there is the whole range of tactical maneuvers that Neumann and Morgenstern's theory of games has uncovered. In the multidimensional real world there are many ways to teach a lesson, especially when the pupil is eager to learn.

COLUMBIA UNIVERSITY

APPENDIX

The summary descriptions of the industries used in Part II are based upon indicated references and C. L. James, *Industrial Concentration and Tariffs*, T.N.E.C. Monograph No. 10 (Washington, 1940); *The Structure of Industry*, T.N.E.C. Monograph No. 27 (Washington, 1941); and C. Wilcox, *Competition and Monopoly in American Industry*, Monograph No. 21 (Washington, 1940), which may be referred to for information on imports, concentration ratios, and general market structures, respectively. Price quotations are from the Bureau of Labor Statistics bulletins, *Wholesale Prices*. In the few cases where price quotations begin in 1931, the number of price quotations reported in Table 1 is 96/77 of the actual number. Unless otherwise noted, quantity data are from S. Fabricant's *The Output of Manufacturing Industries, 1899–1937* (New York: National Bureau of Economic Research, 1940).

ALUMINUM:

The Aluminum Company of America produced all new aluminum during the period and also dominated the scrap market.

Quantity: production (*Minerals Yearbook*)

D. H. Wallace, *Market Control in the Aluminum Industry* (Cambridge: Harvard University Press, 1937)

BANANAS:

In 1936 United Fruit handled 60 per cent, and Standard Fruit and Steamship 30 per cent, of the bananas imported.

Prices: Jamaica 9's to July, 1931, then Honduras (spliced for continuity)

Quantities: imports (*Statistical Abstract*)

BORIC ACID:

In 1937 there were only three producers. Pacific Coast Borax produced half of the total, American Potash and Chemical about 40 per cent, and Stauffer Chemical the remainder.

C. L. James, *op. cit.*, chap. v

CANS:

In 1937 American Can produced about half, and Continental Can about one-quarter, of total output. The latter company also produced cans for Campbell Soup on a fixed-fee basis. McKeesport Tin Plate was third, with about 10 per cent of output, and Owens-Illinois Can was fourth, with less than 5 per cent. There were also fourteen smaller companies.

Standard Statistics Company, *Standard Corporation Reports*

CEMENT:

In 1931 the leading companies in the northeastern section and their percentages of sales were Lehigh, 19.1; Universal Atlas, 15.2; International, 8.1; Penn-Dixie, 7.9; Alpha, 6.7; a total of 57.0 per cent. The next seven mills (it is not clear that each was separately owned), with individual percentages ranging from 3.6 down to 2.4, totaled another 20.3 per cent.

Prices: Northampton

Quantities: production, northeastern section (*Minerals Yearbook*)
Federal Trade Commision, *Cement Industry* (73d Cong., 1st sess., Senate Doc. 71 [Washington, 1933])

COPPER:
In 1947 the leading companies and their percentages of total production were Kennecott Copper, 35.9; Anaconda, 22.9; Phelps Dodge, 18.8; Calumet and Hecla, 4.5.
Quantities: production (*Minerals Yearbook*)
The Structure of Industry, pp. 248–49

GASOLINE:
In 1938 the leading companies in the Pennsylvania-Delaware area and their percentages of sales were Atlantic Refining, 21.9; Standard Oil of New Jersey, 14.5; Gulf Oil, 10.2; Sun Oil, 9.8; Standard Oil of Indiana, 8.5; Consolidated Oil, 7.6; Socony-Vacuum, 6.8; Texas, 4.8; Tide Water, 3.4; Pure Oil, 2.1; and Cities Service, 2.3. In 1926 Atlantic's percentage was 44.5 and Gulf Oil's, 20.8.
Prices: Pennsylvania
Quantities: consumption in Pennsylvania and Delaware (*Minerals Yearbook*)
Federal Trade Commission, *Report on Distribution Methods and Costs*, Part IV (Washington, 1944), p. 52

GRAIN-BINDER:
In 1935 the leading companies and their percentages of total sales were International Harvester, 67.2; Deere, 24.7; and there were also four other companies.
Quantities: production (1933 estimated from *Census of Manufactures*)
Federal Trade Commission, *Report on the Agricultural Implement and Machinery Business* (75th Cong., 3d sess., House Doc. 702 [Washington, 1938]), p. 153

LINOLEUM:
In 1937 there were only four producers of inlaid linoleum. Armstrong Cork and Congoleum Nairn supplied most of the output.
Prices: 1931 on
Quantities: production, 1931 on
Standard Statistics Company, *Standard Corporation Reports*

NEWSPRINT:
In 1928 the leading firms and their percentages of the total production in Canada and the United States were International Paper, 14; Canadian Power and Paper, 12; Abitibi, 11; Great Northern, 9; Crown Zellerbach, 8; Minnesota and Ontario, 5; Price, 5; and Powell River, 4. Crown Zellerbach operated only on the Pacific Coast, where it supplied 70 per cent of the total.
Quantities: domestic production plus imports (the latter from *Statistical Abstract*)
Federal Trade Commission, *Newsprint Paper Industry* (71st Cong., spec. sess., Senate Doc. 214 [Washington, 1930]), pp. 18 ff.

NICKEL:
The International Nickel Company produces about 90 per cent of the output of North America, and its leading rival, Falconbridge Nickel Mines, sells chiefly in Europe.
Quantities: domestic production plus imports minus exports (*Minerals Yearbook*)
A. Skelton in *International Control in the Non-ferrous Metals*, ed. W. Y. Elliott (New York: Macmillan Co., 1937), Part II, chap. v
Report of Commissioner, Combines Investigation Act, *Canada and International Cartels* (Ottowa, 1945), p. 31

PLASTER:
In 1937 United States Gypsum produced almost half the output. National Gypsum and Certain-teed Products and Celotex are other large producers of gypsum products and together account for almost 40 per cent of 1937 output of plaster. The four firms produced 83.4 per cent of total output.
Quantities: production (1933 estimated from *Minerals Yearbook*)

PLATE GLASS:
In 1935 Libby-Owens-Ford and Pittsburgh Plate Glass produced 95 per cent of the output of plate glass; their outputs were about equal. The remainder of the industry consisted of three firms, of which one (Ford Motor) produced for its own use.
Prices: 3–5 square feet
Quantities: production (United States Tariff Commission study [cited below], p. 91; 1936 used in lieu of unknown 1937 data)
United States Tariff Commission, *Flat Glass and Related Glass Products* (2d ser.; Rept. No. 123 [Washington, 1937]), p. 24
"Life Goes On," *Fortune*, January, 1934, p. 43

PLOWS:
In 1936 the leading firms and their percentages of total sales were International Harvester, 17.5; Oliver, 16.7; Unknown,

15 to 20 (judging from the 1937 concentration ratio of 65.7); Deere, 12.2; Avery, 3.5; and Minneapolis-Moline, 2.5. It is not certain that the latter two are fifth and sixth in size.

Prices: walking, two-horse

Federal Trade Commission, *Agricultural Implements* (73d Cong., 1st sess., Senate Doc. 71 [Washington, 1933]), p. 151

RAYON:

In 1935 the capacities of the leading firms for producing yarn were American Viscose, 34.8; Du Pont Rayon, 17.6; Celanese, 12.8; North American, 7.3; Industrial Rayon, 6.1. Four smaller firms had an additional 14.9 per cent of capacity. Output was fairly close to capacity in this year.

Prices: 300 denier, first quality

Quantities: production of yarn (*Chemical and Metallurgical Engineering*, February, 1943, p. 116)

The Structure of Industry, pp. 263–64

SOAP:

In 1931 Proctor and Gamble sold about 40 per cent, Colgate-Palmolive-Peet about 24 per cent, and Lever Brothers about 14 per cent of total soap. In 1935 the four largest firms produced 73.5 per cent of all soap (which is believed to be less concentrated than hand soap) and the eight largest firms 83.1 per cent.

Prices: 1931 on, toilet soap

Quantities: production, 1931 on

"Proctor and Gamble," *Fortune*, December, 1931, p. 97

STARCH:

In 1937 Corn Products Refining Company made more than half of the total sales. The other large firms are A. E. Staley Manufacturing, Penick and Ford, and American Maize Products, with about one-third of total sales. There were also seven smaller companies.

C. L. James, *op. cit.*, p. 15

SULPHUR:

In 1937 Texas Gulf Sulphur supplied 64 per cent of total output, Freeport Sulphur, 26 per cent, and two other companies another 9 per cent.

Minerals Yearbook

TIRES:

In 1933 the leading companies and their percentages of the industry's capacity were Goodyear, 26.4; Firestone, 13.6; United States, 12.3; Goodrich, 12.0; Fisk, 9.1; Kelly-Springfield, 3.5; Mansfield, 2.8; General Tire, 2.6.

Prices: baloon (spliced for continuity)

W. H. Gross, *Evidence Study No. 36 of the Rubber Tire Manufacturing Industry* (Washington: N.R.A. Division of Review [October, 1935]), p. 5

TRACTORS:

In 1935 the leading companies and their percentages of total sales were International Harvester, 49.5; Deere, 24.5; Allis-Chalmers, 9.5; J. I. Case, 7.1. In 1929 International Harvester's percentage was 59.9 and Deere's, 21.1.

Prices: 10–20 horse-power

Federal Trade Commission, *Agricultural Implements*, p. 153

WINDOW GLASS:

In 1935 the industry was composed of twelve companies with twenty-one plants, of which thirteen were in operation. Libby-Owens-Ford, Pittsburgh Plate Glass, and American Window Glass produced more than 75 per cent of total output. In 1936 four other companies organized a common sales company (Fourco Glass Company) which bought up several idle plants. These four companies comprised virtually the entire industry thereafter.

Price: Single B

United States Tariff Commission, *Flat Glass*, p. 24

[9]

THE JOURNAL OF
POLITICAL ECONOMY

Volume LXIX JUNE 1961 Number 3

THE ECONOMICS OF INFORMATION[1]

GEORGE J. STIGLER
University of Chicago

One should hardly have to tell academicians that information is a valuable resource: knowledge *is* power. And yet it occupies a slum dwelling in the town of economics. Mostly it is ignored: the best technology is assumed to be known; the relationship of commodities to consumer preferences is a datum. And one of the information-producing industries, advertising, is treated with a hostility that economists normally reserve for tariffs or monopolists.

There are a great many problems in economics for which this neglect of ignorance is no doubt permissible or even desirable. But there are some for which this is not true, and I hope to show that some important aspects of economic organization take on a new meaning when they are considered from the viewpoint of the search for information. In the present paper I shall attempt to analyze systematically one important problem of information—the ascertainment of market price.

[1] I have benefited from comments of Gary Becker, Milton Friedman, Zvi Griliches, Harry Johnson, Robert Solow, and Lester Telser.

I. THE NATURE OF SEARCH

Prices change with varying frequency in all markets, and, unless a market is completely centralized, no one will know all the prices which various sellers (or buyers) quote at any given time. A buyer (or seller) who wishes to ascertain the most favorable price must canvass various sellers (or buyers)—a phenomenon I shall term "search."

The amount of dispersion of asking prices of sellers is a problem to be discussed later, but it is important to emphasize immediately the fact that dispersion is ubiquitous even for homogeneous goods. Two examples of asking prices, of consumer and producer goods respectively, are displayed in Table 1. The automobile prices (for an identical model) were those quoted with an average amount of "higgling": their average was $2,436, their range from $2,350 to $2,515, and their standard deviation $42. The prices for anthracite coal were bids for federal government purchases and had a mean of $16.90 per ton, a range from $15.46 to $18.92, and a standard deviation of $1.15. In both cases the range of prices was significant on almost any criterion.

Price dispersion is a manifestation—and, indeed, it is the measure—of ignorance in the market. Dispersion is a biased measure of ignorance because there is never absolute homogeneity in

TABLE 1

ASKING PRICES FOR TWO COMMODITIES

A. CHEVROLETS, CHICAGO, FEBRUARY, 1959*

Price (Dollars)	No. of Dealers
2,350–2,400	4
2,400–2,450	11
2,450–2,500	8
2,500–2,550	4

B. ANTHRACITE COAL, DELIVERED (WASHINGTON, D.C.), APRIL, 1953†

Price per Ton (Dollars)	No. of Bids
15.00–15.50	2
15.50–16.00	2
16.00–16.50	2
16.50–17.00	3
17.00–18.00	1
18.00–19.00	4

* Allen F. Jung, "Price Variations Among Automobile Dealers in Metropolitan Chicago," *Journal of Business*, XXXIII (January, 1960), 31–42.

† Supplied by John Flueck

the commodity if we include the terms of sale within the concept of the commodity. Thus, some automobile dealers might perform more service, or carry a larger range of varieties in stock, and a portion of the observed dispersion is presumably attributable to such differences. But it would be metaphysical, and fruitless, to assert that all dispersion is due to heterogeneity.

At any time, then, there will be a frequency distribution of the prices quoted by sellers. Any buyer seeking the commodity would pay whatever price is asked by the seller whom he happened to canvass, if he were content to buy from the first seller. But, if the dispersion of price quotations of sellers is at all large (relative to the cost of search), it will pay, on average, to canvass several sellers. Consider the following primitive example: let sellers be equally divided between asking prices of \$2 and \$3. Then the distribution of minimum prices, as search is lengthened, is shown in Table 2. The buyer who canvasses two sellers instead of one has an expected saving of 25 cents per unit, etc.

The frequency distributions of asking (and offering) prices have not been studied sufficiently to support any hypothesis as to their nature. Asking prices are probably skewed to the right, as a rule, because the seller of reproducible goods will have some minimum but no maximum limit on the price he can accept. If

TABLE 2

DISTRIBUTION OF HYPOTHETICAL MINIMUM PRICES BY NUMBERS OF BIDS CANVASSED

No. of Prices Canvassed	Probability of Minimum Price of \$2.00	Probability of Minimum Price of \$3.00	Expected Minimum Price
1	.5	.5	\$2.50
2	.75	.25	2.25
3	.875	.125	2.125
4	.9375	.0625	2.0625
∞	1.0	0	2.00

the distribution of asking prices is normal, the distributions of minimum prices encountered in searches of one, two, and three sellers will be those displayed in Figure 1. If the distribution is rectangular, the corresponding distributions would be those shown in Panel B. The latter assumption does not receive strong support from the evidence, but it will be used for a time because of its algebraic simplicity.

In fact, if sellers' asking prices (p) are uniformly distributed between zero and one, it can be shown that:[2] (1) The dis-

[2] If $F(p)$ is the cumulative-frequency function of p, the probability that the minimum of n observations will be greater than p is

$$[1 - F(p)]^n = \left[\int^1 dx\right]^n .$$

tribution of minimum prices with n searches is

$$n(1-p)^{n-1}, \tag{1}$$

(2) the average minimum price is

$$\frac{1}{n+1},$$

and (3) the variance of the average minimum price is

$$\frac{n}{(n+1)^2(n+2)}.$$

Whatever the precise distribution of prices, it is certain that increased search will yield diminishing returns as measured by the expected reduction in the minimum asking price. This is obviously true of the rectangular distribution, with an expected minimum price of $1/(n+1)$ with n searches, and also of the normal distributions.[3] In fact, if a distribution of asking prices did not display this property, it would be an unstable distribution for reasons that will soon be apparent.[4]

For any buyer the expected savings from an additional unit of search will be approximately the quantity (q) he wishes to purchase times the expected reduction in price as a result of the search,[5] or

$$q\left|\frac{\partial P_{\min}}{\partial_n}\right|. \tag{2}$$

The expected saving from given search will be greater, the greater the dispersion of prices. The saving will also obviously be greater, the greater the expenditure on the commodity. Let us defer for a time the problem of the time period to which the expenditure refers, and hence the amount of expenditure, by considering the purchase of an indivisible, infrequently purchased good—say, a used automobile.

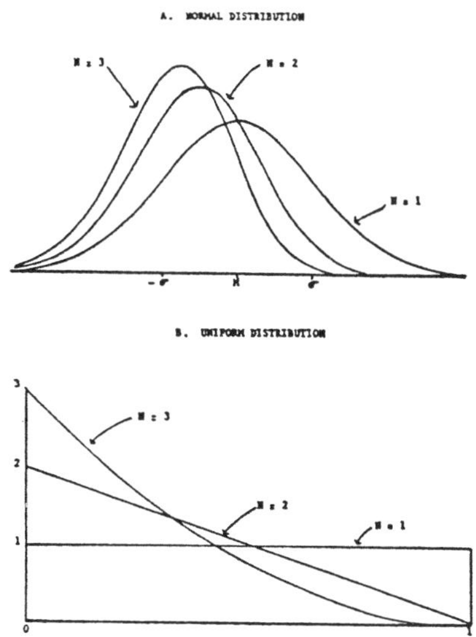

FIG. 1.—Distribution of minimum prices with varying amounts of search.

[3] The expected minimum prices with a normal distribution of mean M and standard deviation σ are

Search	Expected Minimum Price
1	M
2	$M - .564\sigma$
3	$M - .846\sigma$
4	$M - 1.029\sigma$
5	$M - 1.163\sigma$
6	$M - 1.267\sigma$
7	$M - 1.352\sigma$
8	$M - 1.423\sigma$
9	$M - 1.485\sigma$
10	$M - 1.539\sigma$

Robert Solow has pointed out that the expected value of the minimum of a random sample of n observations,

$$E(n) = n\int_0^{\infty} p(1-F)^{n-1}F'dp,$$

is a decreasing function of n, and

$$[E(n+2) - E(n+1)] - [E(n+1) - E(n)]$$

is positive so the minimum decreases at a decreasing rate. The proofs involve the fact that the density function for the rth observation from the maximum in a sample of n is

$$n\binom{n-1}{r-1}F^{n-r}(1-F)^{r-1}F'dp.$$

[5] The precise savings will be (a) the reduction in price times the quantity which would be purchased at the higher price—the expression in the text—*plus* (b) the average saving on the additional purchases induced by the lower price. I neglect this quantity, which will generally be of a smaller order of magnitude.

The cost of search, for a consumer, may be taken as approximately proportional to the number of (identified) sellers approached, for the chief cost is time. This cost need not be equal for all consumers, of course: aside from differences in tastes, time will be more valuable to a person with a larger income. If the cost of search is equated to its expected marginal return, the optimum amount of search will be found.[6]

Of course, the sellers can also engage in search and, in the case of unique items, will occasionally do so in the literal fashion that buyers do. In this—empirically unimportant—case, the optimum amount of search will be such that the marginal cost of search equals the expected increase in receipts, strictly parallel to the analysis for buyers.

With unique goods the efficiency of personal search for either buyers or sellers is extremely low, because the identity of potential sellers is not known—the cost of search must be divided by the fraction of potential buyers (or sellers) in the population which is being searched. If I plan to sell a used car and engage in personal search, less than one family in a random selection of one hundred families is a potential buyer of even a popular model within the next month. As a result, the cost of search is increased more than one hundredfold per price quotation.

The costs of search are so great under these conditions that there is powerful inducement to localize transactions as a device for identifying potential buyers and sellers. The medieval markets commonly increased their efficiency in this respect by prohibiting the purchase or sale of the designated commodities within a given radius of the market or on non-market days. The market tolls that were frequently levied on sellers (even in the absence of effective restrictions on non-market transactions) were clear evidence of the value of access to the localized markets.

[6] Buyers often pool their knowledge and thus reduce the effective cost of search; a few remarks are made on this method below.

Advertising is, of course, the obvious modern method of identifying buyers and sellers: the *classified* advertisements in particular form a meeting place for potential buyers and sellers. The identification of buyers and sellers reduces drastically the cost of search. But advertising has its own limitations: advertising itself is an expense, and one essentially independent of the value of the item advertised. The advertising of goods which have few potential buyers relative to the circulation of the advertising medium is especially expensive. We shall temporarily put advertising aside and consider an alternative.

The alternative solution is the development of specialized traders whose chief service, indeed, is implicitly to provide a meeting place for potential buyers and sellers. A used-car dealer, turning over a thousand cars a year, and presumably encountering three or five thousand each of buying and selling bids, provides a substantial centralization of trading activity. Let us consider these dealer markets, which we shall assume to be competitive in the sense of there being many independent dealers.

Each dealer faces a distribution of (for example) buyers' bids and can vary his selling prices with a corresponding effect upon purchases. Even in the markets for divisible (and hence non-unique) goods there will be some scope for higgling (discrimination) in each individual transaction: the buyer has a maximum price given by the lowest price he encounters among the dealers he has searched (or plans to search), but no minimum price. But let us put this range of indeterminacy aside, perhaps by assuming that the dealer finds discrimination too expensive,[7] and inquire how the demand curve facing a dealer is determined.

Each dealer sets a selling price, p, and makes sales to all buyers for whom this is the minimum price. With a uniform distribution of asking prices by dealers, the number of buyers of a total of N_b possible buyers who will purchase from him is

$$N_i = K N_b n (1 - p)^{n-1}, \qquad (3)$$

where K is a constant.[8] The number of buyers from a dealer increases as his price is reduced, and at an increasing rate.[9] Moreover, with the uniform distribution of asking prices, the number of buyers increases with increased search if the price is below the reciprocal of the amount of search.[10] We should generally expect the high-price sellers to be small-volume sellers.

The stability of any distribution of asking prices of dealers will depend upon the costs of dealers. If there are constant returns to scale, the condition of equal rates of return dictates that the difference between a dealer's buying and selling prices be a constant. This condition cannot in general be met: any dealer can buy low, and sell high, provided he is content with a small volume of transactions, and he will then be earning more than costs (including a competitive rate of return). No other dealer can eliminate this non-competitive rate of profit, although by making the same price bids he can share the volume of business, or by asking lower prices he can increase the rewards to search and hence increase the amount of search.

With economies of scale, the competition of dealers will eliminate the profitability of quoting very high selling and very low buying prices and will render impossible some of the extreme price bids. On this score, the greater the decrease in average cost with volume, the smaller will be the dispersion of prices.[11] Many distributions of prices will be inconsistent with any possible cost conditions of dealers,[12] and it is not evident that strict equalities of rates of return for dealers are generally possible.

If economies of scale in dealing lead to

[7] This is the typical state of affairs in retailing xcept for consumer durable goods.

[8] Since $n(1 - p)^{n-1}$ is a density function, we must multiply it by a dp which represents the range of prices between adjacent price quotations. In addition, if two or more sellers quote an identical price, they will share the sales, so $K = dp/r$, where r is the number of firms quoting price p.

[9] For

$$\frac{\partial N_i}{\partial p} = -\frac{(n-1)\,N_i}{(1-p)} < 0\,,$$

and

$$\frac{\partial^2 N_i}{\partial p^2} = \frac{(n-1)(n-2)\,N_i}{(1-p)^2} > 0$$

if $n > 2$.

[10] Let

$$\log N_i = \log K + \log N_b + \log n + (n-1)\log(1-p)\,.$$

Then

$$\frac{1}{N_i}\frac{\partial N_i}{\partial n} = \frac{1}{n} + \log(1-p) = \frac{1}{n} - p\,,$$

approximately.

[11] This argument assumes that dealers will discover unusually profitable bids, given the buyers' search, which is, of course, only partly true: there is also a problem of dealers' search with respect to prices.

[12] With the rectangular distribution of asking prices, if each buyer purchases the same number of units, the elasticity of demand falls continuously with price, so that, if average cost equaled price at every rate of sales (with one seller at each price), marginal costs would have to be negative at large outputs. But, of course, the number of sellers can be less at lower prices.

a smaller dispersion of asking prices than do constant costs of dealing, similarly greater amounts of search will lead to a smaller dispersion of observed selling prices by reducing the number of purchasers who will pay high prices. Let us consider more closely the determinants of search.

DETERMINANTS OF SEARCH

The equation defining optimum search is unambiguous only if a unique purchase is being made—a house, a particular used book, etc. If purchases are repetitive, the volume of purchases based upon the search must be considered.

If the correlation of asking prices of dealers in successive time periods is perfect (and positive!), the initial search is the only one that need be undertaken. In this case the expected savings of search will be the present value of the discounted savings on all future purchases, the future savings extending over the life of the buyer or seller (whichever is shorter).[13] On the other hand, if asking prices are uncorrelated in successive time periods, the savings from search will pertain only to that period,[14] and search in each period is independent of previous experience. If the correlation of successive prices is positive, customer search will be larger in the initial period than in subsequent periods.[15]

The correlation of successive asking prices of sellers is usually positive in the handful of cases I have examined. The rank correlation of anthracite price bids (Table 1) in 1953 with those in 1954 was .68 for eight bidders; that for Chevrolet dealers in Chicago February and August of 1959 was .33 for twenty-nine dealers—but, on the other hand, it was zero for Ford dealers for the same dates. Most observed correlations will, of course, be positive because of stable differences in the products or services, but our analysis is restricted to conditions of homogeneity.

As a rule, positive correlations should exist with homogeneous products. The amount of search will vary among individuals because of differences in their expenditures on a commodity or differences in cost of search. A seller who wishes to obtain the continued patronage of those buyers who value the gains of search more highly or have lower costs of search must see to it that he is quoting relatively low prices. In fact, goodwill may be defined as continued patronage by customers without continued search (that is, no more than occasional verification).

A positive correlation of successive asking prices justifies the widely held view that inexperienced buyers (tourists)

[13] Let the expected minimum price be $p_1 = f(n)_1$ in period 1 (with $f' < 0$) and let the expected minimum price in period 2, with r a measure of the correlation between sellers' successive prices, be

$$p_2 = \left(\frac{p_1}{f(n_2)}\right)^r f(n_2) .$$

If the cost of search is λ per unit, total expenditures for a fixed quantity of purchases (Q) per unit of time are, neglecting interest,

$$E = Q(p_1 + p_2) + \lambda(n_1 + n_2) .$$

Expenditures are a minimum when

$$\frac{\partial E}{\partial n_1} = Qf'(n_1) + Qr[f(n_1)]^{r-1} \times [f(n_2)]^{1-r} f'(n_1) + \lambda = 0$$

and

$$\frac{\partial E}{\partial n_2} = (1 - r)Q[f(n_1)]^r \times [f(n_2)]^{-r} f'(n_2) + \lambda = 0 .$$

If $r = 1$, $n_2 = 0$, and n_1 is determined by $Qf'(n_1) = -\lambda/2$, the cost of search is effectively halved.

[14] See n. 13; if $r = 0$, $n_1 = n_2$.

[15] Let $f(n) = e^{-n}$. Then, in the notation of our previous footnotes,

$$n_1 - n_2 = \frac{2r}{1 - r} ,$$

approximately.

pay higher prices in a market than do experienced buyers.[16] The former have no accumulated knowledge of asking prices, and even with an optimum amount of search they will pay higher prices on average. Since the variance of the expected minimum price decreases with additional search, the prices paid by inexperienced buyers will also have a larger variance.

If a buyer enters a wholly new market, he will have no idea of the dispersion of prices and hence no idea of the rational amount of search he should make. In such cases the dispersion will presumably be estimated by some sort of sequential process, and this approach would open up a set of problems I must leave for others to explore. But, in general, one approaches a market with some general knowledge of the amount of dispersion, for dispersion itself is a function of the average amount of search, and this in turn is a function of the nature of the commodity:

1. The larger the fraction of the buyer's expenditures on the commodity, the greater the savings from search and hence the greater the amount of search.
2. The larger the fraction of repetitive (experienced) buyers in the market, the greater the effective amount of search (with positive correlation of successive prices).
3. The larger the fraction of repetitive sellers, the higher the correlation between successive prices, and hence, by condition (2), the larger the amount of accumulated search.[17]
4. The cost of search will be larger, the larger the geographical size of the market.

An increase in the number of buyers has an uncertain effect upon the dispersion of asking prices. The sheer increase in numbers will lead to an increase in the number of dealers and, *ceteris paribus*, to a larger range of asking prices. But, quite aside from advertising, the phenomenon of pooling information will increase. Information is pooled when two buyers compare prices: if each buyer canvasses s sellers, by combining they effectively canvass $2s$ sellers, duplications aside.[18] Consumers compare prices of some commodities (for example, liquor) much more often than of others (for example, chewing gum)—in fact, pooling can be looked upon as a cheaper (and less reliable) form of search.

SOURCES OF DISPERSION

One source of dispersion is simply the cost to dealers of ascertaining rivals' asking prices, but even if this cost were zero the dispersion of prices would not vanish. The more important limitation is provided by buyers' search, and, if the conditions and participants in the market were fixed in perpetuity, prices would immediately approach uniformity. Only those differences could persist which did not remunerate additional search. The condition for optimum search would be (with perfect correlation of successive prices):

$$q\left|\frac{\partial p}{\partial n}\right| = i \times \text{marginal cost of search},$$

where i is the interest rate. If an additional search costs \$1, and the interest rate is 5 per cent, the expected reduction in price with one more search would at equilibrium be equal to $\$0.05/q$—a quantity which would often be smaller than the smallest unit of currency. But, indivisibilities aside, it would normally be

[16] For that matter, a negative correlation would have the same effects.

[17] If the number of sellers (s) and the asking-price distributions are the same in two periods, but k are new sellers, the average period-1 buyer will have lost proportion k/s of his period-1 search.

[18] Duplications will occur more often than random processes would suggest, because pooling is more likely between buyers of similar location, tastes, etc.

unprofitable for buyers or sellers to eliminate all dispersion.

The maintenance of appreciable dispersion of prices arises chiefly out of the fact that knowledge becomes obsolete. The conditions of supply and demand, and therefore the distribution of asking prices, change over time. There is no method by which buyers or sellers can ascertain the new average price in the market appropriate to the new conditions except by search. Sellers cannot maintain perfect correlation of successive prices, even if they wish to do so, because of the costs of search. Buyers accordingly cannot make the amount of investment in search that perfect correlation of prices would justify. The greater the instability of supply and/or demand conditions, therefore, the greater the dispersion of prices will be.

In addition, there is a component of ignorance due to the changing identity of buyers and sellers. There is a flow of new buyers and sellers in every market, and they are at least initially uninformed on prices and by their presence make the information of experienced buyers and sellers somewhat obsolete.

The amount of dispersion will also vary with one other characteristic which is of special interest: the size (in terms of both dollars and number of traders) of the market. As the market grows in these dimensions, there will appear a set of firms which specialize in collecting and selling information. They may take the form of trade journals or specialized brokers. Since the cost of collection of information is (approximately) independent of its use (although the cost of dissemination is not), there is a strong tendency toward monopoly in the provision of information: in general, there will be a "standard" source for trade information.

II. ADVERTISING

Advertising is, among other things, a method of providing potential buyers with knowledge of the identity of sellers. It is clearly an immensely powerful instrument for the elimination of ignorance—comparable in force to the use of the book instead of the oral discourse to communicate knowledge. A small $5 advertisement in a metropolitan newspaper reaches (in the sense of being read) perhaps 25,000 readers, or fifty readers per penny, and, even if only a tiny fraction are potential buyers (or sellers), the economy they achieve in search, as compared with uninstructed solicitation, may be overwhelming.

Let us begin with advertisements designed only to identify sellers; the identification of buyers will not be treated explicitly, and the advertising of price will be discussed later. The identification of sellers is necessary because the identity of sellers changes over time, but much more because of the turnover of buyers. In every consumer market there will be a stream of new buyers (resulting from immigration or the attainment of financial maturity) requiring knowledge of sellers, and, in addition, it will be necessary to refresh the knowledge of infrequent buyers.

Suppose, what is no doubt too simple, that a given advertisement of size a will inform c per cent of the potential buyers in a given period, so $c = g(a)$.[19] This contact function will presumably show diminishing returns, at least beyond a certain size of advertisement. A certain fraction, b, of potential customers will be "born" (and "die") in a stable population, where "death" includes not only

[19] The effectiveness of the advertisement is also a function of the skill with which it is done and of the fraction of potential buyers who read the medium, but such elaborations are put aside.

departure from the market but forgetting the seller. The value of b will obviously vary with the nature of the commodity; for example, it will be large for commodities which are seldom purchased (like a house). In a first period of advertising (at a given rate) the number of potential customers reached will be cN, if N is the total number of potential customers. In the second period $cN(1-b)$ of these potential customers will still be informed, cbN new potential customers will be informed, and

$$c[(1-b)n - cN(1-b)]$$

old potential customers will be reached for the first time, or a total of

$$cN[1+(1-b)(1-c)] .$$

This generalizes, for k periods, to

$$cN[1+(1-b)(1-c) + \ldots + (1-b)^{k-1}(1-c)^{k-1}] ,$$

and, if k is large, this approaches

$$\frac{cN}{1-(1-c)(1-b)} = \lambda N . \quad (4)$$

The proportion (λ) of potential buyers informed of the advertiser's identity thus depends upon c and b.

If each of r sellers advertises the same amount, λ is the probability that any one seller will inform any buyer. The distribution of N potential buyers by the number of contacts achieved by r sellers is given by the binomial distribution:

$$N(\lambda + [1-\lambda])^r ,$$

with, for example,

$$\frac{Nr!}{m!(r-m)!} \lambda^m (1-\lambda)^{r-m}$$

buyers being informed of exactly m sellers' identities. The number of sellers known to a buyer ranges from zero to r, with an average of $r\lambda$ sellers and a variance of $r\lambda(1-\lambda)$.[20]

The amount of relevant information in the market, even in this simple model, is not easy to summarize in a single measure—a difficulty common to frequency distributions. If all buyers wished to search s sellers, all buyers knowing less than s sellers would have inadequate information, and all who knew more than s sellers would have redundant information, although the redundant information would not be worthless.[21] Since the value of information is the amount by which it reduces the expected cost to the buyer of his purchases, if these expected reductions are $\Delta C_1, \Delta C_2, \ldots$, for searches of $1, 2, \ldots$, the value of the information to buyers is approximately

$$\sum_{m=1}^{r} \frac{r!}{m!(r-m)!} \lambda^m (1-\lambda)^{r-m} \Delta C_m .$$

The information possessed by buyers, however, is not simply a matter of chance; those buyers who spend more on the commodity, or who search more for a given expenditure, will also search more for advertisements. The buyers with more information will, on average, make more extensive searches, so the value of information will be greater than this last formula indicates.

We may pause to discuss the fact that advertising in, say, a newspaper is normally "paid" for by the seller. On our analysis, the advertising is valuable to the buyer, and he would be willing to pay

[20] This approach has both similarities and contrasts to that published by S. A. Ozga, "Imperfect Markets through Lack of Knowledge," *Quarterly Journal of Economics*, LXXIV (February, 1960), 29–52.

[21] The larger the number of sellers known, the larger is the range of prices among the sellers and the lower the expected minimum price after s searches. But this effect will normally be small.

more for a paper with advertisements than for one without. The difficulty with having the sellers insert advertisements "free" and having the buyer pay for them directly is that it would be difficult to ration space on this basis: the seller would have an incentive to supply an amount of information (or information of a type) the buyer did not wish, and, since numerous advertisements are supplied jointly, the buyer could not register clearly his preferences regarding advertising. (Catalogues, however, are often sold to buyers.) Charging the seller for the advertisements creates an incentive for him to supply to the buyer only the information which is desired.

It is commonly complained that advertising is jointly supplied with the commodity in the sense that the buyer must pay for both even though he wishes only the latter. The alternative of selling the advertising separately from the commodity, however, would require that the advertising of various sellers (of various commodities) would be supplied jointly: the economies of disseminating information in a general-purpose periodical are so great that some form of jointness is inescapable. But the common complaint is much exaggerated: the buyer who wishes can search out the seller who advertises little (but, of course, enough to be discoverable), and the latter can sell at prices lower by the savings on advertising.

These remarks seem most appropriate to newspaper advertisements of the "classified" variety; what of the spectacular television show or the weekly comedian? We are not equipped to discuss advertising in general because the problem of quality has been (and will continue to be) evaded by the assumption of homogeneous goods. Even within our narrower framework, however, the use of entertainment to attract buyers to information is a comprehensible phenomenon. The assimilation of information is not an easy or pleasant task for most people, and they may well be willing to pay more for the information when supplied in an enjoyable form. In principle, this complementary demand for information and entertainment is exactly analogous to the complementary demand of consumers for commodities and delivery service or air-conditioned stores. One might find a paradox in the simultaneous complaints of some people that advertising is too elaborate and school *houses* too shoddy.

A monopolist will advertise (and price the product) so as to maximize his profits,

$$\pi = Npq\lambda - \phi(N\lambda q) - ap_a ,$$

where $p = f(q)$ is the demand curve of the individual buyer, $\phi(Nq\lambda)$ is production costs other than advertising, and ap_a is advertising expenditures. The maximum profit conditions are

$$\frac{\partial \pi}{\partial q} = N\lambda\left(p + q\frac{\partial p}{\partial q}\right) - \phi' N\lambda = 0 \quad (5)$$

and

$$\frac{\partial \pi}{\partial a} = Npq\frac{\partial \lambda}{\partial a} - \phi' Nq\frac{\partial \lambda}{\partial a} - p_a = 0 . \quad (6)$$

Equation (5) states the usual marginal cost–marginal revenue equality, and equation (6) states the equality of (price − marginal cost) with the marginal cost $[p_a/Nq(\partial\lambda/\partial a)]$ of advertising.[22]

[22] The marginal revenue from advertising expenditure,

$$\frac{Npq}{p_a}\frac{\partial \lambda}{\partial a},$$

equals the absolute value of the elasticity of demand by equations (5) and (6); see R. Dorfman and P. O. Steiner, "Optimal Advertising and Optimal Quality," *American Economic Review*, XLIV (1954), 826.

With the Cournot spring (where production costs $\phi = 0$) the monopolist advertises up to the point where price equals the marginal cost of informing a buyer: the monopolist will not (cannot) exploit ignorance as he exploits desire. The monopolist will advertise more, the higher the "death" rate (b), unless it is very high relative to the "contact" rate (c).[23] The monopolistic situation does not invite comparison with competition because an essential feature—the value of search in the face of price dispersion—is absent.

A highly simplified analysis of advertising by the competitive firm is presented in the Appendix. On the assumption that all firms are identical and that all buyers have identical demand curves and search equal amounts, we obtain the maximum-profit equation:

$$\text{Production cost} = p\left(1 + \frac{1}{\eta_{qp} + \eta_{Kp}}\right), \quad (7)$$

where η_{qp} is the elasticity of a buyer's demand curve and η_{K_p} is the elasticity of the fraction of buyers purchasing from the seller with respect to his price. The latter elasticity will be of the order of magnitude of the number of searches made by a buyer. With a uniform distribution of asking prices, increased search will lead to increased advertising by low-price sellers and reduced advertising by high-price sellers. The amount of advertising by a firm decreases as the number of firms increases.

Price advertising has a decisive influence on the dispersion of prices. Search now becomes extremely economical, and the question arises why, in the absence of differences in quality of products, the dispersion does not vanish. And the answer is simply that, if prices are advertised by a large portion of the sellers, the price differences diminish sharply. That they do not wholly vanish (in a given market) is due simply to the fact that no combination of advertising media reaches all potential buyers within the available time.

Assuming, as we do, that all sellers are equally convenient in location, must we say that some buyers are perverse in not reading the advertisements? Obviously not, for the cost of keeping currently informed about all articles which an individual purchases would be prohibitive. A typical household probably buys several hundred different items a month, and, if, on average, their prices change (in some outlets) only once a month, the number of advertisements (by at least several sellers) which must be read is forbiddingly large.

The seller's problem is even greater: he may sell two thousand items (a modest number for a grocery or hardware store), and to advertise each on the occasion of a price change—and frequently enough thereafter to remind buyers of his price—would be impossibly expensive. To keep the buyers in a market informed on the current prices of all items of consumption would involve perhaps a thousandfold increase of newspaper advertising.

From the manufacturer's viewpoint, uncertainty concerning his price is clearly disadvantageous. The cost of search is a cost of purchase, and consumption will therefore be smaller, the greater the dispersion of prices and the greater the optimum amount of search. This is presumably one reason (but, I conjecture, a very minor one) why uniform prices are set by

[23] Differentiating equation (6) with respect to b, we find that $\partial a/\partial b$ is positive or negative according as

$$b \lessgtr \frac{c}{1-c}.$$

If $c \geq \frac{1}{2}$, the derivative must be positive.

sellers of nationally advertised brands: if they have eliminated price variation, they have reduced the cost of the commodity (including search) to the buyer, even if the dealers' margins average somewhat more than they otherwise would.

The effect of advertising prices, then, is equivalent to that of the introduction of a very large amount of search by a large portion of the potential buyers. It follows from our discussion in Section I that the dispersion of asking prices will be much reduced. Since advertising of prices will be devoted to products for which the marginal value of search is high, it will tend to reduce dispersion most in commodities with large aggregate expenditures.

III. CONCLUSIONS

The identification of sellers and the discovery of their prices are only one sample of the vast role of the search for information in economic life. Similar problems exist in the detection of profitable fields for investment and in the worker's choice of industry, location, and job. The search for knowledge on the quality of goods, which has been studiously avoided in this paper, is perhaps no more important but, certainly, analytically more difficult. Quality has not yet been successfully specified by economics, and this elusiveness extends to all problems in which it enters.

Some forms of economic organization may be explicable chiefly as devices for eliminating uncertainties in quality. The department store, as Milton Friedman has suggested to me, may be viewed as an institution which searches for the superior qualities of goods and guarantees that they are good quality. "Reputation" is a word which denotes the persistence of quality, and reputation commands a price (or exacts a penalty) because it economizes on search. When economists deplore the reliance of the consumer on reputation—although they choose the articles they read (and their colleagues) in good part on this basis—they implicitly assume that the consumer has a large laboratory, ready to deliver current information quickly and gratuitously.

Ignorance is like subzero weather: by a sufficient expenditure its effects upon people can be kept within tolerable or even comfortable bounds, but it would be wholly uneconomic entirely to eliminate all its effects. And, just as an analysis of man's shelter and apparel would be somewhat incomplete if cold weather is ignored, so also our understanding of economic life will be incomplete if we do not systematically take account of the cold winds of ignorance.

APPENDIX

Under competition, the amount of advertising by any one seller (i) can be determined as follows. Each buyer will engage in an amount s of search, which is determined by the factors discussed above (Sec. 1). He will on average know

$$(r-1)\lambda+\lambda_i$$

sellers, where λ_i is defined by equation (4) for seller i. Hence,

$$\frac{\lambda_i}{(r-1)\lambda+\lambda_i}$$

per cent of buyers who know seller i will canvass him on one search, and

$$\left(1-\frac{\lambda_i}{(r-1)\lambda+\lambda_i}\right)^s$$

per cent of the buyers who know i will not canvass him in s searches,

$$s\leq (r-1)\lambda+\lambda_i\,.$$

Therefore, of the buyers who know i, the proportion who will canvass him at least once is[24]

$$1-\left(1-\frac{\lambda_i}{(r-1)\lambda+\lambda_i}\right)^s.$$

If we approximate

$$\frac{\lambda_i}{(r-1)\lambda+\lambda_i}$$

by

$$\frac{\lambda_i}{r\lambda}$$

and take only the first two terms of the binomial expansion, this becomes

$$\frac{s\lambda_i}{r\lambda}.$$

The receipts of any seller then become the product of (1) The number of buyers canvassing him,

$$\frac{s\lambda_i}{r\lambda}\lambda_i N = T_i,$$

(2) the fraction K of those canvassing him who buy from him, where K depends upon his relative price (and the amount of search and the number of rivals), and (3) sales to each customer, pq. If $\phi(T_i Kq)$ is production costs and ap_a advertising costs, profits are

$$\pi = T_i K p q - \phi(T_i K q) - a p_a .$$

The conditions for maximum profits are

$$\frac{\partial\pi}{\partial p} = T_i\left(K\frac{\partial pq}{\partial p}+pq\frac{\partial K}{\partial p}\right) - T_i\phi'\left(K\frac{\partial q}{\partial p}+q\frac{\partial K}{\partial p}\right)=0 \qquad (8)$$

and

$$\frac{\partial\pi}{\partial a} = Kpq\frac{\partial T_i}{\partial a} - \phi' K q\frac{\partial T_i}{\partial a} - p_a = 0\,. \qquad (9)$$

[24] The formula errs slightly in allowing the multiple canvass of one seller by a buyer.

The former equation can be rewritten in elasticities as

$$\phi' = p\left(1+\frac{1}{\eta_{qp}+\eta_{Kp}}\right) \qquad (8a)$$

Price exceeds marginal cost, not simply by $(-p/\eta_{qp})$ as with monopoly, but by the smaller amount

$$\frac{-p}{\eta_{qp}+\eta_{Kp}},$$

where η_{Kp} will generally be of the order of magnitude of the number of searches made by a buyer.[25] Equation (2) states the equality of the marginal revenue of advertising with its marginal cost. By differentiating equation (2) with respect to s and taking ϕ' as constant, it can be shown that increased search by buyers will lead to increased advertising by low-price sellers and reduced advertising by high-price sellers (with a uniform distribution of prices).[26]

By the same method it may be shown that the amount of advertising by the firm will decrease as the number of rivals increases.[27] The aggregate amount of advertising by the industry may either increase or decrease with an increase in the number of firms, s, depending on the relationship between λ and a.

[25] In the case of the uniform distribution, η_{Kp} is

$$\frac{-(s-1)p}{1-p}.$$

[26] The derivative $\partial a/\partial s$ has the sign of $(1+\eta_{Ks})$, and this elasticity equals

$$1+s\log[1-p]$$

with a uniform distribution of prices.

[27] By differentiation of equation (2) with respect to r one gets

$$r\frac{\partial a}{\partial r}\left\{\lambda_i\frac{\partial^2\lambda_i}{\partial a^2}+\left(\frac{\partial\lambda_i}{\partial a}\right)^2\right\} = \lambda_i\frac{\partial\lambda_i}{\partial a}\left(1-\frac{r}{K}\frac{\partial K}{\partial r}\right).$$

The term in brackets on the left side is negative by the stability condition; the right side is positive.

[10]

INFORMATION IN THE LABOR MARKET

GEORGE J. STIGLER[1]
University of Chicago

THE young person entering the labor market for the first time has an immense number of potential employers, scarce as they may seem the first day. If he is an unskilled or a semi-skilled worker, the number of potential employers is strictly in the millions. Even if he has a specialized training, the number of potential employers will be in the thousands: the young Ph.D. in economics, for example, has scores of colleges and universities, dozens of governmental agencies, hundreds of business firms, and the Ford Foundation as potential employers. As the worker becomes older the number of potential employers may shrink more often than it grows, but the number will seldom fall to even a thousand.

No worker, unless his degree of specialization is pathological, will ever be able to become informed on the prospective earnings which would be obtained from every one of these potential employers at any given time, let alone keep this information up to date. He faces the problem of how to acquire information on the wage rates, stability of employment, conditions of employment, and other determinants of job choice, and how to keep this information current. I shall concentrate attention on the determination of wage rates.

I. THE DISPERSION OF WAGE RATES

Even with strict homogeneity of commodities, we usually find some dispersion in the prices which are offered by sellers or buyers. Only if either buyers have complete knowledge of all sellers' offers, or all sellers have complete knowledge of all buyers' offers, will there be a single price. Complete knowledge, however, is seldom possessed, simply because it costs more to learn of alternative prices than (at the margin) this information yields.[2]

The labor markets display the same characteristics, but their analysis is much complicated by the lack of homogeneity of the workers (and, to a much lesser extent, of non-wage conditions of employment). In order to form some estimate of the nature of the "pure" dispersion of wages due to imperfect knowledge, we shall begin with a very special class of college graduates.

A tolerably pure estimate of the dispersion of wage offers to homogeneous labor is provided by the contemporary offers to the same person. For forty-four graduates of the Graduate School of Business at the University of Chicago who received 144 offers (in 1960 and 1961) from corporations, the standard deviation of monthly rates was $43. The mean offer was $540.7, so the coefficient of variation was 7.9 per cent.[3]

[1] I am deeply indebted to Claire Friedland for the statistical work in this paper. H. Gregg Lewis made very helpful comments on an earlier version.

[2] The argument is elaborated in my "The Economics of Information," *Journal of Political Economy*, June 1961.

[3] There was no systematic or significant difference in the standard deviations for those who received 2, 3, 4, or 5 or more offers:

No. of Offers	No. of Students	Standard Deviation
2	17	$46
3	13	35
4	7	49
5 or more	7	43

The basic data were made available by courtesy of David Huntington of the Placement Bureau of the Graduate School of Business.

Since this job market was completely localized in one office, and there is considerable intercommunication among the national companies whose representatives solicit prospective employees (and among prospective employees), this appears to be a conservative estimate of the gross dispersion for given quality. The fact that each student on average solicited only 2.25 offers works in the same direction. The differences in the attractiveness of non-wage elements of the various jobs, however, are impossible to discover.[4] On balance it appears that the true dispersion is substantially underestimated, and later evidence suggests that it may be much larger in less organized markets.

Unfortunately, distributions of offers to given individuals are not available for any large occupational group or any extended geographical market. One must deal with offers (or wage rates paid) by individual employers or groups of employers, and the dispersion of such offers may be either larger or smaller than the true distribution we desire. The dispersion of distributions of company average offers will be larger insofar as they reflect differences in quality of workers (or of jobs),[5] or cover several labor markets; the dispersion will be smaller insofar as intracompany dispersion is eliminated. In our sample of business graduates, the standard deviation of the average offers of companies is $40, compared with that of $43 for given students. Although no unique relationship between these dispersions can be assumed, we can and will assume that for similar labor markets they are reasonably well correlated.

[4] The extent to which initial wage rates are reliable indexes of subsequent wage rates is investigated below.

[5] The variance of offers, within a given specialty, is usually much larger between than "within" individuals who have received multiple offers.

The dispersion of wage offers in the small Chicago sample is approximately equal to that of the national sample of wage offers made each year by Frank Endicott.[6] The coefficients of variation of groups other than engineers range from 6.4 per cent to 9.1 per cent (Table 1); the corresponding figure for our sample was 7.3 per cent.

TABLE 1

MONTHLY HIRING RATES OF LARGE CORPORATIONS FOR COLLEGE GRADUATES, 1958–60

Occupation	No. of Companies	1958	1959	1960
	1. Mean Salaries			
Engineers	66	$472	$493	$515
Accountants	40	421	435	457
Salesmen	29	410	426	447
General business	41	403	416	431
	2. Coefficient of Variation (Per Cent)			
Engineers	66	4.04	4.22	4.26
Accountants	40	6.45	6.93	6.42
Salesmen	29	8.78	8.18	9.11
General business	41	8.60	8.96	8.64

Source: Endicott Survey worksheets. All companies here included reported in each of the three years.

If the expected period of employment exceeds one year (as it does), the worker must also make an estimate of future wage differences among employers. Endicott's data permit an estimate of the correlation of successive annual rates (Table 2). The correlations are high, and—what is more surprising—two of the four cases show no tendency to diminish when the time period is lengthened to two years. If the correlations were to remain high for long periods, the

[6] We are indebted to Endicott for permission to examine the company reports for three years.

differences in wages would presumably reflect compensating differences in the non-wage terms of employment. But the normal pattern surely is one of declining correlation coefficients as the period is lengthened, if only as a Galton regression phenomenon.

Differences in initial wage rates would also be offset by different rates of increase in wages, so the present values of different jobs could still be equal. Endicott's survey for 1960 reported the

TABLE 2

CORRELATION COEFFICIENTS OF SALARY RATES IN 1958, 1959, AND 1960 FOR COLLEGE GRADUATES

Occupation	No. of Companies	Correlation Coefficient		
		1958 and 1959	1959 and 1960	1958 and 1960
Engineers.......	66	.660	.761	.577
Accountants....	40	.723	.872	.720
Sales...........	29	.849	.885	.871
General business.	41	.853	.891	.873

Source: Same as Table 1.

average salary paid to college graduates after one year of service, and these salaries may be compared with those paid initially. The relationship for accountants was

$$W_2 = 24.71 + \underset{(.062)}{1.039}W_1 , \qquad (N = 67),$$

where W_2 was the wage in 1960 and W_1 the wage in 1959; the relationship is close (r = .900). So far as these data go, they suggest that initial wage rates are a good predictor of wage rates in the following year.

These fragments illustrate rather than prove the existence of substantial dispersion in hiring rates for homogeneous labor. This dispersion cannot be measured precisely, but is of the order of magnitude of 5–10 per cent even in so well organized a market as that of college graduates at a single university.

II. THE PROBLEM OF INFORMATION

A worker will search for wage offers (and an employer will search for wage demands) until the expected marginal return equals the marginal cost of search. Under what conditions will this search eliminate all dispersion of wage rates for homogeneous labor?

The conditions are severe. It is not sufficient for demand and supply to have been stable indefinitely long, and hence "the" equilibrium wage not to have changed for an indefinitely long period, in order to eliminate all dispersion. If workers were to change employment (perhaps because of improving skills) or employers were to change identity (because of the turnover of firms), it still would not pay to search enough to eliminate all dispersion. But if these changes were infrequent—say, once every three years or more—the dispersion of wage rates would be fairly small, although not negligible.[7] Changes in jobs due to

[7] With a rectangular wage offer distribution between 0 and 1, the average maximum wage encountered in n searches is $n/(n + 1)$, so the expected marginal wage rate gain from $(n + 1)$ searches is

$$\frac{n+1}{n+2} - \frac{n}{n+1} = \frac{1}{(n+1)(n+2)},$$

which, multiplied by the expected duration of employment, is the marginal income gain from search. If employment is expected to last m days, and the cost of search is k days, the amount of search will be given by

$$\frac{m}{(n+1)(n+2)} = \frac{kn}{n+1},$$

or n is approximately $\sqrt{m/k}$, or (say) 25 with three years of expected employment, and k = 1. The coef-

changes in workers' tastes and abilities and employers' identities therefore set some minimum on the dispersion of wage rates. If the market has appreciable geographical extent, transportation costs of workers (and plants) add to this minimum dispersion.

The fluctuations of supply-and-demand conditions add a new source of dispersion. The information of the worker (and employer) now becomes obsolete with time: there will be changes in the level of wages and in the relative wage rates of different employers (and workers) which call for additional search. The more rapidly "the" equilibrium wage rate changes, the smaller the returns from search and hence the smaller the amount of search that will be undertaken—and the larger the resulting wage dispersion.

The subsequent analysis is devoted to an application of this approach to the costs and returns from search for various types of workers. The unavailability of a temporal sequence of closely spaced wage distributions makes it impossible to explore the effects of rates of change of equilibrium prices on the amount of dispersion.

THE RETURNS FROM SEARCH BY WORKERS

We shall begin our analysis of the returns from search by forming some estimate of the magnitude of the return as a function of the amount of search. To this end, let us assume that the wage offers by all possible employers are normally distributed.[8] Then the expected maximum wage offer (w_m) a man will encounter in n searches is approximately[9]

$$w_m = .65n^{.37}\,\sigma_w + \bar{w}\,,$$

and the marginal wage rate increase from one additional search is

$$\frac{\partial w_n}{\partial n} = \frac{.24\sigma_w}{n^{.63}}\,.$$

If $\sigma_w = \bar{w}/10$, the marginal wage rate gain from additional search is:

Search (n)	Marginal Wage Rate Gain
5	.0087 $\bar{w}$
10	.0056 $\bar{w}$
15	.0044 $\bar{w}$
20	.0036 $\bar{w}$

If the annual wage rate is $6,000, the marginal wage rate gain is therefore of the order of $20 to $50 in this range of search.

If the structure of employer wage offers were permanently fixed, and if the worker lived forever, the marginal income gain from additional search would be simply the capitalized value of the marginal *wage-rate* gain. If the structure were permanent and the duration of employment t_o years, the marginal *income* gain would be the value of the corresponding annuity, namely,

$$\frac{\partial w_n}{\partial n}\,\frac{(1+i)^{t_o}-1}{i(1+i)^{t_o}}\,.$$

---

ficient of variation of wages is

$$\sqrt{\frac{n}{(n+1)^2(n+2)}}\;\frac{n+1}{n} = \frac{1}{\sqrt{n(n+2)}} = \sqrt{\frac{k}{m}}\,,$$

which would be 4 per cent in our example. This argument is an adaptation of that in "The Economics of Information," *op. cit.*, p. 215.

[8] The Chicago student wage offers are consistent with this assumption, and it seems intuitively more plausible than the rectangular distribution which was used (for algebraic convenience) in "The Economics of Information" and in n. 7.

[9] The expression is simply an approximation (for $3 < n < 20$) to the mean maximum observation from a normal population in random samples of size n; the precise values are given in W. J. Dixon and F. J. Massey, *Introduction to Statistical Analysis* (New York, 1957), p. 407.

In this extreme case of a permanent wage structure, the order of magnitude of the marginal income gain from search is illustrated by the following table, where $\sigma_w = \bar{w}/10$ and i = 6 per cent.

Prospective Years of Employment	Amount of Search	
	5 Employers	15 Employers
3	.023 $\bar{w}$	.012 $\bar{w}$
5	.037 $\bar{w}$	.018 $\bar{w}$
10	.064 $\bar{w}$	.032 $\bar{w}$

For the $6,000 salary level, these marginal income gains run from $66 (fifteen employers, three years) to $384 (five employers, ten years).

But these gains are exaggerated because there is not a perfect correlation between the wage offers of employers in successive time periods. The employers themselves do not know wage offers sufficiently well to preserve a perfect correlation, even if they mysteriously wished it, and the appearance of new employers adds a further reason for continued search by the worker.

When the correlation of successive wage offers is positive but less than unity it will still pay the worker to search more intensively in the earlier periods because this search will have some value in subsequent periods. In a simple two-period model, the details of which are given in the appendix, the increased search in the first period due to correlation of wage rates will increase the expected maximum wage offer in the proportion $br^2/(1\text{-}b)$, or approximately $r^2/2$. If r = .5, the amount of search in period 1 will be increased by 20 per cent, with roughly a 12 per cent increase in salary.

It would be possible to analyze a variety of phenomena in the light of the correlation of successive wage offers. For example, the higher the correlation, the longer the expected tenure of a worker with a company, and therefore the lower the quit rate. Unfortunately there are no published data, so far as I know, which allow calculation of the correlations, although of course these data dwell in the worksheets of numerous wage surveys.

As a poor substitute, one can examine the average wage rates (measured by earnings per worker) on a geographical basis. The average earnings per worker in a state will be an index of wage rates in the given industry, and it will be a better index the more similar the occupational and wage structures of the industry in various states. A sample of such calculations is reported in Table 3.

Several features of these geographical patterns are noteworthy. The dispersion of earnings among states is much smaller in the recent period, and the decline occurred in twenty-one of twenty-five industries. The inference is that the national market has become more perfect, and the inference is commended by the fact that costs of movement have fallen substantially relative to wage rates over the period. The correlation coefficients reveal a slight decline on average, although they are based upon a seven-year interval in the later period (including a year of turbulent demobilization) as against a five-year interval in the earlier period.[10] The comparison timidly suggests that the difference in earnings increasingly represents differences in the quality of labor rather than in its compensation.

The most direct implication of the formal analysis is that the gains from search are larger the longer the prospective period of employment. When search is more extensive, however, the disper-

[10] The industries are also more homogeneous in the later period, and this serves to increase the correlation coefficients.

sion of maximum wage rates will be smaller—the lowest wage offers will more often be rejected for known better offers.[11] So the realized dispersion of wage rates should be smaller the longer the prospective period of employment. Several tests of this implication can be made.

Women generally expect to stay in the labor force a shorter period than men do, so among homogeneous groups of men and women we should expect that the latter have larger dispersions. The occupational wage surveys do reveal this expected difference.[12] The major difficulty in making extensive tests of this prediction is that the tabulated Census

[11] Or, more precisely, the distribution of maximum offers has a variance that decreases as the number of searches increases.

[12] For example, hourly earnings of shipping packers in manufacturing in Chicago have the following characteristics:

	1952	1957
Males:		
Interquartile range	23.4¢	43.8¢
Median rate	144.2	182.0
Interquartile ratio (per cent)	16.2	24.1
Females:		
Interquartile range	28.4¢	45.8¢
Median rate	109.8	175.7
Interquartile ratio (per cent)	25.9	26.1

Source: Bureau of Labor Statistics, Bulls. 1105 and 1202–15.

With normally distributed variates, the interquartile ratio is 1.35 times the coefficient of variation.

TABLE 3

CHARACTERISTICS OF AVERAGE EARNINGS IN SELECTED MANUFACTURING INDUSTRIES, 1904–9 AND 1947–54

(Identical States)

Industry	No. of States	Correlation Coefficients		Average Coefficient of Variation (Per Cent)	
		1904 and 1909	1947 and 1954	1904 and 1909	1947 and 1954
Non-ferrous foundries	8	.895	.663	15.3	8.7
Motor vehicles and equipment	9	.349	.106	8.9	4.9
Structural clay products	23	.982	.938	29.4	19.3
Ship and boat building	9	.894	.703	17.6	10.6
Rubber products	8	.270	.672	8.1	6.4
Musical instruments and parts	7	.953	.460	25.7	8.7
Confectionery products	17	.819	.876	15.3	17.8
Beer and ale	12	.921	.834	15.4	10.8
Mattresses and bedsprings	9	.830	.906	22.0	22.9
Furniture and fixtures, excluding mattresses and bedsprings	33	.941	.912	26.2	17.0
Fertilizers	13	.905	.952	20.4	20.4
Meat products	29	.728	.922	18.5	15.8
Flour and meal	14	.935	.530	21.8	12.0
Bakery products	20	.952	.918	18.2	12.6
Bottled soft drinks	15	.954	.874	20.1	18.4
Manufactured ice	21	.926	.854	22.8	25.5
Woolen and worsted fabrics	8	.987	.844	17.6	8.7
Knitting mills	17	.955	.774	23.5	11.2
Paperboard containers	18	.906	.926	17.1	14.0
Printing and publishing	47	.912	.906	21.3	11.8
Drugs and medicines	13	.725	.924	16.2	14.0
Soap and related products	10	.950	.681	14.8	12.0
Paints and allied products	15	.742	.870	18.4	11.2
Leather tanning and finishing	9	.968	.906	19.0	13.8
Footwear (except rubber)	12	.932	.703	13.1	9.2
Average		.853	.786	18.7	13.5

data on earnings (in 1940 and 1950) do not allow the removal of the effects of age (men have a much wider dispersion of ages) and of race (Negro women are a larger fraction of the female labor force than Negro men are of the male labor force).[13]

Similar comparisons can be made of younger and older workers. The coefficient of variation increases with age for engineers (see Table 4). The coefficient

TABLE 4

MONTHLY ENGINEERING EARNINGS, BY AGE, 1929

Age	Mean Monthly Earnings	Standard Deviation	Coefficient of Variation (Per Cent)
23	161.0	85.1*	52.9*
24–25	189.5	58.2	30.7
26–27	230.1	86.4	37.6
28–31	282.8	117.5	41.6
32–35	349.9	175.7	50.2
36–39	400.0	221.6	55.4
40–47	464.1	294.5	63.5
48–55	510.0	346.0	67.8
56–63	544.3	399.8	73.4
64 or more	487.6	356.3	73.1

Source: A. Fraser, Jr., "Employment and Earnings in the Engineering Profession, 1929 to 1934," Bureau of Labor Statistics, Bull. No. 682, 233, Table 2.

* This class appears to be heterogeneous: two of the respondents had salaries 20 standard deviations above the mean.

of variation of 1949 earnings of plumbers and pipefitters was 40.8 per cent; that of apprentices was 32.9 per cent.[14] The dispersion of salaries of college teachers is larger the higher the rank (and age) of the teacher.[15] A more powerful test would be provided by a comparison of wages of students in summer employment with young men of the same age who had permanently left school.

Our original estimate of the coefficient of variation of earnings in section 1 was of the order of 10 per cent. The differences cited above—for example, 60 per cent versus 30 per cent for engineers of fifty-five and twenty-five years of age—might suggest a much larger estimate of the effects of ignorance. These gross dispersions are due to at least three different components, however, only the first two of which involve information:

i. The dispersion of earnings of engineers increases with age because younger engineers make more extensive search than older engineers.
ii. The difference in ability of engineers becomes better known as they become older (and have worked longer for a given employer).[16]

[13] A moderately extensive analysis was made of dispersions of income in 1949 in large cities for selected occupations, and an analysis was made of earnings in 1939 for waiters and waitresses. The 1949 data showed larger dispersions for women than for men; the 1939 data for the one occupation showed the opposite. The heterogeneity of age and race (and in 1940 the inclusion of self-employed workers) are such that I believe the results are wholly inconclusive. For the same reason, the consistently smaller *average* wages of women (which are predicted by the theory) are not supporting evidence.

[14] On the other hand, the coefficients of variation for machinists and tool makers (30.1 per cent) and apprentices (29.7 per cent) were essentially identical. These are all United States data, influenced by extent of part-time work (which was much higher among apprentices than among machinists).

[15] The interquartile ratios $[(Q_3 - Q_1)/Q_2]$ of academic salaries in 1959–60 were:

Rank	Per Cent	
	Men	Women
Professor	33.0	31.8
Associate professor	23.3	26.2
Assistant professor	19.7	24.2
Instructor	19.3	21.7

These calculations are based upon National Education Association, Higher Education Series, Research Report, 1960–R3. See also my *Trends in Employment in the Service Industries* (New York: National Bureau of Economic Research, 1956), p. 128.

The smaller dispersion of salaries of women professors is found in every type of college and university reported. Women make up less than one-twelfth of the full professors and more than twice as large a fraction even of associate professors. The roles of ability and discrimination in producing this reversal of the basic pattern would be interesting to know.

[16] This increased dispersion in earnings due to better recognition of differences in ability (the search for information on the quality of workers) is of course to be reckoned as a reduction in the dispersion of earnings of homogeneous workers.

iii. The older engineers have made different amounts of "on-the-job" investment in training, which serves to increase their dispersion of abilities, a phenomenon discussed in Professor Mincer's paper.

The disentanglement of the second and third components of dispersion is especially difficult. We reach again the conclusion that the differences in quality of workers cast a deep shadow over all measures of pure dispersion due to differences in knowledge (or, for that matter, due to other forms of investment).

The effect of the absolute level of earnings, which may also enter into the determination of the gain from search, will be considered in the next section.

THE COSTS OF SEARCH

The larger the cost of search the less search will be undertaken by a worker at a given level of dispersion of employers' wage offers. These costs will vary systematically with various characteristics of occupations.

When prospective employers of a worker are readily identified—which is partly associated with how specialized a worker is—search for a job is more economical: one does not have to waste inquiries on wholly irrelevant possibilities. We should therefore expect the dispersion of actual wage rates to be less the more easily the employers are identified.

This prediction is supported by several analyses of earnings in the twenty metropolitan areas in 1950. Domestic servants have higher coefficients of variation than laundry operatives in nineteen of twenty areas (with means of 75.2 per cent and 54.0 per cent, respectively). The confirmation is less emphatic in the comparison of taxi drivers with truck drivers (the former have lower coefficients of variation in thirteen of twenty regions, but the means are virtually identical: 44.2 per cent and 45.7 per cent).[17]

The costs of search are also lower the higher the probability that a given, identified employer is taking on men. This would argue that in periods of expanding employment the dispersion of wages will be smaller. But unemployment among a class of workers also works in the opposite direction to reduce the cost of search. Within local markets the cost of search is primarily a cost in time, to be valued (at least approximately) by the mean wage rate, as a measure of the leisure value of time. But for the unemployed worker, this alternative cost of leisure is negligible. In the search in other labor markets, however, both transportation costs and foregone earnings must be incurred.[18]

The effects of the level of earnings on the amount of search are equally difficult to disentangle. If the absolute dispersion (σ_w) is proportional to the mean wage, the mean wage affects costs and returns from search proportionately, and there is no effect on the amount of search. On the other hand, it appears to have been the regular practice for employment agencies to charge a fee that is a higher percentage of larger initial salaries—the fee is progressive.[19] The simplest explanation would be that the expected duration of employment is greater the higher the initial wage rate. On the whole, this kind of evidence seems much more persuasive than that based on interoccupational comparisons.

[17] These Census data are moderately more persuasive than those rejected earlier because differences due to race, part-time work, and age are smaller.

[18] Hence the mean wage rates for given work should vary more among establishments in an extensive area than within a single labor market.

[19] P. H. Douglas and A. Director, *The Problem of Unemployment* (1931), p. 267.

The search for information may take forms other than direct solicitation: newspaper advertisements, employment agencies, employer search, and the myriad forms of pooling of information by workers. Some require little expenditure of time and—if used alone—would lead us to expect that the dispersion of wage rates should be equal in absolute terms (standard deviations, not coefficients of variation) for workers at different wage levels. Such information, however, is incomplete and limited, and if more is needed solicitation is eventually resorted to. The marginal cost of search may rise as search increases.

The private employment agencies offer a fertile field for investigation from this viewpoint. Their *raison d'être* is information, and they should have specialized in the occupations in which information is most difficult for the employer or worker to obtain. Their fees, indeed, would provide a direct estimate of the marginal cost of information in these occupations.

III. THE EMPLOYERS' SEARCH

There is direct search by employers, wholly comparable to that of workers, in certain industries. College teaching is an obvious example: the employer canvasses graduate schools, professional journals, and the like for potential employees and invites them in to be looked over. This kind of direct solicitation is most probable when the workers are highly specialized, of course.

The main reason for workers undertaking the burden of solicitation is that it is cheaper for them than for employers. When an employer has numerous employees the probability that a given employer needs additional workers is much greater than the probability that a given worker will accept a job offer. The identification problem is usually also less for a worker than for an employer—the fraction of wasted search will be much smaller for a steelworker than for a steel company. But where the number of employees per employer approaches unity (domestic service, vice-presidents in charge of marketing), the employer usually takes on some or all of the task of search.

The employers' search involves more than the identification of potential workers: they must be "processed" to a degree set by the personnel practices, and there are training costs (including low productivity) for a time. Walter Oi estimates that the initial hiring and training cost per worker was (in 1951) about $382 for International Harvester, the cost rising rapidly with the level of skill.[20]

One way to reduce hiring costs is to pay higher relative wages. Not only is the quit rate of existing workers reduced by high wages, but on average, more obviously high-quality workers will accept offers. Wage rates and skilled search are substitutes for the employer: the more efficiently he detects workers of superior quality the less he need pay for such quality.

The small company has distinct advantages in the hiring process, so far as judging the quality of workers is concerned. The employer can directly observe the performance of the new worker and need not resort to expensive and uncertain rating practices to estimate the workers' performance. It is well known that wage rates are less in small plants than in large, and the difference reflects at least in part (and perhaps in whole) the lower costs to the small-scale employer of judging quality. A similar result obtains with respect to dispersion of

[20] "Labor as a Quasi-Fixed Factor of Production" (unpublished Ph.D. dissertation, University of Chicago, 1961).

wages: a sample of such data is given in Table 5. Men should in general enter smaller companies the greater their ability.

These last remarks represent in a sense a contradiction to the main argument of this paper. For previously I have accepted wage dispersion as a measure of ignorance but now take it as a measure of ability (less dispersion implies greater ignorance). The contradiction is only superficial because the problem of information on quality has been replacing that of information on price, and heterogeneity of quality has replaced homogeneity. Yet this shift poses again the central difficulty with which we began: the entanglement of quality and price variation in labor markets.

TABLE 5

COEFFICIENTS OF VARIATION OF HOURLY WAGE RATES OF MALE EMPLOYEES IN SELECTED MANUFACTURING INDUSTRIES BY CLASS OF WORKER

INDUSTRY AND EMPLOYER	NO. OF PLANTS	COEFFICIENT OF VARIATION (PER CENT)		
		Skilled	Semiskilled	Unskilled
Radios:				
Two largest companies	2	12.8	16.7	13.8
Other companies	22	24.6	24.9	20.9
Soap:				
Large companies	13	15.1	16.8	17.2
Other companies	59	25.6	24.5	23.3
Explosives:				
Three largest companies	28	16.2	14.1	15.8
Other companies	23	19.8	17.4	19.5
Meatpacking:				
Four largest companies	59	....	20.4	....
Small companies	182	....	28.1	....

Source: *Hourly Earnings of Employees in Large and Small Enterprises* ("Temporary National Economic Committee Monograph," No. 14, 1948), pp. 21, 54, 59, 66, 70. The same pattern holds without exception for female employees. The meatpacking data refer to the northern wage district, and to all employees.

IV. INFORMATION AS CAPITAL

The information a man possesses on the labor market is capital: it was produced at the cost of search, and it yields a higher wage rate than on average would be received in its absence.

From the viewpoint of the individual worker, the capital value of his knowledge can be calculated by the usual method of valuing an asset; that is, discounting its future revenue. In section 1, above, we gave the marginal income gain from search as

$$\frac{\partial w_m}{\partial n}\frac{(1+i)^{t_o}-1}{i(1+i)^{t_o}}.$$

that is, the marginal wage-rate gain times the present value of an annuity of duration t_o. The total income gained is the integral of this expression over the range of search, or

$$(w_m-\bar{w})\frac{(1+i)^{t_o}-1}{i(1+i)^{t_o}}.$$

This formula, as we observed, is an overestimate to the extent that future wage rates paid by various employers are not perfectly correlated with present wage rates. Conversely, if the duration of work with one employer is t_o, there will be some value to the knowledge presently acquired, in the search for alternative employments after t_o. This offset will be larger the larger the correlation of wage offers over time.

The duration of given jobs varies systematically with age and skill. Gladys Palmer's study suggested an average duration of a job of about three years for men between the ages of twenty-five and thirty-four, rising to six years for men over sixty-five.[21] The turnover of jobs is higher among unskilled workers than among skilled workers. If the worker has a prospective job duration of three years, and the coefficient of variation of wage offers is 10 per cent, the capital value of his knowledge, by the above formula (with $i = .06$), would be

$.32\ \bar{w}$ if 5 wage offers are found,

$.47\ \bar{w}$ if 15 wage offers are found.

If such numbers are applied to the entire labor force, one gets an aggregate of private capital in laborer's information on the order of $100 billion.

The employer has a corresponding capital value of information: it is equal to the present value of the savings in wage rates for given quality of workers (or the superior quality of workers at given wage rates). The larger the amount of search by workers, the less will be the opportunity (or the greater the cost) for the employer to achieve a given saving in wage rates. The division of the investment in information between employers and workers will be determined by institutional characteristics of the market: where it is more economical for one party to acquire the information, the other party will make relatively small investments.

From the social viewpoint, the return from investment in information consists in a more efficient allocation of the labor force: the better informed the labor market, the closer each worker's (marginal) product is to its maximum at any given time. From this viewpoint, the function of information is to prevent less efficient employers from obtaining labor, and inefficient workers from obtaining the better jobs. In a regime of ignorance, Enrico Fermi would have been a gardener, Von Neumann a checkout clerk at a drugstore.

The social capital is not necessarily equal to the sum of the private capitals. If most workers search intensively, employers who offer low wage rates will be unable to fill their jobs and will be forced either to close down or to raise wage rates—so if I enter the labor market and do not search, I nevertheless profit from others' knowledge of the market. This effect arises because of the existence of the economies of scale.

The amounts and kinds of information needed for the efficient allocation of labor, whether judged from the viewpoint of the laborer, the employer, or the community, extend far beyond the determination of wage rates. The kinds and amounts of skill men should acquire pose parallel informational problems, and so too do the non-monetary conditions of employment. The traditional literature has not done these problems justice. It is doubtful that justice would be more closely approached by making exaggerated claims of the importance of the problem of information. There is no exaggeration however, in the suggestion that the analysis of the precise problems of information and of the methods an economy uses to deal with them appears to be a highly rewarding area for future research.

[21] *Labor Mobility in Six Cities* (New York, 1954), p. 53. The durations are biased downward for the younger men because not all were in the labor force for an entire decade.

APPENDIX

Let n_1 and n_2 be the search in the two periods, λ the average cost of search. Then the "profit" of a worker from search, neglecting interest, is

$$\pi = w_1 + w_2 - \lambda(n_1 + n_2),$$

where

$$w_1 = a n_1^b,$$

$$w_2 = a(n_2 + r^2 n_1)^b.$$

For a maximum,

$$\frac{\partial \pi}{\partial n_1} = a b n_1^{b-1} + a b (n_2 + r^2 n_1)^{b-1} r^2 - \lambda = 0. \quad (1)$$

$$\frac{\partial \pi}{\partial n_2} = a b (n_2 + r^2 n_1)^{b-1} - \lambda = 0. \quad (2)$$

Equating values of λ,

$$n_2 = n_1 \{ (1 - r^2)^{1/(1-b)} - r^2 \}. \quad (3)$$

It follows from (3) that $n_2 = n_1$ when $r = 0$. It can be shown that if $r = 1$, $n_2 = 0$,[22] and

$$n_1 = \left(\frac{\lambda}{2ab}\right)^{1/(b-1)}.$$

Search in period 1 makes a marginal wage contribution of

$$\frac{\partial w_2}{\partial n_1} = a b (n_2 + r^2 n_1)^{b-1} r^2$$

in period 2. The optimum amount of search in period 1, from equations (1) and (2), is

$$n_1 = \left(\frac{\lambda}{ab}\right)^{1/(b-1)} (1 - r^2)^{1/(b-1)}. \quad (4)$$

The wage rate in period 1 with a correlation of r exceeds that with no correlation in the proportion

$$\frac{a(\lambda/ab)^{b/(b-1)}(1 - r^2)^{b/(b-1)} - a(\lambda/ab)^{b/(b-1)}}{a(\lambda/ab)^{b/(b-1)}},$$

or by $(1 - r^2)^{b/(b-1)} - 1$, or approximately by $br^2/(1 - b)$.

[22] If r approaches unity, equations (1) and (2) yield

$$\frac{ab}{n_1^{1-b}} = 0,$$

or n_1 becomes infinite, and by equation (2),

$$n_2 + r^2 n_1 = \left(\frac{\lambda}{ab}\right)^{1/(b-1)}$$

so n_2/n_1 approaches $-r^2$ as n_1 approaches infinity. Since n_2 has a minimum of zero, n_1 is fixed by (1) at the expression in the text.

[11]

A THEORY OF OLIGOPOLY

GEORGE J. STIGLER[1]
University of Chicago

NO ONE has the right, and few the ability, to lure economists into reading another article on oligopoly theory without some advance indication of its alleged contribution. The present paper accepts the hypothesis that oligopolists wish to collude to maximize joint profits. It seeks to reconcile this wish with facts, such as that collusion is impossible for many firms and collusion is much more effective in some circumstances than in others. The reconciliation is found in the problem of policing a collusive agreement, which proves to be a problem in the theory of information. A considerable number of implications of the theory are discussed, and a modest amount of empirical evidence is presented.

I. THE TASK OF COLLUSION

A satisfactory theory of oligopoly cannot begin with assumptions concerning the way in which each firm views its interdependence with its rivals. If we adhere to the traditional theory of profit-maximizing enterprises, then behavior is no longer something to be assumed but rather something to be deduced. The firms in an industry will behave in such a way, given the demand-and-supply functions (including those of rivals), that their profits will be maximized.

The combined profits of the entire set of firms in an industry are maximized when they act together as a monopolist. At least in the traditional formulation of the oligopoly problem, in which there are no major uncertainties as to the profit-maximizing output and price at any time, this familiar conclusion seems inescapable. Moreover, the result holds for any number of firms.

Our modification of this theory consists simply in presenting a systematic account of the factors governing the feasibility of collusion, which like most things in this world is not free. Before we do so, it is desirable to look somewhat critically at the concept of homogeneity of products, and what it implies for profit-maximizing. We shall show that collusion normally involves much more than "the" price.

Homogeneity is commonly defined in terms of identity of products or of (what is presumed to be equivalent) pairs of products between which the elasticity of substitution is infinite. On either definition it is the behavior of buyers that is decisive. Yet it should be obvious that products may be identical to any or every buyer while buyers may be quite different from the viewpoint of sellers.

This fact that every transaction involves two parties is something that economists do not easily forget. One would therefore expect a definition of homogeneity also to be two-sided: if the products are what sellers offer, and the purchase commitments are what the buyers offer, full homogeneity clearly involves infinite elasticities of substitution between both products and purchase

[1] I am indebted to Claire Friedland for the statistical work and to Harry Johnson for helpful criticisms.

commitments. In other words, two products are homogeneous to a buyer if he is indifferent between all combinations of x of one and (say) $20 - x$ of the other, at a common price. Two purchase commitments are homogeneous to a seller if he is indifferent between all combinations of y of one and (say) $20 - y$ of the other, at a common price. Full homogeneity is then defined as homogeneity both in products (sellers) and purchase commitments (buyers).

The heterogeneity of purchase commitments (buyers), however, is surely often at least as large as that of products within an industry, and sometimes vastly larger. There is the same sort of personal differentia of buyers as of sellers—ease in making sales, promptness of payment, penchant for returning goods, likelihood of buying again (or buying other products). In addition there are two differences among buyers which are pervasive and well recognized in economics:

1. The size of purchase, with large differences in costs of providing lots of different size.
2. The urgency of purchase, with possibly sufficient differences in elasticity of demand to invite price discrimination.

It is one thing to assert that no important market has homogeneous transactions, and quite another to measure the extent of the heterogeneity. In a regime of perfect knowledge, it would be possible to measure heterogeneity by the variance of prices in transactions; in a regime of imperfect knowledge, there will be dispersion of prices even with transaction homogeneity.[2]

The relevance of heterogeneity to collusion is this: It is part of the task of maximizing industry profits to employ a price structure that takes account of the larger differences in the costs of various classes of transactions. Even with a single, physically homogeneous product the profits will be reduced if differences among buyers are ignored. A simple illustration of this fact is given in the Appendix; disregard of differences among buyers proves to be equivalent to imposing an excise tax upon them, but one which is not collected by the monopolist. A price structure of some complexity will usually be the goal of collusive oligopolists.

II. THE METHODS OF COLLUSION

Collusion of firms can take many forms, of which the most comprehensive is outright merger. Often merger will be inappropriate, however, because of diseconomies of scale,[3] and at certain times and places it may be forbidden by law. Only less comprehensive is the cartel with a joint sales agency, which again has economic limitations—it is ill suited to custom work and creates serious administrative costs in achieving quality standards, cost reductions, product innovations, etc. In deference to American antitrust policy, we shall assume that the collusion takes the form of joint determination of outputs and prices by ostensibly independent firms, but we shall not take account of the effects of the legal prohibitions until later. Oligopoly existed before 1890, and has existed in countries that have never had an antitrust policy.

The colluding firms must agree upon the price structure appropriate to the transaction classes which they are prepared to recognize. A complete profit-maximizing price structure may have

[2] Unless one defines heterogeneity of transactions to include also differences in luck in finding low price sellers; see my "Economics of Information," *Journal of Political Economy*, June, 1961.

[3] If the firms are multiproduct, with different product structures, the diseconomies of merger are not strictly those of scale (in any output) but of firm size measured either absolutely or in terms of variety of products.

almost infinitely numerous price classes: the firms will have to decide upon the number of price classes in the light of the costs and returns from tailoring prices to the diversity of transactions. We have already indicated by hypothetical example (see Appendix) that there are net profits to be obtained by catering to differences in transactions. The level of collusive prices will also depend upon the conditions of entry into the industry as well as upon the elasticities of demand.

Let us assume that the collusion has been effected, and a price structure agreed upon. It is a well-established proposition that if any member of the agreement can secretly violate it, he will gain larger profits than by conforming to it.[4] It is, moreover, surely one of the axioms of human behavior that all agreements whose violation would be profitable to the violator must be enforced. The literature of collusive agreements, ranging from the pools of the 1880's to the electrical conspiracies of recent times, is replete with instances of the collapse of conspiracies because of "secret" price-cutting. This literature is biased: conspiracies that are successful in avoiding an amount of price-cutting which leads to collapse of the agreement are less likely to be reported or detected. But no conspiracy can neglect the problem of enforcement.

Enforcement consists basically of detecting significant deviations from the agreed-upon prices. Once detected, the deviations will tend to disappear because they are no longer secret and will be matched by fellow conspirators if they are not withdrawn. If the enforcement is weak, however—if price-cutting is detected only slowly and incompletely—the conspiracy must recognize its weakness: it must set prices not much above the competitive level so the inducements to price-cutting are small, or it must restrict the conspiracy to areas in which enforcement can be made efficient.

Fixing market shares is probably the most efficient of all methods of combating secret price reductions. No one can profit from price-cutting if he is moving along the industry demand curve,[5] once a maximum profit price has been chosen. With inspection of output and an appropriate formula for redistribution of gains and losses from departures from quotas, the incentive to secret price-cutting is eliminated. Unless inspection of output is costly or ineffective (as with services), this is the ideal method of enforcement, and is widely used by legal cartels. Unfortunately for oligopolists, it is usually an easy form of collusion to detect, for it may require side payments among firms and it leaves indelible traces in the output records.

Almost as efficient a method of eliminating secret price-cutting is to assign each buyer to a single seller. If this can be done for all buyers, short-run price-cutting no longer has any purpose. Long-run price-cutting will still be a serious possibility if the buyers are in competition: lower prices to one's own customers can then lead to an expansion of their share of their market, so the price-cutter's long-run demand curve will be more elastic than that of the industry. Long-run price-cutting is likely to be important, however, only where sellers are providing a major cost component to the buyer.

There are real difficulties of other sorts

[4] If price is above marginal cost, marginal revenue will be only slightly less than price (and hence above marginal cost) for price cuts by this one seller.

[5] More precisely, he is moving along a demand curve which is a fixed share of the industry demand, and hence has the same elasticity as the industry curve at every price.

to the sellers in the assignment of buyers. In general the fortunes of the various sellers will differ greatly over time: one seller's customers may grow threefold, while another seller's customers shrink by half. If the customers have uncorrelated fluctuations in demand, the various sellers will experience large changes in relative outputs in the short run.[6] Where the turnover of buyers is large, the method is simply impracticable.

Nevertheless, the conditions appropriate to the assignment of customers will exist in certain industries, and in particular the geographical division of the market has often been employed. Since an allocation of buyers is an obvious and easily detectible violation of the Sherman Act, we may again infer that an efficient method of enforcing a price agreement is excluded by the antitrust laws. We therefore turn to other techniques of enforcement, but we shall find that the analysis returns to allocation of buyers.

In general the policing of a price agreement involves an audit of the transactions prices. In the absence or violation of antitrust laws, actual inspection of the accounting records of sellers has been employed by some colluding groups, but even this inspection gives only limited assurance that the price agreement is adhered to.[7] Ultimately there is no substitute for obtaining the transaction prices from the buyers.

An oligopolist will not consider making secret price cuts to buyers whose purchases fall below a certain size relative to his aggregate sales. The ease with which price-cutting is detected by rivals is decisive in this case. If p is the probability that some rival will hear of one such price reduction, $1 - (1 - p)^n$ is the probability that a rival will learn of at least one reduction if it is given to n customers. Even if p is as small as 0.01, when n equals 100 the probability of detection is .634, and when n equals 1000 it is .99996. No one has yet invented a way to advertise price reductions which brings them to the attention of numerous customers but not to that of any rival.[8]

It follows that oligopolistic collusion will often be effective against small buyers even when it is ineffective against large buyers. When the oligopolists sell to numerous small retailers, for example, they will adhere to the agreed-upon price, even though they are cutting prices to larger chain stores and industrial buyers. This is a first empirical implication of our theory. Let us henceforth exclude small buyers from consideration.

The detection of secret price-cutting will of course be as difficult as interested people can make it. The price-cutter will certainly protest his innocence, or, if this would tax credulity beyond its taxable capacity, blame a disobedient subordinate. The price cut will often take the indirect form of modifying some nonprice dimension of the transaction. The customer may, and often will, divulge price reductions, in order to have them matched by others, but he will learn from experience if each disclosure is followed by the withdrawal of the lower price offer. Indeed the buyer will frequently

[6] When the relative outputs of the firms change, the minimum cost condition of equal marginal costs for all sellers is likely to be violated. Hence industry profits are not maximized.

[7] The literature and cases on "open-price associations" contain numerous references to the collection of prices from sellers (see Federal Trade Commission, *Open-Price Trade Associations* [Washington, 1929], and cases cited).

[8] This argument applies to size of buyer relative to the individual seller. One can also explain the absence of higgling in small transactions because of the costs of bargaining, but this latter argument turns on the absolute size of the typical transaction, not its size relative to the seller.

fabricate wholly fictitious price offers to test the rivals. Policing the collusion sounds very much like the subtle and complex problem presented in a good detective story.

There is a difference: In our case the man who murders the collusive price will receive the bequest of patronage. The basic method of detection of a price-cutter must be the fact that he is getting business he would otherwise not obtain. No promises of lower prices that fail to shift some business can be really effective—either the promised price is still too high or it is simply not believed.

Our definition of perfect collusion, indeed, must be that no buyer changes sellers voluntarily. There is no competitive price-cutting if there are no shifts of buyers among sellers.

To this rule that price-cutting must be inferred from shifts of buyers there is one partial exception, but that an important one. There is one type of buyer who usually reveals the price he pays, and does not accept secret benefices: the government. The system of sealed bids, publicly opened with full identification of each bidder's price and specifications, is the ideal instrument for the detection of price-cutting. There exists no alternative method of secretly cutting prices (bribery of purchasing agents aside). Our second empirical prediction, then, is that collusion will always be more effective against buyers who report correctly and fully the prices tendered to them.[9]

It follows from the test of the absence of price competition by buyer loyalty—and this is our third major empirical prediction—that collusion is severely limited (under present assumptions excluding market-sharing) when the significant buyers constantly change identity. There exist important markets in which the (substantial) buyers do change identity continuously, namely, in the construction industries. The building of a plant or an office building, for example, is an essentially non-repetitive event, and rivals cannot determine whether the successful bidder has been a price-cutter unless there is open bidding to specification.

The normal market, however, contains both stability and change. There may be a small rate of entry of new buyers. There will be some shifting of customers even in a regime of effective collusion, for a variety of minor reasons we can lump together as "random factors." There will often be some sharing of buyers by several sellers—a device commending itself to buyers to increase the difficulty of policing price agreements. We move then to the world of circumstantial evidence, or, as it is sometimes called, of probability.

III. THE CONDITIONS FOR DETECTING SECRET PRICE REDUCTIONS

We shall investigate the problem of detecting secret price-cutting with a simplified model, in which all buyers and all sellers are initially of equal size. The number of buyers per seller—recalling that we exclude from consideration all buyers who take less than (say) 0.33 per cent of a seller's output—will range from 300 down to perhaps 10 or 20 (since we wish to avoid the horrors of full bilateral oligopoly). A few of these buyers are new, but over moderate periods of time most are "old," although some of these old customers will shift among suppliers. A potential secret price-cutter has then three groups of customers who would increase their patronage if given secret price cuts: the old customers of rivals;

[9] The problem implicitly raised by these remarks is why all sales to the government are not at collusive prices. Part of the answer is that the government is usually not a sufficiently large buyer of a commodity to remunerate the costs of collusion.

the old customers who would normally leave him; and new customers.

Most old buyers will deal regularly with one or a few sellers, in the absence of secret price-cutting. There may be no secret price-cutting because a collusive price is adhered to, or because only an essentially competitive price can be obtained. We shall show that the loyalty of customers is a crucial variable in determining which price is approached. We need to know the probability that an old customer will buy again from his regular supplier at the collusive price, in the absence of secret price-cutting.

The buyer will set the economies of repetitive purchase (which include smaller transaction costs and less product-testing) against the increased probability of secret price-cutting that comes from shifting among suppliers. From the viewpoint of any one buyer, this gain will be larger the larger the number of sellers and the smaller the number of buyers, as we shall show below. The costs of shifting among suppliers will be smaller the more homogeneous the goods and the larger the purchases of the buyer (again an inverse function of his size). Let us label this probability of repeat purchases p. We shall indicate later how this probability could be determined in a more general approach.

The second component of sales of a firm will be its sales to new buyers and to the floating old customers of rivals. Here we assume that each seller is equally likely to make a sale, in the absence of price competition.

Let us proceed to the analysis. There are n_0 "old" buyers and n_n new customers, with $n_n = \lambda n_0$ and n_s sellers. A firm may look to three kinds of evidence on secret price-cutting, and therefore by symmetry to three potential areas to practice secret price-cutting.

1. *The behavior of its own old customers.*—It has, on average, n_0/n_s such customers, and expects to sell to $m_1 = pn_0/n_s$ of them in a given round of transactions, in the absence of price cutting. The variance of this number of customers is

$$\sigma_1^2 = \frac{(1-p)pn_0}{n_s}.$$

The probability of the firm losing more old customers than

$$\frac{(1-p)n_0}{n_s} + k\sigma_1$$

is given by the probability of values greater than k. The expected number of these old customers who will shift to any one rival is, say,

$$m_2 = \frac{1}{n_s - 1}\left[\frac{(1-p)n_0}{n_s} + k\sigma_1\right],$$

with a variance

$$\sigma_2^2 = \frac{n_s - 2}{(n_s - 1)^2}\left[\frac{(1-p)n_0}{n_s} + k\sigma_1\right].$$

The probability that any rival will obtain more than $m_2 + r\sigma_2$ of these customers is determined by r. We could now choose those combinations of k and r that fix a level of probability for the loss of a given number of old customers to any one rival beyond which secret price-cutting by this rival will be inferred. This is heavy arithmetic, however, so we proceed along a less elegant route.

Let us assume that the firm's critical value for the loss of old customers, beyond which it infers secret price-cutting, is

$$\frac{(1-p)n_0}{n_s} + \sigma_1 = \frac{(1-p)n_0}{n_s}\left[1 + \sqrt{\left(\frac{p}{1-p}\frac{n_s}{n_0}\right)}\right] = \frac{(1-p)n_0}{n_s}(1+\theta),$$

that is, one standard deviation above the mean. Any one rival will on average attract

$$m_2 = \frac{1}{n_s - 1}\left[\frac{(1-p)n_0}{n_s} + \sigma_1\right]$$

of these customers, with a variance of

$$\sigma_2^2 = \frac{n_s - 2}{(n_s - 1)^2}\left[\frac{(1-p)n_0}{n_s} + \sigma_1\right].$$

Let the rival be suspected of price-cutting if he obtains more than $(m_2 + \sigma_2)$ customers, that is, if the probability of any larger number is less than about 30 per cent. The joint probability of losing one standard deviation more than the average number of old customers and a rival obtaining one standard deviation more than his average share is about 10 per cent. The average sales of a rival are n_0/n_s, ignoring new customers. The maximum number of buyers any seller can obtain from one rival without exciting suspicion, minus the number he will on average get without price-cutting ($[1 - p]n_0/n_s\ [n_s - 1]$), expressed as a ratio to his average sales, is

$$\frac{[\theta(1-p)n_0/(n_s - 1)n_s + \sigma_2]}{n_0/n_s}.$$

This criterion is tabulated in Table 1.

TABLE 1

PERCENTAGE GAINS IN SALES FROM UNDETECTED PRICE-CUTTING BY A FIRM

Criterion I: $\frac{1}{(n_s - 1)}\left[\theta(1-p) + \sqrt{\frac{n_s(n_s - 2)(1-p)(1+\theta)}{n_0}}\right] \qquad \theta = \sqrt{\frac{p}{1-p}\frac{n_s}{n_0}}$

Probability of Repeat Sales (p)	No. of Buyers (n_0)	No. of Sellers					
		2	3	4	5	10	20
p=0.95	20	6.9	11.3	11.3	11.4	11.8	12.7
	30	5.6	8.9	8.8	8.8	9.0	9.6
	40	4.9	7.5	7.4	7.4	7.5	7.9
	50	4.4	6.6	6.5	6.4	6.5	6.8
	100	3.1	4.4	4.3	4.3	4.2	4.4
	200	2.2	3.0	2.9	2.8	2.8	2.8
	400	1.5	2.1	2.0	1.9	1.8	1.8
p=0.90	20	9.5	14.8	14.7	14.6	14.8	15.7
	30	7.8	11.7	11.5	11.4	11.4	12.0
	40	6.7	10.0	9.7	9.6	9.5	9.9
	50	6.0	8.8	8.6	8.4	8.3	8.6
	100	4.2	6.0	5.8	5.6	5.4	5.5
	200	3.0	4.1	3.9	3.8	3.6	3.6
	400	2.1	2.8	2.7	2.6	2.4	2.4
p=0.80	20	12.6	19.3	18.9	18.7	18.6	19.4
	30	10.3	15.4	15.0	14.7	14.5	15.0
	40	8.9	13.1	12.7	12.5	12.2	12.5
	50	8.0	11.6	11.2	11.0	10.6	10.8
	100	5.7	8.0	7.7	7.4	7.1	7.1
	200	4.0	5.5	5.3	5.1	4.8	4.7
	400	2.8	3.8	3.6	3.5	3.2	3.2
p=0.70	20	14.5	22.3	21.8	21.5	21.2	21.9
	30	11.8	17.8	17.3	17.0	16.6	16.9
	40	10.2	15.2	14.8	14.5	14.0	14.2
	50	9.2	13.5	13.1	12.8	12.3	12.4
	100	6.5	9.3	9.0	8.7	8.2	8.2
	200	4.6	6.5	6.2	6.0	5.6	5.5
	400	3.2	4.5	4.3	4.2	3.8	3.7

The entries in Table 1 are measures of the maximum additional sales obtainable by secret price-cutting (expressed as a percentage of average sales) from any one rival beyond which that rival will infer that the price-cutting is taking place. Since the profitability of secret price-cutting depends upon the amount of business one can obtain (as well as upon the excess of price over marginal cost), we may also view these numbers as the measures of the incentive to engage in secret price-cutting. Three features of the tabulation are noteworthy:

a) The gain in sales from any one rival by secret price-cutting is not very sensitive to the number of rivals, given the number of customers and the probability of repeat sales. The aggregate gain in sales of a firm from price-cutting—its total incentive to secret price-cutting—is the sum of the gains from each rival, and therefore increases roughly in proportion to the number of rivals.

b) The incentive to secret price-cutting falls as the number of customers per seller increases—and falls roughly in inverse proportion to the square root of the number of buyers.

c) The incentive to secret price-cutting rises as the probability of repeat purchases falls, but at a decreasing rate.

We have said that the gain to old buyers from shifting their patronage among sellers will be that it encourages secret price-cutting by making it more difficult to detect. Table 1 indicates that there are diminishing returns to increased shifting: The entries increase at a decreasing rate as p falls. In a fuller model we could introduce the costs of shifting among suppliers and determine p to maximize expected buyer gains. The larger the purchases of a buyer, when buyers are of unequal size, however, the greater is the prospect that his shifts will induce price-cutting.

In addition it is clear that, when the number of sellers exceeds two, it is possible for two or more firms to pool information and thus to detect less extreme cases of price-cutting. For example, at the given probability levels, the number of old customers that any one rival should be able to take from a firm was shown to be at most

$$(1-p)\frac{n_0(1+\theta)}{n_s-1},$$

with variance

$$\frac{(n_s-2)(1-p)(1+\theta)}{(n_s-1)^2}\,n_0.$$

At the same probability level, the average number of old customers that one rival should be able to take from T firms is at most

$$\frac{T(1-p)n_0}{n_s-T}\left(1+\frac{\theta}{\sqrt{T}}\right),$$

with the variance

$$\frac{(n_s-T-1)}{(n_s-T)^2}(1-p)\left(1+\frac{\theta}{\sqrt{T}}\right)n_0T.$$

Each of these is smaller than the corresponding expression for one seller when expressed as a fraction of the customers lost by each of the firms pooling information.

There are of course limits to such pooling of information: not only does it become expensive as the number of firms increases, but also it produces less reliable information, since one of the members of the pool may himself be secretly cutting prices. Some numbers illustrative of the effect of pooling will be given at a later point.

2. *The attraction of old customers of other firms is a second source of evidence of price-cutting.*—If a given rival has not cut prices, he will on average lose $(1-p)$ (n_0/n_s) customers, with a variance of σ_1^2. The number of customers he will retain with secret price-cutting cannot exceed

a level at which the rivals suspect the price-cutting. Any one rival will have little basis for judging whether he is getting a fair share of this firm's old customers, but they can pool their information and then in the aggregate they will expect the firm to lose at least $(1 - p)(n_0/n_s) - 2\sigma_1$ customers, at the 5 per cent probability level. Hence the secret price-cutter can retain at most $2\sigma_1$ of his old customers (beyond his average number), which as a fraction of his average sales (ignoring new customers) is

$$\frac{2\sigma_1}{n_0/n_s} = 2\sqrt{\frac{(1-p)pn_s}{n_0}}.$$

This is tabulated as Table 2.

TABLE 2

OLD CUSTOMERS THAT A SECRET PRICE-CUTTER CAN RETAIN, AS A PERCENTAGE OF AVERAGE SALES

Criterion II: $2\sqrt{\frac{p(1-p)}{2}\frac{n_s}{n_0}}$

Probability That Old Customer Will Remain Loyal (p)	No. of Old Customers per Seller (n_0/n_s)			
	10	20	50	100
0.95	13.8	9.7	6.2	4.4
.90	19.0	13.4	8.5	6.0
.85	22.6	16.0	10.1	7.1
.80	25.3	17.9	11.3	8.0
.75	27.4	19.4	12.2	8.7
.70	29.0	20.5	13.0	9.2
.65	30.2	21.3	13.5	9.5
.60	31.0	21.9	13.9	9.8
.55	31.5	22.2	14.1	10.0
0.50	31.6	22.4	14.1	10.0

If the entries in Table 2 are compared with those in Table 1,[10] it is found that a price-cutter is easier to detect by his gains at the expense of any one rival than by his unusual proportion of repeat sales. This second criterion will therefore seldom be useful.

3. *The behavior of new customers is a third source of information on price-cutting.*—There are n_n new customers per period,[11] equal to λn_0. A firm expects, in the absence of price-cutting, to sell to

$$m_3 = \frac{1}{n_s}\lambda n_0$$

of these customers, with a variance of

$$\sigma_3^2 = \left(1 - \frac{1}{n_s}\right)\frac{\lambda n_0}{n_s}.$$

If the rivals pool information (without pooling, this area could not be policed effectively), this firm cannot obtain more than $m_3 + 2\sigma_3$ customers without being deemed a price-cutter, using again a 5 per cent probability criterion. As a percentage of the firm's total sales, the maximum sales above the expected number in the absence of price cutting are then

$$\frac{2\sigma_3}{n_0(1+\lambda)/n_s} = \frac{2}{1+\lambda}\sqrt{\frac{(n_s-1)\lambda}{n_0}}.$$

We tabulate this criterion as Table 3.

Two aspects of the incentive to cut prices (or equivalently the difficulty of detecting price cuts) to new customers are apparent: the incentive increases rapidly with the number of sellers[12] and the

[10] For example, take $p = .95$. The entry for 10 customers per seller is 13.8 in Table 2—this is the maximum percentage of average sales that can be obtained by price reductions to old customers. The corresponding entries in Table 1 are 6.9 (2 sellers, 20 buyers), 8.9 (3 and 30), 7.4 (4 and 40), 6.4 (5 and 50), 4.2 (10 and 100), etc. Multiplying each entry in Table 1 by $(n_s - 1)$, we get the maximum gain in sales (without detection) by attracting customers of rivals, and beyond 2 sellers the gains are larger by this latter route. Since Table 1 is based upon a 10 per cent probability level, strict comparability requires that we use 1.6 σ, instead of 2 σ, in Table 2, which would reduce the entries by one-fifth.

[11] Unlike old customers, whose behavior is better studied in a round of transactions, the new customers are a flow whose magnitude depends much more crucially on the time period considered. The annual flow of new customers is here taken (relative to the number of old customers) as the unit.

[12] And slowly with the number of sellers if customers per seller are held constant.

incentive increases with the rate of entry of new customers. As usual the incentive falls as the absolute number of customers per seller rises. If the rate of entry of new buyers is 10 per cent or more, price-cutting to new customers allows larger sales increases without detection that can be obtained by attracting customers of rivals (compare Tables 1 and 3).

Of the considerable number of directions in which this model could be enlarged, two will be presented briefly.

The first is inequality in the size of firms. In effect this complication has already been introduced by the equivalent device of pooling information. If we tabulate the effects of pooling of information by K firms, the results are equivalent to having a firm K times as large as the other firms. The number of old customers this large firm can lose to any one small rival (all of whom are equal in size) is given, in Table 4, as a percentage of the average number of old customers of the small firm; the column labeled $K = 1$ is of course the case analyzed in Table 1.

The effects of pooling on the detection of price-cutting are best analyzed by

TABLE 3

MAXIMUM ADDITIONAL NEW CUSTOMERS (AS A PERCENTAGE OF AVERAGE SALES) OBTAINABLE BY SECRET PRICE-CUTTING

$$\textit{Criterion III: } \frac{2}{1+\lambda}\sqrt{\frac{\lambda(n_s-1)}{n_0}}$$

Rate of Appearance of New Buyers (λ)	No. of Old Buyers (n_0)	No. of Sellers					
		2	3	4	5	10	20
1/100	20	4.4	6.3	7.7	8.9	13.3	19.3
	30	3.6	5.1	6.3	7.2	10.8	15.8
	40	3.1	4.4	5.4	6.3	9.4	13.6
	50	2.8	4.0	4.8	5.6	8.4	12.2
	100	2.0	2.8	3.4	4.0	5.9	8.6
	200	1.4	2.0	2.4	2.8	4.2	6.1
	400	1.0	1.4	1.7	2.0	3.0	4.3
1/10	20	12.9	18.2	22.3	25.7	38.6	56.0
	30	10.5	14.8	18.2	21.0	31.5	45.8
	40	9.1	12.9	15.8	18.2	27.3	39.6
	50	8.1	11.5	14.1	16.3	24.4	35.4
	100	5.8	8.1	10.0	11.5	17.2	25.1
	200	4.1	5.8	7.0	8.1	12.2	17.7
	400	2.9	4.1	5.0	5.8	8.6	12.5
1/5	20	16.7	23.6	28.9	33.3	50.0	72.6
	30	13.6	19.2	23.6	27.2	40.8	59.3
	40	11.8	16.7	20.4	23.6	35.4	51.4
	50	10.5	14.9	18.3	21.1	31.6	46.0
	100	7.4	10.5	12.9	14.9	22.4	32.5
	200	5.3	7.4	9.1	10.5	15.8	23.0
	400	3.7	5.3	6.4	7.4	11.2	16.2
1/4	20	17.9	25.3	31.0	35.8	53.7	78.0
	30	14.6	20.7	25.3	29.2	43.8	63.7
	40	12.6	17.9	21.9	25.3	38.0	55.1
	50	11.3	16.0	19.6	22.6	33.9	49.3
	100	8.0	11.3	13.9	16.0	24.0	34.9
	200	5.7	8.0	9.8	11.3	17.0	24.7
	400	4.0	5.7	6.9	8.0	12.0	17.4

comparing Table 4 with Table 1. If there are 100 customers and 10 firms (and $p = 0.9$), a single firm can increase sales by 5.4 per cent by poaching on one rival, or about 50 per cent against all rivals (Table 1). If 9 firms combine, the maximum amount the single firm can gain by secret price-cutting is 28.9 per cent (Table 4). With 20 firms and 200 customers, a single firm can gain 3.6 per cent from each rival, or about 30 per cent from 9 rivals; if these rivals merge, the corresponding figure falls to 14.0 per cent. The pooling of information therefore reduces substantially the scope for secret price-cutting.

This table exaggerates the effect of inequality of firm size because it fails to take account of the fact that the number of customers varies with firm size, on our argument that only customers above a certain size relative to the seller are a

TABLE 4

PERCENTAGE GAINS IN SALES FROM UNDETECTED PRICE-CUTTING BY A SMALL FIRM

Criterion IV:

$$\frac{1}{n_s - K}\left[\theta(1-p)\sqrt{K} + \sqrt{\frac{n_s K(1-p)(n_s - K - 1)(1 + \theta/\sqrt{K})}{n_0}}\right]$$

$$\theta = \sqrt{\frac{p}{1-p}\frac{n_s}{n_0}}$$

Probability of Repeat Sales (p)	No. of Firms ($n_s - K + 1$)	Buyers per Small Seller (n_0/n_s)	Size of Large Firm (K)			
			1	2	5	9
$p=0.9$	2	10	9.5	13.4	21.2	28.5
		30	5.5	7.7	12.2	16.4
		50	4.2	6.0	9.5	12.7
	3	10	11.7	15.8	23.9	31.4
		30	6.3	8.7	13.3	17.6
		50	4.8	6.6	10.2	13.5
	4	10	9.7	13.1	19.7	25.7
		30	5.2	7.1	10.9	14.4
		50	4.0	5.4	8.3	11.0
	10	10	5.4	7.2	10.7	14.0
		30	2.9	3.9	5.9	7.7
		50	2.2	2.9	4.5	5.9
$p=0.8$	2	10	12.6	17.9	28.3	37.9
		30	7.3	10.3	16.3	21.9
		50	5.7	8.0	12.6	17.0
	3	10	15.4	21.0	32.1	42.3
		30	8.4	11.6	18.0	23.9
		50	6.4	8.9	13.8	18.4
	4	10	12.7	17.3	26.3	34.7
		30	6.9	9.5	14.7	19.5
		50	5.3	7.3	11.3	15.0
	10	10	7.1	9.5	14.4	18.9
		30	3.8	5.2	8.0	10.6
		50	2.9	4.0	6.1	8.1

feasible group for secret price-cutting. The small firm can find it attractive to cut prices to buyers which are not large enough to be potential customers by price-cutting for the large seller.

The temporal pattern of buyers' behavior provides another kind of information: What is possibly due to random fluctuation in the short run cannot with equal probability be due to chance if repeated. Thus the maximum expected loss of old customers to a rival in one round of transactions is (at the 1σ level)

$$\frac{n_0}{(n_s-1)n_s}(1-p)(1+\theta),$$

but for T consecutive periods the maximum expected loss is (over T periods)

$$\frac{T}{n_s-1}(1-p)\frac{n_0}{n_s}[1+\theta\sqrt{T}],$$

with a variance of

$$\sigma_5{}^2=\frac{(n_s-2)}{(n_s-1)^2}T(1-p)\frac{n_0}{n_s}[1+\theta\sqrt{T}].$$

This source of information is of minor efficacy in detecting price-cutting unless the rounds of successive transactions are numerous—that is, unless buyers purchase (enter contracts) frequently.

Our approach has certain implications for the measurement of concentration, if we wish concentration to measure likelihood of effective collusion. In the case of new customers, for example, let the probability of attracting a customer be proportional to the firm's share of industry output (s). Then the variance of the firm's share of sales to new customers will be $n_n s(1-s)$, and the aggregate for the industry will be

$$C=n_n\sum_1^r s(1-s)$$

for r firms. This expression equals $n_n(1-H)$, where

$$H=\Sigma s^2$$

is the Herfindahl index of concentration. The same index holds, as an approximation, for potential price-cutting to attract old customers.[13]

The foregoing analysis can be extended to non-price variables, subject to two modifications. The first modification is that there be a definite joint profit-maximizing policy upon which the rivals can agree. Here we may expect to encounter a spectrum of possibilities, ranging from a clearly defined optimum policy (say, on favorable legislation) to a nebulous set of alternatives (say, directions of research).[14] Collusion is less feasible, the less clear the basis on which it should proceed. The second modification is that

[13] A similar argument leads to a measure of concentration appropriate to potential price-cutting for old customers. Firm i will lose

$$(1-p)n_0 s_i$$

old customers, and firm j will gain

$$(1-p)n_0\frac{s_i s_j}{1-s_i}$$

of them, with a variance

$$(1-p)n_0\frac{s_i s_j}{1-s_i}\left(1-\frac{s_j}{1-s_i}\right).$$

If we sum over all i ($\neq j$), we obtain the variance of firm j's sales to old customers of rivals

$$(1-p)n_0 s_j(1+H-2s_j),$$

to an approximation, and summing over all j, we have the concentration measure,

$$(1-p)n_0(1-H).$$

The agreement of this measure with that for new customers is superficial: that for new customers implicitly assumes pooling of information and that for old customers does not.

[14] Of course, price itself usually falls somewhere in this range rather than at the pole. The traditional assumption of stationary conditions conceals this fact.

the competitive moves of any one firm will differ widely among non-price variables in their detectability by rivals. Some forms of non-price competition will be easier to detect than price-cutting because they leave visible traces (advertising, product quality, servicing, etc.) but some variants will be elusive (reciprocity in purchasing, patent licensing arrangements). The common belief that non-price competition is more common than price competition is therefore not wholly in keeping with the present theory. Those forms that are suitable areas for collusion will have less competition; those which are not suitable will have more competition.

TABLE 5

RESIDUALS FROM REGRESSION OF ADVERTISING RATES ON CIRCULATION*

No. of Evening Papers	n	Mean Residual (Logarithm)	Standard Deviation of Mean
One	23	0.0211	0.0210
With morning paper	10	− .0174	.0324
Without morning paper	13	.0507	.0233
Two	30	−0.0213	0.0135

* The regression equation is

$$\log R = 5.194 - \underset{(.620)}{1.688} \log c + \underset{(.063)}{.139} (\log c)^2 ,$$

where R is the 5 M milline rate and c is circulation.

Source: American Association of Advertising Agencies, *Market and Newspaper Statistics*, Vol. VIIIa (1939).

IV. SOME FRAGMENTS OF EVIDENCE

Before we seek empirical evidence on our theory, it is useful to report two investigations of the influence of numbers of sellers on price. These investigations have an intrinsic interest because, so far as I know, no systematic analysis of the effect of numbers has hitherto been made.

The first investigation was of newspaper advertising rates, as a function of the number of evening newspapers in a city. Advertising rates on a milline basis are closely (and negatively) related to circulation, so a regression of rates on circulation was made for fifty-three cities in 1939. The residuals (in logarithmic form) from this regression equation are tabulated in Table 5. It will be observed that rates are 5 per cent above the average in one-newspaper towns and 5 per cent below the average in two-newspaper towns, and the towns with one evening paper but also an independent morning paper fall nearly midway between these points. Unfortunately there were too few cities with more than two evening newspapers to yield results for larger numbers of firms.

The second investigation is of spot commercial rates on AM radio stations in the four states of Ohio, Indiana, Michigan, and Illinois. The basic equation introduces, along with number of rivals, a series of other factors (power of station, population of the county in which the station is located, etc.). Unfortunately the number of stations is rather closely correlated with population ($r^2 = .796$ in the logarithms). The general result, shown in Table 6, is similar to that for newspapers: the elasticity of price with respect to number of rivals is quite small (−.07). Here the range of stations in a county was from 1 to 13.

Both studies suggest that the level of prices is not very responsive to the actual number of rivals. This is in keeping with the expectations based upon our model, for that model argues that the number of buyers, the proportion of new buyers, and the relative sizes of firms are as important as the number of rivals.

To turn to the present theory, the only test covering numerous industries so far devised has been one based upon profitability. This necessarily rests upon company data, and it has led to the exclusion of a large number of industries for which the companies do not operate in a well-defined industry. For example, the larger steel and chemical firms operate in a series of markets in which their position ranges from monopolistic to competitive. We have required of each industry that the earnings of a substantial fraction of the companies in the industry (measured by output) be determined by the profitability of that industry's products, that is, that we have a fair share of the industry and the industry's product is the dominant product of the firms.

Three measures of profitability are given in Table 7: (1) the rate of return on all capital (including debt), (2) the rate of return on net worth (stockholders' equity); (3) the ratio of market value to book value of the common stock.

In addition, two measures of concentration are presented: (1) the conventional measure, the share of output produced by the four leading firms; and (2) the Herfindahl index, *H*.

The various rank correlations are given in Table 8. The various concentration measures, on the one hand, and the various measures of profitability, on the other hand, are tolerably well correlated.[15] All show the expected positive relationship. In general the data suggest that there is no relationship between profitability and concentration if *H* is less than 0.250 or the share of the four largest firms is less than about 80 per cent. These data, like those on advertising rates, confirm our theory only in the sense that they support theories which assert that competition increases with number of firms.

Our last evidence is a study of the prices paid by buyers of steel products in 1939, measured relative to the quoted prices (Table 9). The figure of 8.3 for hot-

TABLE 6

REGRESSION OF AM SPOT COMMERCIAL RATES (26 TIMES) AND STATION CHARACTERISTICS, 1961

($n = 345$)

Independent Variables*	Regression Coefficient	Standard Error
1. Logarithm of population of county, 1960	.238	0.026
2. Logarithm of kilowatt power of station	.206	.015
3. Dummy variables of period of broadcasting:		
a) Sunrise to sunset	−.114	.025
b) More than (*a*), less than 18 hours	−.086	.027
c) 18–21 hours	−.053	.028
4. Logarithm of number of stations in county	−.074	0.046
	R^2= .743	

* Dependent variable: logarithm of average rate, May 1, 1961 (dollars).

Source: "Spot Radio Rates and Data," *Standard Rate and Data Service, Inc.*, Vol. XLIII, No. 5 (May 1961).

[15] The concentration measures have a rank correlation of .903. The profitability measures have the following rank correlations:

	Return on All Assets	Ratio of Market to Book Value
Return on net worth	.866	.872
Ratio of market to book value	.733	....

TABLE 7

PROFITABILITY AND CONCENTRATION DATA

Industry*	Concentration (1954)		Average Rate of Return (1953–57)		Ratio of Market Value to Book Value (1953–57)
	Share of Top 4	H†	All Assets	Net Worth	
Sulfur mining (4)	98	0.407	19.03	23.85	3.02
Automobiles (3)	98	.369	11.71	20.26	2.30
Flat glass (3)	90	.296	11.79	16.17	2.22
Gypsum products (2)	90	.280	12.16	20.26	1.83
Primary aluminum (4)	98	.277	6.87	13.46	2.48
Metal cans (4)	80	.260	7.27	13.90	1.60
Chewing gum (2)	86	.254	13.50	17.06	2.46
Hard-surface floor coverings (3)	87	.233	6.56	7.59	0.98
Cigarettes (5)	83	.213	7.23	11.18	1.29
Industrial gases (3)	84	.202	8.25	11.53	1.33
Corn wet milling (3)	75	.201	9.17	11.55	1.48
Typewriters (3)	83	.198	3.55	5.39	0.84
Domestic laundry equipment (2)	68	.174	9.97	17.76	1.66
Rubber tires (9)	79	.171	7.86	14.02	1.70
Rayon fiber (4)	76	.169	5.64	6.62	0.84
Carbon black (2)	73	.152	8.29	9.97	1.40
Distilled liquors (6)	64	0.118	6.94	7.55	0.77

* The number of firms is given in parentheses after the industry title. Only those industries are included for which a substantial share (35 per cent or more) of the industry's sales is accounted for by the firms in the sample, and these firms derive their chief revenues (50 per cent or more) from the industry in question.

† *H* is Herfindahl index.

TABLE 8

RANK CORRELATIONS OF MEASURES OF PROFITABILITY AND MEASURES OF CONCENTRATION

Measure of Concentration	Measure of Profitability		
	Rate of Return on All Assets	Rate of Return on Net Worth	Ratio of Market Value to Book Value
Share of output produced by four largest firms	.322	.507	.642
Herfindahl index (*H*)	.524	.692	.730

TABLE 9

PRICES OF STEEL PRODUCTS, 1939, AND INDUSTRY STRUCTURE, 1938

Product Class	Prices, 2d Quarter, 1939 (Per Cent)		Herfindahl Index	Output in 1939 Relative to 1937
	Average Discount from List Price	Standard Deviation		
Hot-rolled sheets	8.3	7.3	0.0902	1.14
Merchant bars	1.2	4.5	.1517	0.84
Hot-rolled strip	8.5	8.3	.1069	0.56
Plates	2.6	4.8	.1740	0.85
Structural shapes	3.2	4.3	.3280	0.92
Cold-rolled strip	8.8	9.8	.0549	0.88
Cold-rolled sheets	5.8	5.0	.0963	1.14
Cold-finished bars	0.9	3.4	0.0964	0.83

Source: Prices: "Labor Department Examines Consumers' Prices of Steel Products," *Iron Age*, April 25, 1946; industry structure: 1938 capacity data from *Directory of Iron and Steel Works of the United States and Canada*; output: *Annual Statistical Report, American Iron and Steel Institute* (New York, 1938, 1942).

rolled sheets, for example, represents an average of 8.3 per cent reduction from quoted prices, ***paid by buyers***, with a standard deviation of 7.3 per cent of quoted prices. The rate of price-cutting is almost perfectly correlated with the standard deviation of transaction prices, as we should expect: the less perfect the market knowledge, the more extensive the price-cutting.

In general, the more concentrated the industry structure (measured by the Herfindahl index), the larger were the price reductions. Although there were no extreme departures from this relationship, structural shapes and hot-rolled strip had prices somewhat lower than the average relationship, and cold finished bars prices somewhat higher than expected, and the deviations are not accounted for by the level of demand (measured by 1939 sales relative to 1937 sales). The number of buyers could not be taken into account, but the BLS study states:

> The extent of price concessions shown by this study is probably understated because certain very large consumers in the automobile and container industries were excluded from the survey. This omission was at the request of the OPA which contemplated obtaining this information in connection with other studies. Since a small percentage of steel consumers, including these companies, accounts for a large percentage of steel purchased, prices paid by a relatively few large consumers have an important influence upon the entire steel price structure. Very large steel consumers get greater reductions from published prices than smaller consumers, often the result of competitive bidding by the mills for the large volume of steel involved. One very large steel consumer, a firm that purchased over 2 pct of the total consumption of hot and cold-rolled sheets in 1940, refused to give purchase prices. This firm wished to protect its suppliers, fearing that "certain transactions might be revealed which would break confidence" with the steel mills. However, this company did furnish percent changes of prices paid for several steel products which showed that for some products prices advanced markedly, and in one case, nearly 50 pct. The great price advances for this company indicate that it was receiving much larger concessions than smaller buyers.[16]

These various bits of evidence are fairly favorable to the theory, but they do not constitute strong support. More powerful tests will be feasible when the electrical equipment triple-damage suits are tried.[17] The great merit of our theory, in fact, is that it has numerous testable hypotheses, unlike the immortal theories that have been traditional in this area.

[16] See "Labor Department Examines Consumers' Prices of Steel Products," *op. cit.*, p. 133.

[17] For example, it will be possible to test the prediction that prices will be higher and less dispersed in sales on public bids than in privately negotiated sales, and the prediction that price-cutting increases as the number of buyers diminishes.

APPENDIX

The importance of product heterogeneity for profit-maximizing behavior cannot well be established by an a priori argument. Nevertheless, the following simple exposition of the implications for profitability of disregarding heterogeneity may have some heuristic value. The analysis, it will be observed, is formally equivalent to that of the effects of an excise tax on a monopolist.

Assume that a monopolist makes men's suits, and that he makes only one size of suit. This is absurd behavior, but the picture of the sadistic monopolist who disregards consumer desires has often made fugitive appearances in the literature so the problem has some interest of its own. The demand curve of a consumer for suits that fit, $f(p)$, would now be reduced because he would have to incur some alteration cost a in order to wear the suit. His effective demand would therefore decline to $f(p + a)$. Assume further that the marginal cost of suits is constant (m), and that it would be the same if the monopolist were to make suits of various sizes.

The effect on profits of a uniform product—uniform is an especially appropriate word here—can be shown graphically (Fig. 1). The decrease in quantity sold, with a linear demand curve, is

$$MB = \tfrac{1}{2} a f'(p) \; .$$

The decrease in the price received by the monopolist is

$$DN = \frac{MB}{f'(p)} - a = -\frac{a}{2},$$

so if π is profit per unit, and q is output, the relative decline in total profit is approximately

$$\frac{\Delta\pi}{\pi} + \frac{\Delta q}{q},$$

or

$$\frac{MB}{OB} + \frac{ND}{AD}.$$

Since

$$OB = \frac{f(m)}{2}$$

$$AD = -\frac{p}{\eta},$$

where η is the elasticity of demand, the relative decline of profits with a uniform product is

$$\frac{af'(p)}{f(m)} + \frac{a\eta}{2p} = \frac{a\eta}{2p} + \frac{a\eta}{2p}$$

$$= \frac{a\eta}{p}.$$

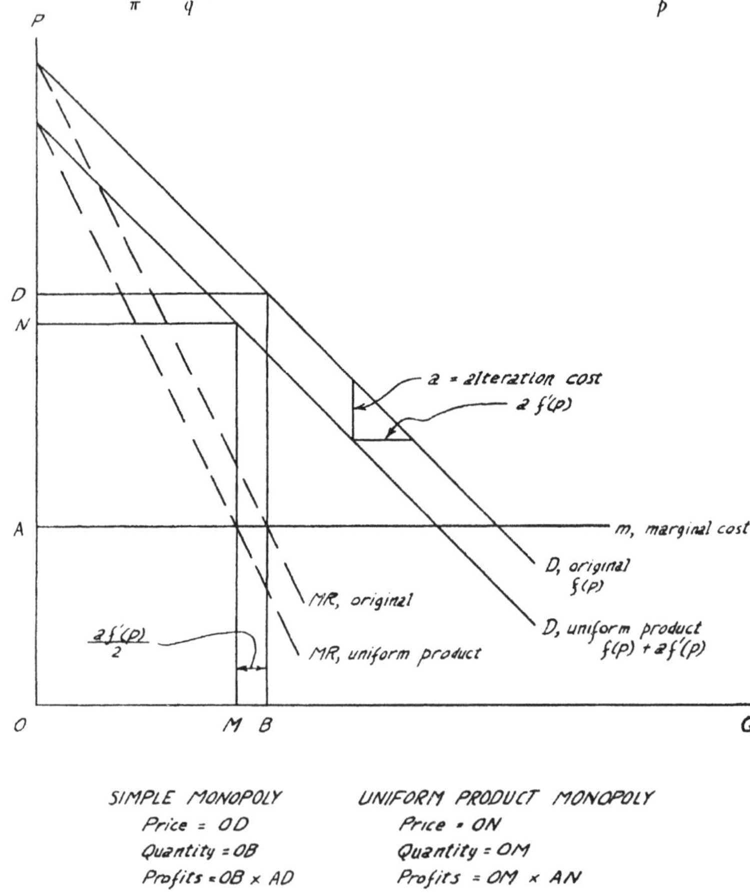

FIG. 1

The loss from imposed uniformity is therefore proportional to the ratio of alteration costs to price.

Our example is sufficiently unrealistic to make any quantitative estimate uninteresting. In general one would expect an upper limit to the ratio a/p, because it becomes cheaper to resort to other goods (custom tailoring in our example), or to abandon the attempt to find appropriate goods. The loss of profits of the monopolist will be proportional to the average value of a/p, and this will be smaller, the smaller the variation in buyers' circumstances.

Still, monopolists are lucky if their long-run demand curves have an elasticity only as large as -5, and then even a ratio of a to p of 1/40 will reduce their profits by 12 per cent. The general conclusion I wish to draw is that a monopolist who does not cater to the diversities of his buyers' desires will suffer a substantial decline in his profits.

[12]

The theory of economic regulation

George J. Stigler

The University of Chicago

The potential uses of public resources and powers to improve the economic status of economic groups (such as industries and occupations) are analyzed to provide a scheme of the demand for regulation. The characteristics of the political process which allow relatively small groups to obtain such regulation is then sketched to provide elements of a theory of supply of regulation. A variety of empirical evidence and illustration is also presented.

■ The state—the machinery and power of the state—is a potential resource or threat to every industry in the society. With its power to prohibit or compel, to take or give money, the state can and does selectively help or hurt a vast number of industries. That political juggernaut, the petroleum industry, is an immense consumer of political benefits, and simultaneously the underwriters of marine insurance have their more modest repast. The central tasks of the theory of economic regulation are to explain who will receive the benefits or burdens of regulation, what form regulation will take, and the effects of regulation upon the allocation of resources.

Regulation may be actively sought by an industry, or it may be thrust upon it. A central thesis of this paper is that, as a rule, regulation is acquired by the industry and is designed and operated primarily for its benefit. There are regulations whose net effects upon the regulated industry are undeniably onerous; a simple example is the differentially heavy taxation of the industry's product (whiskey, playing cards). These onerous regulations, however, are exceptional and can be explained by the same theory that explains beneficial (we may call it "acquired") regulation.

Two main alternative views of the regulation of industry are widely held. The first is that regulation is instituted primarily for the protection and benefit of the public at large or some large subclass of the public. In this view, the regulations which injure the public—as when the oil import quotas increase the cost of petroleum products to America by $5 billion or more a year—are costs of some social goal (here, national defense) or, occasionally, perversions of the regulatory philosophy. The second view is essentially that the political process defies rational explanation: "politics" is an imponderable, a constantly and unpredictably shifting mixture of forces of the most diverse nature, comprehending acts of great moral virtue (the emancipation of slaves) and of the most vulgar venality (the congressman feathering his own nest).

The author obtained the B.B.A. degree from the University of Washington, the M.B.A. degree from Northwestern, and the Ph.D. degree from the University of Chicago. He is presently Charles R. Walgreen Distinguished Service Professor of American Institutions at the University of Chicago, and has published numerous articles and texts in the field of economics. Dr. Stigler is Vice Chairman of the Securities Investor Protective Commission.

why does not the powerful industry which obtained this expensive program instead choose direct cash subsidies from the public treasury? The "protection of the public" theory of regulation must say that the choice of import quotas is dictated by the concern of the federal government for an adequate domestic supply of petroleum in the event of war—a remark calculated to elicit uproarious laughter at the Petroleum Club. Such laughter aside, if national defense were the goal of the quotas, a tariff would be a more economical instrument of policy: it would retain the profits of exclusion for the treasury. The non-rationalist view would explain the policy by the inability of consumers to measure the cost to them of the import quotas, and hence their willingness to pay $5 billion in higher prices rather than the $2.5 billion in cash that would be equally attractive to the industry. Our profit-maximizing theory says that the explanation lies in a different direction: the present members of the refining industries would have to share a cash subsidy with all new entrants into the refining industry.[1] Only when the elasticity of supply of an industry is small will the industry prefer cash to controls over entry or output.

This question, why does an industry solicit the coercive powers of the state rather than its cash, is offered only to illustrate the approach of the present paper. We assume that political systems are rationally devised and rationally employed, which is to say that they are appropriate instruments for the fulfillment of desires of members of the society. This is not to say that the state will serve any person's concept of the public interest: indeed the problem of regulation is the problem of discovering when and why an industry (or other group of like-minded people) is able to use the state for its purposes, or is singled out by the state to be used for alien purposes.

1. What benefits can a state provide to an industry?

■ The state has one basic resource which in pure principle is not shared with even the mightiest of its citizens: the power to coerce. The state can seize money by the only method which is permitted by the laws of a civilized society, by taxation. The state can ordain the physical movements of resources and the economic decisions of households and firms without their consent. These powers provide the possibilities for the utilization of the state by an industry to increase its profitability. The main policies which an industry (or occupation) may seek of the state are four.

The most obvious contribution that a group may seek of the government is a direct subsidy of money. The domestic airlines received "air mail" subsidies (even if they did not carry mail) of $1.5 billion through 1968. The merchant marine has received construction and operation subsidies reaching almost $3 billion since World War II. The education industry has long shown a masterful skill in obtaining public funds: for example, universities and colleges have received federal funds exceeding $3 billion annually in recent years, as well as subsidized loans for dormitories and other construction. The veterans of wars have often received direct cash bonuses.

[1] The domestic producers of petroleum, who also benefit from the import quota, would find a tariff or cash payment to domestic producers equally attractive. If their interests alone were consulted, import quotas would be auctioned off instead of being given away.

We have already sketched the main explanation for the fact that an industry with power to obtain governmental favors usually does not use this power to get money: unless the list of beneficiaries can be limited by an acceptable device, whatever amount of subsidies the industry can obtain will be dissipated among a growing number of rivals. The airlines quickly moved away from competitive bidding for air mail contracts to avoid this problem.[2] On the other hand, the premier universities have not devised a method of excluding other claimants for research funds, and in the long run they will receive much-reduced shares of federal research monies.

The second major public resource commonly sought by an industry is control over entry by new rivals. There is considerable, not to say excessive, discussion in economic literature of the rise of peculiar price policies (limit prices), vertical integration, and similar devices to retard the rate of entry of new firms into oligopolistic industries. Such devices are vastly less efficacious (economical) than the certificate of convenience and necessity (which includes, of course, the import and production quotas of the oil and tobacco industries).

The diligence with which the power of control over entry will be exercised by a regulatory body is already well known. The Civil Aeronautics Board has not allowed a single new trunk line to be launched since it was created in 1938. The power to insure new banks has been used by the Federal Deposit Insurance Corporation to reduce the rate of entry into commercial banking by 60 percent.[3] The interstate motor carrier history is in some respects even more striking, because no even ostensibly respectable case for restriction on entry can be developed on grounds of scale economies (which are in turn adduced to limit entry for safety or economy of operation). The number of federally licensed common carriers is shown in Figure 1: the immense growth of the freight hauled by trucking common carriers has been associated with a steady secular decline of numbers of such carriers. The number of applications for new certificates has been in excess of 5000 annually in recent years: a rigorous proof that hope springs eternal in an aspiring trucker's breast.

We propose the general hypothesis: every industry or occupation that has enough political power to utilize the state will seek to control entry. In addition, the regulatory policy will often be so fashioned as to retard the rate of growth of new firms. For example, no new savings and loan company may pay a dividend rate higher than that prevailing in the community in its endeavors to attract deposits.[4] The power to limit selling expenses of mutual funds, which is soon to be conferred upon the Securities and Exchange Commission, will serve to limit the growth of small mutual funds and hence reduce the sales costs of large funds.

One variant of the control of entry is the protective tariff (and the corresponding barriers which have been raised to interstate movements of goods and people). The benefits of protection to an industry, one might think, will usually be dissipated by the entry of new domestic producers, and the question naturally arises: Why does the industry not also seek domestic entry controls? In a few industries

[2] See [7], pp. 60 ff.

[3] See [10].

[4] The Federal Home Loan Bank Board is the regulatory body. It also controls the amount of advertising and other areas of competition.

FIGURE 1

CERTIFICATES FOR INTERSTATE MOTOR CARRIERS

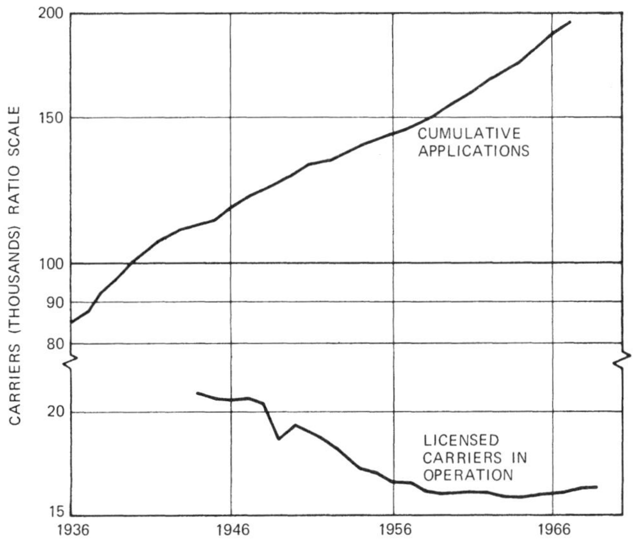

SOURCE: TABLE 5

(petroleum) the domestic controls have been obtained, but not in most. The tariff will be effective if there is a specialized domestic resource necessary to the industry; oil-producing lands is an example. Even if an industry has only durable specialized resources, it will gain if its contraction is slowed by a tariff.

A third general set of powers of the state which will be sought by the industry are those which affect substitutes and complements. Crudely put, the butter producers wish to suppress margarine and encourage the production of bread. The airline industry actively supports the federal subsidies to airports; the building trade unions have opposed labor-saving materials through building codes. We shall examine shortly a specific case of inter-industry competition in transportation.

The fourth class of public policies sought by an industry is directed to price-fixing. Even the industry that has achieved entry control will often want price controls administered by a body with coercive powers. If the number of firms in the regulated industry is even moderately large, price discrimination will be difficult to maintain in the absence of public support. The prohibition of interest on demand deposits, which is probably effective in preventing interest payments to most non-business depositors, is a case in point. Where there are no diseconomies of large scale for the individual firm (e.g., a motor trucking firm can add trucks under a given license as common carrier), price control is essential to achieve more than competitive rates of return.

☐ **Limitations upon political benefits.** These various political boons are not obtained by the industry in a pure profit-maximizing form. The political process erects certain limitations upon the exercise of cartel policies by an industry. These limitations are of three sorts.

TABLE 1

IMPORT QUOTAS OF REFINERIES AS PERCENT OF DAILY INPUT OF PETROLEUM (DISTRICTS I – IV, JULY 1, 1959 – DEC. 31, 1959)

SIZE OF REFINERY (THOUSANDS OF BARRELS)	PERCENT QUOTA
0–10	11.4
10–20	10.4
20–30	9.5
30–60	8.5
60–100	7.6
100–150	6.6
150–200	5.7
200–300	4.7
300 AND OVER	3.8

SOURCE: HEARING, SELECT COMMITTEE ON SMALL BUSINESS, U. S. CONGRESS, 88th CONG., 2nd SESS., AUG. 10 AND 11, 1964, [12] P. 121.

First, the distribution of control of the industry among the firms in the industry is changed. In an unregulated industry each firm's influence upon price and output is proportional to its share of industry output (at least in a simple arithmetic sense of direct capacity to change output). The political decisions take account also of the political strength of the various firms, so small firms have a larger influence than they would possess in an unregulated industry. Thus, when quotas are given to firms, the small firms will almost always receive larger quotas than cost-minimizing practices would allow. The original quotas under the oil import quota system will illustrate this practice (Table 1). The smallest refiners were given a quota of 11.4 percent of their daily consumption of oil, and the percentage dropped as refinery size rose.[5] The pattern of regressive benefits is characteristic of public controls in industries with numerous firms.

Second, the procedural safeguards required of public processes are costly. The delays which are dictated by both law and bureaucratic thoughts of self-survival can be large: Robert Gerwig found the price of gas sold in interstate commerce to be 5 to 6 percent higher than in intrastate commerce because of the administrative costs (including delay) of Federal Power Commission reviews [5].

Finally, the political process automatically admits powerful outsiders to the industry's councils. It is well known that the allocation of television channels among communities does not maximize industry revenue but reflects pressures to serve many smaller communities. The abandonment of an unprofitable rail line is an even more notorious area of outsider participation.

These limitations are predictable, and they must all enter into the calculus of the profitability of regulation of an industry.

□ **An illustrative analysis.** The recourse to the regulatory process is of course more specific and more complex than the foregoing sketch

[5] The largest refineries were restricted to 75.7 percent of their historical quota under the earlier voluntary import quota plan.

suggests. The defensive power of various other industries which are affected by the proposed regulation must also be taken into account. An analysis of one aspect of the regulation of motor trucking will illustrate these complications. At this stage we are concerned only with the correspondence between regulations and economic interests; later we shall consider the political process by which regulation is achieved.

The motor trucking industry operated almost exclusively within cities before 1925, in good part because neither powerful trucks nor good roads were available for long-distance freight movements. As these deficiencies were gradually remedied, the share of trucks in intercity freight movements began to rise, and by 1930 it was estimated to be 4 percent of ton-miles of intercity freight. The railroad industry took early cognizance of this emerging competitor, and one of the methods by which trucking was combatted was state regulation.

By the early 1930's all states regulated the dimensions and weight of trucks. The weight limitations were a much more pervasive control over trucking than the licensing of common carriers because even the trucks exempt from entry regulation are subject to the limitations on dimensions and capacity. The weight regulations in the early 1930's are reproduced in the appendix (Table 6). Sometimes the participation of railroads in the regulatory process was incontrovertible: Texas and Louisiana placed a 7000-pound payload limit on trucks serving (and hence competing with) two or more railroad stations, and a 14,000-pound limit on trucks serving only one station (hence, not competing with it).

We seek to determine the pattern of weight limits on trucks that would emerge in response to the economic interests of the concerned parties. The main considerations appear to be the following:

(1) Heavy trucks would be allowed in states with a substantial number of trucks on farms: the powerful agricultural interests would insist upon this. The 1930 Census reports nearly one million trucks on farms. One variable in our study will be, for each state, trucks per 1000 of agricultural population.[6]

(2) Railroads found the truck an effective and rapidly triumphing competitor in the shorter hauls and hauls of less than carload traffic, but much less effective in the carload and longer-haul traffic. Our second variable for each state is, therefore, length of average railroad haul.[7] The longer the average rail haul is, the less the railroads will be opposed to trucks.

(3) The public at large would be concerned by the potential damage done to the highway system by heavy trucks. The better the state highway system, the heavier the trucks that would be permitted. The percentage of each state's highways that had a high type surface is the third variable. Of course good highways are more likely to exist where the potential contribution of trucks to a state's economy is greater, so the causation may be looked at from either direction.

[6] The ratio of trucks to total population would measure the product of (1) the importance of trucks to farmers, and (2) the importance of farmers in the state. For reasons given later, we prefer to emphasize (1).

[7] This is known for each railroad, and we assume that (1) the average holds within each state, and (2) two or more railroads in a state may be combined on the basis of mileage. Obviously both assumptions are at best fair approximations.

We have two measures of weight limits on trucks, one for 4-wheel trucks (X_1) and one for 6-wheel trucks (X_2). We may then calculate two equations,

$$X_1 \text{ (or } X_2) = a + bX_3 + cX_4 + dX_5 ,$$

where

X_3 = trucks per 1000 agricultural labor force, 1930 ,
X_4 = average length of railroad haul of freight traffic, 1930,
X_5 = percentage of state roads with high-quality surface, 1930.

(All variables are fully defined and their state values given in Table 7 on page 20.)

The three explanatory variables are statistically significant, and each works in the expected direction. The regulations on weight were less onerous; the larger the truck population in farming, the less competitive the trucks were to railroads (i.e., the longer the rail hauls), and the better the highway system (see Table 2).

□ The foregoing analysis is concerned with what may be termed the industrial demand for governmental powers. Not every industry will have a significant demand for public assistance (other than money!), meaning the prospect of a substantial increase in the present value of the enterprises even if the governmental services could be obtained gratis (and of course they have costs to which we soon turn). In some economic activities entry of new rivals is extremely difficult to control—consider the enforcement problem in restricting the supply of domestic servants. In some industries the substitute products cannot be efficiently controlled—consider the competition offered to bus lines by private car-pooling. Price fixing is not feasible where every

TABLE 2

REGRESSION ANALYSIS OF STATE WEIGHT LIMITS ON TRUCKS
(T VALUES UNDER REGRESSION COEFFICIENTS)

DEPENDENT VARIABLE	N	CONSTANT	X_3	X_4	X_5	R^2
X_1	48	12.28 (4.87)	0.0336 (3.99)	0.0287 (2.77)	0.2641 (3.04)	0.502
X_2	46	10.34 (1.57)	0.0437 (2.01)	0.0788 (2.97)	0.2528 (1.15)	0.243

X_1 = WEIGHT LIMIT ON 4-WHEEL TRUCKS (THOUSANDS OF POUNDS), 1932-33
X_2 = WEIGHT LIMIT ON 6-WHEEL TRUCKS (THOUSANDS OF POUNDS), 1932-33
X_3 = TRUCKS ON FARMS PER 1,000 AGRICULTURAL LABOR FORCE, 1930
X_4 = AVERAGE LENGTH OF RAILROAD HAUL OF FREIGHT (MILES), 1930
X_5 = PERCENT OF STATE HIGHWAYS WITH HIGH-TYPE SURFACE, DEC. 31, 1930

SOURCES: X_1 AND X_2: THE MOTOR TRUCK RED BOOK AND DIRECTORY [11], 1934 EDITION, P. 85-102, AND U.S. DEPT. OF AGRIC., BUR. OF PUBLIC ROADS, DEC. 1932 [13].

X_3: CENSUS OF AGRICULTURE, 1930, VOL. IV, [14].

X_4: A.A.R.R., BUR. OF RAILWAY ECONOMICS, RAILWAY MILEAGE BY STATES, DEC. 31, 1930 [1] AND U.S.I.C.C., STATISTICS OF RAILWAYS IN THE U.S., 1930 [18].

X_5: STATISTICAL ABSTRACT OF THE U.S., 1932 [16].

unit of the product has a different quality and price, as in the market for used automobiles. In general, however, most industries will have a positive demand price (schedule) for the services of government.

2. The costs of obtaining legislation

■ When an industry receives a grant of power from the state, the benefit to the industry will fall short of the damage to the rest of the community. Even if there were no deadweight losses from acquired regulation, however, one might expect a democratic society to reject such industry requests unless the industry controlled a majority of the votes.[8] A direct and informed vote on oil import quotas would reject the scheme. (If it did not, our theory of rational political processes would be contradicted.) To explain why many industries are able to employ the political machinery to their own ends, we must examine the nature of the political process in a democracy.

A consumer chooses between rail and air travel, for example, by voting with his pocketbook: he patronizes on a given day that mode of transportation he prefers. A similar form of economic voting occurs with decisions on where to work or where to invest one's capital. The market accumulates these economic votes, predicts their future course, and invests accordingly.

Because the political decision is coercive, the decision process is fundamentally different from that of the market. If the public is asked to make a decision between two transportation media comparable to the individual's decision on how to travel—say, whether airlines or railroads should receive a federal subsidy—the decision must be abided by everyone, travellers and non-travellers, travellers this year and travellers next year. This compelled universality of political decisions makes for two differences between democratic political decision processes and market processes.

(1) The decisions must be made simultaneously by a large number of persons (or their representatives): the political process demands simultaneity of decision. If *A* were to vote on the referendum today, *B* tomorrow, *C* the day after, and so on, the accumulation of a majority decision would be both expensive and suspect. (*A* might wish to cast a different vote now than last month.)

The condition of simultaneity imposes a major burden upon the political decision process. It makes voting on specific issues prohibitively expensive: it is a significant cost even to engage in the transaction of buying a plane ticket when I wish to travel; it would be stupendously expensive to me to engage in the physically similar transaction of voting (i.e., patronizing a polling place) whenever a number of my fellow citizens desired to register their views on railroads versus airplanes. To cope with this condition of simultaneity, the voters must employ representatives with wide discretion and must eschew direct expressions of marginal changes in preferences. This characteristic also implies that the political decision does not predict voter desires and make preparations to fulfill them in advance of their realization.

[8] If the deadweight loss (of consumer and producer surplus) is taken into account, even if the oil industry were in the majority it would not obtain the legislation if there were available some method of compensation (such as sale of votes) by which the larger damage of the minority could be expressed effectively against the lesser gains of the majority.

(2) The democratic decision process must involve "all" the community, not simply those who are directly concerned with a decision. In a private market, the non-traveller never votes on rail versus plane travel, while the huge shipper casts many votes each day. The political decision process cannot exclude the uninterested voter: the abuses of any exclusion except self-exclusion are obvious. Hence, the political process does not allow participation in proportion to interest and knowledge. In a measure, this difficulty is moderated by other political activities besides voting which do allow a more effective vote to interested parties: persuasion, employment of skilled legislative representatives, etc. Nevertheless, the political system does not offer good incentives like those in private markets to the acquisition of knowledge. If I consume ten times as much of public service A (streets) as of B (schools), I do not have incentives to acquire corresponding amounts of knowledge about the public provision of these services.[9]

These characteristics of the political process can be modified by having numerous levels of government (so I have somewhat more incentive to learn about local schools than about the whole state school system) and by selective use of direct decision (bond referenda). The chief method of coping with the characteristics, however, is to employ more or less full-time representatives organized in (disciplined by) firms which are called political parties or machines.

The representative and his party are rewarded for their discovery and fulfillment of the political desires of their constituency by success in election and the perquisites of office. If the representative could confidently await reelection whenever he voted against an economic policy that injured the society, he would assuredly do so. Unfortunately virtue does not always command so high a price. If the representative denies ten large industries their special subsidies of money or governmental power, they will dedicate themselves to the election of a more complaisant successor: the stakes are that important. This does not mean that every large industry can get what it wants or all that it wants: it does mean that the representative and his party must find a coalition of voter interests more durable than the anti-industry side of every industry policy proposal. A representative cannot win or keep office with the support of the sum of those who are opposed to: oil import quotas, farm subsidies, airport subsidies, hospital subsidies, unnecessary navy shipyards, an inequitable public housing program, and rural electrification subsidies.

The political decison process has as its dominant characteristic infrequent, universal (in principle) participation, as we have noted: political decisions must be infrequent and they must be global. The voter's expenditure to learn the merits of individual policy proposals and to express his preferences (by individual and group representation as well as by voting) are determined by expected costs and returns, just as they are in the private marketplace. The costs of comprehensive information are higher in the political arena because information must be sought on many issues of little or no direct concern to the individual, and accordingly he will know little about most matters before the legislature. The expressions of preferences in voting will be less precise than the expressions of preferences in the

[9] See [2].

marketplace because many uninformed people will be voting and affecting the decision.[10]

The channels of political decision-making can thus be described as gross or filtered or noisy. If everyone has a negligible preference for policy A over B, the preference will not be discovered or acted upon. If voter group X wants a policy that injures non-X by a small amount, it will not pay non-X to discover this and act against the policy. The system is calculated to implement all strongly felt preferences of majorities and many strongly felt preferences of minorities but to disregard the lesser preferences of majorities and minorities. The filtering or grossness will be reduced by any reduction in the cost to the citizen of acquiring information and expressing desires and by any increase in the probability that his vote will influence policy.

The industry which seeks political power must go to the appropriate seller, the political party. The political party has costs of operation, costs of maintaining an organization and competing in elections. These costs of the political process are viewed excessively narrowly in the literature on the financing of elections: elections are to the political process what merchandizing is to the process of producing a commodity, only an essential final step. The party maintains its organization and electoral appeal by the performance of costly services to the voter at all times, not just before elections. Part of the costs of services and organization are borne by putting a part of the party's workers on the public payroll. An opposition party, however, is usually essential insurance for the voters to discipline the party in power, and the opposition party's costs are not fully met by public funds.

The industry which seeks regulation must be prepared to pay with the two things a party needs: votes and resources. The resources may be provided by campaign contributions, contributed services (the businessman heads a fund-raising committee), and more indirect methods such as the employment of party workers. The votes in support of the measure are rallied, and the votes in opposition are dispersed, by expensive programs to educate (or uneducate) members of the industry and of other concerned industries.

These costs of legislation probably increase with the size of the industry seeking the legislation. Larger industries seek programs which cost the society more and arouse more opposition from substantially affected groups. The tasks of persuasion, both within and without the industry, also increase with its size. The fixed size of the political "market," however, probably makes the cost of obtaining legislation increase less rapidly than industry size. The smallest industries are therefore effectively precluded from the political process unless they have some special advantage such as geographical concentration in a sparsely settled political subdivision.

If a political party has in effect a monopoly control over the governmental machine, one might expect that it could collect most of the benefits of regulation for itself. Political parties, however, are

[10] There is an organizational problem in any decision in which more than one vote is cast. If because of economies of scale it requires a thousand customers to buy a product before it can be produced, this thousand votes has to be assembled by some entrepreneur. Unlike the political scene, however, there is no need to obtain the consent of the remainder of the community, because they will bear no part of the cost.

perhaps an ideal illustration of Demsetz' theory of natural monopoly [4]. If one party becomes extortionate (or badly mistaken in its reading of effective desires), it is possible to elect another party which will provide the governmental services at a price more closely proportioned to costs of the party. If entry into politics is effectively controlled, we should expect one-party dominance to lead that party to solicit requests for protective legislation but to exact a higher price for the legislation.

The internal structure of the political party, and the manner in which the perquisites of office are distributed among its members, offer fascinating areas for study in this context. The elective officials are at the pinnacle of the political system—there is no substitute for the ability to hold the public offices. I conjecture that much of the compensation to the legislative leaders takes the form of extra-political payments. Why are so many politicians lawyers?—because everyone employs lawyers, so the congressman's firm is a suitable avenue of compensation, whereas a physician would have to be given bribes rather than patronage. Most enterprises patronize insurance companies and banks, so we may expect that legislators commonly have financial affiliations with such enterprises.

The financing of industry-wide activities such as the pursuit of legislation raises the usual problem of the free rider.[11] We do not possess a satisfactory theory of group behavior—indeed this theory is the theory of oligopoly with one addition: in the very large number industry (e.g., agriculture) the political party itself will undertake the entrepreneurial role in providing favorable legislation. We can go no further than the infirmities of oligopoly theory allow, which is to say, we can make only plausible conjectures such as that the more concentrated the industry, the more resources it can invest in the campaign for legislation.

☐ **Occupational licensing.** The licensing of occupations is a possible use of the political process to improve the economic circumstances of a group. The license is an effective barrier to entry because occupational practice without the license is a criminal offense. Since much occupational licensing is performed at the state level, the area provides an opportunity to search for the characteristics of an occupation which give it political power.

Although there are serious data limitations, we may investigate several characteristics of an occupation which should influence its ability to secure political power:

(1) *The size of the occupation.* Quite simply, the larger the occupation, the more votes it has. (Under some circumstances, therefore, one would wish to exclude non-citizens from the measure of size.)

(2) *The per capita income of the occupation.* The income of the occupation is the product of its number and average income, so this variable and the preceding will reflect the total income of the occupation. The income of the occupation is presumably an index of the probable rewards of successful political action: in the absence of specific knowledge of supply and demand functions, we expect

[11] The theory that the lobbying organization avoids the "free-rider" problem by selling useful services was proposed by Thomas G. Moore [8] and elaborated by Mancur Olson [9]. The theory has not been tested empirically.

licensing to increase each occupation's equilibrium income by roughly the same proportion. In a more sophisticated version, one would predict that the less the elasticity of demand for the occupation's services, the more profitable licensing would be. One could also view the income of the occupation as a source of funds for political action, but if we view political action as an investment this is relevant only with capital-market imperfections.[12]

The average income of occupational members is an appropriate variable in comparisons among occupations, but it is inappropriate to comparisons of one occupation in various states because real income will be approximately equal (in the absence of regulation) in each state.

(3) *The concentration of the occupation in large cities.* When the occupation organizes a campaign to obtain favorable legislation, it incurs expenses in the solicitation of support, and these are higher for a diffused occupation than a concentrated one. The solicitation of support is complicated by the free-rider problem in that individual members cannot be excluded from the benefits of legislation even if they have not shared the costs of receiving it. If most of the occupation is concentrated in a few large centers, these problems (we suspect) are much reduced in intensity: regulation may even begin at the local governmental level. We shall use an orthodox geographical concentration measure: the share of the occupation of the state in cities over 100,000 (or 50,000 in 1900 and earlier).

(4) *The presence of a cohesive opposition to licensing.* If an occupation deals with the public at large, the costs which licensing imposes upon any one customer or industry will be small and it will not be economic for that customer or industry to combat the drive for licensure. If the injured group finds it feasible and profitable to act jointly, however, it will oppose the effort to get licensure, and (by increasing its cost) weaken, delay, or prevent the legislation. The same attributes—numbers of voters, wealth, and ease of organization—which favor an occupation in the political arena, of course, favor also any adversary group. Thus, a small occupation employed by only one industry which has few employers will have difficulty in getting licensure; whereas a large occupation serving everyone will encounter no organized opposition.

An introductory statistical analysis of the licensing of select occupations by states is summarized in Table 3. In each occupation the dependent variable for each state is the year of first regulation of entry into the occupation. The two independent variables are

(1) the ratio of the occupation to the total labor force of the state in the census year nearest to the median year of regulation,

(2) the fraction of the occupation found in cities over 100,000 (over 50,000 in 1890 and 1900) in that same year.

---

[12] Let n = the number of members of the profession and y = average income. We expect political capacity to be in proportion to (ny) so far as benefits go, but to reflect also the direct value of votes, so the capacity becomes proportional to $(n^a y)$ with $a > 1$.

TABLE 3

INITIAL YEAR OF REGULATION AS A FUNCTION OF RELATIVE SIZE OF OCCUPATION AND DEGREE OF URBANIZATION

OCCUPATION	NUMBER OF STATES LICENSING	MEDIAN CENSUS YEAR OF LICENSING	REGRESSION COEFFICIENTS (AND T-VALUES)		R^2
			SIZE OF OCCUPATION (RELATIVE TO LABOR FORCE)	URBANIZATION (SHARE OF OCCUPATION IN CITIES OVER 100,000*)	
BEAUTICIANS	48	1930	–4.03 (2.50)	5.90 (1.24)	0.125
ARCHITECTS	47	1930	–24.06 (2.15)	–6.29 (0.84)	0.184
BARBERS	46	1930	–1.31 (0.51)	–26.10 (2.37)	0.146
LAWYERS	29	1890	–0.26 (0.08)	–65.78 (1.70)	0.102
PHYSICIANS	43	1890	0.64 (0.65)	–23.80 (2.69)	0.165
EMBALMERS	37	1910	3.32 (0.36)	–4.24 (0.44)	0.007
REGISTERED NURSES	48	1910	–2.08 (2.28)	–3.36 (1.06)	0.176
DENTISTS	48	1900	2.51 (0.44)	–22.94 (2.19)	0.103
VETERINARIANS	40	1910	–10.69 (1.94)	–37.16 (4.20)	0.329
CHIROPRACTORS	48	1930	–17.70 (1.54)	11.69 (1.25)	0.079
PHARMACISTS	48	1900	–4.19 (1.50)	–6.84 (0.80)	0.082

SOURCES: THE COUNCIL OF STATE GOVERNMENTS, "OCCUPATIONAL LICENSING LEGISLATION IN THE STATES", 1952 [3], AND U.S. CENSUS OF POPULATION [15], VARIOUS YEARS.

* 50,000 IN 1890 AND 1900.

We expect these variables to be negatively associated with year of licensure, and each of the nine statistically significant regression coefficients is of the expected sign.

The results are not robust, however: the multiple correlation coefficients are small, and over half of the regression coefficients are not significant (and in these cases often of inappropriate sign). Urbanization is more strongly associated than size of occupation with licensure.[13] The crudity of the data may be a large source of these disappointments: we measure, for example, the characteristics of the barbers in each state in 1930, but 14 states were licensing barbers by 1910. If the states which licensed barbering before 1910 had relatively more barbers, or more highly urbanized barbers, the predictions

[13] We may pool the occupations and assign dummy variables for each occupation; the regression coefficients then are:

size of occupation relative to labor force: -0.450 ($t = 0.59$)
urbanization : -12.133 ($t = 4.00$).

Thus urbanization is highly significant, while size of occupation is not significant.

would be improved. The absence of data for years between censuses and before 1890 led us to make only the cruder analysis.[14]

In general, the larger occupations were licensed in earlier years.[15] Veterinarians are the only occupation in this sample who have a well-defined set of customers, namely livestock farmers, and licensing was later in those states with large numbers of livestock relative to rural population. The within-occupation analyses offer some support for the economic theory of the supply of legislation.

A comparison of different occupations allows us to examine several other variables. The first is income, already discussed above. The second is the size of the market. Just as it is impossible to organize an effective labor union in only one part of an integrated market, so it is impossible to regulate only one part of the market. Consider an occupation—junior business executives will do—which has a national market with high mobility of labor and significant mobility of employers. If the executives of one state were to organize, their scope for effective influence would be very small. If salaries were raised above the competitive level, employers would often recruit elsewhere so the demand elasticity would be very high.[16] The third variable is stability of occupational membership: the longer the members are in the occupation, the greater their financial gain from control of entry. Our regrettably crude measure of this variable is based upon the number of members aged 35–44 in 1950 and aged 45–54 in 1960: the closer these numbers are, the more stable the membership of the occupation. The data for the various occupations are given in Table 4.

The comparison of licensed and unlicensed occupations is consistently in keeping with our expectations:

(1) the licensed occupations have higher incomes (also before licensing, one may assume),

(2) the membership of the licensed occupations is more stable (but the difference is negligible in our crude measure),

(3) the licensed occupations are less often employed by business enterprises (who have incentives to oppose licensing),

(4) all occupations in national markets (college teachers, engineers, scientists, accountants) are unlicensed or only partially licensed.

---

[14] A more precise analysis might take the form of a regression analysis such as:

$$\text{Year of licensure} = \text{constant} + b_1\,(\text{year of critical size of occupation}) + b_2\,(\text{year of critical urbanization of occupation}),$$

where the critical size and urbanization were defined as the mean size and mean urbanization in the year of licensure.

[15] Lawyers, physicians, and pharmacists were all relatively large occupations by 1900, and nurses also by 1910. The only large occupation to be licensed later was barbers; the only small occupation to be licensed early was embalmers.

[16] The regulation of business in a partial market will also generally produce very high supply elasticities within a market: if the price of the product (or service) is raised, the pressure of excluded supply is very difficult to resist. Some occupations are forced to reciprocity in licensing, and the geographical dispersion of earnings in licensed occupations, one would predict, is not appreciably different than in unlicensed occupations with equal employer mobility. Many puzzles are posed by the interesting analysis of Arlene S. Holen in [6], pp. 492-98.

TABLE 4

CHARACTERISTICS OF LICENSED AND UNLICENSED PROFESSIONAL OCCUPATIONS, 1960

OCCUPATION	MEDIAN AGE (YEARS)	MEDIAN EDUCATION (YEARS)	MEDIAN EARNINGS (50-52 WKS.)	INSTABILITY OF MEMBERSHIP*	PERCENT NOT SELF-EMPLOYED	PERCENT IN CITIES OVER 50,000	PERCENT OF LABOR FORCE
LICENSED:							
ARCHITECTS	41.7	16.8	$ 9,090	0.012	57.8%	44.1%	0.045%
CHIROPRACTORS	46.5	16.4	6,360	0.053	5.8	30.8	0.020
DENTISTS	45.9	17.3	12,200	0.016	9.4	34.5	0.128
EMBALMERS	43.5	13.4	5,990	0.130	52.8	30.2	0.055
LAWYERS	45.3	17.4	10,800	0.041	35.8	43.1	0.308
PROF. NURSES	39.1	13.2	3,850	0.291	91.0	40.6	0.868
OPTOMETRISTS	41.6	17.0	8,480	0.249	17.5	34.5	0.024
PHARMACISTS	44.9	16.2	7,230	0.119	62.3	40.0	0.136
PHYSICIANS	42.8	17.5	14,200	0.015	35.0	44.7	0.339
VETERINARIANS	39.2	17.4	9,210	0.169	29.5	14.4	0.023
AVERAGE	43.0	16.3	8,741	0.109	39.7	35.7	0.195
PARTIALLY LICENSED:							
ACCOUNTANTS	40.4	14.9	6,450	0.052	88.1	43.5	0.698
ENGINEERS	38.3	16.2	8,490	0.023	96.8	31.6	1.279
ELEM. SCHOOL TEACHERS	43.1	16.5	4,710	(a)	99.1	18.8	1.482
AVERAGE	40.6	15.9	6,550	0.117(b)	94.7	34.6	1.153
UNLICENSED:							
ARTISTS	38.0	14.2	5,920	0.103	77.3	45.7	0.154
CLERGYMEN	43.3	17.0	4,120	0.039	89.0	27.2	0.295
COLLEGE TEACHERS	40.3	17.4	7,500	0.085	99.2	36.0	0.261
DRAFTSMEN	31.2	12.9	5,990	0.098	98.6	40.8	0.322
REPORTERS & EDITORS	39.4	15.5	6,120	0.138	93.9	43.3	0.151
MUSICIANS	40.2	14.8	3,240	0.081	65.5	37.7	0.289
NATURAL SCIENTISTS	35.9	16.8	7,490	0.264	96.3	32.7	0.221
AVERAGE	38.3	15.5	5,768	0.115	88.5	37.6	0.242

(*) 1-R, WHERE R = RATIO: 1960 AGE 45-54 TO 1950 AGE 35-44.

(a) NOT AVAILABLE SEPARATELY; TEACHERS N.E.C. (INCL. SECONDARY SCHOOL AND OTHER) = 0.276

(b) INCLUDES FIGURE FOR TEACHERS N.E.C. IN NOTE (a)

SOURCE: U.S. CENSUS OF POPULATION, [15], 1960.

The size and urbanization of the three groups, however, are unrelated to licensing. The inter-occupational comparison therefore provides a modicum of additional support for our theory of regulation.

3. Conclusion

■ The idealistic view of public regulation is deeply imbedded in professional economic thought. So many economists, for example, have denounced the ICC for its pro-railroad policies that this has become a cliché of the literature. This criticism seems to me exactly as appropriate as a criticism of the Great Atlantic and Pacific Tea Company for selling groceries, or as a criticism of a politician for currying popular support. The fundamental vice of such criticism is that it misdirects attention: it suggests that the way to get an ICC which is not subservient to the carriers is to preach to the commissioners or to the people who appoint the commissioners. The only way to get a different commission would be to change the political support for the Commission, and reward commissioners on a basis unrelated to their services to the carriers.

Until the basic logic of political life is developed, reformers will be ill-equipped to use the state for their reforms, and victims of the pervasive use of the state's support of special groups will be helpless to protect themselves. Economists should quickly establish the license to practice on the rational theory of political behavior.

Appendix

TABLE 5

COMMON, CONTRACT AND PASSENGER MOTOR CARRIERS, 1935–1969[1]

YEAR ENDING	CUMULATIVE APPLICATIONS			OPERATING CARRIERS	
	GRAND-FATHER	NEW	TOTAL	APPROVED APPLICATIONS[3]	NUMBER IN OPERATION[2]
OCT. 1936	82,827	1,696	84,523	–	–
1937	83,107	3,921	87.028	1;114	–
1938	85,646	6,694	92,340	20,398	–
1939	86,298	9,636	95,934	23,494	–
1940	87,367	12,965	100,332	25,575	–
1941	88,064	16,325	104,389	26,296	–
1942	88,702	18,977	107,679	26,683	–
1943	89,157	20,007	109,164	27,531	–
1944	89,511	21,324	110,835	27,177	21,044
1945	89,518	22,829	112,347		20,788
1946	89,529	26,392	115,921		20,632
1947	89,552	29,604	119,156		20,665
1948	89,563	32,678	122,241		20,373
1949	89,567	35,635	125,202		18,459
1950	89,573	38,666	128,239		19,200
1951	89,574	41,889	131,463		18,843
1952	(89,574)[4]	44,297	133,870		18,408
1953	"	46,619	136,192		17,869
1954	"	49,146	138,719		17,080
1955	"	51,720	141,293		16,836
JUNE 1956	"	53,640	143,213		16,486
1957	"	56,804	146,377		16,316
1958	"	60,278	149,851		16,065
1959	"	64,171	153,744		15,923
1960	"	69,205	158,778		15,936
1961	"	72,877	162,450		15,967
1962	"	76,986	166,559		15,884
1963	"	81,443	171,016		15,739
1964	"	86,711	176,284		15,732
1965	"	93,064	182,637		15,755
1966	"	101,745	191,318		15,933
1967	"	106,647	196,220		16,003
1968	"	(6)	(6)		16,230[5]
1969	"	(6)	(6)		16,318[5]

SOURCE: U.S. INTERSTATE COMMERCE COMMISSION ANNUAL REPORTS [17].

1 EXCLUDING BROKERS AND WITHIN-STATE CARRIERS.

2 PROPERTY CARRIERS WERE THE FOLLOWING PERCENTAGES OF ALL OPERATING CARRIERS: 1944–93.4%; 1950–92.4%; 1960–93.0%; 1966–93.4%.

3 ESTIMATED.

4 NOT AVAILABLE; ASSUMED TO BE APPROXIMATELY CONSTANT.

5 1968 AND 1969 FIGURES ARE FOR NUMBER OF CARRIERS REQUIRED TO FILE ANNUAL REPORTS.

6 NOT AVAILABLE COMPARABLE TO PREVIOUS YEARS; APPLICATIONS FOR PERMANENT AUTHORITY DISPOSED OF (I.E., FROM NEW AND PENDING FILES) 1967-69 ARE AS FOLLOWS: 1967–7,049; 1968–5,724; 1969–5,186.

TABLE 6

WEIGHT LIMITS ON TRUCKS, 1932-33*, BY STATES (BASIC DATA FOR TABLE 2).

STATE	MAXIMUM WEIGHT (IN LBS.)		STATE	MAXIMUM WEIGHT (IN LBS.)	
	4-WHEEL[1]	6-WHEEL[2]		4-WHEEL[1]	6-WHEEL[2]
ALABAMA	20,000	32,000	NEBRASKA	24,000	40,000
ARIZONA	22,000	34,000	NEVADA	25,000	38,000
ARKANSAS	22,200	37,000	NEW HAMPSHIRE	20,000	20,000
CALIFORNIA	22,000	34,000	NEW JERSEY	30,000	30,000
COLORADO	30,000	40,000	NEW MEXICO	27,000	45,000
CONNECTICUT	32,000	40,000	NEW YORK	33,600	44,000
DELAWARE	26,000	38,000	NO. CAROLINA	20,000	20,000
FLORIDA	20,000	20,000	NO. DAKOTA	24,000	48,000
GEORGIA	22,000	39,600	OHIO	24,000	24,000
IDAHO	24,000	40,000	OKLAHOMA	20,000	20,000
ILLINOIS	24,000	40,000	OREGON	25,500	42,500
INDIANA	24,000	40,000	PENNSYLVANIA	26,000	36,000
IOWA	24,000	40,000	RHODE ISLAND	28,000	40,000
KANSAS	24,000	34,000	SO. CAROLINA	20,000	25,000
KENTUCKY	18,000	18,000	SO. DAKOTA	20,000	20,000
LOUISIANA	13,400	N. A.	TENNESSEE	20,000	20,000
MAINE	18,000	27,000	TEXAS	13,500	N. A.
MARYLAND	25,000	40,000	UTAH	26,000	34,000
MASSACHUSETTS	30,000	30,000	VERMONT	20,000	20,000
MICHIGAN	27,000	45,000	VIRGINIA	24,000	35,000
MINNESOTA	27,000	42,000	WASHINGTON	24,000	34,000
MISSISSIPPI	18,000	22,000	WEST VA.	24,000	40,000
MISSOURI	24,000	24,000	WISCONSIN	24,000	36,000
MONTANA	24,000	34,000	WYOMING	27,000	30,000

* RED BOOK [11] FIGURES ARE REPORTED (P. 89) AS "BASED ON THE STATE'S INTERPRETATIONS OF THEIR LAWS [1933] AND ON PHYSICAL LIMITATIONS OF VEHICLE DESIGN AND TIRE CAPACITY." PUBLIC ROADS [13] FIGURES ARE REPORTED (P. 167) AS "AN ABSTRACT OF STATE LAWS, INCLUDING LEGISLATION PASSED IN 1932."

1. 4-WHEEL: THE SMALLEST OF THE FOLLOWING 3 FIGURES WAS USED:

(A) MAXIMUM GROSS WEIGHT (AS GIVEN IN RED BOOK, P. 90-91).

(B) MAXIMUM AXLE WEIGHT (AS GIVEN IN RED BOOK, P. 90-91), MULTIPLIED BY 1.5 (SEE RED BOOK, P. 89).

(C) MAXIMUM GROSS WEIGHT (AS GIVEN IN RED BOOK, P. 93).

EXCEPTIONS: TEXAS AND LOUISIANA–SEE RED BOOK, P. 91.

2. 6-WHEEL: MAXIMUM GROSS WEIGHT AS GIVEN IN PUBLIC ROADS, P. 167. THESE FIGURES AGREE IN MOST CASES WITH THOSE SHOWN IN RED BOOK, P. 93, AND WITH PUBLIC ROADS MAXIMUM AXLE WEIGHTS MULTIPLIED BY 2.5 (SEE RED BOOK, P. 93). TEXAS AND LOUISIANA ARE EXCLUDED AS DATA ARE NOT AVAILABLE TO CONVERT FROM PAYLOAD TO GROSS WEIGHT LIMITS.

TABLE 7

INDEPENDENT VARIABLES
(BASIC DATA FOR TABLE 2 – CONT'D)

STATE	TRUCKS ON FARMS PER 1,000 AGRICULTURAL LABOR FORCE	AVERAGE LENGTH OF RAILROAD HAUL OF FREIGHT (MILES)	PERCENT OF STATE HIGHWAYS WITH HIGH-TYPE SURFACE
ALABAMA	26.05	189.4	1.57
ARIZONA	79.74	282.2	2.60
ARKANSAS	28.62	233.1	1.72
CALIFORNIA	123.40	264.6	13.10
COLORADO	159.50	244.7	0.58
CONNECTICUT	173.80	132.6	7.98
DELAWARE	173.20	202.7	21.40
FLORIDA	91.41	184.1	8.22
GEORGIA	32.07	165.7	1.60
IDAHO	95.89	243.6	0.73
ILLINOIS	114.70	207.9	9.85
INDIANA	120.20	202.8	6.90
IOWA	98.73	233.3	3.39
KANSAS	146.70	281.5	0.94
KENTUCKY	20.05	227.5	1.81
LOUISIANA	31.27	201.0	1.94
MAINE	209.30	120.4	1.87
MARYLAND	134.20	184.1	12.90
MASSACHUSETTS	172.20	144.7	17.70
MICHIGAN	148.40	168.0	6.68
MINNESOTA	120.40	225.6	1.44
MISSISSIPPI	29.62	164.9	1.14
MISSOURI	54.28	229.7	2.91
MONTANA	183.80	266.5	0.09
NEBRASKA	132.10	266.9	0.41
NEVADA	139.40	273.2	0.39
NEW HAMPSHIRE	205.40	129.0	3.42
NEW JERSEY	230.20	137.6	23.30
NEW MEXICO	90.46	279.0	0.18
NEW YORK	220.50	163.3	21.50
NO. CAROLINA	37.12	171.5	8.61
NO. DAKOTA	126.40	255.1	0.01
OHIO	125.80	194.2	11.20
OKLAHOMA	78.18	223.3	1.42
OREGON	118.90	246.2	3.35
PENNSYLVANIA	187.60	166.5	9.78
RHODE ISLAND	193.30	131.0	20.40
SO. CAROLINA	20.21	169.8	2.82
SO. DAKOTA	113.40	216.6	0.04
TENNESSEE	23.98	191.9	3.97
UTAH	101.70	235.7	1.69
VERMONT	132.20	109.7	2.26
VIRGINIA	71.88	229.8	2.86
WASHINGTON	180.90	254.4	4.21
WEST VIRGINIA	62.88	218.7	8.13
WISCONSIN	178.60	195.7	4.57
WYOMING	133.40	286.7	0.08

(1) AVERAGE LENGTH OF RR HAUL OF (REVENUE) FREIGHT = AVERAGE DISTANCE IN MILES EACH TON IS CARRIED = RATIO OF NUMBER OF TON-MILES TO NUMBER OF TONS CARRIED. FOR EACH STATE, AVERAGE LENGTH OF HAUL WAS OBTAINED BY WEIGHTING AVERAGE LENGTH OF HAUL OF EACH COMPANY BY THE NUMBER OF MILES OF LINE OPERATED BY THAT COMPANY IN THE STATE (ALL FOR CLASS I RR'S).

(2) PERCENTAGE OF STATE ROADS WITH HIGH-QUALITY SURFACE: WHERE HIGH-QUALITY (HIGH-TYPE) SURFACE CONSISTS OF BITUMINOUS MACADAM, BITUMINOUS CONCRETE, SHEET ASPHALT, PORTLAND CEMENT CONCRETE, AND BLOCK PAVEMENTS. ALL STATE RURAL ROADS, BOTH LOCAL AND STATE HIGHWAYS SYSTEMS, ARE INCLUDED.

References

1. Association of American Railroads, Bureau of Railway Economics. *Railway Mileage by States.* Washington, D. C.: December 31, 1930.
2. Becker, G. S. "Competition and Democracy." *Journal of Law and Economics,* October 1958.
3. The Council of State Governments. "Occupational Licensing Legislation in the States." 1952.
4. Demsetz, H., "Why Regulate Utilities?" *Journal of Law and Economics,* April 1968.
5. Gerwig, R. W. "Natural Gas Production: A Study of Costs of Regulation." *Journal of Law and Economics,* October 1962, pp. 69-92.
6. Holen, A. S. "Effects of Professional Licensing Arrangements on Interstate Labor Mobility and Resource Allocation." *Journal of Political Economy,* Vol. 73 (1915), pp. 492-98.
7. Keyes, L. S. *Federal Control of Entry into Air Transportation.* Cambridge, Mass.: Harvard University Press, 1951.
8. Moore, T. G. "The Purpose of Licensing." *Journal of Law and Economics,* October 1961.
9. Olson, M. *The Logic of Collective Action.* Cambridge, Mass.: Harvard University Press, 1965.
10. Peltzman, S. "Entry in Commercial Banking." *Journal of Law and Economics,* October 1965.
11. *The Motor Truck Red Book and Directory,* 1934 Edition, pp. 85–102.
12. U. S. Congress, Select Committee on Small Business. *Hearings,* 88th Congress, 2nd Session, August 10 and 11, 1964.
13. U. S. Department of Agriculture, Bureau of Public Roads. *Public Roads.* Washington, D. C.: U. S. Government Printing Office, December 1932.
14. U. S. Department of Commerce, Bureau of the Census. *United States Census of Agriculture, 1930,* Vol. 4. Washington, D. C.: U. S. Government Printing Office, 1930.
15. ———. *United States Census of Population.* Washington, D. C.: U. S. Government Printing Office, appropriate years.
16. ———, Bureau of Foreign and Domestic Commerce. *Statistical Abstract of the U. S., 1932.* Washington, D. C.: U. S. Government Printing Office, 1932.
17. U. S. Interstate Commerce Commission. *Annual Report.* Washington, D. C.: U. S. Government Printing Office, appropriate years.
18. ———. *Statistics of Railways in the United States, 1930.* Washington, D. C.: U. S. Government Printing Office, 1930.

Part III
Ronald H. Coase

Introduction to Part III: Ronald H. Coase (b. 1910)

Ronald Coase was born in Willesden, London, UK in 1910. He went to school in London and won a place at a high (secondary) school which, at that time, allowed pupils after they had completed their secondary education to study as external students of the University of London for a year. Coase reports that this prompted the first of a number of fortunate incidents that shaped his career as an economist (Nobel Foundation, 2010). His initial intention was to take a degree in history but a late start at high school meant that he had not taken the required prior course in Latin. As an alternative Coase chose chemistry – a subject in which he had demonstrated some earlier promise – but he found the associated mathematics 'not to my taste'. This left him with only one option: commerce. He passed his first year's work and enrolled at the London School of Economics (LSE) (part of the University of London) to continue as an undergraduate on a bachelor of commerce degree. He was awarded a BCom by the University of London in 1932. In 1951 he was awarded a PhD in economics by the same institution.

Coase's first academic appointment was as an assistant lecturer at the Dundee School of Economics and Commerce in 1932. In 1934 he was appointed as assistant lecturer at the University of Liverpool and in 1935 he returned to the London School of Economics, initially as an assistant lecturer, then lecturer (1938) and finally reader (1947). During the Second World War he did statistical work at the Forestry Commission and in the Offices of the War Cabinet. His war service lasted from 1940 to 1946. In 1951, Coase left the UK for the USA, where he was appointed Professor of Economics at Buffalo University, New York. In 1958 he moved to the University of Virginia as professor, and in 1964 he joined the University of Chicago, first as professor and from 1971 as the Clifton R. Musser Professor of Economics. Coase spent 1991 as Distinguished Professor (visiting) of Law and Economics at the University of Kansas. Since 1982 he has been Clifton R. Musser Professor Emeritus of Economics and Senior Fellow in Law and Economics at Chicago.

Among Coase's offices and honours are honorary degrees from a number of universities around the world. He is a distinguished fellow of the American Economic Association and a fellow of the American Academy of Arts and Sciences. Coase is also an honorary fellow of the LSE, a corresponding fellow of the British Academy and a Membre Titulaire of the European Academy. In 1980 he won the Law and Economics Center Prize from the University of Miami and in 1988 he received the D. Francis Bustin Prize from the University of Chicago. In 1991 Coase was awarded the Nobel Memorial Prize in Economics 'for his discovery and clarification of the significance of transaction costs and property rights for the institutional structure and functioning of the economy' (Nobel Foundation, 2010).

As noted, Coase spent the first year of his undergraduate career as an external student of the University of London. He then took the usual two further years to complete his degree. However, university regulations required him to be 'resident' at the LSE for three years before he could graduate. This presented Coase with the problem of finding something to do to fulfil his final year of residence. Again, Coase records an incident of serendipity that would decisively influence his life and career. He confesses that even as late as five months before his final examinations his 'notions on how the economy worked were extremely woolly' (Coase, 1992, p. 715). However, attending the seminars of a newly appointed professor – Arnold Plant – proved to be a turning point. Plant introduced Coase to Adam Smith's 'invisible hand' and gave him a revelatory and 'coherent view of the economic system'. It seems that Coase also impressed Plant, as under his influence the University of London awarded Coase a Sir Ernest Cassel Travelling Scholarship. Coase used this to spend a year in the USA doing the research that would many years later form a major part of his Nobel citation. Before learning of his award, Coase had planned to spend his last year as an undergraduate studying industrial law, and he observes that 'had I done so I would undoubtedly have gone on to become a lawyer' (Nobel Foundation, 2010).

Coase travelled to the USA intent on 'studying the structure of American industries, with the aim of discovering why industries were organized in different ways' (Nobel Foundation, 2010). He was also exercised by a puzzle posed for him by the teachings of Smith (and Plant). The metaphorical invisible hand demonstrated the power that the competitive process had to organize and coordinate production. But in his visits to American firms and factories, Coase was meeting a tier of management whose very function was also to coordinate and organize: 'Why was it needed if the pricing system provided all the coordination necessary?' (Coase, 1992, p. 715). The answer to this question, Coase realized, was that 'there were costs of using the price mechanism. What the prices are have to be discovered. There are negotiations to be undertaken, contracts have to be drawn up, inspections have to be made … and so on. These costs have come to be known as transaction costs' (ibid.). In his 1937 paper in *Economica*, 'The Nature of the Firm' (paper 13), cited by the Royal Swedish Academy of Sciences as part of the reason for his Nobel award, Coase argues that it is the presence of transaction costs that explains the very existence of firms: the contractual and other tasks and processes that give rise to such costs are simply more efficiently managed by the institution of the firm. Markets and the individuals within them could do the job but less efficiently. Coase (1992, p. 716) characterizes the firm as a 'little planned society'; he argues that the boundary between what is done through the market and what is done by the firm is decided by the competitive process.

Coase's Nobel citation makes reference to one other paper: 'The Problem of Social Cost' (paper 14), published in the *Journal of Law and Economics* (which Coase was later to edit) in 1960. This work gave rise to the famous Coase theorem, which Coase himself credits to fellow Nobel Laureate, George Stigler (see entry for Stigler in the present volume and Stigler, 1989). Coase's purpose in the 'Problem of Social Cost' paper was to offer a critique of the convention established by A.C. Pigou that, in the presence of negative externalities, some form of corrective government action – such as the imposition of a tax – could 'internalize' and therefore limit damage to third parties. Coase showed that, where transaction costs are zero, negotiations freely entered into by the offending and offended parties will both eliminate negative externalities and provide for an efficient allocation of resources. Moreover, Coase was able to demonstrate that this outcome would occur however property rights are defined between the parties. For example, a firm at risk of polluting a river would be willing to compensate the riparian owner were a pollution event to arise. On the other hand, if the firm were the riparian owner, then a third-party river user would be willing to pay it to take steps not to pollute. Payments in either direction would vary according to the value each side placed on its output (the firm), or amenity (the river user): the most valued option prevails regardless of who has rights over the river. Of course, where transaction costs *are* present, affected parties may find it too costly or difficult to undertake the necessary negotiations. In such circumstances, Coase recognized that the assignment of property rights can affect resource allocation and, as Brunner (1992, p. 10) notes, 'The social problem then is the optimal assignment of rights'. For Coase (1992, p. 718), and those his work has encouraged, this raises the significance of the links between economics and the institutional arena where rights are decided: that of the law. In a wonderful passage from his Nobel lecture he emphasizes the importance of the institutional context for economic analysis:

> It makes little sense for economists to discuss the process of exchange without specifying the institutional setting within which the trading takes place, since this affects the incentives to produce and the costs of transacting. I think this is now beginning to be recognized and made crystal-clear by what is going on in Eastern Europe today. The time has surely gone in which economists could analyze in great detail two individuals exchanging nuts for berries on the edge of the forest and then feel that their analysis of the process of exchange was complete, illuminating though this analysis may be in certain respects.

Brunner (1992, p. 10) has called 'The Problem of Social Cost', one of the outstanding papers published in the postwar period. Blaug (1998, p.41) is perhaps even more fulsome:

> It is rare for a single article to generate an entire branch of economics, much less two branches of economics, but the Economics of Property Rights ... and The Economics of Law ... two rapidly growing sub-disciplines within economics in the last decade or so, can be traced directly to Coase's article on social cost ...

Posner (1993, p. 195) claims that it 'is widely believed to be the most frequently cited article in all of economics'.

Coase's other notable work includes a study of the allocation of the radio frequency spectrum in the USA published as 'The Federal Communications Commission' in the *Journal of Law and Economics* in 1959. Against the grain of popular wisdom at the time in the industry and in government circles, Coase argued in the paper 'that it would be better if use of the spectrum was determined by the pricing system and was awarded to the highest bidder' (Nobel Foundation, 2010). He relates an interesting story of an invitation from a number of Chicago economists (Coase was then at the University of Virginia) to discuss what they thought was an error in this work. At the meeting, Coase persuaded his critics that he was in the right and he was asked to write up his argument for a second paper in the *Journal of Law and Economics*. This subsequently appeared in 1960 as 'The Problem of Social Cost'. Coase supposes that without the prompt from Chicago his most famous paper would never have been written (Nobel Foundation, 2010). The central argument in 'The Federal Communications Commission' is itself of some contemporary relevance. The economist consultants to the British government on its auction of the '3rd generation' mobile phone licences – which raised some £22.5 billion ($34bn) or 2.5 per cent of UK GDP – cite Coase as the original advocate of the kind of work on which they were engaged (see Binmore and Klemperer, 2002).

Coase's lifetime work has been drawn together in two volumes: Coase (1988; 1994). The former includes his two classic articles from 1937 and 1960. The latter consists of 15 essays in which Coase evaluates the contributions of outstanding economists, including Adam Smith, Alfred Marshall and George Stigler. The legacy of Coase in economic analysis is explored in a collection of 40 articles edited by Steven Medema (1995).

Main Published Works

(1937), 'The Nature of the Firm', *Economica*, **4**, November, pp. 386–405.
(1959), 'The Federal Communications Commission', *Journal of Law and Economics*, **2**, October, pp. 1–40.
(1960), 'The Problem of Social Cost', *Journal of Law and Economics*, **3**, October, pp. 1–44.
(1988), *The Firm, the Market and the Law*, Chicago, IL: University of Chicago Press.
(1992), 'The Institutional Structure of Production', *American Economic Review*, **82**, September, pp. 713–19.
(1994), *Essays on Economics and Economists*, Chicago, IL: University of Chicago Press.

Secondary Literature

Barzel, Y. and L.A. Kochin (1992), 'Ronald Coase on the Nature of Social Cost as a Key to the Problem of the Firm', *Scandinavian Journal of Economics*, **94** (1), pp. 19–31.
Binmore, K. and P. Klemperer (2002), 'The Biggest Auction Ever: the Sale of the British 3G Telecom Licences', *Economic Journal*, **112**, March, C74–C96.
Brunner, K. (1992), 'Ronald Coase: Old Fashioned Scholar', *Scandinavian Journal of Economics*, **94** (1), pp. 7–17.
Medema, S.G. (ed.) (1995), *The Legacy of Ronald Coase in Economic Analysis*, Aldershot, UK and Brookfield, VT, USA: Edward Elgar.
Nobel Foundation (2010), Official Web Site, www.nobelprize.org.
Posner, R.A. (1993), 'Ronald Coase and Methodology', *Journal of Economic Perspectives*, **7**, Fall, pp. 195–210.
Stigler, G.J. (1989), 'Two Notes on the Coase Theorem', *Yale Law Journal*, **99**, December, pp. 631–3.

[13]

The Nature of the Firm

By R. H. Coase

Economic theory has suffered in the past from a failure to state clearly its assumptions. Economists in building up a theory have often omitted to examine the foundations on which it was erected. This examination is, however, essential not only to prevent the misunderstanding and needless controversy which arise from a lack of knowledge of the assumptions on which a theory is based, but also because of the extreme importance for economics of good judgment in choosing between rival sets of assumptions. For instance, it is suggested that the use of the word "firm" in economics may be different from the use of the term by the "plain man."[1] Since there is apparently a trend in economic theory towards starting analysis with the individual firm and not with the industry,[2] it is all the more necessary not only that a clear definition of the word "firm" should be given but that its difference from a firm in the "real world," if it exists, should be made clear. Mrs. Robinson has said that "the two questions to be asked of a set of assumptions in economics are: Are they tractable? and: Do they correspond with the real world?"[3] Though, as Mrs. Robinson points out, "more often one set will be manageable and the other realistic," yet there may well be branches of theory where assumptions may be both manageable and realistic. It is hoped to show in the following paper that a definition of a firm may be obtained which is not only realistic in that it corresponds to what is meant by a firm in the real world, but is tractable by two of the most powerful instruments of economic analysis developed by Marshall, the idea of the margin and that of substitution, together giving the idea of substitution at

[1] Joan Robinson, *Economics is a Serious Subject*, p. 12.
[2] See N. Kaldor, "The Equilibrium of the Firm," *Economic Journal*, March, 1934.
[3] Op. cit., p. 6.

the margin.[1] Our definition must, of course, "relate to formal relations which are capable of being *conceived* exactly."[2]

I

It is convenient if, in searching for a definition of a firm, we first consider the economic system as it is normally treated by the economist. Let us consider the description of the economic system given by Sir Arthur Salter.[3] "The normal economic system works itself. For its current operation it is under no central control, it needs no central survey. Over the whole range of human activity and human need, supply is adjusted to demand, and production to consumption, by a process that is automatic, elastic and responsive." An economist thinks of the economic system as being co-ordinated by the price mechanism and society becomes not an organisation but an organism.[4] The economic system "works itself." This does not mean that there is no planning by individuals. These exercise foresight and choose between alternatives. This is necessarily so if there is to be order in the system. But this theory assumes that the direction of resources is dependent directly on the price mechanism. Indeed, it is often considered to be an objection to economic planning that it merely tries to do what is already done by the price mechanism.[5] Sir Arthur Salter's description, however, gives a very incomplete picture of our economic system. Within a firm, the description does not fit at all. For instance, in economic theory we find that the allocation of factors of production between different uses is determined by the price mechanism. The price of factor *A* becomes higher in *X* than in *Y*. As a result, *A* moves from *Y* to *X* until the difference between the prices in *X* and *Y*, except in so far as it compensates for other differential advantages, disappears. Yet in the real world, we find that there are many areas where this does not apply. If a workman moves from department *Y* to department *X*, he does not go because of a change in relative prices, but because he is ordered to do so. Those who

[1] J. M. Keynes, *Essays in Biography*, pp. 223–4.

[2] L. Robbins, *Nature and Significance of Economic Science*, p. 63.

[3] This description is quoted with approval by D. H. Robertson, *Control of Industry*, p. 85, and by Professor Arnold Plant, "Trends in Business Administration," ECONOMICA, February, 1932. It appears in *Allied Shipping Control*, pp. 16–17.

[4] See F. A. Hayek, "The Trend of Economic Thinking," ECONOMICA, May, 1933.

[5] See F. A. Hayek, op. cit.

object to economic planning on the grounds that the problem is solved by price movements can be answered by pointing out that there is planning within our economic system which is quite different from the individual planning mentioned above and which is akin to what is normally called economic planning. The example given above is typical of a large sphere in our modern economic system. Of course, this fact has not been ignored by economists. Marshall introduces organisation as a fourth factor of production; J. B. Clark gives the co-ordinating function to the entrepreneur; Professor Knight introduces managers who co-ordinate. As D. H. Robertson points out, we find "islands of conscious power in this ocean of unconscious co-operation like lumps of butter coagulating in a pail of buttermilk."[1] But in view of the fact that it is usually argued that co-ordination will be done by the price mechanism, why is such organisation necessary? Why are there these "islands of conscious power"? Outside the firm, price movements direct production, which is co-ordinated through a series of exchange transactions on the market. Within a firm, these market transactions are eliminated and in place of the complicated market structure with exchange transactions is substituted the entrepreneur-co-ordinator, who directs production.[2] It is clear that these are alternative methods of co-ordinating production. Yet, having regard to the fact that if production is regulated by price movements, production could be carried on without any organisation at all, well might we ask, why is there any organisation?

Of course, the degree to which the price mechanism is superseded varies greatly. In a department store, the allocation of the different sections to the various locations in the building may be done by the controlling authority or it may be the result of competitive price bidding for space. In the Lancashire cotton industry, a weaver can rent power and shop-room and can obtain looms and yarn on credit.[3] This co-ordination of the various factors of production is, however, normally carried out without the intervention of the price mechanism. As is evident, the amount of "vertical" integration, involving as it does

[1] Op. cit., p. 85.

[2] In the rest of this paper I shall use the term entrepreneur to refer to the person or persons who, in a competitive system, take the place of the price mechanism in the direction of resources.

[3] *Survey of Textile Industries*, p. 26.

the supersession of the price mechanism, varies greatly from industry to industry and from firm to firm.

It can, I think, be assumed that the distinguishing mark of the firm is the supersession of the price mechanism. It is, of course, as Professor Robbins points out, "related to an outside network of relative prices and costs,"[1] but it is important to discover the exact nature of this relationship. This distinction between the allocation of resources in a firm and the allocation in the economic system has been very vividly described by Mr. Maurice Dobb when discussing Adam Smith's conception of the capitalist: "It began to be seen that there was something more important than the relations inside each factory or unit captained by an undertaker; there were the relations of the undertaker with the rest of the economic world outside his immediate sphere . . . . the undertaker busies himself with the division of labour inside each firm and he plans and organises consciously," but "he is related to the much larger economic specialisation, of which he himself is merely one specialised unit. Here, he plays his part as a single cell in a larger organism, mainly unconscious of the wider rôle he fills."[2]

In view of the fact that while economists treat the price mechanism as a co-ordinating instrument, they also admit the co-ordinating function of the "entrepreneur," it is surely important to enquire why co-ordination is the work of the price mechanism in one case and of the entrepreneur in another. The purpose of this paper is to bridge what appears to be a gap in economic theory between the assumption (made for some purposes) that resources are allocated by means of the price mechanism and the assumption (made for other purposes) that this allocation is dependent on the entrepreneur-co-ordinator. We have to explain the basis on which, in practice, this choice between alternatives is effected.[3]

[1] Op. cit., p. 71.

[2] *Capitalist Enterprise and Social Progress*, p. 20. Cf., also, Henderson, *Supply and Demand*, pp. 3–5.

[3] It is easy to see when the State takes over the direction of an industry that, in planning it, it is doing something which was previously done by the price mechanism. What is usually not realised is that any business man in organising the relations between his departments is also doing something which could be organised through the price mechanism. There is therefore point in Mr. Durbin's answer to those who emphasise the problems involved in economic planning that the same problems have to be solved by business men in the competitive system. (See "Economic Calculus in a Planned Economy," *Economic Journal*, December, 1936.) The important difference between these two cases is that economic planning is imposed on industry while firms arise voluntarily because they represent a more efficient method of organising production. In a competitive system, there is an "optimum" amount of planning!

II

Our task is to attempt to discover why a firm emerges at all in a specialised exchange economy. The price mechanism (considered purely from the side of the direction of resources) might be superseded if the relationship which replaced it was desired for its own sake. This would be the case, for example, if some people preferred to work under the direction of some other person. Such individuals would accept less in order to work under someone, and firms would arise naturally from this. But it would appear that this cannot be a very important reason, for it would rather seem that the opposite tendency is operating if one judges from the stress normally laid on the advantage of "being one's own master."[1] Of course, if the desire was not to be controlled but to control, to exercise power over others, then people might be willing to give up something in order to direct others; that is, they would be willing to pay others more than they could get under the price mechanism in order to be able to direct them. But this implies that those who direct pay in order to be able to do this and are not paid to direct, which is clearly not true in the majority of cases.[2] Firms might also exist if purchasers preferred commodities which are produced by firms to those not so produced; but even in spheres where one would expect such preferences (if they exist) to be of negligible importance, firms are to be found in the real world.[3] Therefore there must be other elements involved.

The main reason why it is profitable to establish a firm would seem to be that there is a cost of using the price mechanism. The most obvious cost of "organising" production through the price mechanism is that of discovering what the relevant prices are.[4] This cost may be reduced but it will not be eliminated by the emergence of specialists who will sell this information. The costs of negotiating and

[1] Cf. Harry Dawes, "Labour Mobility in the Steel Industry," *Economic Journal*, March, 1934, who instances "the trek to retail shopkeeping and insurance work by the better paid of skilled men due to the desire (often the main aim in life of a worker) to be independent" (p. 86).

[2] None the less, this is not altogether fanciful. Some small shopkeepers are said to earn less than their assistants.

[3] G. F. Shove, "The Imperfection of the Market : a Further Note," *Economic Journal*, March, 1933, p. 116, note 1, points out that such preferences may exist, although the example he gives is almost the reverse of the instance given in the text.

[4] According to N. Kaldor, [A Classificatory Note of the Determinateness of Equilibrium," *Review of Economic Studies*, February, 1934, it is one of the assumptions of static theory that "All the relevant prices are known to all individuals." But this is clearly not true of the real world.

concluding a separate contract for each exchange transaction which takes place on a market must also be taken into account.[1] Again, in certain markets, e.g., produce exchanges, a technique is devised for minimising these contract costs; but they are not eliminated. It is true that contracts are not eliminated when there is a firm but they are greatly reduced. A factor of production (or the owner thereof) does not have to make a series of contracts with the factors with whom he is co-operating within the firm, as would be necessary, of course, if this co-operation were as a direct result of the working of the price mechanism. For this series of contracts is substituted one. At this stage, it is important to note the character of the contract into which a factor enters that is employed within a firm. The contract is one whereby the factor, for a certain remuneration (which may be fixed or fluctuating), agrees to obey the directions of an entrepreneur *within certain limits*.[2] The essence of the contract is that it should only state the limits to the powers of the entrepreneur. Within these limits, he can therefore direct the other factors of production.

There are, however, other disadvantages—or costs—of using the price mechanism. It may be desired to make a long-term contract for the supply of some article or service. This may be due to the fact that if one contract is made for a longer period, instead of several shorter ones, then certain costs of making each contract will be avoided. Or, owing to the risk attitude of the people concerned, they may prefer to make a long rather than a short-term contract. Now, owing to the difficulty of forecasting, the longer the period of the contract is for the supply of the commodity or service, the less possible, and indeed, the less desirable it is for the person purchasing to specify what the other contracting party is expected to do. It may well be a matter of indifference to the person supplying the service or commodity which of several courses of action is taken, but not to the purchaser of that service or commodity. But the purchaser will not know which of these several courses he will want the supplier to take. Therefore,

[1] This influence was noted by Professor Usher when discussing the development of capitalism. He says: "The successive buying and selling of partly finished products were sheer waste of energy." (*Introduction to the Industrial History of England*, p. 13). But he does not develop the idea nor consider why it is that buying and selling operations still exist.

[2] It would be possible for no limits to the powers of the entrepreneur to be fixed. This would be voluntary slavery. According to Professor Batt, *The Law of Master and Servant*, p. 18, such a contract would be void and unenforceable.

the service which is being provided is expressed in general terms, the exact details being left until a later date. All that is stated in the contract is the limits to what the persons supplying the commodity or service is expected to do. The details of what the supplier is expected to do is not stated in the contract but is decided later by the purchaser. When the direction of resources (within the limits of the contract) becomes dependent on the buyer in this way, that relationship which I term a " firm " may be obtained.[1] A firm is likely therefore to emerge in those cases where a very short term contract would be unsatisfactory. It is obviously of more importance in the case of services—labour—than it is in the case of the buying of commodities. In the case of commodities, the main items can be stated in advance and the details which will be decided later will be of minor significance.

We may sum up this section of the argument by saying that the operation of a market costs something and by forming an organisation and allowing some authority (an " entrepreneur ") to direct the resources, certain marketing costs are saved. The entrepreneur has to carry out his function at less cost, taking into account the fact that he may get factors of production at a lower price than the market transactions which he supersedes, because it is always possible to revert to the open market if he fails to do this.

The question of uncertainty is one which is often considered to be very relevant to the study of the equilibrium of the firm. It seems improbable that a firm would emerge without the existence of uncertainty. But those, for instance, Professor Knight, who make the *mode of payment* the distinguishing mark of the firm—fixed incomes being guaranteed to some of those engaged in production by a person who takes the residual, and fluctuating, income—would appear to be introducing a point which is irrelevant to the problem we are considering. One entrepreneur may sell his services to another for a certain sum of money, while the payment to his employees may be mainly or wholly a share in profits.[2] The significant question would

[1] Of course, it is not possible to draw a hard and fast line which determines whether there is a firm or not. There may be more or less direction. It is similar to the legal question of whether there is the relationship of master and servant or principal and agent. See the discussion of this problem below.

[2] The views of Professor Knight are examined below in more detail.

appear to be why the allocation of resources is not done directly by the price mechanism.

Another factor that should be noted is that exchange transactions on a market and the same transactions organised within a firm are often treated differently by Governments or other bodies with regulatory powers. If we consider the operation of a sales tax, it is clear that it is a tax on market transactions and not on the same transactions organised within the firm. Now since these are alternative methods of "organisation"—by the price mechanism or by the entrepreneur—such a regulation would bring into existence firms which otherwise would have no *raison d'être*. It would furnish a reason for the emergence of a firm in a specialised exchange economy. Of course, to the extent that firms already exist, such a measure as a sales tax would merely tend to make them larger than they would otherwise be. Similarly, quota schemes, and methods of price control which imply that there is rationing, and which do not apply to firms producing such products for themselves, by allowing advantages to those who organise within the firm and not through the market, necessarily encourage the growth of firms. But it is difficult to believe that it is measures such as have been mentioned in this paragraph which have brought firms into existence. Such measures would, however, tend to have this result if they did not exist for other reasons.

These, then, are the reasons why organisations such as firms exist in a specialised exchange economy in which it is generally assumed that the distribution of resources is "organised" by the price mechanism. A firm, therefore, consists of the system of relationships which comes into existence when the direction of resources is dependent on an entrepreneur.

The approach which has just been sketched would appear to offer an advantage in that it is possible to give a scientific meaning to what is meant by saying that a firm gets larger or smaller. A firm becomes larger as additional transactions (which could be exchange transactions co-ordinated through the price mechanism) are organised by the entrepreneur and becomes smaller as he abandons the organisation of such transactions. The question which arises is whether it is possible to study the forces which determine the size of the firm. Why does the entrepreneur not organise one less transaction or one more? It is interesting to note that Professor Knight considers that:

> "the relation between efficiency and size is one of the most serious problems of theory, being, in contrast with the relation for a plant, largely a matter of personality and historical accident rather than of intelligible general principles. But the question is peculiarly vital because the possibility of monopoly gain offers a powerful incentive to *continuous and unlimited* expansion of the firm, which force must be offset by some equally powerful one making for decreased efficiency (in the production of money income) with growth in size, if even boundary competition is to exist."[1]

Professor Knight would appear to consider that it is impossible to treat scientifically the determinants of the size of the firm. On the basis of the concept of the firm developed above, this task will now be attempted.

It was suggested that the introduction of the firm was due primarily to the existence of marketing costs. A pertinent question to ask would appear to be (quite apart from the monopoly considerations raised by Professor Knight), why, if by organising one can eliminate certain costs and in fact reduce the cost of production, are there any market transactions at all?[2] Why is not all production carried on by one big firm? There would appear to be certain possible explanations.

First, as a firm gets larger, there may be decreasing returns to the entrepreneur function, that is, the costs of organising additional transactions within the firm may rise.[3] Naturally, a point must be reached where the costs of organising an extra transaction within the firm are equal to the costs involved in carrying out the transaction in the open market, or, to the costs of organising by another entrepreneur. Secondly, it may be that as the transactions which are organised increase, the entrepreneur fails to place the factors of production in the uses where their value

[1] *Risk, Uncertainty and Profit*, Preface to the Re-issue, London School of Economics Series of Reprints, No. 16, 1933.

[2] There are certain marketing costs which could only be eliminated by the abolition of "consumers' choice" and these are the costs of retailing. It is conceivable that these costs might be so high that people would be willing to accept rations because the extra product obtained was worth the loss of their choice.

[3] This argument assumes that exchange transactions on a market can be considered as homogeneous; which is clearly untrue in fact. This complication is taken into account below.

is greatest, that is, fails to make the best use of the factors of production. Again, a point must be reached where the loss through the waste of resources is equal to the marketing costs of the exchange transaction in the open market or to the loss if the transaction was organised by another entrepreneur. Finally, the supply price of one or more of the factors of production may rise, because the "other advantages" of a small firm are greater than those of a large firm.[1] Of course, the actual point where the expansion of the firm ceases might be determined by a combination of the factors mentioned above. The first two reasons given most probably correspond to the economists' phrase of "diminishing returns to management."[2]

The point has been made in the previous paragraph that a firm will tend to expand until the costs of organising an extra transaction within the firm become equal to the costs of carrying out the same transaction by means of an exchange on the open market or the costs of organising in another firm. But if the firm stops its expansion at a point below the costs of marketing in the open market and at a point equal to the costs of organising in another firm, in most cases (excluding the case of "combination"[3]), this will imply that there is a market transaction between these two producers, each of whom could organise it at less than the actual marketing costs. How is the paradox to be resolved? If we consider an example the reason for this will become clear. Suppose *A* is buying a product from *B* and that both *A* and *B* could organise this marketing transaction at less than its present cost. *B*, we can assume, is not organising one process or stage of production, but several. If *A* therefore wishes to avoid a market transaction, he will have to take over all the processes of production controlled by *B*. Unless *A* takes over all the processes of

[1] For a discussion of the variation of the supply price of factors of production to firms of varying size, see E. A. G. Robinson, *The Structure of Competitive Industry*. It is sometimes said that the supply price of organising ability increases as the size of the firm increases because men prefer to be the heads of small independent businesses rather than the heads of departments in a large business. See Jones, *The Trust Problem*, p. 531, and Macgregor, *Industrial Combination*, p. 63. This is a common argument of those who advocate Rationalisation. It is said that larger units would be more efficient, but owing to the individualistic spirit of the smaller entrepreneurs, they prefer to remain independent, apparently in spite of the higher income which their increased efficiency under Rationalisation makes possible.

[2] This discussion is, of course, brief and incomplete. For a more thorough discussion of this particular problem, see N. Kaldor, "The Equilibrium of the Firm," *Economic Journal*, March, 1934, and E. A. G. Robinson, "The Problem of Management and the Size of the Firm," *Economic Journal*, June, 1934.

[3] A definition of this term is given below.

production, a market transaction will still remain, although it is a different product that is bought. But we have previously assumed that as each producer expands he becomes less efficient; the additional costs of organising extra transactions increase. It is probable that *A*'s cost of organising the transactions previously organised by *B* will be greater than *B*'s cost of doing the same thing. *A* therefore will take over the whole of *B*'s organisation only if his cost of organising *B*'s work is not greater than *B*'s cost by an amount equal to the costs of carrying out an exchange transaction on the open market. But once it becomes economical to have a market transaction, it also pays to divide production in such a way that the cost of organising an extra transaction in each firm is the same.

Up to now it has been assumed that the exchange transactions which take place through the price mechanism are homogeneous. In fact, nothing could be more diverse than the actual transactions which take place in our modern world. This would seem to imply that the costs of carrying out exchange transactions through the price mechanism will vary considerably as will also the costs of organising these transactions within the firm. It seems therefore possible that quite apart from the question of diminishing returns the costs of organising certain transactions within the firm may be greater than the costs of carrying out the exchange transactions in the open market. This would necessarily imply that there were exchange transactions carried out through the price mechanism, but would it mean that there would have to be more than one firm? Clearly not, for all those areas in the economic system where the direction of resources was not dependent directly on the price mechanism could be organised within one firm. The factors which were discussed earlier would seem to be the important ones, though it is difficult to say whether "diminishing returns to management" or the rising supply price of factors is likely to be the more important.

Other things being equal, therefore, a firm will tend to be larger:

(*a*) the less the costs of organising and the slower these costs rise with an increase in the transactions organised.

(*b*) the less likely the entrepreneur is to make mistakes and the smaller the increase in mistakes with an increase in the transactions organised.

(*c*) the greater the lowering (or the less the rise) in the supply price of factors of production to firms of larger size.

Apart from variations in the supply price of factors of production to firms of different sizes, it would appear that the costs of organising and the losses through mistakes will increase with an increase in the spatial distribution of the transactions organised, in the dissimilarity of the transactions, and in the probability of changes in the relevant prices.[1] As more transactions are organised by an entrepreneur, it would appear that the transactions would tend to be either different in kind or in different places. This furnishes an additional reason why efficiency will tend to decrease as the firm gets larger. Inventions which tend to bring factors of production nearer together, by lessening spatial distribution, tend to increase the size of the firm.[2] Changes like the telephone and the telegraph which tend to reduce the cost of organising spatially will tend to increase the size of the firm. All changes which improve managerial technique will tend to increase the size of the firm.[3-4]

It should be noted that the definition of a firm which was given above can be used to give more precise meanings to the terms "combination" and "integration."[5] There is a combination when transactions which were previously

[1] This aspect of the problem is emphasised by N. Kaldor, op. cit. Its importance in this connection had been previously noted by E. A. G. Robinson, *The Structure of Competitive Industry*, pp. 83–106. This assumes that an increase in the probability of price movements increases the costs of organising within a firm more than it increases the cost of carrying out an exchange transaction on the market—which is probable.

[2] This would appear to be the importance of the treatment of the technical unit by E. A. G. Robinson, op. cit., pp. 27–33. The larger the technical unit, the greater the concentration of factors and therefore the firm is likely to be larger.

[3] It should be noted that most inventions will change both the costs of organising and the costs of using the price mechanism. In such cases, whether the invention tends to make firms larger or smaller will depend on the relative effect on these two sets of costs. For instance, if the telephone reduces the costs of using the price mechanism more than it reduces the costs of organising, then it will have the effect of reducing the size of the firm.

[4] An illustration of these dynamic forces is furnished by Maurice Dobb, *Russian Economic Development*, p. 68. "With the passing of bonded labour the factory, as an establishment where work was organised under the whip of the overseer, lost its *raison d'être* until this was restored to it with the introduction of power machinery after 1846." It seems important to realise that the passage from the domestic system to the factory system is not a mere historical accident, but is conditioned by economic forces. This is shown by the fact that it is possible to move from the factory system to the domestic system, as in the Russian example, as well as *vice versa*. It is the essence of serfdom that the price mechanism is not allowed to operate. Therefore, there has to be direction from some organiser. When, however, serfdom passed, the price mechanism was allowed to operate. It was not until machinery drew workers into one locality that it paid to supersede the price mechanism and the firm again emerged.

[5] This is often called "vertical integration," combination being termed "lateral integration."

organised by two or more entrepreneurs become organised by one. This becomes integration when it involves the organisation of transactions which were previously carried out between the entrepreneurs on a market. A firm can expand in either or both of these two ways. The whole of the "structure of competitive industry" becomes tractable by the ordinary technique of economic analysis.

III

The problem which has been investigated in the previous section has not been entirely neglected by economists and it is now necessary to consider why the reasons given above for the emergence of a firm in a specialised exchange economy are to be preferred to the other explanations which have been offered.

It is sometimes said that the reason for the existence of a firm is to be found in the division of labour. This is the view of Professor Usher, a view which has been adopted and expanded by Mr. Maurice Dobb. The firm becomes "the result of an increasing complexity of the division of labour . . . . The growth of this economic differentiation creates the need for some integrating force without which differentiation would collapse into chaos ; and it is as the integrating force in a differentiated economy that industrial forms are chiefly significant."[1] The answer to this argument is an obvious one. The "integrating force in a differentiated economy" already exists in the form of the price mechanism. It is perhaps the main achievement of economic science that it has shown that there is no reason to suppose that specialisation must lead to chaos.[2] The reason given by Mr. Maurice Dobb is therefore inadmissible. What has to be explained is why one integrating force (the entrepreneur) should be substituted for another integrating force (the price mechanism).

The most interesting reasons (and probably the most widely accepted) which have been given to explain this fact are those to be found in Professor Knight's *Risk, Uncertainty and Profit*. His views will be examined in some detail.

[1] Op. cit., p. 10. Professor Usher's views are to be found in his *Introduction to the Industrial History of England*, pp. 1–18.

[2] Cf. J. B. Clark, *Distribution of Wealth*, p. 19, who speaks of the theory of exchange as being the "theory of the organisation of industrial society."

Professor Knight starts with a system in which there is no uncertainty:

"acting as individuals under absolute freedom but without collusion men are supposed to have organised economic life with the primary and secondary division of labour, the use of capital, etc., developed to the point familiar in present-day America. The principal fact which calls for the exercise of the imagination is the internal organisation of the productive groups or establishments. With uncertainty entirely absent, every individual being in possession of perfect knowledge of the situation, there would be no occasion for anything of the nature of responsible management or control of productive activity. Even marketing transactions in any realistic sense would not be found. The flow of raw materials and productive services to the consumer would be entirely automatic."[1]

Professor Knight says that we can imagine this adjustment as being "the result of a long process of experimentation worked out by trial-and-error methods alone," while it is not necessary "to imagine every worker doing exactly the right thing at the right time in a sort of 'pre-established harmony' with the work of others. There might be managers, superintendents, etc., for the purpose of co-ordinating the activities of individuals," though these managers would be performing a purely routine function, "without responsibility of any sort."[2]

Professor Knight then continues:

"With the introduction of uncertainty—the fact of ignorance and the necessity of acting upon opinion rather than knowledge—into this Eden-like situation, its character is entirely changed . . . . With uncertainty present doing things, the actual execution of activity, becomes in a real sense a secondary part of life; the primary problem or function is deciding what to do and how to do it."[3]

This fact of uncertainty brings about the two most important characteristics of social organisation.

"In the first place, goods are produced for a market, on the basis of entirely impersonal prediction of wants, not for the satisfaction of the wants of the producers themselves. The producer takes the responsibility of

[1] *Risk, Uncertainty and Profit*, p. 267.
[2] Op. cit., pp. 267–8.
[3] Op. cit., p. 268.

forecasting the consumers' wants. In the second place, the work of forecasting and at the same time a large part of the technological direction and control of production are still further concentrated upon a very narrow class of the producers, and we meet with a new economic functionary, the entrepreneur. . . . . When uncertainty is present and the task of deciding what to do and how to do it takes the ascendancy over that of execution the internal organisation of the productive groups is no longer a matter of indifference or a mechanical detail. Centralisation of this deciding and controlling function is imperative, a process of 'cephalisation' is inevitable."[1]

The most fundamental change is:

"the system under which the confident and venturesome assume the risk or insure the doubtful and timid by guaranteeing to the latter a specified income in return for an assignment of the actual results. . . . With human nature as we know it it would be impracticable or very unusual for one man to guarantee to another a definite result of the latter's actions without being given power to direct his work. And on the other hand the second party would not place himself under the direction of the first without such a guarantee. . . . The result of this manifold specialisation of function is the enterprise and wage system of industry. Its existence in the world is the direct result of the fact of uncertainty."[2]

These quotations give the essence of Professor Knight's theory. The fact of uncertainty means that people have to forecast future wants. Therefore, you get a special class springing up who direct the activities of others to whom they give guaranteed wages. It acts because good judgment is generally associated with confidence in one's judgment.[3]

Professor Knight would appear to leave himself open to criticism on several grounds. First of all, as he himself points out, the fact that certain people have better judgment or better knowledge does not mean that they can only get an income from it by themselves actively taking part in production. They can sell advice or knowledge. Every business buys the services of a host of advisers. We can imagine a system where all advice or knowledge was bought

[1] Op. cit., pp. 268–95.

[2] Op. cit., pp. 269–70.

[3] Op. cit., p. 270.

as required. Again, it is possible to get a reward from better knowledge or judgment not by actively taking part in production but by making contracts with people who are producing. A merchant buying for future delivery represents an example of this. But this merely illustrates the point that it is quite possible to give a guaranteed reward providing that certain acts are performed without directing the performance of those acts. Professor Knight says that "with human nature as we know it it would be impracticable or very unusual for one man to guarantee to another a definite result of the latter's actions without being given power to direct his work." This is surely incorrect. A large proportion of jobs are done to contract, that is, the contractor is guaranteed a certain sum providing he performs certain acts. But this does not involve any direction. It does mean, however, that the system of relative prices has been changed and that there will be a new arrangement of the factors of production.[1] The fact that Professor Knight mentions that the "second party would not place himself under the direction of the first without such a guarantee" is irrelevant to the problem we are considering. Finally, it seems important to notice that even in the case of an economic system where there is no uncertainty Professor Knight considers that there would be co-ordinators, though they would perform only a routine function. He immediately adds that they would be "without responsibility of any sort," which raises the question by whom are they paid and why? It seems that nowhere does Professor Knight give a reason why the price mechanism should be superseded.

IV

It would seem important to examine one further point and that is to consider the relevance of this discussion to the general question of the "cost-curve of the firm."

It has sometimes been assumed that a firm is limited in size under perfect competition if its cost curve slopes upward,[2] while under imperfect competition, it is limited

[1] This shows that it is possible to have a private enterprise system without the existence of firms. Though, in practice, the two functions of enterprise, which actually influences the system of relative prices by forecasting wants and acting in accordance with such forecasts, and management, which accepts the system of relative prices as being given, are normally carried out by the same persons, yet it seems important to keep them separate in theory. This point is further discussed below.

[2] See Kaldor, op. cit., and Robinson, *The Problem of Management and the Size of the Firm.*

in size because it will not pay to produce more than the output at which marginal cost is equal to marginal revenue.[1] But it is clear that a firm may produce more than one product and, therefore, there appears to be no *prima facie* reason why this upward slope of the cost curve in the case of perfect competition or the fact that marginal cost will not always be below marginal revenue in the case of imperfect competition should limit the size of the firm.[2] Mrs. Robinson[3] makes the simplifying assumption that only one product is being produced. But it is clearly important to investigate how the number of products produced by a firm is determined, while no theory which assumes that only one product is in fact produced can have very great practical significance.

It might be replied that under perfect competition, since everything that is produced can be sold at the prevailing price, then there is no need for any other product to be produced. But this argument ignores the fact that there may be a point where it is less costly to organise the exchange transactions of a new product than to organise further exchange transactions of the old product. This point can be illustrated in the following way. Imagine, following von Thunen, that there is a town, the consuming centre, and that industries are located around this central point in rings. These conditions are illustrated in the following diagram in which *A*, *B* and *C* represent different industries.

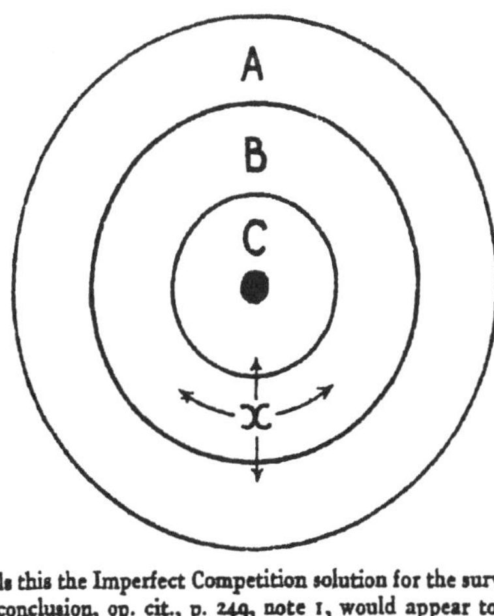

[1] Mr. Robinson calls this the Imperfect Competition solution for the survival of the small firm.

[2] Mr. Robinson's conclusion, op. cit., p. 249, note 1, would appear to be definitely wrong. He is followed by Horace J. White, Jr., "Monopolistic and Perfect Competition," *American Economic Review*, December, 1936, p. 645, note 27. Mr. White states "It is obvious that the size of the firm is limited in conditions of monopolistic competition."

[3] *Economics of Imperfect Competition.*

Imagine an entrepreneur who starts controlling exchange transactions from *x*. Now as he extends his activities in the same produce (*B*), the cost of organising increases until at some point it becomes equal to that of a dissimilar product which is nearer. As the firm expands, it will therefore from this point include more than one product (*A* and *C*). This treatment of the problem is obviously incomplete,[1] but it is necessary to show that merely proving that the cost curve turns upwards does not give a limitation to the size of the firm. So far we have only considered the case of perfect competition; the case of imperfect competition would appear to be obvious.

To determine the size of the firm, we have to consider the marketing costs (that is, the costs of using the price mechanism), and the costs of organising of different entrepreneurs and then we can determine how many products will be produced by each firm and how much of each it will produce. It would, therefore, appear that Mr. Shove[2] in his article on "Imperfect Competition" was asking questions which Mrs. Robinson's cost curve apparatus cannot answer. The factors mentioned above would seem to be the relevant ones.

V

Only one task now remains; and that is, to see whether the concept of a firm which has been developed fits in with that existing in the real world. We can best approach the question of what constitutes a firm in practice by considering the legal relationship normally called that of "master and servant" or "employer and employee."[3] The essentials of this relationship have been given as follows:

"(1) the servant must be under the duty of rendering personal services to the master or to others on behalf

[1] As has been shown above, location is only one of the factors influencing the cost of organising.

[2] G. F. Shove, "The Imperfection of the Market," *Economic Journal*, March, 1933, p. 115. In connection with an increase in demand in the suburbs and the effect on the price charged by suppliers, Mr. Shove asks ". . . . why do not the old firms open branches in the suburbs?" If the argument in the text is correct, this is a question which Mrs. Robinson's apparatus cannot answer.

[3] The legal concept of "employer and employee" and the economic concept of a firm are not identical, in that the firm may imply control over another person's property as well as over their labour. But the identity of these two concepts is sufficiently close for an examination of the legal concept to be of value in appraising the worth of the economic concept.

of the master, otherwise the contract is a contract for sale of goods or the like.

(2) The master must have the right to control the servant's work, either personally or by another servant or agent. It is this right of control or interference, of being entitled to tell the servant when to work (within the hours of service) and when not to work, and what work to do and how to do it (within the terms of such service) which is the dominant characteristic in this relation and marks off the servant from an independent contractor, or from one employed merely to give to his employer the fruits of his labour. In the latter case, the contractor or performer is not under the employer's control in doing the work or effecting the service; he has to shape and manage his work so as to give the result he has contracted to effect."[1]

We thus see that it is the fact of direction which is the essence of the legal concept of "employer and employee," just as it was in the economic concept which was developed above. It is interesting to note that Professor Batt says further:

"That which distinguishes an agent from a servant is not the absence or presence of a fixed wage or the payment only of commission on business done, but rather the freedom with which an agent may carry out his employment."[2]

We can therefore conclude that the definition we have given is one which approximates closely to the firm as it is considered in the real world.

Our definition is, therefore, realistic. Is it manageable? This ought to be clear. When we are considering how large a firm will be the principle of marginalism works smoothly. The question always is, will it pay to bring an extra exchange transaction under the organising authority? At the margin, the costs of organising within the firm will be equal either to the costs of organising in another firm or to the costs involved in leaving the transaction to be "organised" by the price mechanism. Business men will be constantly experimenting, controlling more or less, and in this way, equilibrium will be maintained. This gives the position of equilibrium for static analysis. But

[1] Batt, *The Law of Master and Servant*, p. 6.

[2] Op. cit., p. 7.

it is clear that the dynamic factors are also of considerable importance, and an investigation of the effect changes have on the cost of organising within the firm and on marketing costs generally will enable one to explain why firms get larger and smaller. We thus have a theory of moving equilibrium. The above analysis would also appear to have clarified the relationship between initiative or enterprise and management. Initiative means forecasting and operates through the price mechanism by the making of new contracts. Management proper merely reacts to price changes, rearranging the factors of production under its control. That the business man normally combines both functions is an obvious result of the marketing costs which were discussed above. Finally, this analysis enables us to state more exactly what is meant by the "marginal product" of the entrepreneur. But an elaboration of this point would take us far from our comparatively simple task of definition and clarification.

[14]

The Journal of

LAW & ECONOMICS

VOLUME III OCTOBER 1960

THE PROBLEM OF SOCIAL COST

R. H. COASE
University of Virginia

I. The Problem To Be Examined[1]

This paper is concerned with those actions of business firms which have harmful effects on others. The standard example is that of a factory the smoke from which has harmful effects on those occupying neighbouring properties. The economic analysis of such a situation has usually proceeded in terms of a divergence between the private and social product of the factory, in which economists have largely followed the treatment of Pigou in *The Economics of Welfare*. The conclusions to which this kind of analysis seems to have led most economists is that it would be desirable to make the owner of the factory liable for the damage caused to those injured by the smoke, or alternatively, to place a tax on the factory owner varying with the amount of smoke produced and equivalent in money terms to the damage it would cause, or finally, to exclude the factory from residential districts (and presumably from other

[1] This article, although concerned with a technical problem of economic analysis, arose out of the study of the Political Economy of Broadcasting which I am now conducting. The argument of the present article was implicit in a previous article dealing with the problem of allocating radio and television frequencies (The Federal Communications Commission, 2 J. Law & Econ. [1959]) but comments which I have received seemed to suggest that it would be desirable to deal with the question in a more explicit way and without reference to the original problem for the solution of which the analysis was developed.

areas in which the emission of smoke would have harmful effects on others). It is my contention that the suggested courses of action are inappropriate, in that they lead to results which are not necessarily, or even usually, desirable.

II. The Reciprocal Nature of the Problem

The traditional approach has tended to obscure the nature of the choice that has to be made. The question is commonly thought of as one in which A inflicts harm on B and what has to be decided is: how should we restrain A? But this is wrong. We are dealing with a problem of a reciprocal nature. To avoid the harm to B would inflict harm on A. The real question that has to be decided is: should A be allowed to harm B or should B be allowed to harm A? The problem is to avoid the more serious harm. I instanced in my previous article[2] the case of a confectioner the noise and vibrations from whose machinery disturbed a doctor in his work. To avoid harming the doctor would inflict harm on the confectioner. The problem posed by this case was essentially whether it was worth while, as a result of restricting the methods of production which could be used by the confectioner, to secure more doctoring at the cost of a reduced supply of confectionery products. Another example is afforded by the problem of straying cattle which destroy crops on neighbouring land. If it is inevitable that some cattle will stray, an increase in the supply of meat can only be obtained at the expense of a decrease in the supply of crops. The nature of the choice is clear: meat or crops. What answer should be given is, of course, not clear unless we know the value of what is obtained as well as the value of what is sacrificed to obtain it. To give another example, Professor George J. Stigler instances the contamination of a stream.[3] If we assume that the harmful effect of the pollution is that it kills the fish, the question to be decided is: is the value of the fish lost greater or less than the value of the product which the contamination of the stream makes possible. It goes almost without saying that this problem has to be looked at in total *and* at the margin.

III. The Pricing System with Liability for Damage

I propose to start my analysis by examining a case in which most economists would presumably agree that the problem would be solved in a completely satisfactory manner: when the damaging business has to pay for all damage caused *and* the pricing system works smoothly (strictly this means that the operation of a pricing system is without cost).

A good example of the problem under discussion is afforded by the case of straying cattle which destroy crops growing on neighbouring land. Let us suppose that a farmer and a cattle-raiser are operating on neighbouring proper-

[2] Coase, The Federal Communications Commission, 2 J. Law & Econ. 26–27 (1959).

[3] G. J. Stigler, The Theory of Price 105 (1952).

ties. Let us further suppose that, without any fencing between the properties, an increase in the size of the cattle-raiser's herd increases the total damage to the farmer's crops. What happens to the marginal damage as the size of the herd increases is another matter. This depends on whether the cattle tend to follow one another or to roam side by side, on whether they tend to be more or less restless as the size of the herd increases and on other similar factors. For my immediate purpose, it is immaterial what assumption is made about marginal damage as the size of the herd increases.

To simplify the argument, I propose to use an arithmetical example. I shall assume that the annual cost of fencing the farmer's property is $9 and that the price of the crop is $1 per ton. Also, I assume that the relation between the number of cattle in the herd and the annual crop loss is as follows:

Number in Herd (Steers)	Annual Crop Loss (Tons)	Crop Loss per Additional Steer (Tons)
1	1	1
2	3	2
3	6	3
4	10	4

Given that the cattle-raiser is liable for the damage caused, the additional annual cost imposed on the cattle-raiser if he increased his herd from, say, 2 to 3 steers is $3 and in deciding on the size of the herd, he will take this into account along with his other costs. That is, he will not increase the size of the herd unless the value of the additional meat produced (assuming that the cattle-raiser slaughters the cattle), is greater than the additional costs that this will entail, including the value of the additional crops destroyed. Of course, if, by the employment of dogs, herdsmen, aeroplanes, mobile radio and other means, the amount of damage can be reduced, these means will be adopted when their cost is less than the value of the crop which they prevent being lost. Given that the annual cost of fencing is $9, the cattle-raiser who wished to have a herd with 4 steers or more would pay for fencing to be erected and maintained, assuming that other means of attaining the same end would not do so more cheaply. When the fence is erected, the marginal cost due to the liability for damage becomes zero, except to the extent that an increase in the size of the herd necessitates a stronger and therefore more expensive fence because more steers are liable to lean against it at the same time. But, of course, it may be cheaper for the cattle-raiser not to fence and to pay for the damaged crops, as in my arithmetical example, with 3 or fewer steers.

It might be thought that the fact that the cattle-raiser would pay for all crops damaged would lead the farmer to increase his planting if a cattle-raiser came to occupy the neighbouring property. But this is not so. If the crop was previously sold in conditions of perfect competition, marginal cost was equal to price for the amount of planting undertaken and any expansion would have reduced the profits of the farmer. In the new situation, the existence of crop damage would mean that the farmer would sell less on the open market but his receipts for a given production would remain the same, since the cattle-raiser would pay the market price for any crop damaged. Of course, if cattle-raising commonly involved the destruction of crops, the coming into existence of a cattle-raising industry might raise the price of the crops involved and farmers would then extend their planting. But I wish to confine my attention to the individual farmer.

I have said that the occupation of a neighbouring property by a cattle-raiser would not cause the amount of production, or perhaps more exactly the amount of planting, by the farmer to increase. In fact, if the cattle-raising has any effect, it will be to decrease the amount of planting. The reason for this is that, for any given tract of land, if the value of the crop damaged is so great that the receipts from the sale of the undamaged crop are less than the total costs of cultivating that tract of land, it will be profitable for the farmer and the cattle-raiser to make a bargain whereby that tract of land is left uncultivated. This can be made clear by means of an arithmetical example. Assume initially that the value of the crop obtained from cultivating a given tract of land is $12 and that the cost incurred in cultivating this tract of land is $10, the net gain from cultivating the land being $2. I assume for purposes of simplicity that the farmer owns the land. Now assume that the cattle-raiser starts operations on the neighbouring property and that the value of the crops damaged is $1. In this case $11 is obtained by the farmer from sale on the market and $1 is obtained from the cattle-raiser for damage suffered and the net gain remains $2. Now suppose that the cattle-raiser finds it profitable to increase the size of his herd, even though the amount of damage rises to $3; which means that the value of the additional meat production is greater than the additional costs, including the additional $2 payment for damage. But the total payment for damage is now $3. The net gain to the farmer from cultivating the land is still $2. The cattle-raiser would be better off if the farmer would agree not to cultivate his land for any payment less than $3. The farmer would be agreeable to not cultivating the land for any payment greater than $2. There is clearly room for a mutually satisfactory bargain which would lead to the abandonment of cultivation.[4] But the same argument applies not only to the whole tract cultivated by the farmer but also to any

[4] The argument in the text has proceeded on the assumption that the alternative to cultivation of the crop is abandonment of cultivation altogether. But this need not be so. There may be crops which are less liable to damage by cattle but which would not be as profitable as the crop grown in the absence of damage. Thus, if the cultivation of a new crop would yield a return to the farmer of $1 instead of $2, and the size of the herd which would cause $3 damage with the old crop would cause $1 damage with the new crop, it would be profitable to the cattle-raiser to pay any sum less than $2 to induce the farmer

subdivision of it. Suppose, for example, that the cattle have a well-defined route, say, to a brook or to a shady area. In these circumstances, the amount of damage to the crop along the route may well be great and if so, it could be that the farmer and the cattle-raiser would find it profitable to make a bargain whereby the farmer would agree not to cultivate this strip of land.

But this raises a further possibility. Suppose that there is such a well-defined route. Suppose further that the value of the crop that would be obtained by cultivating this strip of land is $10 but that the cost of cultivation is $11. In the absence of the cattle-raiser, the land would not be cultivated. However, given the presence of the cattle-raiser, it could well be that if the strip was cultivated, the whole crop would be destroyed by the cattle. In which case, the cattle-raiser would be forced to pay $10 to the farmer. It is true that the farmer would lose $1. But the cattle-raiser would lose $10. Clearly this is a situation which is not likely to last indefinitely since neither party would want this to happen. The aim of the farmer would be to induce the cattle-raiser to make a payment in return for an agreement to leave this land uncultivated. The farmer would not be able to obtain a payment greater than the cost of fencing off this piece of land nor so high as to lead the cattle-raiser to abandon the use of the neighbouring property. What payment would in fact be made would depend on the shrewdness of the farmer and the cattle-raiser as bargainers. But as the payment would not be so high as to cause the cattle-raiser to abandon this location and as it would not vary with the size of the herd, such an agreement would not affect the allocation of resources but would merely alter the distribution of income and wealth as between the cattle-raiser and the farmer.

I think it is clear that if the cattle-raiser is liable for damage caused and the pricing system works smoothly, the reduction in the value of production elsewhere will be taken into account in computing the additional cost involved in increasing the size of the herd. This cost will be weighed against the value of the additional meat production and, given perfect competition in the cattle industry, the allocation of resources in cattle-raising will be optimal. What needs to be emphasized is that the fall in the value of production elsewhere which would be taken into account in the costs of the cattle-raiser may well be less than the damage which the cattle would cause to the crops in the ordinary course of events. This is because it is possible, as a result of market transactions, to discontinue cultivation of the land. This is desirable in all

to change his crop (since this would reduce damage liability from $3 to $1) and it would be profitable for the farmer to do so if the amount received was more than $1 (the reduction in his return caused by switching crops). In fact, there would be room for a mutually satisfactory bargain in all cases in which a change of crop would reduce the amount of damage by more than it reduces the value of the crop (excluding damage)—in all cases, that is, in which a change in the crop cultivated would lead to an increase in the value of production.

cases in which the damage that the cattle would cause, and for which the cattle-raiser would be willing to pay, exceeds the amount which the farmer would pay for use of the land. In conditions of perfect competition, the amount which the farmer would pay for the use of the land is equal to the difference between the value of the total production when the factors are employed on this land and the value of the additional product yielded in their next best use (which would be what the farmer would have to pay for the factors). If damage exceeds the amount the farmer would pay for the use of the land, the value of the additional product of the factors employed elsewhere would exceed the value of the total product in this use after damage is taken into account. It follows that it would be desirable to abandon cultivation of the land and to release the factors employed for production elsewhere. A procedure which merely provided for payment for damage to the crop caused by the cattle but which did not allow for the possibility of cultivation being discontinued would result in too small an employment of factors of production in cattle-raising and too large an employment of factors in cultivation of the crop. But given the possibility of market transactions, a situation in which damage to crops exceeded the rent of the land would not endure. Whether the cattle-raiser pays the farmer to leave the land uncultivated or himself rents the land by paying the land-owner an amount slightly greater than the farmer would pay (if the farmer was himself renting the land), the final result would be the same and would maximise the value of production. Even when the farmer is induced to plant crops which it would not be profitable to cultivate for sale on the market, this will be a purely short-term phenomenon and may be expected to lead to an agreement under which the planting will cease. The cattle-raiser will remain in that location and the marginal cost of meat production will be the same as before, thus having no long-run effect on the allocation of resources.

IV. The Pricing System with No Liability for Damage

I now turn to the case in which, although the pricing system is assumed to work smoothly (that is, costlessly), the damaging business is not liable for any of the damage which it causes. This business does not have to make a payment to those damaged by its actions. I propose to show that the allocation of resources will be the same in this case as it was when the damaging business was liable for damage caused. As I showed in the previous case that the allocation of resources was optimal, it will not be necessary to repeat this part of the argument.

I return to the case of the farmer and the cattle-raiser. The farmer would suffer increased damage to his crop as the size of the herd increased. Suppose that the size of the cattle-raiser's herd is 3 steers (and that this is the size of the herd that would be maintained if crop damage was not taken into account). Then the farmer would be willing to pay up to $3 if the cattle-raiser would reduce his herd to 2 steers, up to $5 if the herd were reduced to 1 steer and would pay up to $6 if cattle-raising was abandoned. The cattle-raiser would therefore receive $3 from the farmer if he kept 2 steers instead of 3. This $3 foregone is therefore part of the cost incurred in keeping the third steer. Whether the $3 is a payment which the cattle-raiser has to make if he adds the third steer to his herd (which it would be if the cattle-raiser was liable to the farmer for damage caused to the crop) or whether it is a sum of money which he would have received if he did not keep a third steer (which it would be if the cattle-raiser was not liable to the farmer for damage caused to the crop) does not affect the final result. In both cases $3 is part of the cost of adding a third steer, to be included along with the other costs. If the increase in the value of production in cattle-raising through increasing the size of the herd from 2 to 3 is greater than the additional costs that have to be incurred (including the $3 damage to crops), the size of the herd will be increased. Otherwise, it will not. The size of the herd will be the same whether the cattle-raiser is liable for damage caused to the crop or not.

It may be argued that the assumed starting point—a herd of 3 steers—was arbitrary. And this is true. But the farmer would not wish to pay to avoid crop damage which the cattle-raiser would not be able to cause. For example, the maximum annual payment which the farmer could be induced to pay could not exceed $9, the annual cost of fencing. And the farmer would only be willing to pay this sum if it did not reduce his earnings to a level that would cause him to abandon cultivation of this particular tract of land. Furthermore, the farmer would only be willing to pay this amount if he believed that, in the absence of any payment by him, the size of the herd maintained by the cattle raiser would be 4 or more steers. Let us assume that this is the case. Then the farmer would be willing to pay up to $3 if the cattle raiser would reduce his herd to 3 steers, up to $6 if the herd were reduced to 2 steers, up to $8 if one steer only were kept and up to $9 if cattle-raising were abandoned. It will be noticed that the change in the starting point has not altered the amount which would accrue to the cattle-raiser if he reduced the size of his herd by any given amount. It is still true that the cattle-raiser could receive an additional $3 from the farmer if he agreed to reduce his herd from 3 steers to 2 and that the $3 represents the value of the crop that would be destroyed by adding the third steer to the herd. Although a different belief on the part of the farmer (whether justified or not) about the size of the herd that the cattle-raiser would maintain in the absence of payments from him may affect the total payment he can be induced to pay, it is not true that this different belief would have any effect on the size of the herd that the cattle-raiser will actually keep. This will be the same as it would be if the cattle-raiser had to pay for damage caused by his cattle, since a receipt foregone of a given amount is the equivalent of a payment of the same amount.

It might be thought that it would pay the cattle-raiser to increase his herd above the size that he would wish to maintain once a bargain had been made, in order to induce the farmer to make a larger total payment. And this may be true. It is similar in nature to the action of the farmer (when the cattle-raiser was liable for damage) in cultivating land on which, as a result of an agreement with the cattle-raiser, planting would subsequently be abandoned (including land which would not be cultivated at all in the absence of cattle-raising). But such manoeuvres are preliminaries to an agreement and do not affect the long-run equilibrium position, which is the same whether or not the cattle-raiser is held responsible for the crop damage brought about by his cattle.

It is necessary to know whether the damaging business is liable or not for damage caused since without the establishment of this initial delimitation of rights there can be no market transactions to transfer and recombine them. But the ultimate result (which maximises the value of production) is independent of the legal position if the pricing system is assumed to work without cost.

V. The Problem Illustrated Anew

The harmful effects of the activities of a business can assume a wide variety of forms. An early English case concerned a building which, by obstructing currents of air, hindered the operation of a windmill.[5] A recent case in Florida concerned a building which cast a shadow on the cabana, swimming pool and sunbathing areas of a neighbouring hotel.[6] The problem of straying cattle and the damaging of crops which was the subject of detailed examination in the two preceding sections, although it may have appeared to be rather a special case, is in fact but one example of a problem which arises in many different guises. To clarify the nature of my argument and to demonstrate its general applicability, I propose to illustrate it anew by reference to four actual cases.

Let us first reconsider the case of *Sturges v. Bridgman*[7] which I used as an illustration of the general problem in my article on "The Federal Communications Commission." In this case, a confectioner (in Wigmore Street) used two mortars and pestles in connection with his business (one had been in operation in the same position for more than 60 years and the other for more than 26 years). A doctor then came to occupy neighbouring premises (in Wimpole Street). The confectioner's machinery caused the doctor no harm until, eight years after he had first occupied the premises, he built a consulting room at the end of his garden right against the confectioner's kitchen. It was then found that the noise and vibration caused by the confectioner's machin-

[5] See Gale on Easements 237–39 (13th ed. M. Bowles 1959).

[6] See Fontainebleu Hotel Corp. v. Forty-Five Twenty-Five, Inc., 114 So. 2d 357 (1959).

[7] 11 Ch. D. 852 (1879).

ery made it difficult for the doctor to use his new consulting room. "In particular . . . the noise prevented him from examining his patients by auscultation[8] for diseases of the chest. He also found it impossible to engage with effect in any occupation which required thought and attention." The doctor therefore brought a legal action to force the confectioner to stop using his machinery. The courts had little difficulty in granting the doctor the injunction he sought. "Individual cases of hardship may occur in the strict carrying out of the principle upon which we found our judgment, but the negation of the principle would lead even more to individual hardship, and would at the same time produce a prejudicial effect upon the development of land for residential purposes."

The court's decision established that the doctor had the right to prevent the confectioner from using his machinery. But, of course, it would have been possible to modify the arrangements envisaged in the legal ruling by means of a bargain between the parties. The doctor would have been willing to waive his right and allow the machinery to continue in operation if the confectioner would have paid him a sum of money which was greater than the loss of income which he would suffer from having to move to a more costly or less convenient location or from having to curtail his activities at this location or, as was suggested as a possibility, from having to build a separate wall which would deaden the noise and vibration. The confectioner would have been willing to do this if the amount he would have to pay the doctor was less than the fall in income he would suffer if he had to change his mode of operation at this location, abandon his operation or move his confectionery business to some other location. The solution of the problem depends essentially on whether the continued use of the machinery adds more to the confectioner's income than it subtracts from the doctor's.[9] But now consider the situation if the confectioner had won the case. The confectioner would then have had the right to continue operating his noise and vibration-generating machinery without having to pay anything to the doctor. The boot would have been on the other foot: the doctor would have had to pay the confectioner to induce him to stop using the machinery. If the doctor's income would have fallen more through continuance of the use of this machinery than it added to the income of the confectioner, there would clearly be room for a bargain whereby the doctor paid the confectioner to stop using the machinery. That is to say, the circumstances in which it would not pay the confectioner to continue to use the machinery and to compensate the doctor for the losses that this would bring (if the doctor had the right to prevent the confectioner's using his

[8] Auscultation is the act of listening by ear or stethoscope in order to judge by sound the condition of the body.

[9] Note that what is taken into account is the change in income after allowing for alterations in methods of production, location, character of product, etc.

machinery) would be those in which it would be in the interest of the doctor to make a payment to the confectioner which would induce him to discontinue the use of the machinery (if the confectioner had the right to operate the machinery). The basic conditions are exactly the same in this case as they were in the example of the cattle which destroyed crops. With costless market transactions, the decision of the courts concerning liability for damage would be without effect on the allocation of resources. It was of course the view of the judges that they were affecting the working of the economic system—and in a desirable direction. Any other decision would have had "a prejudicial effect upon the development of land for residential purposes," an argument which was elaborated by examining the example of a forge operating on a barren moor, which was later developed for residual purposes. The judges' view that they were settling how the land was to be used would be true only in the case in which the costs of carrying out the necessary market transactions exceeded the gain which might be achieved by any rearrangement of rights. And it would be desirable to preserve the areas (Wimpole Street or the moor) for residential or professional use (by giving non-industrial users the right to stop the noise, vibration, smoke, etc., by injunction) only if the value of the additional residential facilities obtained was greater than the value of cakes or iron lost. But of this the judges seem to have been unaware.

Another example of the same problem is furnished by the case of *Cooke v. Forbes*.[10] One process in the weaving of cocoa-nut fibre matting was to immerse it in bleaching liquids after which it was hung out to dry. Fumes from a manufacturer of sulphate of ammonia had the effect of turning the matting from a bright to a dull and blackish colour. The reason for this was that the bleaching liquid contained chloride of tin, which, when affected by sulphuretted hydrogen, is turned to a darker colour. An injunction was sought to stop the manufacturer from emitting the fumes. The lawyers for the defendant argued that if the plaintiff "were not to use . . . a particular bleaching liquid, their fibre would not be affected; that their process is unusual, not according to the custom of the trade, and even damaging to their own fabrics." The judge commented: ". . . it appears to me quite plain that a person has a right to carry on upon his own property a manufacturing process in which he uses chloride of tin, or any sort of metallic dye, and that his neighbour is not at liberty to pour in gas which will interfere with his manufacture. If it can be traced to the neighbour, then, I apprehend, clearly he will have a right to come here and ask for relief." But in view of the fact that the damage was accidental and occasional, that careful precautions were taken and that there was no exceptional risk, an injunction was refused, leaving the plaintiff to bring an action for damages if he wished. What the subsequent developments

[10] L. R. 5 Eq. 166 (1867–1868).

were I do not know. But it is clear that the situation is essentially the same as that found in ***Sturges v. Bridgman,*** except that the cocoa-nut fibre matting manufacturer could not secure an injunction but would have to seek damages from the sulphate of ammonia manufacturer. The economic analysis of the situation is exactly the same as with the cattle which destroyed crops. To avoid the damage, the sulphate of ammonia manufacturer could increase his precautions or move to another location. Either course would presumably increase his costs. Alternatively he could pay for the damage. This he would do if the payments for damage were less than the additional costs that would have to be incurred to avoid the damage. The payments for damage would then become part of the cost of production of sulphate of ammonia. Of course, if, as was suggested in the legal proceedings, the amount of damage could be eliminated by changing the bleaching agent (which would presumably increase the costs of the matting manufacturer) and if the additional cost was less than the damage that would otherwise occur, it should be possible for the two manufacturers to make a mutually satisfactory bargain whereby the new bleaching agent was used. Had the court decided against the matting manufacturer, as a consequence of which he would have had to suffer the damage without compensation, the allocation of resources would not have been affected. It would pay the matting manufacturer to change his bleaching agent if the additional cost involved was less than the reduction in damage. And since the matting manufacturer would be willing to pay the sulphate of ammonia manufacturer an amount up to his loss of income (the increase in costs or the damage suffered) if he would cease his activities, this loss of income would remain a cost of production for the manufacturer of sulphate of ammonia. This case is indeed analytically exactly the same as the cattle example.

Bryant v. Lefever[11] raised the problem of the smoke nuisance in a novel form. The plaintiff and the defendants were occupiers of adjoining houses, which were of about the same height.

> Before 1876 the plaintiff was able to light a fire in any room of his house without the chimneys smoking; the two houses had remained in the same condition some thirty or forty years. In 1876 the defendants took down their house, and began to rebuild it. They carried up a wall by the side of the plaintiff's chimneys much beyond its original height, and stacked timber on the roof of their house, and thereby caused the plaintiff's chimneys to smoke whenever he lighted fires.

The reason, of course, why the chimneys smoked was that the erection of the wall and the stacking of the timber prevented the free circulation of air. In a trial before a jury, the plaintiff was awarded damages of £40. The case then went to the Court of Appeals where the judgment was reversed. Bramwell, L.J., argued:

[11] 4 C.P.D. 172 (1878–1879).

. . . it is said, and the jury have found, that the defendants have done that which caused a nuisance to the plaintiff's house. We think there is no evidence of this. No doubt there is a nuisance, but it is not of the defendant's causing. They have done nothing in causing the nuisance. Their house and their timber are harmless enough. It is the plaintiff who causes the nuisance by lighting a coal fire in a place the chimney of which is placed so near the defendants' wall, that the smoke does not escape, but comes into the house. Let the plaintiff cease to light his fire, let him move his chimney, let him carry it higher, and there would be no nuisance. Who then, causes it? It would be very clear that the plaintiff did, if he had built his house or chimney after the defendants had put up the timber on theirs, and it is really the same though he did so before the timber was there. But (what is in truth the same answer), if the defendants cause the nuisance, they have a right to do so. If the plaintiff has not the right to the passage of air, except subject to the defendants' right to build or put timber on their house, then his right is subject to their right, and though a nuisance follows from the exercise of their right, they are not liable.

And Cotton, L.J., said:

Here it is found that the erection of the defendants' wall has sensibly and materially interfered with the comfort of human existence in the plaintiff's house, and it is said this is a nuisance for which the defendants are liable. Ordinarily this is so, but the defendants have done so, not by sending on to the plaintiff's property any smoke or noxious vapour, but by interrupting the egress of smoke from the plaintiff's house in a way to which . . . the plaintiff has no legal right. The plaintiff creates the smoke, which interferes with his comfort. Unless he has . . . a right to get rid of this in a particular way which has been interfered with by the defendants, he cannot sue the defendants, because the smoke made by himself, for which he has not provided any effectual means of escape, causes him annoyance. It is as if a man tried to get rid of liquid filth arising on his own land by a drain into his neighbour's land. Until a right had been acquired by user, the neighbour might stop the drain without incurring liability by so doing. No doubt great inconvenience would be caused to the owner of the property on which the liquid filth arises. But the act of his neighbour would be a lawful act, and he would not be liable for the consequences attributable to the fact that the man had accumulated filth without providing any effectual means of getting rid of it.

I do not propose to show that any subsequent modification of the situation, as a result of bargains between the parties (conditioned by the cost of stacking the timber elsewhere, the cost of extending the chimney higher, etc.), would have exactly the same result whatever decision the courts had come to since this point has already been adequately dealt with in the discussion of the cattle example and the two previous cases. What I shall discuss is the argument of the judges in the Court of Appeals that the smoke nuisance was not caused by the man who erected the wall but by the man who lit the fires. The novelty of the situation is that the smoke nuisance was suffered by the man who lit the fires and not by some third person. The question is not a trivial one since it lies at the heart of the problem under discussion. Who caused the smoke nuisance? The answer seems fairly clear. The smoke nuisance was caused both by the man who built the wall ***and*** by the man who lit the fires. Given the fires, there would have been no smoke nuisance without the wall; given the wall, there would have been no smoke nuisance without the fires. Eliminate the wall *or* the fires and the smoke nuisance would disappear. On the marginal principle it is clear that ***both*** were responsible and ***both*** should be forced to include the loss of amenity due to the smoke as a cost in deciding whether to continue the activity which gives rise to the smoke. And given the possibility of market transactions, this is what would in fact happen. Although the wall-builder was not liable legally for the nuisance, as the man with the smoking chimneys would presumably be willing to pay a sum equal to the monetary worth to him of eliminating the smoke, this sum would therefore become for the wall-builder, a cost of continuing to have the high wall with the timber stacked on the roof.

The judges' contention that it was the man who lit the fires who alone caused the smoke nuisance is true only if we assume that the wall is the given factor. This is what the judges did by deciding that the man who erected the higher wall had a legal right to do so. The case would have been even more interesting if the smoke from the chimneys had injured the timber. Then it would have been the wall-builder who suffered the damage. The case would then have closely paralleled *Sturges v. Bridgman* and there can be little doubt that the man who lit the fires would have been liable for the ensuing damage to the timber, in spite of the fact that no damage had occurred until the high wall was built by the man who owned the timber.

Judges have to decide on legal liability but this should not confuse economists about the nature of the economic problem involved. In the case of the cattle and the crops, it is true that there would be no crop damage without the cattle. It is equally true that there would be no crop damage without the crops. The doctor's work would not have been disturbed if the confectioner had not worked his machinery; but the machinery would have disturbed no one if the doctor had not set up his consulting room in that particular place. The matting was blackened by the fumes from the sulphate of ammonia manufacturer; but no damage would have occurred if the matting manufacturer had not chosen to hang out his matting in a particular place and to use a particular bleaching agent. If we are to discuss the problem in terms of causation, both parties cause the damage. If we are to attain an optimum allocation of resources, it is therefore desirable that both parties should take the harmful effect (the nuisance) into account in deciding on their course of action. It is one of the beauties of a smoothly operating pricing system that, as has already been explained, the fall in the value of production due to the harmful effect would be a cost for both parties.

Bass v. Gregory[12] will serve as an excellent final illustration of the problem. The plaintiffs were the owners and tenant of a public house called the Jolly Anglers. The defendant was the owner of some cottages and a yard adjoining the Jolly Anglers. Under the public house was a cellar excavated in the rock. From the cellar, a hole or shaft had been cut into an old well situated in the defendant's yard. The well therefore became the ventilating shaft for the cellar. The cellar "had been used for a particular purpose in the process of brewing, which, without ventilation, could not be carried on." The cause of the action was that the defendant removed a grating from the mouth of the well, "so as to stop or prevent the free passage of air from [the] cellar upwards through the well. . . ." What caused the defendant to take this step is not clear from the report of the case. Perhaps "the air . . . impregnated by the brewing operations" which "passed up the well and out into the open air" was offensive to him. At any rate, he preferred to have the well in his yard stopped up. The court had first to determine whether the owners of the public house could have a legal right to a current of air. If they were to have such a right, this case would have to be distinguished from *Bryant v. Lefever* (already considered). This, however, presented no difficulty. In this case, the current of air was confined to "a strictly defined channel." In the case of *Bryant v. Lefever,* what was involved was "the general current of air common to all mankind." The judge therefore held that the owners of the public house could have the right to a current of air whereas the owner of the private house in *Bryant v. Lefever* could not. An economist might be tempted to add "but the air moved all the same." However, all that had been decided at this stage of the argument was that there could be a legal right, not that the owners of the public house possessed it. But evidence showed that the shaft from the cellar to the well had existed for over forty years and that the use of the well as a ventilating shaft must have been known to the owners of the yard since the air, when it emerged, smelt of the brewing operations. The judge therefore held that the public house had such a right by the "doctrine of lost grant." This doctrine states "that if a legal right is proved to have existed and been exercised for a number of years the law ought to presume that it had a legal origin."[13] So the owner of the cottages and yard had to unstop the well and endure the smell.

[12] 25 Q.B.D. 481 (1890).

[13] It may be asked why a lost grant could not also be presumed in the case of the confectioner who had operated one mortar for more than 60 years. The answer is that until the doctor built the consulting room at the end of his garden there was no nuisance. So the nuisance had not continued for many years. It is true that the confectioner in his affidavit referred to "an invalid lady who occupied the house upon one occasion, about thirty years before" who "requested him if possible to discontinue the use of the mortars before eight o'clock in the morning" and that there was some evidence that the garden wall had been subjected to vibration. But the court had little difficulty in disposing of this line of argument: ". . . this vibration, even if it existed at all, was so slight, and the com-

The reasoning employed by the courts in determining legal rights will often seem strange to an economist because many of the factors on which the decision turns are, to an economist, irrelevant. Because of this, situations which are, from an economic point of view, identical will be treated quite differently by the courts. The economic problem in all cases of harmful effects is how to maximise the value of production. In the case of *Bass v. Gregory* fresh air was drawn in through the well which facilitated the production of beer but foul air was expelled through the well which made life in the adjoining houses less pleasant. The economic problem was to decide which to choose: a lower cost of beer and worsened amenities in adjoining houses or a higher cost of beer and improved amenities. In deciding this question, the "doctrine of lost grant" is about as relevant as the colour of the judge's eyes. But it has to be remembered that the immediate question faced by the courts is ***not*** what shall be done by whom ***but*** who has the legal right to do what. It is always possible to modify by transactions on the market the initial legal delimitation of rights. And, of course, if such market transactions are costless, such a rearrangement of rights will always take place if it would lead to an increase in the value of production.

VI. The Cost of Market Transactions Taken into Account

The argument has proceeded up to this point on the assumption (explicit in Sections III and IV and tacit in Section V) that there were no costs involved in carrying out market transactions. This is, of course, a very unrealistic assumption. In order to carry out a market transaction it is necessary to discover who it is that one wishes to deal with, to inform people that one wishes to deal and on what terms, to conduct negotiations leading up to a bargain, to draw up the contract, to undertake the inspection needed to make sure that the terms of the contract are being observed, and so on. These operations are often extremely costly, sufficiently costly at any rate to prevent many transactions that would be carried out in a world in which the pricing system worked without cost.

In earlier sections, when dealing with the problem of the rearrangement of legal rights through the market, it was argued that such a rearrangement would be made through the market whenever this would lead to an increase in the value of production. But this assumed costless market transactions. Once the costs of carrying out market transactions are taken into account it is clear that such a rearrangement of rights will only be undertaken when the increase in the value of production consequent upon the rearrangement

plaint, if it can be called a complaint, of the invalid lady . . . was of so trifling a character, that . . . the Defendant's acts would not have given rise to any proceeding either at law or in equity" (11 Ch.D. 863). That is, the confectioner had not committed a nuisance until the doctor built his consulting room.

is greater than the costs which would be involved in bringing it about. When it is less, the granting of an injunction (or the knowledge that it would be granted) or the liability to pay damages may result in an activity being discontinued (or may prevent its being started) which would be undertaken if market transactions were costless. In these conditions the initial delimitation of legal rights does have an effect on the efficiency with which the economic system operates. One arrangement of rights may bring about a greater value of production than any other. But unless this is the arrangement of rights established by the legal system, the costs of reaching the same result by altering and combining rights through the market may be so great that this optimal arrangement of rights, and the greater value of production which it would bring, may never be achieved. The part played by economic considerations in the process of delimiting legal rights will be discussed in the next section. In this section, I will take the initial delimitation of rights and the costs of carrying out market transactions as given.

It is clear that an alternative form of economic organisation which could achieve the same result at less cost than would be incurred by using the market would enable the value of production to be raised. As I explained many years ago, the firm represents such an alternative to organising production through market transactions.[14] Within the firm individual bargains between the various cooperating factors of production are eliminated and for a market transaction is substituted an administrative decision. The rearrangement of production then takes place without the need for bargains between the owners of the factors of production. A landowner who has control of a large tract of land may devote his land to various uses taking into account the effect that the interrelations of the various activities will have on the net return of the land, thus rendering unnecessary bargains between those undertaking the various activities. Owners of a large building or of several adjoining properties in a given area may act in much the same way. In effect, using our earlier terminology, the firm would acquire the legal rights of all the parties and the rearrangement of activities would not follow on a rearrangement of rights by contract, but as a result of an administrative decision as to how the rights should be used.

It does not, of course, follow that the administrative costs of organising a transaction through a firm are inevitably less than the costs of the market transactions which are superseded. But where contracts are peculiarly difficult to draw up and an attempt to describe what the parties have agreed to do or not to do (e.g. the amount and kind of a smell or noise that they may make or will not make) would necessitate a lengthy and highly involved document, and, where, as is probable, a long-term contract would be desir-

[14] See Coase, The Nature of the Firm, 4 Economica, New Series, 386 (1937). Reprinted in Readings in Price Theory, 331 (1952).

able;[15] it would be hardly surprising if the emergence of a firm or the extension of the activities of an existing firm was not the solution adopted on many occasions to deal with the problem of harmful effects. This solution would be adopted whenever the administrative costs of the firm were less than the costs of the market transactions that it supersedes and the gains which would result from the rearrangement of activities greater than the firm's costs of organising them. I do not need to examine in great detail the character of this solution since I have explained what is involved in my earlier article.

But the firm is not the only possible answer to this problem. The administrative costs of organising transactions within the firm may also be high, and particularly so when many diverse activities are brought within the control of a single organisation. In the standard case of a smoke nuisance, which may affect a vast number of people engaged in a wide variety of activities, the administrative costs might well be so high as to make any attempt to deal with the problem within the confines of a single firm impossible. An alternative solution is direct Government regulation. Instead of instituting a legal system of rights which can be modified by transactions on the market, the government may impose regulations which state what people must or must not do and which have to be obeyed. Thus, the government (by statute or perhaps more likely through an administrative agency) may, to deal with the problem of smoke nuisance, decree that certain methods of production should or should not be used (e.g. that smoke preventing devices should be installed or that coal or oil should not be burned) or may confine certain types of business to certain districts (zoning regulations).

The government is, in a sense, a super-firm (but of a very special kind) since it is able to influence the use of factors of production by administrative decision. But the ordinary firm is subject to checks in its operations because of the competition of other firms, which might administer the same activities at lower cost and also because there is always the alternative of market transactions as against organisation within the firm if the administrative costs become too great. The government is able, if it wishes, to avoid the market altogether, which a firm can never do. The firm has to make market agreements with the owners of the factors of production that it uses. Just as the government can conscript or seize property, so it can decree that factors of production should only be used in such-and-such a way. Such authoritarian methods save a lot of trouble (for those doing the organising). Furthermore, the government has at its disposal the police and the other law enforcement agencies to make sure that its regulations are carried out.

It is clear that the government has powers which might enable it to get some things done at a lower cost than could a private organisation (or at any

[15] For reasons explained in my earlier article, see Readings in Price Theory, n. 14 at 337.

rate one without special governmental powers). But the governmental administrative machine is not itself costless. It can, in fact, on occasion be extremely costly. Furthermore, there is no reason to suppose that the restrictive and zoning regulations, made by a fallible administration subject to political pressures and operating without any competitive check, will necessarily always be those which increase the efficiency with which the economic system operates. Furthermore, such general regulations which must apply to a wide variety of cases will be enforced in some cases in which they are clearly inappropriate. From these considerations it follows that direct governmental regulation will not necessarily give better results than leaving the problem to be solved by the market or the firm. But equally there is no reason why, on occasion, such governmental administrative regulation should not lead to an improvement in economic efficiency. This would seem particularly likely when, as is normally the case with the smoke nuisance, a large number of people are involved and in which therefore the costs of handling the problem through the market or the firm may be high.

There is, of course, a further alternative, which is to do nothing about the problem at all. And given that the costs involved in solving the problem by regulations issued by the governmental administrative machine will often be heavy (particularly if the costs are interpreted to include all the consequences which follow from the Government engaging in this kind of activity), it will no doubt be commonly the case that the gain which would come from regulating the actions which give rise to the harmful effects will be less than the costs involved in Government regulation.

The discussion of the problem of harmful effects in this section (when the costs of market transactions are taken into account) is extremely inadequate. But at least it has made clear that the problem is one of choosing the appropriate social arrangement for dealing with the harmful effects. All solutions have costs and there is no reason to suppose that government regulation is called for simply because the problem is not well handled by the market or the firm. Satisfactory views on policy can only come from a patient study of how, in practice, the market, firms and governments handle the problem of harmful effects. Economists need to study the work of the broker in bringing parties together, the effectiveness of restrictive covenants, the problems of the large-scale real-estate development company, the operation of Government zoning and other regulating activities. It is my belief that economists, and policy-makers generally, have tended to over-estimate the advantages which come from governmental regulation. But this belief, even if justified, does not do more than suggest that government regulation should be curtailed. It does not tell us where the boundary line should be drawn. This, it seems to me, has to come from a detailed investigation of the actual results of handling the problem in different ways. But it would be unfortunate if this investigation were undertaken with the aid of a faulty economic analysis. The aim of this article is to indicate what the economic approach to the problem should be.

VII. The Legal Delimitation of Rights and the Economic Problem

The discussion in Section V not only served to illustrate the argument but also afforded a glimpse at the legal approach to the problem of harmful effects. The cases considered were all English but a similar selection of American cases could easily be made and the character of the reasoning would have been the same. Of course, if market transactions were costless, all that matters (questions of equity apart) is that the rights of the various parties should be well-defined and the results of legal actions easy to forecast. But as we have seen, the situation is quite different when market transactions are so costly as to make it difficult to change the arrangement of rights established by the law. In such cases, the courts directly influence economic activity. It would therefore seem desirable that the courts should understand the economic consequences of their decisions and should, insofar as this is possible without creating too much uncertainty about the legal position itself, take these consequences into account when making their decisions. Even when it is possible to change the legal delimitation of rights through market transactions, it is obviously desirable to reduce the need for such transactions and thus reduce the employment of resources in carrying them out.

A thorough examination of the presuppositions of the courts in trying such cases would be of great interest but I have not been able to attempt it. Nevertheless it is clear from a cursory study that the courts have often recognized the economic implications of their decisions and are aware (as many economists are not) of the reciprocal nature of the problem. Furthermore, from time to time, they take these economic implications into account, along with other factors, in arriving at their decisions. The American writers on this subject refer to the question in a more explicit fashion than do the British. Thus, to quote Prosser on Torts, a person may

> make use of his own property or . . . conduct his own affairs at the expense of some harm to his neighbors. He may operate a factory whose noise and smoke cause some discomfort to others, so long as he keeps within reasonable bounds. It is only when his conduct is unreasonable, *in the light of its utility and the harm which results* [italics added], that it becomes a nuisance. . . . . As it was said in an ancient case in regard to candle-making in a town, "Le utility del chose excusera le noisomeness del stink."
>
> The world must have factories, smelters, oil refineries, noisy machinery and blasting, even at the expense of some inconvenience to those in the vicinity and the

plaintiff may be required to accept some not unreasonable discomfort for the general good.[16]

The standard British writers do not state as explicitly as this that a comparison between the utility and harm produced is an element in deciding whether a harmful effect should be considered a nuisance. But similar views, if less strongly expressed, are to be found.[17] The doctrine that the harmful effect must be substantial before the court will act is, no doubt, in part a reflection of the fact that there will almost always be some gain to offset the harm. And in the reports of individual cases, it is clear that the judges have had in mind what would be lost as well as what would be gained in deciding whether to grant an injunction or award damages. Thus, in refusing to prevent the destruction of a prospect by a new building, the judge stated:

> I know no general rule of common law, which . . . says, that building so as to stop another's prospect is a nuisance. Was that the case, there could be no great towns; and I must grant injunctions to all the new buildings in this town. . . .[18]

In *Webb v. Bird*[19] it was decided that it was not a nuisance to build a schoolhouse so near a windmill as to obstruct currents of air and hinder the working of the mill. An early case seems to have been decided in an opposite direction. Gale commented:

> In old maps of London a row of windmills appears on the heights to the north of London. Probably in the time of King James it was thought an alarming circumstance, as affecting the supply of food to the city, that anyone should build so near them as to take the wind out from their sails.[20]

In one of the cases discussed in section V, *Sturges v. Bridgman*, it seems clear that the judges were thinking of the economic consequences of alternative decisions. To the argument that if the principle that they seemed to be following

[16] See W. L. Prosser, The Law of Torts 398–99, 412 (2d ed. 1955). The quotation about the ancient case concerning candle-making is taken from Sir James Fitzjames Stephen, A General View of the Criminal Law of England 106 (1890). Sir James Stephen gives no reference. He perhaps had in mind *Rex. v. Ronkett*, included in Seavey, Keeton and Thurston, Cases on Torts 604 (1950). A similar view to that expressed by Prosser is to be found in F. V. Harper and F. James, The Law of Torts 67–74 (1956); Restatement, Torts §§826, 827 and 828.

[17] See Winfield on Torts 541–48 (6th ed. T. E. Lewis 1954); Salmond on the Law of Torts 181–90 (12th ed. R.F.V. Heuston 1957); H. Street, The Law of Torts 221–29 (1959).

[18] Attorney General v. Doughty, 2 Ves. Sen. 453, 28 Eng. Rep. 290 (Ch. 1752). Compare in this connection the statement of an American judge, quoted in Prosser, op. cit. supra n. 16 at 413 n. 54: "Without smoke, Pittsburgh would have remained a very pretty village," Musmanno, J., in Versailles Borough v. McKeesport Coal & Coke Co., 1935, 83 Pitts. Leg. J. 379, 385.

[19] 10 C.B. (N.S.) 268, 142 Eng. Rep. 445 (1861); 13 C.B. (N.S.) 841, 143 Eng. Rep. 332 (1863).

[20] See Gale on Easements 238, n. 6 (13th ed. M. Bowles 1959).

were carried out to its logical consequences, it would result in the most serious practical inconveniences, for a man might go—say into the midst of the tanneries of *Bermondsey*, or into any other locality devoted to any particular trade or manufacture of a noisy or unsavoury character, and by building a private residence upon a vacant piece of land put a stop to such trade or manufacture altogether,

the judges answered that

whether anything is a nuisance or not is a question to be determined, not merely by an abstract consideration of the thing itself, but in reference to its circumstances; What would be a nuisance in *Belgrave Square* would not necessarily be so in *Bermondsey;* and where a locality is devoted to a particular trade or manufacture carried on by the traders or manufacturers in a particular and established manner not constituting a public nuisance, Judges and juries would be justified in finding, and may be trusted to find, that the trade or manufacture so carried on in that locality is not a private or actionable wrong.[21]

That the character of the neighborhood is relevant in deciding whether something is, or is not, a nuisance, is definitely established.

He who dislikes the noise of traffic must not set up his abode in the heart of a great city. He who loves peace and quiet must not live in a locality devoted to the business of making boilers or steamships.[22]

What has emerged has been described as "planning and zoning by the judiciary."[23] Of course there are sometimes considerable difficulties in applying the criteria.[24]

An interesting example of the problem is found in *Adams v. Ursell*[25] in which a fried fish shop in a predominantly working-class district was set up near houses of "a much better character." England without fish-and-chips is a contradiction in terms and the case was clearly one of high importance. The judge commented:

It was urged that an injunction would cause great hardship to the defendant and to the poor people who get food at his shop. The answer to that is that it does not follow that the defendant cannot carry on his business in another more suitable place somewhere in the neighbourhood. It by no means follows that because a fried fish shop is a nuisance in one place it is a nuisance in another.

In fact, the injunction which restrained Mr. Ursell from running his shop did not even extend to the whole street. So he was presumably able to move to other premises near houses of "a much worse character," the inhabitants

[21] 11 Ch.D. 865 (1879).

[22] Salmond on the Law of Torts 182 (12th ed. R.F.V. Heuston 1957).

[23] C. M. Haar, Land-Use Planning, A Casebook on the Use, Misuse, and Re-use of Urban Land 95 (1959).

[24] See, for example, Rushmer v. Polsue and Alfieri, Ltd. [1906] 1 Ch. 234, which deals with the case of a house in a quiet situation in a noisy district.

[25] [1913] 1 Ch. 269.

of which would no doubt consider the availability of fish-and-chips to outweigh the pervading odour and "fog or mist" so graphically described by the plaintiff. Had there been no other "more suitable place in the neighbourhood," the case would have been more difficult and the decision might have been different. What would "the poor people" have had for food? No English judge would have said: "Let them eat cake."

The courts do not always refer very clearly to the economic problem posed by the cases brought before them but it seems probable that in the interpretation of words and phrases like "reasonable" or "common or ordinary use" there is some recognition, perhaps largely unconscious and certainly not very explicit, of the economic aspects of the questions at issue. A good example of this would seem to be the judgment in the Court of Appeals in *Andreae v. Selfridge and Company Ltd.*[26] In this case, a hotel (in Wigmore Street) was situated on part of an island site. The remainder of the site was acquired by Selfridges which demolished the existing buildings in order to erect another in their place. The hotel suffered a loss of custom in consequence of the noise and dust caused by the demolition. The owner of the hotel brought an action against Selfridges for damages. In the lower court, the hotel was awarded £4,500 damages. The case was then taken on appeal.

The judge who had found for the hotel proprietor in the lower court said:

> I cannot regard what the defendants did on the site of the first operation as having been commonly done in the ordinary use and occupation of land or houses. It is neither usual nor common, in this country, for people to excavate a site to a depth of 60 feet and then to erect upon that site a steel framework and fasten the steel frames together with rivets. . . . Nor is it, I think, a common or ordinary use of land, in this country, to act as the defendants did when they were dealing with the site of their second operation—namely, to demolish all the houses that they had to demolish, five or six of them I think, if not more, and to use for the purpose of demolishing them pneumatic hammers.

Sir Wilfred Greene, M.R., speaking for the Court of Appeals, first noted

> that when one is dealing with temporary operations, such as demolition and re-building, everybody has to put up with a certain amount of discomfort, because operations of that kind cannot be carried on at all without a certain amount of noise and a certain amount of dust. Therefore, the rule with regard to interference must be read subject to this qualification. . . .

He then referred to the previous judgment:

> With great respect to the learned judge, I take the view that he has not approached this matter from the correct angle. It seems to me that it is not possible to say . . . that the type of demolition, excavation and construction in which the defendant company was engaged in the course of these operations was of such an abnormal and unusual nature as to prevent the qualification to which I have referred coming

[26] [1938] 1 Ch. 1.

into operation. It seems to me that, when the rule speaks of the common or ordinary use of land, it does not mean that the methods of using land and building on it are in some way to be stabilised for ever. As time goes on new inventions or new methods enable land to be more profitably used, either by digging down into the earth or by mounting up into the skies. Whether, from other points of view, that is a matter which is desirable for humanity is neither here nor there; but it is part of the normal use of land, to make use upon your land, in the matter of construction, of what particular type and what particular depth of foundations and particular height of building may be reasonable, in the circumstances, and in view of the developments of the day. . . . Guests at hotels are very easily upset. People coming to this hotel, who were accustomed to a quiet outlook at the back, coming back and finding demolition and building going on, may very well have taken the view that the particular merit of this hotel no longer existed. That would be a misfortune for the plaintiff; but assuming that there was nothing wrong in the defendant company's works, assuming the defendant company was carrying on the demolition and its building, productive of noise though it might be, with all reasonable skill, and taking all reasonable precautions not to cause annoyance to its neighbors, then the planitiff might lose all her clients in the hotel because they have lost the amenities of an open and quiet place behind, but she would have no cause of complaint. . . . [But those] who say that their interference with the comfort of their neighbors is justified because their operations are normal and usual and conducted with proper care and skill are under a specific duty . . . to use that reasonable and proper care and skill. It is not a correct attitude to take to say: 'We will go on and do what we like until somebody complains!' . . . Their duty is to take proper precautions and to see that the nuisance is reduced to a minimum. It is no answer for them to say: 'But this would mean that we should have to do the work more slowly than we would like to do it, or it would involve putting us to some extra expense.' All these questions are matters of common sense and degree, and quite clearly it would be unreasonable to expect people to conduct their work so slowly or so expensively, for the purpose of preventing a transient inconvenience, that the cost and trouble would be prohibitive. . . . In this case, the defendant company's attitude seems to have been to go on until somebody complained, and, further, that its desire to hurry its work and conduct it according to its own ideas and its own convenience was to prevail if there was a real conflict between it and the comfort of its neighbors. That . . . is not carrying out the obligation of using reasonable care and skill. . . . The effect comes to this . . . the plaintiff suffered an actionable nuisance; . . . she is entitled, not to a nominal sum, but to a substantial sum, based upon those principles . . . but in arriving at the sum . . . I have discounted any loss of custom . . . which might be due to the general loss of amenities owing to what was going on at the back. . . .

The upshot was that the damages awarded were reduced from £4,500 to £1,000.

The discussion in this section has, up to this point, been concerned with court decisions arising out of the common law relating to nuisance. Delimitation of rights in this area also comes about because of statutory enactments. Most economists would appear to assume that the aim of governmental action in this field is to extend the scope of the law of nuisance by designating as nuisances activities which would not be recognized as such by the common law. And there can be no doubt that some statutes, for example, the Public Health Acts, have had this effect. But not all Government enactments are of this kind. The effect of much of the legislation in this area is to protect businesses from the claims of those they have harmed by their actions. There is a long list of legalized nuisances.

The position has been summarized in *Halsbury's Laws of England* as follows:

> Where the legislature directs that a thing shall in all events be done or authorises certain works at a particular place for a specific purposes or grants powers with the intention that they shall be exercised, although leaving some discretion as to the mode of exercise, no action will lie at common law for nuisance or damage which is the inevitable result of carrying out the statutory powers so conferred. This is so whether the act causing the damage is authorised for public purposes or private profit. Acts done under powers granted by persons to whom Parliament has delegated authority to grant such powers, for example, under provisional orders of the Board of Trade, are regarded as having been done under statutory authority. In the absence of negligence it seems that a body exercising statutory powers will not be liable to an action merely because it might, by acting in a different way, have minimised an injury.

Instances are next given of freedom from liability for acts authorized:

> An action has been held not to be against a body exercising its statutory powers without negligence in respect of the flooding of land by water escaping from watercourses, from water pipes, from drains, or from a canal; the escape of fumes from sewers; the escape of sewage: the subsidence of a road over a sewer; vibration or noise caused by a railway; fires caused by authorised acts; the pollution of a stream where statutory requirements to use the best known method of purifying before discharging the effluent have been satisfied; interference with a telephone or telegraph system by an elctric tramway; the insertion of poles for tramways in the subsoil; annoyance caused by things reasonably necessary for the excavation of authorised works; accidental damage caused by the placing of a grating in a roadway; the escape of tar acid; or interference with the access of a frontager by a street shelter or safety railings on the edge of a pavement.[27]

The legal position in the United States would seem to be essentially the same as in England, except that the power of the legislatures to authorize what would otherwise be nuisances under the common law, at least without giving compensation to the person harmed, is somewhat more limited, as it is subject to constitutional restrictions.[28] Nonetheless, the power is there and cases more or less identical with the English cases can be found. The

[27] See 30 Halsbury, Law of England 690–91 (3d ed. 1960), Article on Public Authorities and Public Officers.

[28] See Prosser, op. cit. supra n. 16 at 421; Harper and James, op. cit. supra n. 16 at 86–87.

question has arisen in an acute form in connection with airports and the operation of aeroplanes. The case of ***Delta Air Corporation v. Kersey, Kersey v. City of Atlanta***[29] is a good example. Mr. Kersey bought land and built a house on it. Some years later the City of Atlanta constructed an airport on land immediately adjoining that of Mr. Kersey. It was explained that his property was "a quiet, peaceful and proper location for a home before the airport was built, but dust, noises and low flying of airplanes caused by the operation of the airport have rendered his property unsuitable as a home," a state of affairs which was described in the report of the case with a wealth of distressing detail. The judge first referred to an earlier case, ***Thrasher v. City of Atlanta***[30] in which it was noted that the City of Atlanta had been expressly authorized to operate an airport.

> By this franchise aviation was recognised as a lawful business and also as an enterprise affected with a public interest . . . all persons using [the airport] in the manner contemplated by law are within the protection and immunity of the franchise granted by the municipality. An airport is not a nuisance per se, although it might become such from the manner of its construction or operation.

Since aviation was a lawful business affected with a public interest and the construction of the airport was autorized by statûte, the judge next referred to *Georgia Railroad and Banking Co. v. Maddox*[31] in which it was said:

> Where a railroad terminal yard is located and its construction authorized, under statutory powers, if it be constructed and operated in a proper manner, it cannot be adjudged a nuisance. Accordingly, injuries and inconveniences to persons residing near such a yard, from noises of locomotives, rumbling of cars, vibrations produced thereby, and smoke, cinders, soot and the like, which result from the ordinary and necessary, therefore proper, use and operation of such a yard, are not nuisances, but are the necessary concomitants of the franchise granted.

In view of this, the judge decided that the noise and dust complained of by Mr. Kersey "may be deemed to be incidental to the proper operation of an airport, and as such they cannot be said to constitute a nuisance." But the complaint against low flying was different:

> . . . can it be said that flights . . . at such a low height [25 to 50 feet above Mr. Kersey's house] as to be imminently dangerous to . . . life and health . . . are a necessary concomitant of an airport? We do not think this question can be answered in the affirmative. No reason appears why the city could not obtain lands of an area [sufficiently large] . . . as not to require such low flights. . . . For the sake of public convenience adjoining-property owners must suffer such inconvenience from noise and dust as result from the usual and proper operation of an airport, but their private rights are entitled to preference in the eyes of the law where the inconvenience is not one demanded by a properly constructed and operated airport.

[29] Supreme Court of Georgia. 193 Ga. 862, 20 S.E. 2d 245 (1942).

[30] 178 Ga. 514, 173 S.E. 817 (1934).

[31] 116 Ga. 64, 42 S.E. 315 (1902).

Of course this assumed that the City of Atlanta could prevent the low flying and continue to operate the airport. The judge therefore added:

From all that appears, the conditions causing the low flying may be remedied; but if on the trial it should appear that it is indispensable to the public interest that the airport should continue to be operated in its present condition, it may be said that the petitioner should be denied injunctive relief.

In the course of another aviation case, *Smith v. New England Aircraft Co.*,[32] the court surveyed the law in the United States regarding the legalizing of nuisances and it is apparent that, in the broad, it is very similar to that found in England:

It is the proper function of the legislative department of government in the exercise of the police power to consider the problems and risks that arise from the use of new inventions and endeavor to adjust private rights and harmonize conflicting interests by comprehensive statutes for the public welfare. . . . There are . . . analogies where the invasion of the airspace over underlying land by noise, smoke, vibration, dust and disagreeable odors, having been authorized by the legislative department of government and not being in effect a condemnation of the property although in some measure depreciating its market value, must be borne by the landowner without compensation or remedy. Legislative sanction makes that lawful which otherwise might be a nuisance. Examples of this are damages to adjacent land arising from smoke, vibration and noise in the operation of a railroad . . . ; the noise of ringing factory bells . . . ; the abatement of nuisances . . . ; the erection of steam engines and furnaces . . . ; unpleasant odors connected with sewers, oil refining and storage of naphtha. . . .

Most economists seem to be unaware of all this. When they are prevented from sleeping at night by the roar of jet planes overhead (publicly authorized and perhaps publicly operated), are unable to think (or rest) in the day because of the noise and vibration from passing trains (publicly authorized and perhaps publicly operated), find it difficult to breathe because of the odour from a local sewage farm (publicly authorized and perhaps publicly operated) and are unable to escape because their driveways are blocked by a road obstruction (without any doubt, publicly devised), their nerves frayed and mental balance disturbed, they proceed to declaim about the disadvantages of private enterprise and the need for Government regulation.

While most economists seem to be under a misapprehension concerning the character of the situation with which they are dealing, it is also the case that the activities which they would like to see stopped or curtailed may well be socially justified. It is all a question of weighing up the gains that would accrue from eliminating these harmful effects against the gains that accrue from allowing them to continue. Of course, it is likely that an extension of Government economic activity will often lead to this protection against

[32] 270 Mass. 511, 523, 170 N.E. 385, 390 (1930).

action for nuisance being pushed further than is desirable. For one thing, the Government is likely to look with a benevolent eye on enterprises which it is itself promoting. For another, it is possible to describe the committing of a nuisance by public enterprise in a much more pleasant way than when the same thing is done by private enterprise. In the words of Lord Justice Sir Alfred Denning:

> . . . the significance of the social revolution of today is that, whereas in the past the balance was much too heavily in favor of the rights of property and freedom of contract, Parliament has repeatedly intervened so as to give the public good its proper place.[33]

There can be little doubt that the Welfare State is likely to bring an extension of that immunity from liability for damage, which economists have been in the habit of condemning (although they have tended to assume that this immunity was a sign of too little Government intervention in the economic system). For example, in Britain, the powers of local authorities are regarded as being either absolute or conditional. In the first category, the local authority has no discretion in exercising the power conferred on it. "The absolute power may be said to cover all the necessary consequences of its direct operation even if such consequences amount to nuisance." On the other hand, a conditional power may only be exercised in such a way that the consequences do not constitute a nuisance.

> It is the intention of the legislature which determines whether a power is absolute or conditional. . . . [As] there is the possibility that the social policy of the legislature may change from time to time, a power which in one era would be construed as being conditional, might in another era be interpreted as being absolute in order to further the policy of the Welfare State. This point is one which should be borne in mind when considering some of the older cases upon this aspect of the law of nuisance.[34]

It would seem desirable to summarize the burden of this long section. The problem which we face in dealing with actions which have harmful effects is not simply one of restraining those responsible for them. What has to be decided is whether the gain from preventing the harm is greater than the loss which would be suffered elsewhere as a result of stopping the action which produces the harm. In a world in which there are costs of rearranging the rights established by the legal system, the courts, in cases relating to nuisance, are, in effect, making a decision on the economic problem and determining how resources are to be employed. It was argued that the courts are conscious of this and that they often make, although not always in a very explicit fashion, a comparison between what would be gained and what lost by preventing

[33] See Sir Alfred Denning, Freedom Under the Law 71 (1949).

[34] M. B. Cairns, The Law of Tort in Local Government 28–32 (1954).

actions which have harmful effects. But the delimitation of rights is also the result of statutory enactments. Here we also find evidence of an appreciation of the reciprocal nature of the problem. While statutory enactments add to the list of nuisances, action is also taken to legalize what would otherwise be nuisances under the common law. The kind of situation which economists are prone to consider as requiring corrective Government action is, in fact, often the result of Government action. Such action is not necessarily unwise. But there is a real danger that extensive Government intervention in the economic system may lead to the protection of those responsible for harmful effects being carried too far.

VIII. Pigou's Treatment in "The Economics of Welfare"

The fountainhead for the modern economic analysis of the problem discussed in this article is Pigou's *Economics of Welfare* and, in particular, that section of Part II which deals with divergences between social and private net products which come about because

> one person A, in the course of rendering some service, for which payment is made, to a second person B, incidentally also renders services or disservices to other persons (not producers of like services), of such a sort that payment cannot be exacted from the benefited parties or compensation enforced on behalf of the injured parties.[35]

Pigou tells us that his aim in Part II of *The Economics of Welfare* is

> to ascertain how far the free play of self-interest, acting under the existing legal system, tends to distribute the country's resources in the way most favorable to the production of a large national dividend, and how far it is feasible for State action to improve upon 'natural' tendencies.[36]

To judge from the first part of this statement, Pigou's purpose is to discover whether any improvements could be made in the existing arrangements which determine the use of resources. Since Pigou's conclusion is that improvements could be made, one might have expected him to continue by saying that he proposed to set out the changes required to bring them about. Instead, Pigou adds a phrase which contrasts "natural" tendencies with State action, which seems in some sense to equate the present arrangements with "natural" tendencies and to imply that what is required to bring about these improvements is State action (if feasible). That this is more or less Pigou's position is evident from Chapter I of Part II.[37] Pigou starts by referring to "optimistic

[35] A. C. Pigou, The Economics of Welfare 183 (4th ed. 1932). My references will all be to the fourth edition but the argument and examples examined in this article remained substantially unchanged from the first edition in 1920 to the fourth in 1932. A large part (but not all) of this analysis had appeared previously in Wealth and Welfare (1912).

[36] *Id.* at xii.

[37] *Id.* at 127–30.

followers of the classical economists"[38] who have argued that the value of production would be maximised if the Government refrained from any interference in the economic system and the economic arrangements were those which came about "naturally." Pigou goes on to say that if self-interest does promote economic welfare, it is because human institutions have been devised to make it so. (This part of Pigou's argument, which he develops with the aid of a quotation from Cannan, seems to me to be essentially correct.) Pigou concludes:

> But even in the most advanced States there are failures and imperfections. . . . there are many obstacles that prevent a community's resources from being distributed . . . in the most efficient way. The study of these constitutes our present problem. . . . its purposes is essentially practical. It seeks to bring into clearer light some of the ways in which it now is, or eventually may become, feasible for governments to control the play of economic forces in such wise as to promote the economic welfare, and through that, the total welfare, of their citizens as a whole.[39]

Pigou's underlying thought would appear to be: Some have argued that no State action is needed. But the system has performed as well as it has because of State action. Nonetheless, there are still imperfections. What additional State action is required?

If this is a correct summary of Pigou's position, its inadequacy can be demonstrated by examining the first example he gives of a divergence between private and social products.

> It might happen . . . that costs are thrown upon people not directly concerned, through, say, uncompensated damage done to surrounding woods by sparks from railway engines. All such effects must be included—some of them will be positive, others negative elements—in reckoning up the social net product of the marginal increment of any volume of resources turned into any use or place.[40]

The example used by Pigou refers to a real situation. In Britain, a railway does not normally have to compensate those who suffer damage by fire caused by sparks from an engine. Taken in conjunction with what he says in Chapter 9 of Part II, I take Pigou's policy recommendations to be, first, that there should be State action to correct this "natural" situation and, second, that the railways should be forced to compensate those whose woods are burnt. If this is a correct interpretation of Pigou's position, I would argue that the first recommendation is based on a misapprehension of the facts and that the second is not necessarily desirable.

[38] In Wealth and Welfare, Pigou attributes the "optimism" to Adam Smith himself and not to his followers. He there refers to the "highly optimistic theory of Adam Smith that the national dividend, in given circumstances of demand and supply, tends 'naturally' to a maximum" (p. 104).

[39] Pigou, op. cit. supra n. 35 at 129–30.

[40] *Id.* at 134.

Let us consider the legal position. Under the heading "Sparks from engines," we find the following in Halsbury's Laws of England:

> If railway undertakers use steam engines on their railway without express statutory authority to do so, they are liable, irrespective of any negligence on their part, for fires caused by sparks from engines. Railway undertakers are, however, generally given statutory authority to use steam engines on their railway; accordingly, if an engine is constructed with the precautions which science suggests against fire and is used without negligence, they are not responsible at common law for any damage which may be done by sparks. . . . In the construction of an engine the undertaker is bound to use all the discoveries which science has put within its reach in order to avoid doing harm, provided they are such as it is reasonable to require the company to adopt, having proper regard to the likelihood of the damage and to the cost and convenience of the remedy; but it is not negligence on the part of an undertaker if it refuses to use an apparatus the efficiency of which is open to bona fide doubt.

To this general rule, there is a statutory exception arising from the Railway (Fires) Act, 1905, as amended in 1923. This concerns agricultural land or agricultural crops.

> In such a case the fact that the engine was used under statutory powers does not affect the liability of the company in an action for the damage. . . . These provisions, however, only apply where the claim for damage . . . does not exceed £ 200, [£ 100 in the 1905 Act] and where written notice of the occurrence of the fire and the intention to claim has been sent to the company within seven days of the occurrence of the damage and particulars of the damage in writing showing the amount of the claim in money not exceeding £ 200 have been sent to the company within twenty-one days.

Agricultural land does not include moorland or buildings and agricultural crops do not include those led away or stacked.[41] I have not made a close study of the parliamentary history of this statutory exception, but to judge from debates in the House of Commons in 1922 and 1923, this exception was probably designed to help the smallholder.[42]

Let us return to Pigou's example of uncompensated damage to surrounding woods caused by sparks from railway engines. This is presumably intended to show how it is possible "for State action to improve on 'natural' tendencies." If we treat Pigou's example as referring to the position before 1905, or as being an arbitrary example (in that he might just as well have written "surrounding buildings" instead of "surrounding woods"), then it is clear that the reason why compensation was not paid must have been that the railway had statutory authority to run steam engines (which relieved it of liability for fires caused by sparks). That this was the legal position was

[41] See 31 Halsbury, Laws of England 474–75 (3d ed. 1960), Article on Railways and Canals, from which this summary of the legal position, and all quotations, are taken.

[42] See 152 H.C. Deb. 2622–63 (1922); 161 H.C. Deb. 2935–55 (1923).

established in 1860, in a case, oddly enough, which concerned the burning of surrounding woods by a railway,[43] and the law on this point has not been changed (apart from the one exception) by a century of railway legislation, including nationalisation. If we treat Pigou's example of "uncompensated damage done to surrounding woods by sparks from railway engines" literally, and assume that it refers to the period after 1905, then it is clear that the reason why compensation was not paid must have been that the damage was more than £100 (in the first edition of *The Economics of Welfare*) or more than £200 (in later editions) or that the owner of the wood failed to notify the railway in writing within seven days of the fire or did not send particulars of the damage, in writing, within twenty-one days. In the real world, Pigou's example could only exist as a result of a deliberate choice of the legislature. It is not, of course, easy to imagine the construction of a railway in a state of nature. The nearest one can get to this is presumably a railway which uses steam engines "without express statutory authority." However, in this case the railway would be obliged to compensate those whose woods it burnt down. That is to say, compensation would be paid in the absence of Government action. The only circumstances in which compensation would not be paid would be those in which there had been Government action. It is strange that Pigou, who clearly thought it desirable that compensation should be paid, should have chosen this particular example to demonstrate how it is possible "for State action to improve on 'natural' tendencies."

Pigou seems to have had a faulty view of the facts of the situation. But it also seems likely that he was mistaken in his economic analysis. It is not necessarily desirable that the railway should be required to compensate those who suffer damage by fires caused by railway engines. I need not show here that, if the railway could make a bargain with everyone having property adjoining the railway line and there were no costs involved in making such bargains, it would not matter whether the railway was liable for damage caused by fires or not. This question has been treated at length in earlier sections. The problem is whether it would be desirable to make the railway liable in conditions in which it is too expensive for such bargains to be made. Pigou clearly thought it was desirable to force the railway to pay compensation and it is easy to see the kind of argument that would have led him to this conclusion. Suppose a railway is considering whether to run an additional train or to increase the speed of an existing train or to install spark-preventing devices on its engines. If the railway were not liable for fire damage, then, when making these decisions, it would not take into account as a cost the increase in damage resulting from the additional train or the faster train or the failure to install spark-preventing devices. This is the source of the di-

[43] Vaughan v. Taff Vale Railway Co., 3 H. and N. 743 (Ex. 1858) and 5 H. and N. 679 (Ex. 1860).

vergence between private and social net products. It results in the railway performing acts which will lower the value of total production—and which it would not do if it were liable for the damage. This can be shown by means of an arithmetical example.

Consider a railway, which is *not* liable for damage by fires caused by sparks from its engines, which runs two trains per day on a certain line. Suppose that running one train per day would enable the railway to perform services worth $150 per annum and running two trains a day would enable the railway to perform services worth $250 per annum. Suppose further that the cost of running one train is $50 per annum and two trains $100 per annum. Assuming perfect competition, the cost equals the fall in the value of production elsewhere due to the employment of additional factors of production by the railway. Clearly the railway would find it profitable to run two trains per day. But suppose that running one train per day would destroy by fire crops worth (on an average over the year) $60 and two trains a day would result in the destruction of crops worth $120. In these circumstances running one train per day would raise the value of total production but the running of a second train would reduce the value of total production. The second train would enable additional railway services worth $100 per annum to be performed. But the fall in the value of production elsewhere would be $110 per annum; $50 as a result of the employment of additional factors of production and $60 as a result of the destruction of crops. Since it would be better if the second train were not run and since it would not run if the railway were liable for damage caused to crops, the conclusion that the railway should be made liable for the damage seems irresistable. Undoubtedly it is this kind of reasoning which underlies the Pigovian position.

The conclusion that it would be better if the second train did not run is correct. The conclusion that it is desirable that the railway should be made liable for the damage it causes is wrong. Let us change our assumption concerning the rule of liability. Suppose that the railway is liable for damage from fires caused by sparks from the engine. A farmer on lands adjoining the railway is then in the position that, if his crop is destroyed by fires caused by the railway, he will receive the market price from the railway; but if his crop is not damaged, he will receive the market price by sale. It therefore becomes a matter of indifference to him whether his crop is damaged by fire or not. The position is very different when the railway is *not* liable. Any crop destruction through railway-caused fires would then reduce the receipts of the farmer. He would therefore take out of cultivation any land for which the damage is likely to be greater than the net return of the land (for reasons explained at length in Section III). A change from a regime in which the railway is *not* liable for damage to one in which it *is* liable is likely therefore to lead to an increase in the amount of cultivation on lands adjoining the railway. It will also, of course, lead to an increase in the amount of crop destruction due to railway-caused fires.

Let us return to our arithmetical example. Assume that, with the changed rule of liability, there is a doubling in the amount of crop destruction due to railway-caused fires. With one train per day, crops worth $120 would be destroyed each year and two trains per day would lead to the destruction of crops worth $240. We saw previously that it would not be profitable to run the second train if the railway had to pay $60 per annum as compensation for damage. With damage at $120 per annum the loss from running the second train would be $60 greater. But now let us consider the first train. The value of the transport services furnished by the first train is $150. The cost of running the train is $50. The amount that the railway would have to pay out as compensation for damage is $120. It follows that it would not be profitable to run any trains. With the figures in our example we reach the following result: if the railway is not liable for fire-damage, two trains per day would be run; if the railway is liable for fire-damage, it would cease operations altogether. Does this mean that it is better that there should be no railway? This question can be resolved by considering what would happen to the value of total production if it were decided to exempt the railway from liability for fire-damage, thus bringing it into operation (with two trains per day).

The operation of the railway would enable transport services worth $250 to be performed. It would also mean the employment of factors of production which would reduce the value of production elsewhere by $100. Furthermore it would mean the destruction of crops worth $120. The coming of the railway will also have led to the abandonment of cultivation of some land. Since we know that, had this land been cultivated, the value of the crops destroyed by fire would have been $120, and since it is unlikely that the total crop on this land would have been destroyed, it seems reasonable to suppose that the value of the crop yield on this land would have been higher than this. Assume it would have been $160. But the abandonment of cultivation would have released factors of production for employment elsewhere. All we know is that the amount by which the value of production elsewhere will increase will be less than $160. Suppose that it is $150. Then the gain from operating the railway would be $250 (the value of the transport services) minus $100 (the cost of the factors of production) minus $120 (the value of crops destroyed by fire) minus $160 (the fall in the value of crop production due to the abandonment of cultivation) plus $150 (the value of production elsewhere of the released factors of production). Overall, operating the railway will increase the value of total production by $20. With these figures it is clear that it is better that the railway should not be liable for the damage it causes, thus enabling it to operate profitably. Of course, by altering the figures, it could be shown that there are other cases in which it would be desirable that the railway should be liable for the damage it causes. It is enough for my purpose to show that, from an economic point of view, a situation in which there is "uncompensated damage done to surrounding woods by sparks from railway engines" is not necessarily undesirable. Whether it is desirable or not depends on the particular circumstances.

How is it that the Pigovian analysis seems to give the wrong answer? The reason is that Pigou does not seem to have noticed that his analysis is dealing with an entirely different question. The analysis as such is correct. But it is quite illegitimate for Pigou to draw the particular conclusion he does. The question at issue is not whether it is desirable to run an additional train or a faster train or to install smoke-preventing devices; the question at issue is whether it is desirable to have a system in which the railway has to compensate those who suffer damage from the fires which it causes or one in which the railway does not have to compensate them. When an economist is comparing alternative social arrangements, the proper procedure is to compare the total social product yielded by these different arrangements. The comparison of private and social products is neither here nor there. A simple example will demonstrate this. Imagine a town in which there are traffic lights. A motorist approaches an intersection and stops because the light is red. There are no cars approaching the intersection on the other street. If the motorist ignored the red signal, no accident would occur and the total product would increase because the motorist would arrive earlier at his destination. Why does he not do this? The reason is that if he ignored the light he would be fined. The private product from crossing the street is less than the social product. Should we conclude from this that the total product would be greater if there were no fines for failing to obey traffic signals? The Pigovian analysis shows us that it is possible to conceive of better worlds than the one in which we live. But the problem is to devise practical arrangements which will correct defects in one part of the system without causing more serious harm in other parts.

I have examined in considerable detail one example of a divergence between private and social products and I do not propose to make any further examination of Pigou's analytical system. But the main discussion of the problem considered in this article is to be found in that part of Chapter 9 in Part II which deals with Pigou's second class of divergence and it is of interest to see how Pigou develops his argument. Pigou's own description of this second class of divergence was quoted at the beginning of this section. Pigou distinguishes between the case in which a person renders services for which he receives no payment and the case in which a person renders disservices and compensation is not given to the injured parties. Our main attention has, of course, centred on this second case. It is therefore rather astonishing to find, as was pointed out to me by Professor Francesco Forte, that the problem of the smoking chimney—the "stock instance"[44] or "classroom example"[45] of the second case—is used by Pigou as an example of the first case (services rendered without payment) and is never mentioned, at any rate explicitly, in connection with the second case.[46] Pigou points out that factory owners who devote resources to preventing their chimneys from smoking render services for which they receive no payment. The implication, in the light of Pigou's discussion later in the chapter, is that a factory owner with a smokey chimney should be given a bounty to induce him to install smoke-preventing devices. Most modern economists would suggest that the owner of the factory with the smokey chimney should be taxed. It seems a pity that economists (apart from Professor Forte) do not seem to have noticed this feature of Pigou's treatment since a realisation that the problem could be tackled in either of these two ways would probably have led to an explicit recognition of its reciprocal nature.

In discussing the second case (disservices without compensation to those damaged), Pigou says that they are rendered "when the owner of a site in a residential quarter of a city builds a factory there and so destroys a great part of the amenities of neighbouring sites; or, in a less degree, when he uses his site in such a way as to spoil the lighting of the house opposite; or when he invests resources in erecting buildings in a crowded centre, which by contracting the air-space and the playing room of the neighbourhood, tend to injure the health and efficiency of the families living there."[47] Pigou is, of course, quite right to describe such actions as "uncharged disservices." But he is wrong when he describes these actions as "anti-social."[48] They may or may not be. It is necessary to weigh the harm against the good that will result. Nothing could be more "anti-social" than to oppose any action which causes any harm to anyone.

The example with which Pigou opens his discussion of "uncharged disservices" is not, as I have indicated, the case of the smokey chimney but the case of the overrunning rabbits: ". . . incidental uncharged disservices are rendered to third parties when the game-preserving activities of one occupier involve the overrunning of a neighbouring occupier's land by rabbits. . . ." This example is of extraordinary interest, not so much because the economic

[44] Sir Dennis Robertson, I Lectures on Economic Principles 162 (1957).

[45] E. J. Mishan, The Meaning of Efficiency in Economics, 189 The Bankers' Magazine 482 (June 1960).

[46] Pigou, op. cit. supra n. 35 at 184.

[47] *Id.* at 185–86.

[48] *Id.* at 186 n.1. For similar unqualified statements see Pigou's lecture "Some Aspects of the Housing Problem" in B. S. Rowntree and A. C. Pigou, Lectures on Housing, in 18 Manchester Univ. Lectures (1914).

analysis of the case is essentially any different from that of the other examples, but because of the peculiarities of the legal position and the light it throws on the part which economics can play in what is apparently the purely legal question of the delimitation of rights.

The problem of legal liability for the actions of rabbits is part of the general subject of liability for animals.[49] I will, although with reluctance, confine my discussion to rabbits. The early cases relating to rabbits concerned the relations between the lord of the manor and commoners, since, from the thirteenth century on, it became usual for the lord of the manor to stock the commons with conies (rabbits), both for the sake of the meat and the fur. But in 1597, in *Boulston*'s case, an action was brought by one landowner against a neighbouring landowner, alleging that the defendant had made coney-burrows and that the conies had increased and had destroyed the plaintiff's corn. The action failed for the reason that

> . . . so soon as the coneys come on his neighbor's land he may kill them, for they are ferae naturae, and he who makes the coney-boroughs has no property in them, and he shall not be punished for the damage which the coneys do in which he has no property, and which the other may lawfully kill.[50]

As *Boulston*'s case has been treated as binding—Bray, J., in 1919, said that he was not aware that *Boulston*'s case has ever been overruled or questioned[51]—Pigou's rabbit example undoubtedly represented the legal position at the time *The Economics of Welfare* was written.[52] And in this case, it is not far from the truth to say that the state of affairs which Pigou describes came about because of an absence of Government action (at any rate in the form of statutory enactments) and was the result of "natural" tendencies.

Nonetheless, *Boulston*'s case is something of a legal curiousity and Professor Williams makes no secret of his distaste for this decision:

[49] See G. L. Williams, Liability for Animals—An Account of the Development and Present Law of Tortious Liability for Animals, Distress Damage Feasant and the Duty to Fence, in Great Britain, Northern Ireland and the Common Law Dominions (1939). Part Four, "The Action of Nuisance, in Relation to Liability for Animals," 236–62, is especially relevant to our discussion. The problem of liability for rabbits is discussed in this part, 238–47. I do not know how far the common law in the United State regarding liability for animals has diverged from that in Britain. In some Western States of the United States, the English common law regarding the duty to fence has not been followed, in part becanse "the considerable amount of open, uncleared land made it a matter of public policy to allow cattle to run at large" (Williams, *op. cit. supra* 227). This affords a good example of how a different set of circumstances may make it economically desirable to change the legal rule regarding the delimitation of rights.

[50] 5 Coke (Vol. 3) 104 b. 77 Eng. Rep., 216, 217.

[51] See Stearn v. Prentice Bros. Ltd., (1919) 1 K.B., 395, 397.

[52] I have not looked into recent cases. The legal position has also been modified by statutory enactments.

The conception of liability in nuisance as being based upon ownership is the result, apparently, of a confusion with the action of cattle-trespass, and runs counter both to principle and to the medieval authorities on the escape of water, smoke and filth. . . . The prerequisite of any satisfactory treatment of the subject is the final abandonment of the pernicious doctrine in *Boulston*'s case. . . . Once *Boulston*'s case disappears, the way will be clear for a rational restatement of the whole subject, on lines that will harmonize with the principles prevailing in the rest of the law of nuisance.[53]

The judges in *Boulston*'s case were, of course, aware that their view of the matter depended on distinguishing this case from one involving nuisance:

This cause is not like to the cases put, on the other side, of erecting a lime-kiln, dye-house, or the like; for there the annoyance is by the act of the parties who make them; but it is not so here, for the conies of themselves went into the plaintiff's land, and he might take them when they came upon his land, and make profit of them.[54]

Professor Williams comments:

Once more the atavistic idea is emerging that the animals are guilty and not the landowner. It is not, of course, a satisfactory principle to introduce into a modern law of nuisance. If A. erects a house or plants a tree so that the rain runs or drips from it on to B.'s land, this is A.'s act for which he is liable; but if A. introduces rabbits into his land so that they escape from it into B.'s, this is the act of the rabbits for which A. is not liable—such is the specious distinction resulting from *Boulston*'s case.[55]

It has to be admitted that the decision in *Boulston*'s case seems a little odd. A man may be liable for damage caused by smoke or unpleasant smells, without it being necessary to determine whether he owns the smoke or the smell. And the rule in *Boulston*'s case has not always been followed in cases dealing with other animals. For example, in *Bland v. Yates*,[56] it was decided that an injunction could be granted to prevent someone from keeping an *unusual and excessive* collection of manure in which flies bred and which infested a neighbour's house. The question of who owned the flies was not raised. An economist would not wish to object because legal reasoning sometimes appears a little odd. But there is a sound economic reason for supporting Professor Williams' view that the problem of liability for animals (and particularly rabbits) should be brought within the ordinary law of nuisance. The reason is not that the man who harbours rabbits is solely responsible for the damage; the man whose crops are eaten is equally responsible. And given that the costs of market transactions make a rearrange-

[53] Williams, op. cit. supra n. 49 at 242, 258.

[54] Boulston v. Hardy, Cro. Eliz., 547, 548, 77 Eng. Rep. 216.

[55] Williams, op. cit. supra n. 49 at 243.

[56] 58 Sol.J. 612 (1913–1914).

ment of rights impossible, unless we know the particular circumstances, we cannot say whether it is desirable or not to make the man who harbours rabbits responsible for the damage committed by the rabbits on neighbouring properties. The objection to the rule in *Boulston*'s case is that, under it, the harbourer of rabbits can *never* be liable. It fixes the rule of liability at one pole: and this is as undesirable, from an economic point of view, as fixing the rule at the other pole and making the harbourer of rabbits always liable. But, as we saw in Section VII, the law of nuisance, as it is in fact handled by the courts, is flexible and allows for a comparison of the utility of an act with the harm it produces. As Professor Williams says: "The whole law of nuisance is an attempt to reconcile and compromise between conflicting interests. . . ."[57] To bring the problem of rabbits within the ordinary law of nuisance would not mean *inevitably* making the harbourer of rabbits liable for damage committed by the rabbits. This is not to say that the sole task of the courts in such cases is to make a comparison between the harm and the utility of an act. Nor is it to be expected that the courts will always decide correctly after making such a comparison. But unless the courts act very foolishly, the ordinary law of nuisance would seem likely to give economically more satisfactory results than adopting a rigid rule. Pigou's case of the overrunning rabbits affords an excellent example of how problems of law and economics are interrelated, even though the correct policy to follow would seem to be different from that envisioned by Pigou.

Pigou allows one exception to his conclusion that there is a divergence between private and social products in the rabbit example. He adds: ". . . unless . . . the two occupiers stand in the relation of landlord and tenant, so that compensation is given in an adjustment of the rent."[58] This qualification is rather surprising since Pigou's first class of divergence is largely concerned with the difficulties of drawing up satisfactory contracts between landlords and tenants. In fact, all the recent cases on the problem of rabbits cited by Professor Williams involved disputes between landlords and tenants concerning sporting rights.[59] Pigou seems to make a distinction between the case in which no contract is possible (the second class) and that in which the contract is unsatisfactory (the first class). Thus he says that the second class of divergences between private and social net product

> cannot, like divergences due to tenancy laws, be mitigated by a modification of the contractual relation between any two contracting parties, because the divergence arises out of a service or disservice rendered to persons other than the contracting parties.[60]

[57] Williams, op. cit. supra n. 49 at 259.

[58] Pigou, op. cit. supra n. 35 at 185.

[59] Williams, op. cit. supra n. 49 at 244–47.

[60] Pigou, op. cit. supra n. 35 at 192.

But the reason why some activities are not the subject of contracts is exactly the same as the reason why some contracts are commonly unsatisfactory—it would cost too much to put the matter right. Indeed, the two cases are really the same since the contracts are unsatisfactory because they do not cover certain activities. The exact bearing of the discussion of the first class of divergence on Pigou's main argument is difficult to discover. He shows that in some circumstances contractual relations between landlord and tenant may result in a divergence between private and social products.[61] But he also goes on to show that Government-enforced compensation schemes and rent-controls will also produce divergences.[62] Furthermore, he shows that, when the Government is in a similar position to a private landlord, e.g. when granting a franchise to a public utility, exactly the same difficulties arise as when private individuals are involved.[63] The discussion is interesting but I have been unable to discover what general conclusions about economic policy, if any, Pigou expects us to draw from it.

Indeed, Pigou's treatment of the problems considered in this article is extremely elusive and the discussion of his views raises almost insuperable difficulties of interpretation. Consequently it is impossible to be sure that one has understood what Pigou really meant. Nevertheless, it is difficult to resist the conclusion, extroardinary though this may be in an economist of Pigou's stature, that the main source of this obscurity is that Pigou had not thought his position through.

IX. The Pigovian Tradition

It is strange that a doctrine as faulty as that developed by Pigou should have been so influential, although part of its success has probably been due to the lack of clarity in the exposition. Not being clear, it was never clearly wrong. Curiously enough, this obscurity in the source has not prevented the emergence of a fairly well-defined oral tradition. What economists think they learn from Pigou, and what they tell their students, which I term the Pigovian tradition, is reasonably clear. I propose to show the inadequacy of this Pigovian tradition by demonstrating that both the analysis and the policy conclusions which it supports are incorrect.

I do not propose to justify my view as to the prevailing opinion by copious references to the literature. I do this partly because the treatment in the literature is usually so fragmentary, often involving little more than a reference to Pigou plus some explanatory comment, that detailed examination would be inappropriate. But the main reason for this lack of reference is that the doctrine, although based on Pigou, must have been largely the product of an oral tradition. Certainly economists with whom I have discussed these problems have shown a unanimity of opinion which is quite

[61] *Id.* 174–75. [62] *Id.* 177–83. [63] *Id.* 175–77.

remarkable considering the meagre treatment accorded this subject in the literature. No doubt there are some economists who do not share the usual view but they must represent a small minority of the profession.

The approach to the problems under discussion is through an examination of the value of physical production. The private product is the value of the additional product resulting from a particular activity of a business. The social product equals the private product minus the fall in the value of production elsewhere for which no compensation is paid by the business. Thus, if 10 units of a factor (and no other factors) are used by a business to make a certain product with a value of $105; and the owner of this factor is not compensated for their use, which he is unable to prevent; and these 10 units of the factor would yield products in their best alternative use worth $100; then, the social product is $105 minus $100 or $5. If the business now pays for one unit of the factor and its price equals the value of its marginal product, then the social product rises to $15. If two units are paid for, the social product rises to $25 and so on until it reaches $105 when all units of the factor are paid for. It is not difficult to see why economists have so readily accepted this rather odd procedure. The analysis focusses on the individual business decision and since the use of certain resources is not allowed for in costs, receipts are reduced by the same amount. But, of course, this means that the value of the social product has no social significance whatsoever. It seems to me preferable to use the opportunity cost concept and to approach these problems by comparing the value of the product yielded by factors in alternative uses or by alternative arrangements. The main advantage of a pricing system is that it leads to the employment of factors in places where the value of the product yielded is greatest and does so at less cost than alternative systems (I leave aside that a pricing system also eases the problem of the redistribution of income). But if through some God-given natural harmony factors flowed to the places where the value of the product yielded was greatest without any use of the pricing system and consequently there was no compensation, I would find it a source of surprise rather than a cause for dismay.

The definition of the social product is queer but this does not mean that the conclusions for policy drawn from the analysis are necessarily wrong. However, there are bound to be dangers in an approach which diverts attention from the basic issues and there can be little doubt that it has been responsible for some of the errors in current doctrine. The belief that it is desirable that the business which causes harmful effects should be forced to compensate those who suffer damage (which was exhaustively discussed in section VIII in connection with Pigou's railway sparks example) is undoubtedly the result of not comparing the total product obtainable with alternative social arrangements.

The same fault is to be found in proposals for solving the problem of harmful effects by the use of taxes or bounties. Pigou lays considerable stress on this solution although he is, as usual, lacking in detail and qualified in his support.[64] Modern economists tend to think exclusively in terms of taxes and in a very precise way. The tax should be equal to the damage done and should therefore vary with the amount of the harmful effect. As it is not proposed that the proceeds of the tax should be paid to those suffering the damage, this solution is not the same as that which would force a business to pay compensation to those damaged by its actions, although economists generally do not seem to have noticed this and tend to treat the two solutions as being identical.

Assume that a factory which emits smoke is set up in a district previously free from smoke pollution, causing damage valued at $100 per annum. Assume that the taxation solution is adopted and that the factory owner is taxed $100 per annum as long as the factory emits the smoke. Assume further that a smoke-preventing device costing $90 per annum to run is available. In these circumstances, the smoke-preventing device would be installed. Damage of $100 would have been avoided at an expenditure of $90 and the factory-owner would be better off by $10 per annum. Yet the position achieved may not be optimal. Suppose that those who suffer the damage could avoid it by moving to other locations or by taking various precautions which would cost them, or be equivalent to a loss in income of, $40 per annum. Then there would be a gain in the value of production of $50 if the factory continued to emit its smoke and those now in the district moved elesewhere or made other adjustments to avoid the damage. If the factory owner is to be made to pay a tax equal to the damage caused, it would clearly be desirable to institute a double tax system and to make residents of the district pay an amount equal to the additional cost incurred by the factory owner (or the consumers of his products) in order to avoid the damage. In these conditions, people would not stay in the district or would take other measures to prevent the damage from occurring, when the costs of doing so were less than the costs that would be incurred by the producer to reduce the damage (the producer's object, of course, being not so much to reduce the damage as to reduce the tax payments). A tax system which was confined to a tax on the producer for damage caused would tend to lead to unduly high costs being incurred for the prevention of damage. Of course this could be avoided if it were possible to base the tax, not on the damage caused, but on the fall in the value of production (in its widest sense) resulting from the emission of smoke. But to do so would require a detailed knowledge of individual preferences and I am unable to imagine how the data needed for such a taxation system could be assembled. Indeed,

[64] *Id.* 192–4, 381 and Public Finance 94–100 (3d ed. 1947).

the proposal to solve the smoke-pollution and similar problems by the use of taxes bristles with difficulties: the problem of calculation, the difference between average and marginal damage, the interrelations between the damage suffered on different properties, etc. But it is unnecessary to examine these problems here. It is enough for my purpose to show that, even if the tax is exactly adjusted to equal the damage that would be done to neighboring properties as a result of the emission of each additional puff of smoke, the tax would not necessarily bring about optimal conditions. An increase in the number of people living or of business operating in the vicinity of the smoke-emitting factory will increase the amount of harm produced by a given emission of smoke. The tax that would be imposed would therefore increase with an increase in the number of those in the vicinity. This will tend to lead to a decrease in the value of production of the factors employed by the factory, either because a reduction in production due to the tax will result in factors being used elsewhere in ways which are less valuable, or because factors will be diverted to produce means for reducing the amount of smoke emitted. But people deciding to establish themselves in the vicinity of the factory will not take into account this fall in the value of production which results from their presence. This failure to take into account costs imposed on others is comparable to the action of a factory-owner in not taking into account the harm resulting from his emission of smoke. Without the tax, there may be too much smoke and too few people in the vicinity of the factory; but with the tax there may be too little smoke and too many people in the vicinity of the factory. There is no reason to suppose that one of these results is necessarily preferable.

I need not devote much space to discussing the similar error involved in the suggestion that smoke producing factories should, by means of zoning regulations, be removed from the districts in which the smoke causes harmful effects. When the change in the location of the factory results in a reduction in production, this obviously needs to be taken into account and weighed against the harm which would result from the factory remaining in that location. The aim of such regulation should not be to eliminate smoke pollution but rather to secure the optimum amount of smoke pollution, this being the amount which will maximise the value of production.

X. A Change of Approach

It is my belief that the failure of economists to reach correct conclusions about the treatment of harmful effects cannot be ascribed simply to a few slips in analysis. It stems from basic defects in the current approach to problems of welfare economics. What is needed is a change of approach.

Analysis in terms of divergencies between private and social products concentrates attention on particular deficiencies in the system and tends to nourish the belief that any measure which will remove the deficiency is necessarily desirable. It diverts attention from those other changes in the system which are inevitably associated with the corrective measure, changes which may well produce more harm than the original deficiency. In the preceding sections of this article, we have seen many examples of this. But it is not necessary to approach the problem in this way. Economists who study problems of the firm habitually use an opportunity cost approach and compare the receipts obtained from a given combination of factors with alternative business arrangements. It would seem desirable to use a similar approach when dealing with questions of economic policy and to compare the total product yielded by alternative social arrangements. In this article, the analysis has been confined, as is usual in this part of economics, to comparisons of the value of production, as measured by the market. But it is, of course, desirable that the choice between different social arrangements for the solution of economic problems should be carried out in broader terms than this and that the total effect of these arrangements in all spheres of life should be taken into account. As Frank H. Knight has so often emphasized, problems of welfare economics must ultimately dissolve into a study of aesthetics and morals.

A second feature of the usual treatment of the problems discussed in this article is that the analysis proceeds in terms of a comparison between a state of laissez faire and some kind of ideal world. This approach inevitably leads to a looseness of thought since the nature of the alternatives being compared is never clear. In a state of laissez faire, is there a monetary, a legal or a political system and if so, what are they? In an ideal world, would there be a monetary, a legal or a political system and if so, what would they be? The answers to all these questions are shrouded in mystery and every man is free to draw whatever conclusions he likes. Actually very little analysis is required to show that an ideal world is better than a state of laissez faire, unless the definitions of a state of laissez faire and an ideal world happen to be the same. But the whole discussion is largely irrelevant for questions of economic policy since whatever we may have in mind as our ideal world, it is clear that we have not yet discovered how to get to it from where we are. A better approach would seem to be to start our analysis with a situation approximating that which actually exists, to examine the effects of a proposed policy change and to attempt to decide whether the new situation would be, in total, better or worse than the original one. In this way, conclusions for policy would have some relevance to the actual situation.

A final reason for the failure to develop a theory adequate to handle the problem of harmful effects stems from a faulty concept of a factor of production. This is usually thought of as a physical entity which the businessman acquires and uses (an acre of land, a ton of fertiliser) instead of as a right to perform certain (physical) actions. We may speak of a person owning land and using it as a factor of production but what the land-owner in fact possesses is the right to carry out a circumscribed list of actions. The rights of a land-owner are not unlimited. It is not even always possible for him to remove the land to another place, for instance, by quarrying it. And although it may be possible for him to exclude some people from using "his" land, this may not be true of others. For example, some people may have the right to cross the land. Furthermore, it may or may not be possible to erect certain types of buildings or to grow certain crops or to use particular drainage systems on the land. This does not come about simply because of Government regulation. It would be equally true under the common law. In fact it would be true under any system of law. A system in which the rights of individuals were unlimited would be one in which there were no rights to acquire.

If factors of production are thought of as rights, it becomes easier to understand that the right to do something which has a harmful effect (such as the creation of smoke, noise, smells, etc.) is also a factor of production. Just as we may use a piece of land in such a way as to prevent someone else from crossing it, or parking his car, or building his house upon it, so we may use it in such a way as to deny him a view or quiet or unpolluted air. The cost of exercising a right (of using a factor of production) is always the loss which is suffered elsewhere in consequence of the exercise of that right—the inability to cross land, to park a car, to build a house, to enjoy a view, to have peace and quiet or to breathe clean air.

It would clearly be desirable if the only actions performed were those in which what was gained was worth more than what was lost. But in choosing between social arrangements within the context of which individual decisions are made, we have to bear in mind that a change in the existing system which will lead to an improvement in some decisions may well lead to a worsening of others. Furthermore we have to take into account the costs involved in operating the various social arrangements (whether it be the working of a market or of a government department), as well as the costs involved in moving to a new system. In devising and choosing between social arrangements we should have regard for the total effect. This, above all, is the change in approach which I am advocating.